The Lost Library

The Tauber Institute Series
for the Study of European Jewry

Jehuda Reinharz, General Editor
ChaeRan Y. Freeze, Associate Editor
Sylvia Fuks Fried, Associate Editor
Eugene R. Sheppard, Associate Editor

The Tauber Institute Series is dedicated to publishing compelling and innovative approaches to the study of modern European Jewish history, thought, culture, and society. The series features scholarly works related to the Enlightenment, modern Judaism and the struggle for emancipation, the rise of nationalism and the spread of antisemitism, the Holocaust and its aftermath, as well as the contemporary Jewish experience. The series is published under the auspices of the Tauber Institute for the Study of European Jewry — established by a gift to Brandeis University from Dr. Laszlo N. Tauber — and is supported, in part, by the Tauber Foundation and the Valya and Robert Shapiro Endowment.

For the complete list of books that are available in this series,
please see www.upne.com

Dan Rabinowitz
    *The Lost Library: The Legacy of Vilna's Strashun Library in the
    Aftermath of the Holocaust*
Jehuda Reinharz and Yaacov Shavit
    *The Road to September 1939: Polish Jews, Zionists, and the Yishuv
    on the Eve of World War II*
Adi Gordon
    Toward Nationalism's End: An Intellectual Biography of Hans Kohn
Noam Zadoff
    Gershom Scholem: From Berlin to Jerusalem and Back
*Monika Schwarz-Friesel and Jehuda Reinharz
    *Inside the Antisemitic Mind: The Language of Jew-Hatred in
    Contemporary Germany*
Elana Shapira
    *Style and Seduction: Jewish Patrons, Architecture, and Design in
    Fin de Siècle Vienna*
ChaeRan Y. Freeze, Sylvia Fuks Fried, and Eugene R. Sheppard, editors
    The Individual in History: Essays in Honor of Jehuda Reinharz
Immanuel Etkes
    Rabbi Shneur Zalman of Liady: The Origins of Chabad Hasidism

*A Sarnat Library Book

The Lost Library

**The Legacy of
Vilna's Strashun Library
in the Aftermath of the
Holocaust**

DAN RABINOWITZ

BRANDEIS UNIVERSITY PRESS — WALTHAM, MASSACHUSETTS

BRANDEIS UNIVERSITY PRESS

An imprint of University Press of New England

www.upne.com

© 2019 Brandeis University

All rights reserved

Manufactured in the United States of America

Designed by Eric M. Brooks

Typeset in Skolar by Passumpsic Publishing

For permission to reproduce any of the material in this book, contact Permissions, University Press of New England, One Court Street, Suite 250, Lebanon NH 03766; or visit www.upne.com

Library of Congress Cataloging-in-Publication Data

NAMES: Rabinowitz, Dan, 1975– author.

TITLE: The lost library: the legacy of Vilna's Strashun library in the aftermath of the Holocaust / Dan Rabinowitz.

DESCRIPTION: Waltham, Massachusetts: Brandeis University Press, an imprint of University Press of New England, [2019] | Series: The Tauber Institute series for the study of European Jewry | A Sarnat Library book | Includes bibliographical references and index.

IDENTIFIERS: LCCN 2018023866 (print) | LCCN 2018026226 (ebook) | ISBN 9781512603101 (epub) | ISBN 9781512603088 (cloth: alk. paper) | ISBN 9781512603095 (pbk.)

SUBJECTS: LCSH: Strashun Library. | Jewish libraries— Lithuania—Vilnius—History. | Libraries—Destruction and pillage—Lithuania—Vilnius—History—20th century. | Strashun, Mathias, -1885—Library.

CLASSIFICATION: LCC Z675.J4 (ebook) | LCC Z675.J4 R35 2019 (print) | DDC 027.04793—dc23

LC record available at https://lccn.loc.gov/2018023866

5 4 3 2 1

To the memory of

My father-in-law, MELVIN RISHE,
a philanthropist, scholar, and community leader,
whose love for his family knew no bounds

SARA LANDESMAN,
*who fled Europe with the Mir Yeshiva and made her
home in Silver Spring, Maryland, where she welcomed
all in need with open arms and grace*

My grandfather, ELIEZER RABINOWITZ,
*who devoted his life to Jewish education, first in Vilna
as head of the Horev school system and then in the
United States at Ner Israel Rabbinical College*

Contents

Acknowledgments

I wish to express my gratitude to all those who made this book possible: To my wonderful editor Sylvia Fuks Fried, at the Tauber Institute, for her unstinting support, even when the direction and timeline of the book changed. Phyllis Deutsch, whose forbearance and feedback were critical, and Susan Abel. Ryan Cole, for his editorial assistance and advice, and my copyeditor, Elizabeth Forsaith. To the many who provided information, materials, assistance with translations, and archival resources: Zachary Baker, Gunner Berg, Menachem Butler, Kobi Fisher, Louise Fisher at the Israel State Archives, David Fishman, Elisabeth Gallas, Mark Glickman, Ettie Goldwasser, Gershom Gorenberg, Dana Herman, Sharon Horowitz at the Library of Congress, Dovid Katz, Cecile Kuznitz, Fruma Mohrer, Ruth Murphy, Allan Nadler, Carl Rheins, Brad Sabin-Hill, Shaul Seidler-Feller, Billi Shilo, Lyudmila Sholokhova, Frida Shor, Nancy Sinkoff, Daniel Sperber, Shimon Steinmentz, Marek Webb, and Mordechai Zalkin. Eliezer Brodt has been a good friend and unimaginable resource. His contributions are so substantial that they would otherwise require mention on nearly every page. One of the most unexpected and enjoyable aspects of this project was meeting Lara Lempertienė, the director of the Lithuanian National Library's Judaica Research Center; she is a seemingly endless font of information related to Mattityahu, and a scholar and friend. Aaron Taub, who invited me to the Association of Jewish Librarians conference. Eli Genauer, who read and reread the manuscript closely. Zalman Alpert, Hillel Broder, Shawn Fishman, ChaeRan Freeze, Eliezer Katzman, Lisa Leff, Sid Leiman, Matthew Solomson, Rabbi Yehezkel Weinfeld, and the anonymous reader who read the manuscript and provided feedback. The institutions that generously opened their archives: the Lithuanian State Historical Archives and its archivist Galina Baranova; the United States Holocaust Memorial Museum; the National Archives in College Park, Maryland; the Bar-Ilan University Archive of Religious Zionism; the Stanford University Archives; the American Jewish Historical Society Archives; Mossad Harav Kook; the Israel State Archives; and the YIVO Institute for Jewish Research. To my two long-standing book dealers,

Chaim Dzailowsky and Joshua Peirce. My friends Sam G., Sam M., Dave, Edwin, Miriam, Tevi, Reuven, Yuni Aton, Ariel, Yaak, and Rachel, who patiently listened to me over the past year. The anonymous donor who permitted me to travel to various archives and visit Vilna and experience firsthand its charm and history. Finally, to my wife and children for their unstinting support throughout the project, even during long periods of hibernation in the basement office and extended international trips; you are what inspires me, and each of you, in your own special way, is evidence that the legacy of our families' Eastern European pre–World War II heritage will be carried on to the next generations.

Introduction

THE LIBRARY AT THE HEART OF THIS STORY—its books, fate, and symbolism—was the first modern Jewish public library. The Strashun Library began its life deep in Eastern Europe, in Vilna, in what is today the Baltic state of Lithuania, and ranked among the greatest intellectual institutions in all of Jewish Europe. Although a Jewish library, its holdings went well beyond biblical and rabbinic books, encompassing nearly all Jewish and secular genres, in a dozen languages. During World War II, over 90 percent of all Baltic Jews perished, but most of the library survived in a manner that defies credence. A treacherous journey that began in war-torn Vilna was fraught with looting, theft, destruction, efforts to save the books at the risk of life and limb, the fabrication of questionable historical narratives, the subsequent obfuscation of the library's provenance, and international litigation and diplomacy.

Judging a book by its cover, or even simply by its contents, is misleading. Appreciating what lies beneath the surface and who its readers were can be as rewarding as studying the contents of the books themselves. This belief is what drove me to the story of the Strashun Library, my journey beginning with my first significant foray into book collecting.

It was the winter of 1998, and I stood at the foot of the stairs in the basement of a stranger's home in the Boro Park section of Brooklyn, New York. And down the steps came a tall Hasid in full garb: a long black coat, side curls, which in the style of a Sikh were kept under his black hat, and of course, a ZZ Top-esque beard. My first meeting with the Hebrew book-dealer Chaim was a surreal experience.

After spending over a year trying to connect with this man, I received a call from an intermediary, a book collector, informing me that Chaim was in from Israel, his home base, and willing to meet in New York. But the get-together had to be the next day. Immediately I dropped everything and took the train from Washington, DC, to New York. Having never met him in person, I was admittedly guilty of assuming that I would be greeted by the stereotypical bookdealer: scholarly with round glasses slipping off his nose, pale skinned and stooped over from spending too much time indoors rummaging through piles of books, wearing a worn and ill-fitting suit paired with a bow tie. My assumptions about his appearance, it turned out, could not have been more wrong. After I realized that this was in fact the dealer, we began discussing the matter at hand: building my version of a rare book collection.

My bibliographical interests lay not simply in constructing a collection of old books, first editions, and a particular author or subject. Rather, I was interested in a very specific genre: books that were themselves part of a larger historical narrative and contained otherwise undiscovered tales, especially those which appear incongruous with conventional expectations of Hebrew books and Jewish history — books as storytellers. The bookdealer, no stranger to these and himself a bibliophile, immediately knew exactly what I was looking for. In fact, he even had some of them at hand. Irrespective of the garb, I realized I had found the perfect person to assist me in this endeavor.

Among the first books I purchased from Chaim was one that was very representative of my collecting goals, the *Besamim Rosh*. The *Besamim Rosh* was published in Berlin in 1793 and is a compendium of responsa attributed to R. Asher b. Jehiel (ca. 1250/59-1327) (Rosh), one of the greatest Jewish medieval legal scholars. The publisher, R. Saul Berlin (1740-1794), a German rabbi from an aristocratic Jewish family, claimed to have located an Italian sixteenth-century manuscript of 392 of Rosh's responsa. Berlin proceeded to print the responsa with his own extensive notes, under the collective title *Besamim Rosh*.[1] Berlin received endorsements from leading contemporary rabbis attesting to both the authenticity of the manuscript and its discoverer's erudition. Yet almost immediately after the book's publication, questions arose regarding Berlin's attribution of the manuscript. In particular, a few of the responsa appeared to espouse radical legal rulings that were out of character for Rosh as well as his contemporaries. This, in addition to other factors, led some to raise the charge that the *Besamim Rosh* was a forgery; these were not Rosh's responsa but Berlin's.[2] Forgeries of Hebrew religious texts are rare and unexpected, seemingly counter to the morals and ethics that attach to religion, easily piquing my interest in owning this oddity.[3]

What would compel someone to forge responsa? Hebrew books were not hugely profitable, and Saul was already a well-regarded rabbi without the need to gin up material for self-aggrandizement. Although it is impossible to know with certainty Saul's motivations, the falsification can be best understood within the larger historical context: the late eighteenth-century controversy regarding the nascent Jewish Enlightenment, the Haskalah movement, and in particular the form that would come to be known as the Berlin Haskalah. During its early period, adherents of the movement used a variety of methods to expand its ranks. This book was part of that campaign. An early proponent of the movement, Berlin preferred to spread and legitimize the Haskalah by claiming earlier antecedents, located within classic Jewish legal literary genres. In particular, Berlin and his compatriots and contemporaries were keen on conducting a comprehensive reevaluation and reformation of normative Judaism to better fit with modern conventions and philosophy. Nearly every position of the Haskalah found a home in the *Besamim Rosh*. Among the responsa are many that undermined and openly mocked rabbinic authority, and the continued applicability of biblical and rabbinic laws.[4] Not for nothing, one scholar crowned Berlin the "Jewish Voltaire."[5] Nevertheless, Berlin, by attributing these responsa to an unimpeachable source, Rosh, hoped that those who balked at joining the movement because of its novelty could be converted or, at the very least, stop persecuting members of the Haskalah.[6] The book itself, aside from the inherent bibliographical curiosity of the forgery of a religious text, told a larger story that went far beyond its contents and fitted well within my collecting goals.

Tracing the publication history of the *Besamim Rosh* yields yet another unexpected aspect of Hebrew printing: internal or self-censorship. Likely because of the controversy regarding the authenticity of the *Besamim Rosh*, the book was not reprinted until 1881 in Krakow, Poland.[7] The second edition's claim to be a perfect reprint of the first is false. The printer, without acknowledgment, omitted Saul's introduction and two of the more controversial letters. One missing letter channeled the secular Enlightenment and humanistic views regarding suicide, ascribing its motive to mental illness rather than to a rebellion against God.[8] By the same theory, Rosh ostensibly refused to apply normative Jewish law that denied burial in a Jewish cemetery and mourning rites. The second censored responsa suspends the prohibition against traveling on a horse or in a carriage on the Sabbath when one's personal dignity would otherwise suffer. Again, this position echoed that of the secular Enlightenment, emphasizing individual self-respect. The sometime condition of leniency, financial loss, but not humanistic concern, is expressly excluded as a rationale. Suspending this prohibition may have been particularly objectionable because of its historical consciousness in Jewish literature. The infamous heretic of rabbinic Judaism, dating to the Mishnaic period (ca. 200 CE), is Elisha ben Abuyah (Aher—"the other"). He was originally a great scholar, only to rebel later in life and go down the path of heresy. Among the handful of his enumerated sins was riding his horse on the Sabbath. Thus, this responsa implicitly minimizes the severity of the sin of the greatest Jewish heretic. Whatever the reasons behind the Krakow publisher's censorship, it adds another layer to the *Besamim Rosh's* external historical narrative, further aligning the *Besamim Rosh* with my collection goals.

The *Besamim Rosh* was the first book that opened my eyes to the immense power of literature to tell the multilayered and complex history of the Jewish people. I realized that by collecting storied books, I too could possess my own artifacts—albeit through a nonobvious type of artifact: a book that was important, but not only for its contents. This particular volume set me on my quest for storied books and fueled the creation of a library around that genre. It would be another book's story, however, that was the most complex and thrilling book history I had ever come across.

My hunt led me to a huge warehouse in an industrial park in Jerusalem at 2 am on a Monday night in June of 2003. The place and time were attributable to Chaim's eccentricities. Though he carried an excellent selection of books across subjects and time periods, purchasing was never a straightforward process. Rather, orders placed from his catalog were generally met with silence. A month or months later, a package arrived unannounced containing some or all of the requested books. At times, it even contained books requested from prior catalogs from years ago.

As with my initial meeting with Chaim, even traveling to Israel and meeting face to face was not without complications. Phone calls would be met by vague assurances of a meeting time but without concrete details. Instead, as was the case on one occasion, the summons came in the middle of the night without warning. For a book collector, calls like this are routine: if there are books to be found, the time and place are all part of the thrill of the hunt. Thus, I found myself standing in an otherwise abandoned industrial park in front of a huge warehouse in the middle of the night. Immediately on entering the building, I was hit with the distinctive smell of old books; and when the klieg lights blinked on, the sight of hundreds of shelves holding thousands of books greeted me. Despite the late hour, I would spend however long Chaim permitted, going through shelf by shelf searching for storied books for my collection.

I was not disappointed. After an hour, on a high shelf, I located an eighteenth-century Hebrew grammar book by Shlomo Zalman Hanau (1687–1746), *Binyan Shlomo*.[9] Hanau was intensely interested in reviving the role of Hebrew grammar from obscurity in the study of Jewish texts. He wrote a succession of books on the topic; his first, published when he was twenty-one, was *Binyan Shlomo*. On its face, the book is unremarkable, a tome discussing the nuances of Hebrew grammar, much of it focused on medieval texts. This copy, however, contained a page smaller in size than the others, lacking pagination and appearing after the book's ostensible final page.

This page contained a corrigendum to the book, yet not in the traditional sense. This single page was not included in the original printing. Instead, sometime after the book was published, the leaf was inserted into this copy. The reason for the later insertion was that in the author's discussions he cited earlier Hebrew grammarians and at times sharply disagreed with their opinions.[10] Disagreement alone was unremarkable and is among the features that define rabbinic Judaism. Instead, Hanau's tone and language were unusual in their vitriol and tenor. Hanau repeatedly characterized his predecessors' arguments as "devoid of logic," based on "ignorance" and "carelessness," or a "figment of their imagination." Hanau also punned on their names and that of their books to belittle their scholarship. The *bet din* (rabbinical court) of Frankfurt, under whose authority the book was printed, ordered Hanau to take corrective action, express his contrition, and apologize, otherwise they would rescind their endorsements, order the recall of the book, and issue a ban against it. Hanau agreed to do so, and printed the small page at the end of this copy. But rather than simply complying, he deployed a particularly clever stratagem for doing so. The appended page includes an appeal for forgiveness but does not stop there; instead Hanau quotes the allegedly offensive statements, allowing the reader to comprehend every alleged slight, the most salacious material, without having to read through the entire book, subtly undermining any notion of contrition. The rare "apology" page was bound into this copy.[11]

Hanau's sharp tone and unwillingness simply to abide by precedent was a reflection of his views regarding the critical importance of grammar and its role in Jewish life. Were he to pledge fealty to either his predecessors or the current state of the texts, his study would be limited to

אמר המחבר הנה כשלתי בלשוני בהגנות אשר הגנתי על המחברים
והרביתי מלין ונגעתי בכבוד חכמים) הן לא טורד וכחוב[?]
עשיתי זאת ולא עלתה על דעתי שום חתטבת חוץ או פינוג לכוות חכמים
בזלה רק כתבכונתי להלהיב כפם המעיין ולהעיר אוכו לשמוע בלמודים)
על כן בזאתי לבקש מהם מחילה :

על אשר דון יצחק אברבנאל כתבתי לא כדעת ורבר ודבריו לא הטכל
ובמקום אשר כתבתי עליו הנה זאת באתהו מפאת קטרין ידיעתו
שלא ירד לסוף דעת הכביא / וכל זה יגא מאתי כשגגה היוגא מלתכי השליע
ומתטוח אכי לסכיו ומבקש מחילה מעגמותיו הקדושים וזכוח אכי בחכמת
וסכידות הטר שימלח לי הדון על דברים כאלה :

על הכבס אבן עזרא כתבתי לא בטון ברוחב דעתי / ובמקום אשר
ומתעשר ואין כל / ובמקום אשר ואשתמיטתי מקרא מלא / ולא
היה לי להפריו על מדותי להרחיב פי כנד החכם ההוא אשר קטכו עבה
מותני / אף כי חכמתו עמדה לי שלא יקום לדברים כאלה מנד חסכון
ידעתי כי שונג אכי לכל פשע :

על הכב רבינו דוד קמחי כתבתי לפעמים ולא דק / או לא חם לקמחי
סונקמחא עתיכא עין / אומיף מיד ואומיך קמחא / בודא[?]
עזוכיתי הטו אלה שיבלא דברים כאלה שיגלו מפי / שלא לי מרי וסר עוכי וחטאתי
תכופר :

על המדקדק רבי אל[י]' נחור כתבתי לפעמים בדברינו לא בחרתי /
או וטעמו כליר שלמות / או אל[י]' וקין כו / ואף הוא יענה ויאמר
כלתחי :

על הכב בעל שית יצחק כתבתי לפעמים למי מדכים למי שית / או
והלכה שיתה / או וכל השומע יגחק / וכדומה לזה פנעתי בכבוד
הרב אף כי קלותי לדבר כגדו כחמתי כי עשיתי וכבוד הכב ביקוחו חול[?]
בתצלה העליונה ידע ולא איכפת לי וחלילה לי מהחדל לבקש מחילה
מעגמותיו הקדושים ורב שחח על כבודו כבודו מחול :

על שאר המחברים כאשר הגנתי עליאם והוגחתי כוחי בחלק כביד
מה יחד הנני עומד ומתחרט על דברים כאלה וסניחות מי יבן
לכן וזאותי כל יעבוד פי לדבר עוד כדברים האלה וחדל יכפר בעדי :

the abstract, and that was surely not the case for something as fundamental as the composition and rules of the language itself. Hanau eventually would pen books specifically intended to revise the liturgical texts based on grammatical rules. Of course, like *Binyan Shlomo*, those too would be met with substantial opposition. The small page spoke volumes about Hanau's views.[12]

This copy was imprinted with an additional historic artifact. According to the book's ex libris, this copy of *Binyan Shlomo* had most recently belonged to the Central Rabbinical Library at Hechal Shlomo, a religious organization in Jerusalem, whose library holdings, as Chaim informed me, had recently been liquidated. That was not the only book I bought that evening. As I combed through the books, I noticed that others bore the Hechal Shlomo ex libris. But many also included a series of ex libris that were curious in and of themselves. One ex libris in particular was of personal interest, that of Mattityahu Strashun, a nineteenth-century rabbinic scholar from Vilna, Lithuania. He was a prominent community leader, philanthropist, and most relevant to me, a book collector who built a substantial and diverse library. His collection habits were nonconformist and strayed far afield from traditional rabbinic libraries that were limited to that literature. Instead, Mattityahu's criteria went further than a focus on any one single area of literature and permitted him to create a groundbreaking private library that would ultimately have repercussions that reached beyond himself and influenced the entirety of Jewish Vilna. Because of that history, the books with his ex libris were no longer simply rarities; they signified that he was a unique collector for his time and status, and instigated my interest in studying his biography and bibliophilia. The story of those books led to an exploration of the history of Mattityahu's personal library and that of the first Jewish public library–which was created from his collection and through his largess — Vilna's Strashun Library.

The story of Strashun's library, however, begins well before his lifetime; it begins with the long history of Jewish Vilna, which crystallized, in the seventeenth and eighteenth centuries, around the figure of the Vilna Gaon, a distinctly modern progenitor of Strashun. Vilna was an almost mythical city known as the Jerusalem of Lithuania. Vilna was not merely a geographical location; it also represented the ideal space of the Jewish study house, dedicated to rigorous scholarship, intellectual erudition, independence of mind, and the pursuit of knowledge from Torah to mysticism, mathematics to science. This ideal is what allowed for the flourishing of a distinct form of Haskalah, a uniquely Lithuanian expression of Haskalah, which can remain staunchly Orthodox yet explore secular knowledge, to simultaneously embrace the contemporary without abandoning history.[13]

Elijah of Vilna (1720–1797), otherwise known as the Vilna Gaon, was perhaps the best-known personality to emerge from Vilna. He pioneered a program that broadened Jewish study beyond the otherwise historically restricted canon and applied contemporary analytical and research methodologies to the entire corpus of Jewish literature. This approach reinvigorated Jewish study and paved a path for it to endure and thrive into the modern period. He inspired a cadre of scholars that championed that brand of interdisciplinary scholarship, which eventually became synonymous with Vilna.

Strashun was an adherent of that Vilna tradition. Mattityahu did not hold a rabbinic position, and his scholarship found expression in his hundreds of articles that appeared in a variety of forums, and one published book. Those materials display an almost preternatural command of all traditional Jewish sources. He was particularly adept at explicating difficult passages by identifying unknown parallel citations in obscure texts. His writings are replete with discussions of Jewish history, Hebrew poetry, grammar, philology, philosophy, liturgy, bibliography, and regularly used Latin, German, Greek, and Russian sources. His diverse scholarship was fueled by and represented in the holdings of his first-rate library of over eight thousand books and manuscripts, which was unusually wide-ranging for a collector and certainly for the library of a rabbinic scholar.

During his lifetime, Mattityahu's singularly rich collection combined with his virtually open-door policy afforded those who otherwise lacked access to books vital to their respective scholarly passions the opportunity to consult texts. Yet his munificence extended beyond opening his home and library for intellectual pursuits. He envisioned that his personal library would create nothing less than a living monument to scholarship, becoming one of Vilna's greatest institutions and ultimately an embodiment of its unique and elevated status among European Jewry. To reach that goal, he bequeathed his library to the Vilna community and expressly granted the community perpetual and absolute control of the library. He also pledged monies and investment property for the maintenance and expansion of the library, and eventually a special building was erected to house his temple of knowledge. That building—the Strashun Library—matured into a unique institution of Jewish public culture in pre-Holocaust Europe.

The Strashun Library was the first of its kind—a fully public Jewish library operated, owned, and accessible by the entire community. Jewish libraries had existed for centuries, yet prior to the Strashun Library they were private or quasi-private, taking the form of personal libraries; those owned by synagogues, Jewish schools, societies, or institutions; or part of larger study halls. Although in some instances those libraries were funded by the community and the public was granted access, legally speaking, they remained private property. Consequently, these libraries' holdings were necessarily restricted by and subject to the vagaries and ideologies of their respected owners and not their patrons, and were at risk that, at any time, public access could be limited or shut off entirely.

Mattityahu appreciated that nothing less than full public control regarding all aspects of a library qualified as a truly Jewish public library. Obtaining that control required public ownership and not just its financial support, because that relegated the community's role to that of a booster but lacking ultimate authority. A library owned by the community, and no longer the property of a distinct subclass, ensured that the library's holdings would mirror that of the public at large; and artificial access controls could not be implemented without the community's input. The institution's absolute public status would naturally provide a singular space for the ingathering of all of Vilna's diverse population—scholars, laypersons, rich, poor, secular, and religious Jews of all stripes and persuasions—under a single roof.

Over the next century and until the Holocaust, Vilna's unique zeitgeist gave rise to myriad and variegated religious, agnostic, secular and even antireligious, intellectual, political, and social movements, institutions, and organizations. Many significant Jewish personalities hailing from all areas of Jewish scholarship and culture called Vilna home. The Strashun Library became a mecca for those men and women. This neutral meeting place was a microcosm of the larger admixture that defined the Vilna Jewish community. Vilna and the Strashun Library created a symbiotic relationship, each fostering and exemplifying the best of the other. Mattityahu's library, emblematic of his personal version of Vilna, metamorphosed into Vilna's version of itself. The Strashun Library was Vilna's study house in the real and symbolic sense.

The Holocaust put an end to Jewish life in Eastern Europe and decimated Vilna in particular. Yet despite overwhelming odds, including the plunder of the Strashun Library and the complete destruction of its building, a significant portion of the Strashun Library survived intact. In one of the great ironies of the Holocaust, the Strashun Library's survival, as well as that of other European libraries, is largely attributable to the actions of the Nazis themselves.

In Frankfurt, the Nazis established an institute and research library for the study of Jews, its intended purpose to provide "academic" justifications for antisemitism. To fill the library's shelves, a special army unit was established; its mission was to identify and plunder important Jewish books and cultural items. The Strashun Library fell victim to this rapacious campaign, and a substantial portion of its books were sent to Frankfurt. The Nazis took extraordinary measures to ensure the safety of their plundered loot, and much of it survived the war, including the majority of the Strashun Library books. After the war, the Germans' cache of books was discovered by the US Army.

The question of the appropriate heir to Eastern European Jewry, and consequently the most appropriate place for the extant Strashun Library, resulted in a tug-of-war between two Jewish institutions, the YIVO Institute for Jewish Research in New York and Hechal Shlomo in Jerusalem. The ensuing fight over the Strashun Library's remains nearly wiped out its unique symbolism and legacy. In the race for supremacy over the heritage and legacy of the Jewish people, the protagonists lost sight of the meaning of Vilna and its Strashun Library.

YIVO and Hechal Shlomo were institutions that held diametrically opposed views of Eastern European Jewry's prewar legacy and the future of Judaism. Each institution unilaterally crowned itself heir to the no-longer-extant European Jewish experience and the preeminent organization to lead the next generation of Jews. The Strashun Library proved a particularly attractive prize for both, and each expended considerable effort to win the contest for the library.

A modest attempt to simply understand a handful of ex libris that had fallen into my hands, which began life with a Vilna book collector, led me to try to uncover the storied history of the Strashun Library. In the process, I visited multiple state and institutional libraries and archives on three continents, some of which, most notably in the former Soviet Union, have only recently become accessible to researchers. My journey led down a number of rabbit holes, but resulted in a far more nuanced story of the books I discovered at the Jerusalem warehouse. Like the *Besamim Rosh*, that story involved elements of philosophical fraud and censoring facts in furtherance of ideological goals. And once no longer needed for ideological gains, the books were converted into banal financial assets. Yet the story of those books also included how a single collector and his library could evolve into more than the sum of its parts: a representation, and ultimately artifact, of the Vilna Jewish community at large converted the entirety of Vilna into a virtual study hall.

Jewish life in Eastern Europe is a mere shell of its pre-Holocaust glory, most of it lost to the Nazis' attempt to wipe the Jews from the face of the earth. Yet Jews refused to succumb to unprecedented persecution and now have returned to their pre–World War II numbers, albeit in different geographic locales and forms. The Strashun Library, too, has undergone displacement and loss. Notwithstanding the chaos of war and the confusion of its aftermath, contests in auction houses, and the implosion of its guardian institutions and nation-states, the Strashun Library remained and remains indestructible, ever evolving in its symbolism. Those books I held in my hands in the dark of night in the Jerusalem warehouse captured within them not just their own story, but the history of the people of the book.

CHAPTER ONE

Vilna: The Study House

IN THE SUMMER OF 1812, Napoleon Bonaparte marched his battalions eastward, across the Neman River and on toward the city of Vilna,[1] the cultural and political capital of Lithuania. There the French emperor rested a fortnight before pushing on with his ill-fated invasion of Russia.[2] According to legend, what he found there, a city with an expansive and thriving Jewish population, led Napoleon to label Vilna the Jerusalem of the North.[3] Unbeknownst to him, he played an unintentional role in perpetuating Vilna's unique ethos and place in Jewish history.

Vilna is located close to two hundred miles southeast of the Baltic Sea, at the confluence of the Vilna and Neris Rivers. The Vilna River, which likely gave the city its name, is a derivative of the Lithuanian *vilnis*, a surge or flow. If that is correct, that is an apt description of the city's history. Vilna never rested comfortably within clearly defined borders — whether geographical, political, religious, linguistic, ideological, demographic, or cultural — forcing it to constantly straddle the divide, never allowing its inhabitants the luxury of pledging fealty to one side or another. Rather than tearing Vilna asunder, that ever-shifting landscape forged its special and nearly mythical identity. Vilna's lack of hegemony was conversely an opportunity for it to identify and embrace the most beneficial elements that it was exposed to, without regard to where the ideas originated — Vilna "gathers the history of [Eurasia . . .], and streams it into uncharted channels."[4] Vilna came to represent less a geographic location and more "a condition." Vilna was not a frontier or border town; Vilna is perhaps best described as a threshold, "a zone where time and space swell," which "can neither be measured nor localized."[5] According to the Nobel laureate and poet Czesław Miłosz, born in Vilna in 1911, Vilna's specialness was as an "enclave . . . neither Polish nor not-Polish, neither Lithuanian nor not-

Lithuanian, neither a provincial nor capital city . . . an oddity, a city of mixed-up, overlapping regions," which ultimately precipitated the creation of a veritable "Atlantis."[6]

From Vilna's beginning, it was passed from king to king, country to country, and state to empire. Vilna's significance dates to 1323, when it was named the capital of the Grand Duchy of Lithuania. In 1386, the merger of Poland and Lithuania, accomplished in part by the marriage of the king of Lithuania to the queen of Poland, placed Vilna under a single monarch who controlled both countries, although Lithuania remained a separate state. The Union of Lublin, in 1569, resulted in Vilna's becoming part of the newly created Polish-Lithuanian Commonwealth. The third, and final, Partition of Poland in 1795 assimilated Vilna into the Russian Empire. In 1915, during World War I, Vilna was occupied by the Germans. Only in 1918, after switching a half-dozen times between Polish and Russian rule, did Lithuania become an independent republic, with Vilna as its capital. For Vilna, that return to independence was short-lived. Lithuania remained independent until 1939; however, in 1920, Vilna was reincorporated into Poland, where it remained until the onset of World War II. In September 1939, immediately after the signing of the Molotov-Ribbentrop Pact, Vilna came under Soviet control; but three months later, yet again, Vilna regained its independence, albeit for a brief nine months. In July 1940, the Soviets reoccupied Vilna and would remain until displaced by the Germans in June 1941. When the Soviets reconquered Vilna in July 1944, it became part of the USSR. Vilna was returned to independence in 1991, when Lithuania seceded from the USSR, and Vilna was recrowned an independent Lithuania's capital.

Religious diversity has been a hallmark of Vilna. "Located at the frontiers of every spiritual milieu of Europe," Vilna residents included Catholics, Protestants, Byzantine Orthodox, Jews, Karaites, Muslims, and pagans. Acting as a religious threshold "nurtured a landscape of religious tolerance and cultural cross-pollination."[7] This "cross-pollination" is evident within one of Vilna's oldest religious buildings, the Vilnius Cathedral, located at the center of the old city, which dates to the thirteenth century. Its crypt contains a mural from the 1390s, which blends two seemingly mutually exclusive elements. The mural is executed in the Byzantine style, which was at times entirely iconoclastic and even when that was modified, depicted Jesus as invulnerable; nonetheless, the mural employs the Christian perspective of the Crucifixion.[8] Likewise, the first book published in Vilna, in 1522, *Malaia Podorozhnaia Knizhnitsa (The Small*

Travel Book), is a virtual Babel. The book's publisher, Francis Skaryna (ca. 1485/1490 to before 1552), was a humanist scholar who was likely raised Catholic. The book itself was written for a public lay audience and comprised Byzantine Orthodox prayers and a religious calendar, which are printed in Cyrillic characters in the Slavic/Belarussian language.[9]

Jews were among Vilna's most prominent groups, inextricably linked with Lithuania and Vilna from their earliest histories. A Jew was literally the first to put Lithuania on the map. In 1375, a Jewish cartographer, Abraham Cresques from the island of Majorca, created the Catalan Atlas for the Prince of Aragon, and for the first time, marked Lithuania on a map.[10] What began on paper culminated in Jews becoming part of the very fabric of Vilna. In the 1890s, a Danish ethnographer, Age Meyer Benedictsen, visited Vilna and in his subsequent chronicle of his trip, remarked that "Vilna more than anything is the town of the Jews."[11]

Evidence of Jewish settlement in Vilna dates to the mid-fifteenth century.[12] In 1527, however, Jews were officially banned from the city. The ban did not last long, and at least by the mid-1500s, Jews had returned. In 1593, King Sigmund III legally sanctioned Jewish settlement, permitting them to engage in certain trades and commerce, practice religion, and establish a cemetery, synagogue, ritual bath, and meat shops.[13] In 1633, Sigmund's son, Władisłav IV, reaffirmed his father's privileges and granted what is considered "the fundamental charter" of Vilna Jewry.[14] That charter established boundaries for a Jewish ghetto[15] and sanctioned Jewish life in that area. The Jews could operate independently of the municipality, purchase land, engage in previously prohibited trades and professions, and erect a synagogue and other social and religious structures.

The charter set aside only a diminutive area in a triangular shape that restricted the Jews to three narrow streets—Jews Street in the center flanked by Butchers Street (today Marko Antokolskio, after the Jewish sculpture artist), and St. Michael's Street. That area was so confining that it was most easily navigated, not by using the streets, but through a series of interconnected courtyards and alleys. These courtyards, *hoyfs*, became de facto streets to such a degree that building locations were identified by their courtyard's owners, for example, Reb Leib-Leizer's Hoyf, and not their official street addresses.[16] Unlike some other Jewish settlements in Poland and Lithuania, Vilna's Jewish Quarter was in the heart of the city, and Jews were integral to Vilna's character.[17]

The earliest Jewish settlement in Vilna coincided with a general shift in Jewish demographics from Western Europe eastward. During that same time frame, there was also a relocation of the center of Jewish scholarship. From the beginning of the last millennium, traditional rabbinic Jewish scholarship was concentrated in the German lands. But from the late sixteenth century onward, the center of that scholarship migrated eastward, and Poland became ascendant. By the seventeenth century, Poland contained the largest Jewish population in the Diaspora.[18] Vilna too saw its star rise.

Notwithstanding the accuracy of the Napoleonic legend, by the time he entered Vilna, it was an epicenter of Jewish intellectualism, a veritable Jerusalem, influencing the rest of the Jewish world and even regularly receiving pilgrims to visit its institutions and scholars. By the early nineteenth century, Vilna was one of the most important political, cultural, and religious centers in the Russian Empire, and home to its largest Jewish community. In 1818 there were over fourteen thousand Jews in Vilna, who made up 42 percent of its total population. Throughout the nineteenth century, Vilna's Jewish population continued to grow; and at the close of that century, it could count over 61,000 Jews, out of approximately 155,000 Vilna residents.[19]

Vilna's rise to prominence is traceable in no small measure to Elijah of Vilna, a legendary figure of such extraordinary intellect that he was simply referred to as the Gaon, or Genius, of Vilna.[20] Initially a recluse, eschewing public recognition of his intellectual prowess, later in life he took on increasingly more public roles, and to no greater effect than opposing the nascent Hasidic movement.[21] The Gaon's opposition to the movement was rooted in his core belief in the primacy and centrality of Torah study over all other religious practices. The Hasidim, however, espoused a mystically oriented form of Judaism. They emphasized an emotional connection with God, *devekut*, that was achieved through proper intention (*kavanah*) and resulted in a number of novel practices. This theology relegated Torah study to a secondary if not tertiary role in Judaism. The rabbinic scholar no longer occupied a lofty position in the Hasidic movement. The new leaders, *tsaddikim* (holy ones), channeled mysticism to act as intermediaries between the people and God. To the Gaon, the Hasidic movement was nothing less than pure heresy.[22]

In 1772 the Gaon took up the cudgel and led a campaign to stamp out the Hasidim. Vilna and other communities issued bans, burned Hasidic books, and imprisoned their leaders.[23] Ultimately, however, the Gaon was unsuccessful in suppressing the movement, although the Hasidic movement did respond to some of the criticisms and adjusted some of its more extreme practices. The Hasidic movement survived and expanded its ranks and territories, including gaining a foothold in Lithuania. Yet the Gaon's opposition would have further reaching and more lasting effects for the Jews of Vilna. That controversy proved a catalyst—but not the defining feature

—for shaping the contours of the characteristics that became most closely associated with Jews in Lithuania and especially those in Vilna.[24]

In this controversy, the Gaon's adherents were referred to by their stance, Mitnagdim, (those opposed) to the Hasidim. Yet that moniker failed to express the full nature of the personalities of the Jews in Lithuania and Vilna. They were not just reactionary; they carried their own specific characteristics. Instead, they became known as a special class of Jews, Litvaks.

A Litvak's life's focus was on Torah study, whose devotion to God was expressed in *yirah* (fear of God), rather than emotional and experiential *ahavah* (love of God).[25] A Litvak was stereotypically depicted as a cold logician, devoid of an emotional connection to Judaism—one most closely associated with a purely intellectual appreciation of Judaism, a skeptic, and deliberately living an austere and dour existence. Their critics accused Litvaks of leading a dangerous lifestyle, one that would lead only to apostasy. According to those critics, a Litvak was lacking a *yidishe neshome*, an authentic Jewish soul, and was mocked as having instead a *tselem kop*, literally a head with a Christian cross—expressed in the common Hasidic saying "Split the head of a Litvak, and you'll find a cross."[26] A more charitable articulation of the Litvak, and his *tselem kop*, inverts the meaning of *tselem* and connects it to the Hebrew verb *hitzliv*, meaning literally to "cross over or back-and-forth." A Litvak used his *tselem kop* to dissect and analyze every piece of evidence to arrive at the absolute truth.[27] Whether the term *Litvak* carried a positive or negative connotation, from the period of the Gaon onward, Vilna's Jews' self-perception was a fundamentally distinctive articulation of Judaism.

The Litvak's emphasis on intellectualism also encompassed a specific program of Torah study, which was pioneered by the Gaon and that itself was a break with tradition.[28] For centuries scholars severely circumscribed the sorts of Jewish works worthy of study and focused on Talmud and Jewish law, excluding a large part of rabbinic and even biblical literature. The Gaon, however, sought to systematize the study of Jewish texts through the broadening of the corpus and applied himself to otherwise previously ignored areas of Jewish literature: the complete Bible, including the Prophets and Writings, grammar, and even the cantillation marks.[29] According to the Gaon, the entire body of rabbinic literature was interrelated, and neglecting any part necessarily resulted in misunderstanding and misinterpreting the Talmudic and legal texts.[30] Indeed, the Gaon's erudition and mastery of nearly every area of rabbinic Jewish literature is well established, no small feat considering that the literature encompasses the Babylonian Talmud (the most recent English translation and explanatory texts consist of seventy-three volumes), in addition to the more obscure and smaller Jerusalem Talmud (its English translation stands at over twenty-nine volumes), dozens of rabbinic books predating the compiling of the Jerusalem and Babylonian Talmuds, and commentaries written from the eighth century onward, in addition to kabbalistic, legal, and liturgical texts.[31] The Gaon also penned his own commentary on a number of these books,[32] many of which are included in modern editions of Jewish texts.[33]

The Gaon's expansive views regarding Torah study allegedly extended to non-Jewish texts. According to one of his students, Rabbi Barukh of Shklov, the Gaon forcefully advocated for the inclusion of secular texts in Torah study. Barukh claims that "I heard from the Holy One that, to the extent that a person is lacking in knowledge of secular subjects, he will lack one hundredfold in the wisdom of the Torah. For the Torah and secular knowledge are bound together. . . . He commanded me to translate whatever possible of the secular subjects into our holy tongue in order to recover what they [the Gentiles] had devoured . . . so that knowledge should proliferate among our people of Israel."[34]

Beyond expanding the boundaries of relevant texts, the Gaon's approach to study was similarly innovative. He eschewed historically abstract and convoluted analyses (*pilpul*) and instead emphasized a logical and rational text-based (*peshat*) methodology of analysis, one that sought the true meaning of the text and sought to impose a rational system of study.[35] This dedication to rigorous scholarship led to a corresponding emphasis on the accuracy of the text and frequent textual emendations, precipitating reexaminations of seemingly fixed interpretations.[36]

Notwithstanding the Gaon's radical course of study, he remained staunchly Orthodox. His guiding principle was an unwavering commitment to intellectual excellence; and that, from his perspective, required an eccentric approach to the nature of Jewish scholarship and not a reformation of normative Jewish religious practice.

After his death in 1797, the Gaon's reputation spread, and he was subsequently canonized in the pantheon of great Jewish intellectual figures.

Vilna, with its inherent connection to the Gaon, saw its status in world Jewry elevated; the Gaon and Vilna were virtually synonymous.[37] In most of Europe his reputation was symbolic, but in Vilna his pioneering and distinctive form of scholarship made a lasting impression. The Gaon's students, and the circle that formed around them, sought to disseminate and further develop the Gaon's methods and philosophies even as there were divergent opinions regarding the substance and central ideas of his intellectual legacy. Vilna became a breeding ground for nonconventional forms of study that emphasized rational interpretations, historical analysis, and intellectual primacy over mystical practice, and that simultaneously acknowledged and retained the values of traditional scholarship and religious practice and its unique expression of Haskalah.[38] These maskilim sought to recast tradition so that it represented their understanding of a rational Judaism in its purest form.

The Gaon's leading follower, R. Hayim ben Isaac of Volozhin, took two important steps to perpetuate the Gaon's values regarding the ideal form of scholarship.[39] First, Hayim wrote a comprehensive work, *Nefesh ha-Hayim* (*Breath of Life*), which articulated the philosophical underpinnings of the Gaon's ideas regarding the primacy of Torah study and implicitly questioning the Hasidic perspective of Jewish values.[40] *Nefesh ha-Hayim* concentrated on emphasizing the value of Torah study over all else, including prayer. Hayim's discussion incorporated mystical texts that Hasidim had previously interpreted as supportive of their views, providing an implicit rebuttal of their ideas. According to Hayim, *devekut* (cleaving) with God could be achieved solely through Torah study and a lifestyle that emphasized *yirah*, without resorting to alternative modes of religious practice.[41]

Hayim also provided a physical space that fostered the Gaon's ideal of scholarship. In 1802 Hayim established a yeshiva in the town of Volozhin, located over one hundred kilometers from Vilna, that promoted full-time Torah study. Volozhin, like Vilna, served as an intellectual center that emphasized scholarship over all else. Unlike prior yeshivot, Volozhin operated independently—both in terms of funding and oversight—from any single community and without requiring the involvement of the local communal rabbi (although Hayim himself was and remained the rabbi of Volozhin). Historically, yeshivot were supported by the community, and the students relied on the largess of the populace for lodging and food. Hayim's model inverted this relationship, in which he raised the necessary funds to maintain the yeshiva and pay local householders for board.

This independence emancipated the yeshiva students from internal communal issues and financial constraints, allowing them to concentrate on their studies undisturbed.[42] The Gaon too espoused removal from normal societal responsibilities as integral for success in study. Moreover, Hayim ushered in a new ideal of a yeshiva head and shook up the historical communal power structure. No longer was the town rabbi automatically the head of the school; that position must be occupied by a Torah scholar, with the rabbi performing an adjunct role at best.[43] The total effect of the Volozhin yeshiva served to underscore the elevated place of Torah study and Torah scholars. Among the earliest public support for Volozhin came from Vilna, including the Gaon's son R. Abraham.[44]

Hayim may have been the first of the Gaon students to establish a yeshiva and receive the support of Vilna's leaders; however, Vilna in no way ceded its place as the preeminent location of Torah study. Some in Vilna saw Volozhin as a niche institution, with only limited impact on Lithuanian Torah study, and limited in perpetuating the legacy of the Gaon. Evidence of Vilna's continued dominance and elite status was manifest in Vilna's ability to attract the best and the brightest scholars and maintain numerical superiority in students and institutions.[45] In 1822, twenty years after Volozhin was established, according to one observer, "Vilna's greatness is heard from afar, a metropolis, and its reputation is because it is full of outstanding students, scholars, and scribes—Vilna's yeshivot and schools number that of its inhabitants."[46]

Vilna contained the greatest numbers of batei midrash and schools, and also became the mecca for Haskalah, but one that was unique to Vilna. Those maskilim did not seek to uproot tradition, but to recast it so that it represented their understanding of a rational Judaism in its purest form, and saw its antecedents in the Gaon's scholarship. Haskalah, however, is not a uniform term and has been applied to disparate movements. How the Haskalah manifested itself and its particular goals varied widely over time. For example, in the instance of Saul Berlin, Haskalah took on the form of a vehicle for radical religious reforms. Whereas in the case of early and mid-nineteenth-century Vilna, tradition coexisted with the addition of secular studies—channeling the Gaon's unwavering focus on exacting scholarship that necessitated independence of mind and openness to alternative texts and methods. Vilna's form of Haskalah is sometimes referred to as the Haskalah of the North, in contradistinction to that of Berlin, which was characterized by its opposition to religion. Notwithstanding the precise definition of Haskalah, until the mid- to late

nineteenth century, many Vilna maskilim remained religiously observant and felt no need to abandon Judaism while adopting new educational
and philosophical theories.[47]

During the nineteenth century, the Russian government, in fits and
starts, attempted to address the "Jewish question" of how to integrate
Jews into Russian society. Reforms related to this campaign profoundly
affected nearly every aspect of Jewish life: education, family, dress, language, law, rabbinic authority, communal structure, and economic life.[48]
The Jews were subject to numerous draconian laws, including the forced
conscription of Jewish boys from as young as age twelve, with lengths
of service as long as thirty years, the purpose of which was not military,
but to convert Jews.[49] Nonetheless, many of the reforms arguably were
motivated by liberal ideas to modernize Jewish life and were seemingly
aligned with the goals of Haskalah; and members of the Vilna Haskalah
were among its most active proponents and even spearheaded some of
those policies.

Vilna's Haskalah also introduced nontraditional forms of Jewish literature.[50] But unlike in Western Europe, in Vilna, Yiddish and Hebrew
were retained even in those new models.[51] The late nineteenth and early
twentieth century saw many new forms of Jewish literature and substantial modifications in readers' habits. Nonreligious books in Yiddish and
Hebrew became commonplace. These new forms displaced the emphasis
on rabbinic literature, and readership of these books was common among
men and women.[52] Like the incorporation of modernity within the intellectual class of Vilna, these new forms adopted by the masses still were
overshadowed by the substantial popularity of religious texts. Women,
for example, were voracious readers of Yiddish fictional literature, and
yet traditional translations of the Bible and prayer books remained the
most widely sold books.

Many of the Jewish, Hebrew and Yiddish, poets and writers called
Vilna home. Kalman Shulman (1819–1899) studied in the Volozhin Yeshiva and eventually moved to Vilna. He translated into Hebrew many
secular and Jewish history, scientific, and belletristic books, and wrote
his own books on these topics. These books promoted and disseminated
Hebrew literature and general knowledge among Russian Jewry. Shulman coupled his modern approach to literature with a religious lifestyle.
At times he omitted passages from his translations that ran counter to
his personal beliefs.[53] The most important poet of the Haskalah, and according to some the greatest Jewish poet since the Middle Ages, Yehudah

Leib Gordon (1830–1902), was a Vilna native.[54] Avraham Dov Lebensohn (Adam ha-Kohen), a poet and one of the pioneers of Haskalah education, found his success in Vilna.[55] Similarly, the Hebrew novelist Abraham Mapu (1806–1867) briefly lived in Vilna, and his historical romance novel —the most popular Hebrew novel of the nineteenth century, *Ahavat Zion* —was published in Vilna.[56] The first books of Sholem Yankev Abramovitsh (1835–1917), known by his pen name, Mendele Moykher-Sforim, who attended one of Vilna's prominent yeshivot and was one of the founders of modern Yiddish and Hebrew literature, were published in Vilna.[57]

Ayzik Meyer Dik (1807/14?–1893) was an active member of Vilna's Haskalah (and religiously observant) and supported many of the reforms of Alexander II. Dik initially published in Hebrew, but soon afterward switched to Yiddish as his preferred medium. Dik was commissioned to write a weekly booklet of short stories, and he ultimately produced close to four hundred.[58] Literary salons popped up all over Vilna to discuss, debate, and analyze this new literature.[59]

In the mid-nineteenth century, Vilna was home to the largest Jewish publishing house in all of Europe, Romm Press. In 1836, Tsar Nicholas I imposed a comprehensive and severe policy of censorship of Jewish books that shuttered Jewish publishing houses.[60] But Romm Press was immune from that law and was effectively granted a monopoly, which continued until the early 1860s.[61] Romm Press published over fourteen hundred books, and its lasting imprint is on its edition of the Talmud printed from 1880 to 1886.[62] The Talmud not only was printed in Vilna, but also incorporated its scholarship, most obviously with the inclusion of the Gaon's comments on all the tractates from a manuscript written in his hand.[63] But beyond his comments, the Gaon's methodology is front and center. The publisher spent considerable resources to ensure the accuracy of the text and sought out manuscripts in the Vatican Library, among other locations.[64] Subsequently, the publisher became secondary to the city, and that edition simply became known as the Vilna Shas (Talmud). The Vilna Shas remains today the canonical edition of the Talmud.[65]

Romm Press did not limit itself to religious texts. To the contrary, the press published books in Hebrew and Yiddish, across a wide array of subjects and genres. After being rejected by other publishers, Isaac Ber Levinsohn's *Teudah beYisrael*, one of the most influential Haskalah texts, was published twice by Romm Press in the nineteenth century.[66] Numerous Hebrew and Yiddish translations of world literature, science, math, and history are all part of the Romm catalog.[67] Nonetheless, traditional texts still remained popular, yet even those saw changes to accommodate modern sensibilities and tastes. The classic *Tsene Rene*, the Yiddish translation of the Bible aimed at women, underwent revisions in the font, language, and layout that gave it a more Western or modern feel.[68]

In some sense, Romm Press's influence extended to America. During World War I, Americans had difficulty obtaining Hebrew books from Europe. Consequently, in 1921 the Jewish Publication Society (JPS) purchased a high-quality press, of the type that was previously used by only European Hebrew publishers. A former worker at Romm Press, Moses Alperovich, managed the new JPS Press, and he "seemed to embody precisely that cultural transfer from Europe to America that the press . . . as a whole represented."[69]

Access to information rapidly expanded with the introduction of newspapers, another nontraditional aspect of literary culture that rose to prominence in the nineteenth-century Russian Empire. Always striving to find the best medium to spread its ideology, the Haskalah embraced newspapers and journals. One of the first Hebrew weeklies, *Ha-Karmel*, hailed from Vilna and published many articles by leaders of the Vilna Haskalah, and included world news and, at times, supplements in Russian and Yiddish. Many of the leading Hebrew writers contributed to Vilna's progressive Hebrew daily, *Ha-Zeman*.[70] In the early twentieth century, Yiddish dailies would also take hold in Vilna. These furthered the Vilna Jews' access to modern ideas and media with which to readily exchange contemporary viewpoints and spread the reputation of Vilna's Haskalah.[71]

Vilna's location bordering the Russian Empire and Poland, and the ethnically diverse population, led to political foment. Vilna's Lithuanian minority and its prior association with, and proximity to, Poland split the population's allegiances to the Russian Empire. After the Napoleonic Wars, Poland was incorporated into the Russian Empire, but the Russians permitted some limited Polish autonomy and the Polish nobility to retain some of its privileges (the continuation of serfdom and exemptions from military service and taxes). In late 1830, an armed uprising against the Russian Empire began in Poland and spread to Lithuania. After the revolt was crushed, in 1832 Tsar Nicholas I closed the University of Vilnius — established in 1579 and one of the oldest universities in Europe. Jews did not participate in the uprising in any great numbers, and Jewish intellectual life in Vilna was spared from any tsarist retaliation.

The next century saw a rise in Jewish political involvement. By the late 1850s, Polish nationalism was much debated among Vilna's Jews and non-Jews. The members of Vilna's Haskalah also were pulled into the fray. Many maskilim held nationalistic views and fully embraced the Russian Empire, despite many laws that singled out Jews for harsh treatment. To the extent that there were any negative repercussions from those laws, blame was placed on the populace or minor government officials and not the tsar.[72] Nonetheless, by the 1860s, blind fealty to the tsar became more difficult and pushed some to turn toward Poland, which was seen as more liberal. Nonetheless, for some maskilim, allegiance to Poland did not prove fully satisfactory either. Some maskilim elected to embark on new political and nationalist movements that did not require selecting Poland over Russia, and instead found a third way with Zionism or other more neutral movements.[73] Some of the rebellion's underlying issues, and the authors' political views, were portrayed, at times obliquely, in Jewish novels and books of the time, many from Vilna authors.[74]

The rise of a Jewish middle class notwithstanding, most Jews were poor, a not inconsequential number of which lived in abject poverty.[75] Nonetheless, from the early nineteenth century on, Jews controlled Vilna's commercial life. This control was so pervasive that one Russian paper reported the shocking fact that Vilna's denizens shopped following "the religious calendar of the Jewish faith, with Sundays and Christian holidays being the busiest."[76] Johann Peter Frank, a leading Viennese doctor who moved to Vilna in 1804, noted that "in general, the Catholics did not celebrate the Sabbath, because it was a market day when peasants sold their produce."[77]

The economic situation of the Jews, the political climate, and a significant rise in Vilna's population, when Jews were forcibly uprooted from rural areas in the Russian Pale to cities, began to stir Jews into action and spurred the creation of new movements.[78] Vilna saw a substantial rise in its population in the late nineteenth century, and a corresponding rise in participation in a variety of socialist movements.[79] Some maskilim counted economic realities among the issues that must be addressed by the Jews themselves through better education, willingness to work in less traditional occupations, and fluency in the national language.[80] Likewise, in 1870s new Jewish revolutionary and political movements sprang up in Vilna or were initiated by Vilna natives. In 1872, two Aarons, Aaron Lieberman (1843–1880) and Aaron Zundelvich (1854–1923), "led the first revolutionary socialist circle that was also profoundly involved with Jewish culture and languages."[81]

In the fall of 1898, the Jewish Labor Bund, the first formal socialist movement, was founded in Vilna; and quickly the "Bund became the most vibrant Jewish socialist revolutionary movement, and the one destined to have the greatest cultural impact in the non-Soviet parts of Eastern Europe right up to the Second World War."[82] The Bund was a partisan nonreligious organization, which still retained its association with Vilna. After Vilna's governor-general violently reacted to the May Day rally of 1902, a Bundist, Hirsh Lekert, attempted to assassinate the widely reviled governor. But Lekert was "a bootmaker and not a marksman," and he only grazed the governor's hand and foot. Lekert was hung for his actions.[83] Not only was he considered a martyr by those in his party, but "all of the city's Jews" held him up as such.[84]

Vilna also became a major center for Zionism. Hovevei Tzion, a precursor to Herzl's political Zionism, held its third annual conference in Vilna. With the formation of the Zionist movement, Vilna was among the movement's most active local chapters. In 1903 Herzl visited Vilna and was feted like a king. The Mizrachi, a religious Zionist movement, and other splinter movements were founded in Vilna.[85]

These accomplishments and the evolved history of the Jews of Lithuania, and Vilna specifically, leave "no doubt that Lithuanian Jewry's intellectual approach was evident beyond the realm of daily life, and, more prominently, in a number of socio-economic trends and phenomena."[86] Vilna, a city in the far north of Europe, left a profound impact on Jews throughout the Russian Empire and well beyond.

While Vilna's intellectual status within the European Jewish population was initially fueled by religious Jewish scholars such as the Vilna Gaon, by the early twentieth century, that circle had expanded to include secular Jewish thinkers and organizations, writers, musicians, poets, artists, actors, and political movements. Even the Hasidim gained a place within Vilna's Jewish communal administration.[87]

Vilna Jews' pride in their city was so embedded that it spilled over into its literal foundations. Vilna's architecture was striking, and became a unique part of its history. By the early twentieth century, many Vilna Jews viewed "Vilna's history [as] somehow contained within the very fabric of its aged buildings and arched streets."[88] Napoleon's legendary anointment of Vilna as the Jerusalem of Lithuania was on his visit to the Shulhoyf.[89] The Shulhoyf was the heart of the Jewish Quarter and the center of religious, intellectual, and social activities for the entire community. Jews from all walks of life were drawn to it. Those seeking the latest news, "rabbis and scholars, romancers and poets, philosophers and ghetto politicians, would perambulate for an airing, for friendly discussion or for solemn reflection" in the Shulhoyf.[90]

Access to the Shulhoyf was granted through large iron gates fronting Jews Street.[91] The Great Synagogue was directly ahead.[92] The synagogue, an almost-square gabled building, was built in the seventeenth century.[93] Its gables were clad in Doric and Corinthian columns, and it contained space for men and women.[94] In compliance with discriminatory zoning requirements, the building's exterior height was limited to three stories, but burrowing down permitted a five-story interior. To enter required descending ten stairs. The additional interior height was used for great effect, creating "an awe-inspiring atmosphere" and a "sense of force and drama."[95] One rendering, capturing the architecture's actual scale while reducing the congregation to Lilliputian size, emphasizes the enormity of the interior and is evocative of the original Jerusalem Temple's outsized altar and supersized menorah.[96]

Greatness was not simply in its capacity and height, but also in its emotional impact, designed to inspire its patrons' worship. The center of the building was dominated by four enormous Tuscan columns in a square layout supporting a barrel-vaulted ceiling. These supports towered over a smaller structure that ensconced the *bimah* (reader's lectern) beneath. The *bimah* itself was housed in a sumptuously decorated cupola with elements of the late rococo style, and was supported by four Corinthian and eight Tuscan columns.[97] At the front of the synagogue was the ark, reached by ascending a staircase on either side. The ark's detailed millwork and extravagant relief carvings were in stark contrast to its two simple iron doors. Nevertheless, it still rated among the synagogue's most impressive features.[98] When the famous Jewish artist Marc Chagall visited Vilna in 1938, he was inspired to produce a painting of the ark.[99] The overall effect of the interior was undeniable; and per the Napoleon legend, upon glimpsing the interior, "he was rendered speechless with admiration."[100]

The Great Synagogue's combination of unique architectural conventions led to both confusion and inspiration as attested to by an early twentieth-century non-Jewish visitor, Paul Otto Heinrich. When he went looking for the Great Synagogue and related that it proved difficult because unlike "significant [Christian] buildings of Vilna [that were] clearly visible and are easy to find [. . .] the famous Great Synagogue is concealed from the peering eyes of the traveler. [. . . They] might pass it without ever suspect[ing] its existence." To unearth its "mysterious universe" Friday afternoon, right before the onset of the Sabbath, he followed the "enormous crowds of pious Jewish men [as they] rush by," entered the unmarked gate of the Shulhoyf, and realized he had found the ostensibly secret door, "the magic entrance point into the elusive world of the Great Synagogue." Nonetheless, he remained confused: was "it possible that this insignificant house in front of him, which swallows [the] procession of people is the final destination of his exploration?" Yet his patience was rewarded, and he continued to "follow the footsteps of those who had just disappeared inside the building." Wherein he descended "a dark stairway that leads downstairs and then, unexpectedly, it [became] clear what hides behind this narrow walkway. Finally, the Great Temple is found! The building, like a symbol of time when the religion forced its followers to bow their heads, is submerged deep in the ground. Centuries have darkened its walls, but the synagogue has preserved its incredible sense of reverence and piety."[101]

The Great Synagogue was among several intellectually and architecturally significant structures in the Shulhoyf. Immediately after entering the gates of the Shulhoyf,[102] and walking toward the Great Synagogue, one first passed the Gaon's Kloyz (a *kloyz* is a communally supported house of study for elite scholars who eschewed daily life in favor of intense religious study).[103] The kloyz's gabled two-storied architecture was among the "more impressive" synagogue buildings in Vilna.[104] The very chair on which the Gaon sat is allegedly preserved in situ.[105] Merely entering the kloyz "and seeing the old and wise men absorbed in study, one would feel the presence of the soul of the Gaon hovering in that space."[106] The site was of such world renown that its Torah scrolls were dressed in lavish ornaments donated by Americans and other foreigners.[107]

Jewish Vilna was not defined by a single group. An article in the Yiddish press discussing Jewish Vilna's character echoed Miłosz's identification of Vilna's distinctive nature in terms of what it was not. According to the article's author, Jewish Vilna was a rejection of singularity; it was not "the rabbi, the maskil or the Bundist; the old fashioned [free loan societies] or the modern self-help organizations; the 'primitive,' 'dying' Shulhoyf or the institutions of the 'living new Jewish humanist culture.'" Instead, Vilna successfully synthesized all of them. Time itself would prove malleable to Vilna's will, both "a medieval — and yet one of the most modern Jewish cities."[108]

Unlike in other environs, Vilna's modern movements viewed themselves as evolving—not rejecting—its past. The new still remained true to the past, forming additional "links in a golden chain."[109] The Bundist poet Dovid Eynhorn proudly asserted, "In Vilna, the thread between Elijah the prophet and Karl Marx is not broken."[110] A writer, upon visiting a secular Yiddish school, could comfortably proclaim that he saw in it "'the shadows of the Gaon's Kloyz'" and of Vilna's yeshivot, and that "'one learns new, entirely new things, but it's the old sitting and learning, it's the old constancy, it's the Litvak's eternal love for Torah and wisdom.'" The "Torah" may have evolved from the Bible and rabbinic texts to secular Yiddish culture, but nevertheless, "'the soul of Vilna remained the same.'"[111]

There were many other Jewish cities throughout Europe that could boast of substantial achievements, whether literary, cultural, religious, political, or academic. Some might claim title to being the oldest or the largest, being more politically and economically significant, or hosting a greater number of newspapers or theaters, rabbis or scholars. Vilna, however, represented "an idea" rather than any one achievement. "Vilna is a magnificent city, and in it Torah and wisdom have combined from time immemorial. . . . All people, from one end to the other, this one hither and that one thither, work as one, to increase and enhance Torah."[112] Vilna represented the ideal space of the Jewish study house dedicated to rigorous scholarship, intellectual erudition, independence of mind, the pursuit of knowledge of Torah to mysticism, mathematics to science. This ideal is what allowed for the flourishing of the northern Haskalah, which remained staunchly Orthodox yet explored secular knowledge, and subsequently became an intellectual center that shaped every movement, from religious scholarship to socialist reading circles. Vilna lived up to its title of Jerusalem; its walls became the ark within which *everything*, whether people, groups, or buildings, came together and created Vilna's Torah, transforming the city itself into a virtual study hall.[113]

Vilna's unique intellectual lineage, composition, and unconventional foci coincided in one of its preeminent institutions, the first modern Jewish public library.[114] The library was public in every sense of the word: open to all, owned by the entire community and not by any individual person or institution, *and* serving the whole Vilna public. Previously, libraries were owned by associations, schools, study halls, individuals, or institutions.[115] These forms carried with them inherent deficiencies.

The first communally supported Jewish libraries that provided some amount of public access were centered around synagogues and schools, and were referred to as *batei midrash*. The seventeenth and eighteenth centuries provided examples from across Europe, including Italy, Amsterdam, Solanki, and Smyrna. And with the immigration of Jews eastward, in the eighteenth century Poland and Lithuania gained their own batei midrash. Throughout the nineteenth and twentieth centuries, libraries also appeared in Jewish towns and cities in Eastern Europe.[116] Nonetheless, these were not fully public libraries. Jews may have been sponsors and permitted access to these libraries, yet they did not truly serve the needs of the entire Jewish community. Rather, they were typically aimed at scholars and carried only religious texts, nearly always in Hebrew, and no secular books to speak of. To the extent that readers sought out non-traditional books, they did so at their own expense.[117] Especially during the late nineteenth century, with interest in secular and Haskalah literature on the rise, there are examples of yeshiva students sneaking Haskalah books into the batei midrash. This personality, "the disenchanted yeshiva student who immersed himself in secular literature instead of talmudic study . . . [became] one of the most common motifs in Yiddish and Hebrew maskilic literature and memoirs."[118]

Smuggling was only one way this deficiency was addressed. Libraries sponsored by guilds, clubs, and societies that catered to those interested in Yiddish or fiction sprang up in many cities and towns in Eastern Europe. In addition, in the Russian Empire, some Jews had limited access to Russian libraries. Yet in many ways these alternative libraries suffered from the same deficiencies as the batei midrash. Because these libraries were situated within larger institutions, they inevitably reflected the interests of those institutions and not those of the wider public. For example, in the early twentieth century, Avraham Kotik, a Yiddish translator and socialist activist,[119] advocated for the creation of a public library and bemoaned the fact that while batei midrash had been in existence for hundreds of years, they lacked books "for the common Jew; the book that is not religious but secular literature, this book still does not have its own resting place."[120] Even his solution would have created a library that would have contained only secular literature and left the batei midrash with the religious books. The new library would have been no more comprehensive or expressed the needs of the public at large any more than the old. Likewise, Russian libraries carried no Jewish books and were recognized as clearly presenting a divide between the secular and religious.

Finally, because the community exercised only limited powers over these libraries, access was subject to the whims of the individual libraries. In some instances, the libraries were open only during the day, thereby excluding the workers. Other libraries opened for only a few hours a week, and were closed on the Sabbath or holidays, when they would otherwise have had the highest demand. Many existing libraries were deliberately designed to invoke a sense of exclusion of the common reader. And many others charged subscriptions, excluding those who were unable to pay.

These limitations of the late nineteenth-century libraries are evident in the conveyance of one of the greatest Jewish-owned libraries to one Russian institute rather than Jewish organizations, institutions, or communities. Moses Aryeh Löeb Friedland's (1826–1899) library was among the most significant Jewish private libraries in the world, and in 1880 he announced his intention to donate the library to the Russian Imperial Library in St. Petersburg.[121] This decision caused consternation among many Jews, and Friedland was viciously criticized for his actions. He did, however, entertain an alternative destination for his books: a location that aligns with the modern definition of a public library, a model that addresses the many shortfalls of the previous Jewish libraries.

R. David Friedman of Karlin ("Dovidel" Karliner) (1823–1917) wrote Friedland and suggested that he might consider constructing a library in "Jerusalem, the center for Jews and Judaism." He thought that library should be fully public, permitting "the public admission to its collections at regular times," where they would be allowed to use and copy any of the books. Ownership and control would be placed in the hands of the entire community "under the auspices of the Ashkenazi and Sephardi rabbis." That institution would continue to grow organically and flourish because "many other collectors and libraries, would donate their books" to such a prestigious and special library.[122]

Friedland responded that although he valued Friedman's advice, it was unrealistic. Friedland explained that his intent always was to donate his books, and he had conducted a survey of the current state of Jewish libraries throughout Eastern Europe. No existing library met the conditions proposed by Friedman. Jerusalem was infertile ground for birthing that library model, and certainly not for his collection. His collection "included Haskalah literature and books from all nations and in all languages in Hebrew characters." A library with that sort of material might raise the ire of the Jewish religious extremists, who would burn it down "just as they had already done" with a library that contained similar materials. Lacking either an extant institution or a suitable alternative, he was left to donate his collection to the Imperial Library. While imperfect, it fitted many of his criteria, was open to all, had set hours of operation, and employed a staff (who "were kind and lovers of Jewish scholarship") to care for the books. Beyond scholarly concerns, he saw his donation as a positive example of Jewish participation in and devotion to the Russian government and possibly as a way to have a positive impact on broader Russian Jewish policy.[123]

Vilna, the other Jerusalem, proved an ideal location for such a library. That library—a *bibliotheka* and not a bet midrash—channeled Friedman and Friedland's vision, and was public in every sense. The library reflected the heterogeneity of Vilna's Jewish community; and it acknowledged and celebrated the *whole* of Jewish Vilna, and channeled the Gaon's vision of scholarship that sought out all Jewish and secular texts. The library contained books in a variety of languages, including religious, secular, contemporary, and traditional literature, ranging from rare rabbinic books to Yiddish translations of contemporary fiction. The library was fully vested to the community. The library was free and open, without regard to gender, belief, or economics. The library provided a physical address to house the intellectual materials and patrons that formed Vilna's exceptional ethos.

The library's success was a credit to its visionary founder, Mattityahu Strashun, a bibliophile who had amassed a substantial library, a son of Vilna, who merged his ideals of rigorous scholarship, broad intellectual interests, and independence of thought, reflected in a private collection that eventually formed the nucleus of Vilna's public library. The library's massive two-story building was given a space in the venerable Shulhoyf, fronting the Great Synagogue and facing the Gaon's Kloyz.[124] What became Vilna's Strashun Library developed into the material representation of Vilna and created a space for anyone who sought to embrace its intellectual heritage.

Your table was set for all those who seize Torah

Your hand was open to all those who sought wisdom

For all those thirsty for the words of truth, you satisfied
their thirst

For the benefit of those who sought you was the purpose
of your toil

All those who sought your advice you guided with wisdom

The downtrodden you sustained and assisted

The company of maskilim you sought as your friends

Sitting and studying you found respite

The Torah was your treasure and the Commandments
more valuable than pearls

Rare books in numbers you gathered and housed

And upon all them with righteousness you engraved

For complete mastery of wisdom was your wealth

ELIEZER ZWEIFEL, "Kinah le-Moto," *Ha-Assif*

Mattityahu Strashun:
The Book Collector

MATTITYAHU'S FATHER, SAMUEL, was born on the eighteenth of Heshvan, October 24, 1793, in Zaskevichi, Belarus.[1] By the time of his death, in 1872, he was among a small cadre of elite Vilna scholars, and had played an integral role in perpetuating Vilna's intellectual reputation. At Samuel's birth, his path to greatness was nearly impossible to imagine: he was neither a Vilnaite nor even a Strashun. The year of his bar mitzvah, 1806, profoundly altered the path of the rest of his life. In addition to embarking on adulthood, he also married Sara that same year and adopted a new name—his father-in-law's surname, Strashun.[2] His father-in-law, David, a wealthy businessman who owned a distillery and an inn, financially supported Samuel and permitted him to focus entirely on his studies.[3] Five years later, Samuel, accompanied by the rest of the Strashun family, fled from Napoleon's army to Vilna; and once again, Samuel was born anew. He fully embraced the zeitgeist of his new home and modeled his studies after those of its intellectual progenitor, the Gaon. Notwithstanding his immigrant status, Samuel ultimately proved an able student of the Gaon.

When Samuel first arrived in Vilna, he studied independently in his father-in-law's kloyz. In 1825 Samuel began studying in the "Yeshiva of Forty," a yeshiva composed of Vilna's elite scholars. The yeshiva was helmed by R. David Kosover and R. Mordechai Meltzer. Many of Samuel's fellow students went on to become leading rabbis and traditional scholars, in addition to major figures in the Haskalah movement, such as Adam Hakohen.[4]

Samuel was expert at traditional Talmudic scholarship. His erudition was almost legendary, and his Talmudic commentary missed only 4 out of the Talmud's nearly 2,711 pages, a rare feat.[5] His commentary, the best-known and most important of his books, mainly comprised short notes, rather than lengthy expositions, a hallmark of the Gaon's style as well. This reflected a rejection of pilpul—the esoteric study and generally lengthy attempt to bend and massage texts, which demonstrates the intellectual capabilities of the scholar rather than the true meaning of the text or a source-based analysis.

Samuel held liberal views on the sacrosanctity of texts, and he applied the whole of his scholarship to ensuring textual accuracy.[6] Prior to the Gaon, correcting and amending Hebrew texts was highly circumscribed, especially when based on less-appreciated areas of scholarship, such as grammar.[7] Much of Samuel's commentary on the Talmud emphasized textual accuracy and strongly proposed emendations and corrections. His suggested corrections were among the most extensive by Orthodox scholars.[8] Samuel counseled that to properly understand the texts one must "recognize such [textual] errors," whether grammatical or copyist, "and correct them."[9]

Among the literary genres of rabbinic literature that were influenced by the Gaon and common to other Vilna maskilim was the study of midrashic literature. This focus was reflected in the high concentration of midrashic commentaries emanating from Vilna. Samuel was counted among this group and published his own commentary.[10] He could stake his claim among Vilna's "premier intellectuals [who] devoted significant time to editing and explicating a myriad of midrashic texts."[11]

Samuel's literary interests extended to often neglected and even derided corners of Jewish literature. He mastered Hebrew grammar, the Prophets, and the Hagiographa, and was an expert in Jewish history, especially the early rabbinic period. His Talmudic commentary is replete with citations to Hebrew grammar, references to Jewish history, and use of biblical etymology.[12] He was familiar with Latin and spoke Polish fluently.[13]

Samuel was comfortable studying contemporary and controversial books from members of the more radical Haskalah. Judah Leib ben Ze'ev (1764–1811) was part of the Berlin Haskalah circle and was a forceful proponent of revitalizing the Hebrew language. In 1796 he published a grammar primer, *Talmud Lashon ha-Ivri*, that became the most popular such text among the maskilim and was published in numerous editions. Ben Ze'ev also challenged fundamental beliefs, most notably the divine origin of some of the books of the Bible; for example, splintering Isaiah into two parts and advocating that the latter was written long after the traditional dating. Consequently, many traditionalists, and even some Lithuanian maskilim, accused him of heterodox views and considered him a *mumar le-haklits* ("an apostate out of spite").[14] His reputation was such that anything he was involved with was suspect. He was an editor for the Vienna press that first issued an edition of the Talmud with the Gaon's notes. But because of Ben Ze'ev's association, the edition was pilloried by the sons of the Gaon; and according to some, the Hasidim would not use that edition. Indeed, they accused Ben Ze'ev of printing that edition on the Sabbath.[15] Samuel, however, makes use of *Talmud Lashon ha-Ivri* in his Talmudic commentary, albeit without explicit citations.[16]

Similarly, Moses Mendelssohn's Bible translation and commentary, *Netivot Shalom*, generally referred to as the *Biur*, was verboten among certain of Samuel's contemporary Orthodox rabbis. Although some Lithuanian maskilim took a more measured approach, most listed the *Biur* among the most heretical of Jewish books.[17] Samuel used it (and other books from the Berlin maskilim) repeatedly and relied upon it to counter the views of other commentators.[18] Samuel's use of the *Biur* was controversial in his time, and remains so today. Associating Samuel, a well-regarded Orthodox rabbi, with the *Biur* is unconscionable to some. For example, a biography of Samuel, printed in 1957, mentions his use of the *Biur*. That biography was reprinted twice, in 1972 and 1982: both these later editions omit the references to the *Biur*.[19]

Beyond the implicit modern conventions that are associated with Samuel's course of study and theories of textual analysis, he also provided direct material support for the dissemination of the ideas of the Vilna Haskalah. In 1822, Isaac Baer Levinsohn (1788–1860), arguably the father of the Russian Haskalah and known as the Russian Mendelssohn or Mendelssohn of the North, completed *Teudah beYisrael*, the first book to formulate and articulate the movement's ideas and goals.[20]

Levinsohn's intent, as he describes it in his introduction to *Teudah beYisrael*, was to demonstrate that a complete course of Jewish studies includes not only Talmudic and Jewish legal texts, but also Hebrew grammar, languages other than Hebrew, and science. Furthermore, he argued that accepting this educational theory does not conflict with Orthodox Judaism.[21] Consistent with that position, Levinsohn points to the Gaon as a historic precursor to this philosophy. The head of Vilna's rabbinical court at the time, R. Abraham Abele Poswoler (1764–1836), wrote an endorsement for *Teudah beYisrael*, lending credence to Levinsohn's argument. That endorsement was omitted in later editions. Levinsohn, however, challenged the wisdom of that omission. He wrote in the second edition that Poswoler's endorsement was brought up "by the notables of the community of Vilna at a great assembly, saying, 'What is this book? What is its nature? What is its flaw?' To which Poswoler answered publicly: 'There is no flaw in it except that it was not composed by our great Rabbi Eliyahu the Hasid of Vilna.'"[22] Nonetheless, Poswoler's endorsement was never again included.[23]

Many authors of Hebrew literature could not afford to publish their own books, and they solicited *Prenumeranten* (prepublication subscriptions) from sympathetic supporters. Levinsohn was impoverished and sought subscribers to fund the publication. Levinsohn specifically targeted Vilna for his fundraising, and the list of Vilna donors received a special section in the donor roster. Samuel was a subscriber.[24]

Even after collecting the necessary funds, Levinsohn ran into obstacles because of the book's content and message. Despite the backing of Vilna's maskilim and others, that was not enough. Levinsohn struggled in vain to find a printer willing to publish his book. None would accept it because of its content. Not until 1828 was it finally published — in Vilna.[25]

Samuel was willing to acknowledge the theory that underlies *Teudah beYisrael*: shifts in society at large required a reexamination and potential modification of historically held viewpoints and practices (albeit with certain limits). In 1864 Samuel's grandson (the son of his daughter Sarna Itta),[26] Vladimir Osipovich Harkavy (ca. 1846–1911), left Vilna to attend Moscow University.[27] Harkavy was one of many Jews in the late nineteenth century who attended university.[28]

In Vladimir's autobiography, he recalls "vividly" his farewell visit to his seventy-one-year-old grandfather. Samuel gave a daily Talmud class at the Paplavos Kloyz.[29] By the time Vladimir arrived at the kloyz, the class had already assembled. When Vladimir approached his grandfather, Samuel stroked Vladimir's cheek and admitted that "we elderly are afraid of the university; we are fearful that it will take you away from Jewry." Nevertheless, Samuel conceded that "new times and new paths have come, and we cannot oppose you." Samuel then expressed his admiration for science, "especially medicine and astronomy." As he bid his grandson farewell, Samuel implored him "not to forget he is a Jew." The audience was "astonished" at Samuel's moderate and permissive reaction; they expected him to deliver an "irate reprimand, even curses."[30]

Harkavy's story is consistent with the first biography of Samuel. For reasons heretofore unknown, in 1856 the governor of Vilna requested a biography of Samuel. Tzvi Hirsch Katzenellenbogen, a scholar in his own right and friend of Samuel,[31] satisfied the governor's request and described Samuel as "famous for his systematic knowledge of the Talmud and Jewish religious and scientific literature, but knows nothing of secular sciences and languages, nonetheless he is not an enemy of education. [. . .] a noteworthy scholar, devout and honest, and enjoys the reputation and trust of the people. [. . .] Sensible, selfless, independent and of calm character."[32]

Samuel's scholarship was indelibly influenced by his move to Vilna and becoming a member of the Strashun family. Those were native to Mattityahu. He was born on October 1, 1817, during the Sukkot holiday, in his grandfather's house at 3 St. Stephno Street in Vilna.[33] A Strashun and a son of Vilna, Mattityahu preserved and perpetuated his bloodlines, carrying forward to the next generation and beyond the spirit and soul of both—an heir in the fullest sense.[34]

Mattityahu first studied privately, with his father or tutors. His curriculum was determined by his father's scholarship and ranged over a wide variety of subjects, including *Tanakh* (the Bible) (which he committed to memory), Talmud and rabbinic literature (with an emphasis on midrash), Hebrew grammar, mathematics, and geography; and he became fluent in Polish, Russian, Greek, and Latin.[35] By sixteen, his expertise was such that he was already being cited in books.[36]

Mattityahu's works shared similarities with his father's. Mattityahu wrote notes to the Talmud that were published in its most widely accepted version, the Romm Press Vilna Shas, and his notes were well regarded by traditionalists throughout Eastern Europe and the Middle East.[37] But his commentary was published on only three tractates of the Talmud.[38] His main field of study was the non-Talmudic rabbinic texts.[39] Mattityahu is considered the final generation of midrash scholars that can be directly traced back to the Gaon. His sole stand-alone published work, his commentary on *Midrash Rabba, Mattat Yah*, published posthumously in 1893, was closely identified with the scholarship of the Gaon and his students and acolytes.[40]

Mattityahu's rabbinic erudition, secular knowledge, and melding of both is readily apparent in *Mattat Yah*. For example, his philological scholarship commonly discusses Greek and Latin loanwords. The contemporary methods for textual criticism also found a home in his commentary. The identification of parallel texts and discussions of world history, geography, and mathematics all make regular appearances.[41] He was unafraid to amend and correct texts, and did so frequently. He was so certain of his readings that in at least one instance he argues that a note of the Gaon is erroneous because it does not align with Mattityahu's textual reading.[42] And he utilized his mastery of Hebrew bibliography to great effect, comparing various editions and identifying sources that otherwise were unknown to most scholars.[43]

Much of Mattityahu's scholarship was confined to articles in journals and newspapers — traditional and maskilic.[44] Many of these articles were published under pseudonyms, and not all have been identified.[45] Thus, a partial bibliography of his newspaper articles counts 316 entries, although a more precise accounting is 316 separate notes on varied topics that spanned sixty-five issues.[46] For example, one article is counted as thirty-four individual entries.[47] These notes display Mattityahu's breadth of knowledge, which spans traditional medieval Talmudic commentaries such as Rashi and Meiri, to works of the German historian Heinrich Graetz, Karaitica, and Pliny — and frequently applies contemporary methodologies of textual criticism and etymology.[48]

Among Mattityahu's most significant areas of study was Jewish history, particularly the history of Vilna. Samuel Joseph Fuenn (1817/18–1891)[49] wrote a history of Vilna and its personalities, *Kiryah Ne'emanah*. Fuenn asked Mattityahu, a close friend, to provide his comments and notes. In response, Mattityahu penned a lengthy letter, over thirteen pages, of additions that Fuenn published at the beginning of the first edition.[50] When those proved insufficient to convey the full degree of Mattityahu's scholarship in this area, he wrote an additional twenty pages of notes; they were included as a separate supplement to the second edition of the book and independently titled *Rehovot Kiryah*.[51] Yet Mattityahu explained that "even with the addition of those twenty pages, [he] still had not exhausted all of [his] information on the topic."[52]

Mattityahu's erudition in the field of history, coupled with his nearly perfect recall of traditional and deep familiarity with nontraditional Jewish texts, is apparent in his discussions of sixteenth-century Azariah de Rossi's controversial work, *Meor Enayim*. *Meor Enayim* is an encyclopedic book covering a number of topics, and also venturing into sensitive areas of Jewish theology. De Rossi uses both Jewish and non-Jewish sources, and scientifically analyzes the Jewish texts.

Meor Enayim ranks among the most controversial Hebrew books; and according to some traditions, it was condemned to the pyre. De Rossi critically examined the Aggadah (nonlegal portions of Talmudic and rabbinic texts) and concluded that it is permissible to challenge the Talmudic rabbis in this area and that their discussions suffer from a gross ignorance of history. In addition, de Rossi refutes the traditional computation of the age of the universe, the consequence of which is to undermine the entire genre of rabbinic messianic speculation.[53] But de Rossi's application of scientific methods to traditional Torah study was particularly attractive to maskilim, Mattityahu among them.

In 1841 Leopold Zunz, founder of the *Wissenschaft des Judentums* movement, published a biography of de Rossi in the Haskalah journal *Kerem Hemed* (Zunz would later publish an edition of *Meor Enayim*). Zunz sought to demonstrate that, contrary to conventional wisdom, the *Meor Enayim* was widely accepted in traditional Orthodox circles. Zunz identifies numerous seventeenth- and eighteenth-century authors who were familiar with the *Meor Enayim*, and in many instances, borrow from it directly without citation.[54] Mattityahu, then twenty-four, wrote to Zunz and provided additional examples of attributed and unattributed usage of the *Meor Enayim*, which Zunz related in a follow-up article.[55] Later he expanded that list in a lengthy footnote in *Rehovot Kiryah*, where he cites over thirty other authors that used *Meor Enayim* with or without citation.[56] These examples are from across the full spectrum of Jewish literature, legal texts, *derashot*, grammar, Talmudic commentaries, biblical exegeses, and responsa, from the seventeenth century until that time. Mattityahu also identifies some instances where in the same book, de Rossi is disparaged and later quoted without attribution. According to Mattityahu, these are only a fraction of the passages he identified, "but that at present, [he] has forgotten the others."[57]

In a particularly ironic twist, in the Hebrew translation of a biographical sketch of Mattityahu, references to the *Meor Enayim* are replaced with an ellipsis.[58] That is, Mattityahu's attempt to bring to light examples of censorship was itself, for all intents and purposes, censored.

At fourteen, Mattityahu married Sora Chana, whose father, Yosef Elias-berg, was one of wealthiest men in Vilna.[59] Eliasberg's wealth permitted Mattityahu to devote himself to full-time study in Eliasberg's house and likely ceased studying directly under his father's tutelage.[60]

Around that same time, Mattityahu read Levinsohn's *Teudah beYisrael*.[61] He "read the book over and over but still [did] not sate [himself] with it." The book had a profound effect on Mattityahu—it was nothing short of transformative—"it opened [his] eyes, and [he] became a different per-son. [. . .] A marvelous light suddenly drove away the shadows of darkness from [his] eyes. [The] words kindled a holy fire in [his] heart, and this fire will no longer be extinguished."[62]

In 1838 Levinsohn's book, *Bet Yehudah*, was published. The book is a continuation of *Teudah*, but places greater definition on his program. Soon after the publication, Mattityahu wrote Levinsohn directly and expressed appreciation for his books, and especially *Bet Yehudah*. Matti-tyahu traces his path from his initial exposure to Levinsohn's books with *Teudah beYisrael*, and how Mattityahu became a follower of Levinsohn. Mattityahu also took the opportunity to provide his notes and critique of *Teudah beYisrael*. In addition to revealing the extent of Mattityahu's schol-arship, those notes and comments show the full extent of Mattityahu's embrace of Levinsohn.[63]

In discussing a comment by Levinsohn regarding the definition of a rabbinic term, Mattityahu veers off into larger issues. Mattityahu finds support for one of Levinsohn's philological conclusions and in so doing criticizes the Amoraim (rabbinic scholars who were active during the Talmudic period, third to fifth centuries CE) for their lack of integration within Roman society. According to Mattityahu, the Taanim were aware of, and adopted, surnames that the Romans applied to Jews. The Amoraim, however, were so insufficiently engaged with their Roman counterparts to even learn the surnames, let alone adopt them. Mattityahu praises the Taanim, who were fully assimilated and adopted Roman conventions, in contradistinction to the Amoraim, who "changed for the worse."[64] Criti-cism of any of the rabbis, and certainly those from the Talmudic period, was taboo, although this was a hallmark of de Rossi. Moreover, his fierce advocacy for integration and saying that the failure to do so is "a change for the worse" is unusual for Lithuanian maskilim, but there is historical precedent among the Vilna maskilim.[65]

Mattityahu's letter also discusses his personal life and the tragic death of his two infant sons. He ascribed their death to his early marriage, and railed against the practice.[66] His experience and remarks echo those of contemporary maskilim regarding adolescent marriage, many of whom were "bitter about their lost youth [. . . and] waged an unrelenting war against adolescent marriages."[67]

Mattityahu regularly corresponded with other scholars who shared his intellectual outlook. These included leading members of the Haskalah throughout Eastern and Western Europe, such as Shlomo Judah Rapoport, Tzvi Hirsh Chajes, Samuel David Luzzato, and Leopold Zunz. Living outside Vilna and lacking the benefit of its acceptance of Mattityahu's brand of study, some scholars inevitably suffered the wrath of the traditionalists in their respective communities.[68] To avoid persecution, many of his cohorts relegated their views of Haskalah to the private realm of letters. Indeed, letters formed the main medium of communication of the Haskalah in the nineteenth century.[69]

Mattityahu took full advantage of Vilna's more permissive attitudes toward modern scholarship.[70] He was involved with many of the most important issues relating to Haskalah and was comfortable engaging in public debate and defending his liberal positions.[71] For example, among the most contentious issues in Vilna, and throughout Eastern Europe, was the modernization of Jewish education. Many maskilim deplored the traditional heder system, and this was one of Levinsohn's main complaints in his writings. In the 1840s, Nicholas I sought to create a system of government-sponsored Jewish rabbinical schools, the curriculum of which encompassed Jewish and secular subjects and which were operated according to the theories of contemporary educational models. Members of the Vilna Haskalah approached these programs as an opportunity to implement and disseminate Haskalah ideas, and were significantly involved in these projects. Mattityahu actively participated in and helped to establish and financially support two schools in Vilna aligned with the Haskalah, and he taught classes in one.[72] Nonetheless, in accordance with his definition of Haskalah, when he, and others who were similarly wedded to maintaining a religious Orthodox life, perceived a shift in one school's curriculum and a hostility toward traditional Judaism, he resigned from the school.[73]

Mattityahu's delineation of Haskalah's boundaries forced him to defend the honor of deceased R. Menashe of Ilya (1767–1831), a student of the Gaon and a Vilna maskil. Mattityahu had a personal connection to Menashe; he was distantly related and also visited Samuel's house while

Mattityahu was still a youth. During that visit, Menashe tested the young Mattityahu and found him already an erudite scholar. In 1858 R. Mordechai Plungian, a Vilna scholar who worked at Romm Press, published *Ben Porat*, a biography of Menashe. Menashe was portrayed as an adherent of the model of Haskalah that advocated for deviating from the religious norms and argued for fundamental reforms to Judaism. An anonymous article that is attributed to Mattityahu publicly denounced the book in the *Ha-Maggid* newspaper.[74] He alleged that the book was "full of lies and falsehoods, regarding Menashe's life and events, indeed, the author fabricated nearly every single story." Mattityahu's version of Menashe (an assumed adherent of Mattityahu's Vilna Haskalah) was unrecognizable in the biography. Instead, he is treated as a Spinoza or Solomon Maimon. Lest one accuse Mattityahu of extremism, he knew he was not alone and that "the maskilim of the holy city [Vilna] also disapprove of the book, and I have even heard that some have counseled to burn the book."[75] In an unusual twist, in the digital copy of *Ha-Maggid* that appears on the National Library of Israel Historical Jewish Press website, Mattityahu's harsh criticism is censored, literally blacked out.[76] Nevertheless, his criticism of the portrayal of Menashe as anything other than traditional is demonstrative of Mattityahu's firm conviction that an Orthodox lifestyle should be maintained irrespective of his intellectual course of study.

The Orthodox lifestyle, however, did not include nonlegal practices, especially when they coincided with educational concerns. In 1843 a group of Vilna maskilim signed a petition addressed to S. A. Shirinsky-Shikhmatov, the aide to the minister of education, that sought to prohibit wearing Jewish clothing. The rationale for the prohibition was that distinctive dress "is the greatest obstacle to education, and that all measures that are undertaken to train the Jewish people may remain fruitless as long as Jews refuse to dress like [their] cultured fellow-citizens."[77] This proposal was vehemently opposed by many Jews in Lithuania and seen as an affront to Jewish identity.[78] Nonetheless, Mattityahu was among the signatories.

Mattityahu also used his communal positions to instigate change. Autonomous Jewish communities, such as Vilna, historically were controlled by a *kahal* (community board). In 1844 the Russian government abolished the institution of the kahal. Nevertheless, Jewish communities remained essentially autonomous, and the abolition of the kahal created a "self-contradictory situation in which the Jewish community was redefined as just a religious community whose leaders were merely to control matters affecting their 'cult'; at the same time, however, that community was still an autonomous legal entity, responsible for its separate taxation and draft levies and for the policing of its members."[79] In Vilna, that void was filled by the Tzedakah Gedolah organization, which for all intents and purposes replaced the community council.[80] The Tzedakah Gedolah provided for the poor and the upkeep of religious institutions, including the Great Synagogue. It raised funds to finance health care, supply wet-nurses, and provide for orphans, as well as deliver food for Passover for the impoverished of Vilna and Jewish soldiers in the Russian army, and even for the poor from other cities who came to Vilna to receive alms. In 1865 Mattityahu was selected to lead the Tzedakah Gedolah.[81]

As with his scholarship, he applied many beneficial modern conventions to historic institutions and communal practices. When he was first appointed to lead the Tzedakah Gedolah, Vilna's community council, he reversed a hundred years of practice that had allowed the council to operate haphazardly and without rules or protocols. The lack of rigor led to an extraordinary amount of waste. That ended when "Strashun, the first Vilna council member with a European education, altered every aspect of the communal council" and imposed order.[82] Religious judges were regularly called on to render decisions in commercial cases, and Mattityahu removed judges who were insufficiently educated to conduct commercial evaluations and necessary calculations, and replaced them with competent jurists.[83] He also sat on the *hevrah kadisha* (the burial society) board and insisted that they keep books and records which he would regularly audit.[84] In 1869 he was designated by the government to head a committee that would identify cemetery plots and assess burial fees.[85]

Mattityahu's reputation as a well-regarded and fiscally responsible leader spread beyond the Jewish community. In 1873 he was selected to join the Vilna branch of the state bank. In that capacity, he sought to ensure that Jews received state loans. In 1878 he was awarded a gold medal for his meritorious service.[86]

Samuel and Mattityahu rejected alignment with either the traditional Orthodox or the existing Haskalah movements. Instead, they successfully drew upon and melded both, without compromising either one, a hallmark of the Vilna Haskalah. R. Mordechai Aaron Günzburg (1795–1823), a member of the Vilna Haskalah and contemporary of Samuel, addressed German rabbis — those who were proficient in secular studies and influenced by alternative forms of Haskalah — who sought to come to Vilna.

He warned them that secular knowledge alone was insufficient to impress the Vilna maskil. The Germans would be "very welcome [. . . because] they will undoubtedly be able to bring much use." They would find "attentive listeners who will eagerly receive [their] sermons and lectures in the pure German language and diligent pupils who, with great avidity, will study [. . .] the secular sciences which are necessary to us." Nonetheless, Günzburg counseled that the Germans must "bring with [them] Torah, Torah, and Torah" because the title "rabbi" is reserved for those who "apply secular subjects and methods to Torah study." No one is exempt from the dual knowledge requirement, and even "if Aristotle himself should rise from the grave, he also would not be privileged to occupy a rabbinic position among" Vilna Jewry. He "will indeed, be received with the great reverence, as he deserves, but we will not make him a rabbi."[87]

Mattityahu was part of the second generation of Vilna maskilim, many of whom were born into maskilic families and not self-motivated in their affinity toward Haskalah; and he evidenced an even greater degree of openness and acceptance of liberal, contemporary Haskalah positions than his father and his circle of scholars.[88] Although Mattityahu embraced those positions, he still retained the mold of the Vilna Haskalah, remaining steeped in traditional sources and retaining his religious practices. In 1870 one visitor to Mattityahu's home explained that in Vilna there "is not a great difference between the maskil who longs for wisdom and knowledge, and religious men who care for piety and religion. The former does not step out of the crowd (*lifros min ha-tzibur*) and does not break the law in public and the latter does not despise Jewish Enlightenment and does not persecute its followers. [. . . T]he residents of Vilna long in their hearts to unify the values of faith and enlightenment."[89] Nineteenth-century Vilna produced scholars who were a hybrid of traditional and modern values, and a recognizable category of Haskalah.[90]

Despite Mattityahu's centrality to the Vilna community, the contemporaneous recognition of Vilna's brand of Haskalah, and the larger Vilna community's embrace of its adherents, Mattityahu's, and to a lesser degree Samuel's, otherwise uncommon synthesis of traditional and Haskalah views creates a challenge for their biographers and historians. Some ignore discussing Samuel and Mattityahu entirely.[91] For example, Mattityahu was a close colleague of Fuenn: they taught together in the Vilna rabbinical seminary; Mattityahu substantially contributed to Fuenn's *Kiryah Ne'emanah* and his short-lived journal *Pirkhei Tsafon*, as well as his newspaper *Ha-Karmel*; and both were signatories on the 1843 letter to the government regarding modifying Jewish clothing. Nonetheless, Mattityahu is absent from Shmuel Feiner's biography and analysis of Fuenn, which concentrates on his role as a maskil.[92] Others who discussed them are guilty of ignoring and censoring their nonnormative attitudes.[93] Still others exaggerate those and place them both firmly in the Haskalah camp without distinguishing the Vilna Haskalah from the larger movement.[94]

One example captures nearly all of those opinions. A particularly subtle and comprehensive biography and analysis of Mattityahu that respects his dichotomous characteristics was later censored to realign his personality with that of the editors — who were presumably unwilling or unable to appreciate Mattityahu for who he was. Jacob Mark's biography of important nineteenth- and early twentieth-century Jewish personalities, *Gedoylim fun Unzer Tsayt* (*The Great Ones of Our Times*), was originally published in Yiddish in 1925. The first edition divides its subjects into two sections: "rabbis and leaders" and "enlightened intellectuals and activists."[95] Mattityahu appears in the latter section. An abridged Hebrew translation was published in 1958.[96] The Hebrew version entirely omits the biographies of all those in the "enlightened intellectuals and activists" section from this edition of *Gedoylim*, seemingly rejecting the inclusion of those under the rubric of "Great Ones." Nonetheless, Mattityahu's biography remains in this edition.[97] Mattityahu's entry, however, is not a faithful reproduction of the original, and most discussions that would indicate his modernist tendencies have been removed. For example, references to Moses Mendelssohn and Leopold Zunz are replaced with ellipses.[98]

Recently, however, some biographers have begun to reassess and contextualize Samuel and Mattityahu's impact and the scope of their embrace of the Vilna Haskalah.[99] Nonetheless, a comprehensive biography and analysis of the two are still lacking.

From a young age, Mattityahu's appreciation of scholarship fed his book collecting.[100] He understood that if he wanted to be a true Vilna scholar, he would have to develop a rich and diverse repository of knowledge that would enable him to pursue his interests to their fullest, and a library was among the early steps in reaching that goal. After his wedding, which elevated his financial situation, he began collecting in earnest.[101] He spent a significant portion of his money and considerable time amassing his collection.[102]

Mattityahu quickly amassed an impressive library, evidence of which appears in his first published article. In 1836, at age nineteen, he wrote a lengthy letter, which was published in two parts in *Perkhei Tsafon*, Vilna's first maskilic journal.[103] The letter was an attempt to compile a complete bibliography of the medieval philosopher Shem Tov ben Shem Tov (ca. 1390–ca. 1440).[104] In the course of that discussion, Mattityahu applies theories of historicity, bibliography, philology, and non-Hebrew languages to explicate the topic. In addition, he cites a number of books from the sixteenth century and at least two manuscripts.[105] He also references a rare 1557 edition of R. Moses ben Isaac Alashkar's (1466–1542) *Hasagot*, a critique of Shem Tov's *Sefer Emunot*. Because of the book's rarity, Mattityahu took the opportunity to transcribe the publisher's introduction for the reader's benefit.[106] Also, he makes extensive use of Johann Buxtorf the Younger's 1660 Latin translation of Yehuda HaLevi's *Sefer ha-Kuzari*.[107]

Mattityahu closes the article and explains his overarching philosophy on book collecting. He equated knowledge with books and invoked the axiom of the thirteenth-century scholar R. Yitzhak Canponton in his *Darkhei ha-Talmud*: "The bounds of one's knowledge is limited by the scope of his library ... this is the meaning of the rabbinic statement 'more books more wisdom.'"[108] Despite Mattityahu's familiarity with an impressive array of books and editions, in different languages and nontraditional subjects, that were generally unavailable to most scholars, he concluded —in his dense fifteen-page article—that there was still more to say on the subject because his access to books was limited! Mattityahu then lists a handful of books that he had yet to procure, mainly because of a general inability to obtain contemporary scholarly Jewish books from Germany. Most likely the books from Germany are those from Zunz and other members of the Wissenchaft des Judentums school, whose approach to Jewish studies was not confined to the Orthodox interpretive rules within which Levinsohn and other Lithuanian maskilim operated. The enumerated books that appear on his wish list are themselves unusual for a traditional Jewish scholar and include two Bible translations by non-Jews. Collectively the article demonstrates, even before Mattityahu's twentieth birthday, the extent and the diversity of his library and scholarship.

Details on Mattityahu's collection methods are sparse. He purchased at least two personal libraries, was in contact with book dealers, and had access to well-known catalogs of libraries throughout Europe and important bibliographies that presumably enabled him to identify books of interest.[109] We can surmise that his bibliophilic hobby was enabled by Vilna's Hebrew bookstores and a multitude of Jewish printing houses, among the largest and most important in all of Europe.[110] Mattityahu traveled throughout eastern and central Europe and took an annual spa trip, which provided opportunities to collect beyond Vilna.[111]

Mattityahu followed through on his adolescent vision for his library. When he died, at age sixty-eight in 1885, he had amassed over seven thousand books and manuscripts. His collection included five incunabula,[112] approximately three hundred sixteenth-century Hebrew books, and manuscripts written by his father and the Gaon.[113]

The subject matter of his library is incredibly diverse, comprising traditional sources and scholarship on the Bible, Mishnah, Talmud, midrash, responsa, Kabbalah, Jewish philosophy, liturgy, and Jewish history, in addition to poetry, grammar, cemetery histories, works of Spinoza, satire, world history, mathematics, the New Testament, and translations of Hebrew texts into Spanish, Latin, Greek, German, and Arabic. The largest number of books under a single subject heading are responsa, numbering close to five hundred. In addition, his library contained approximately one thousand Judaica books entirely in foreign languages.[114]

Mattityahu's oldest books reflect some of the unique attributes of his library. Counted among those books is the incunabulum *Ha-Kanon ha-Godol* (Naples, 1469–?), which is demonstrative of Mattityahu's eclectic collection habits. The book is a Hebrew translation of the complete Arabic text of the Persian writer and philosopher Avicenna's medical compendium, *Canon medicinae*.[115] Another notable incunabulum is R. Nathan ben Jehiel's dictionary, *Sefer ha-Arukh* (Rome, ca. 1469–1472).[116] This is among the first six Hebrew books ever published. Beyond the book's bibliographical significance, in accordance with Mattityahu's collection criterion, he also held a keen interest in philology; and many of his discussions in articles, and throughout his *Mattat Yah*, are replete with citations to the dictionary.[117] This early edition allowed him to discuss textual variants from this edition to later editions.[118] His hundreds of articles that extensively use many of the books within the collection provide supporting evidence of his library's influence on his scholarship.[119]

Mattityahu's library was not merely an amalgamation of books, it was a reflection of his scholarship and values.[120] According to Mattityahu's model, Canponton, books and knowledge were one and the same. Books themselves, therefore, provided a path to education. The library's composition was deliberately diverse and multilingual. The library also served to promote the ideals of Haskalah through its near-perfect holdings of books written by maskilim or their supporters and the Jewish versions of secular scientific, literary, and medical works. Moreover, it enabled the public to educate themselves with the full gamut of necessary literature, and created a space where people could be exposed to the meaning of the Vilna Haskalah without coercion or governmental involvement.

Mattityahu's home was centrally located at the corner of the prestigious Deutschgasse (also known as Niemiecka Street, and today, Vokiečiu Street) and Dominiku Streets, and abutted the Shulhoyf.[121] Already during his lifetime, his library and his deep knowledge of his books were renowned, and both rabbis and maskilim regularly visited to converse with him and use his library. In 1872 the maskilic writer Peretz Smolenskin described Mattityahu's home as a meeting place for "genuine and false maskilim, religious men and hypocrites, all of whom appeal [to] his kindness and await his nourishment, for he is a generous man and a kind host. And he, in his kindness, does not segregate the worshippers of God from those who do not worship God. All comers are respected, and are not asked about their views."[122] Mattityahu's unique collection, coupled with his attitude, converted his house and library into a public salon.[123]

Mattityahu's welcoming attitude stands in contrast to another contemporary book collector, Baron David Ginzburg, and his treatment of his library. According to one observer, Ginzburg's library in St. Petersburg was for self-aggrandizement, a medium to showcase his own "literary and aesthetic inclinations, . . . [e]verything in the large parlors where the books could be found reeked of wealth and comfort." This atmosphere discouraged all but the "*maskilic* elite" from accessing it.[124] Ginzburg turned his library into a material manifestation of the pilpul style of study that emphasized the intellect of the scholar and ignored the true meaning of the texts and their neutral ability to educate.

Beyond Mattityahu's impact on Vilna's intellectual milieu, it is no exaggeration to state that, without his largess, most if not all of the city's communal institutions might have failed. The scope of his communal involvement and philanthropy was incredible and touched every aspect of Jewish life in Vilna. As discussed, he helmed the two most important communal organizations, the Tzedakah Gedolah and the Hevra Kadisha, and was more than just a functionary; and he used his position and wealth to greatly improve the lives of Vilna's Jews.

In 1827 Nicholas I enacted a policy of mandatory conscription into the Russian army and imposed yearly quotas that communities were required to fulfill. The term of service was twenty-five years. The official induction age was eighteen; nonetheless, Jewish children could be seized as young as twelve (and many times even younger). They would remain in the custody of the army, where they would receive rudimentary education and Christian religious instruction until the official age of induction, whereupon they would begin their twenty-five years of military service. These children, known as cantonists, were for all intents and purposes dead to their families and lost to religion.[125] In many instances, the wealthy paid money to the poor, or in the most egregious instances to bounty hunters, *khappers* (kidnappers), to substitute for their children even if they were otherwise exempt. In 1871, however, the conscription law was "reformed," and the government agreed to a substantial monetary penalty in lieu of service. Mattityahu did not have any living children and was personally unaffected by the cantonist laws. Nonetheless, and contrary to the widespread abuse of the quota system by leaders of the kahal, Mattityahu nearly singlehandedly provided the requisite sum to exempt the entire Vilna population from its quota of fifty-eight conscripts.[126]

Mattityahu's charity extended to supporting intellectual public projects. He was the instigator of Romm Press's publication of the Babylonian Talmud, the Vilna Shas. He decried the lack of affordable editions and insisted that a new edition was critical to permit everyone to study. This edition was incredibly successful, becoming the gold standard for future editions.[127]

After Mattityahu turned sixty, he decided to reduce his communal activities and focus on his scholarship, and he began preparing his Talmudic commentary for printing. His commentary was included in three volumes of the Vilna Shas. He had hoped to continue writing and preparing the remainder of his comments for inclusion in the subsequent volumes of the Vilna Shas, but that did not happen.

After his retirement, the community leaders and rabbis pleaded with Mattityahu to return to his leadership roles. Since his departure, the institutions he had overseen had taken a turn for the worse and needed his oversight. Mattityahu agreed to return, but in only an advisory capacity. Upon his return, he was able to resuscitate the communal institutions, but at great personal cost. He suffered the wrath of his younger brother Yosef, who was upset that Mattityahu had returned to power. In the spring of 1885, Yosef died suddenly, and Mattityahu took his loss very hard. He became distracted, and his memory began to fail.

That same spring of 1885, Mattityahu fell, injuring himself severely. He recovered but was in a weakened state and unable to take his annual summer spa trip. That winter he became ill and was bedridden. His health quickly deteriorated. On November 27, he drew up his last will and testament; and on Saturday night, December 13, he called the members of the Burial Society and the Tzedakah Gedolah to his bedside and requested a cemetery plot next to his father. He died the next day.[128]

Mattityahu's funeral occurred on the morning of Tuesday, December 16. The stores were closed by the order of the community, and the streets around his house were overflowing with mourners; according to one report, an estimated 23,000 people attended his funeral (in 1875, there were 38,900 Jews in Vilna). His death was widely reported in the Jewish newspapers, and his funeral was attended by Jews from all walks of life, "the God-fearing traditionalist and the enlightened Jew, the rich and the poor."[129] Prestigious non-Jews were also in attendance, including the governor-general of Vilna, a member of the Duma, and an official from the state bank.[130] Mattityahu's body was brought into the Great Synagogue—a particularly rare honor, one that was previously accorded to the Vilna Gaon—where the official Vilna preacher at that time, R. Jacob Joseph (later chief rabbi of New York), eulogized Mattityahu.[131] He was also eulogized by the most famous traditional Orthodox Eastern European rabbi, R. Yitzhak Elhanan Spektor, who, although nearly seventy, made the over-sixty-mile trip from Kovno (Kaunas) to Vilna for the funeral;[132] and other prominent rabbis also attended and spoke at his funeral.[133]

Mattityahu was buried between his father and Abraham Abele Poswoler, two Vilna figures who had fostered and guided his life's work, and eloquently expressed his multifaceted influence on Vilna.[134] His loss was felt not only by the inhabitants of Vilna, but also by the city itself, for which it was portrayed as a loss—"Vilna, bitterly cries out, I am bereft of my glory and beauty, they have been extinguished."[135]

Mattityahu's death was not his final act. Rather, he ensured that the exceptional nature of Vilna, which he had embodied during his lifetime—its passion for scholarship, openness to modernity, and heterogeneous constitution—would continue in perpetuity. Mattityahu left a sizable bequest to a variety of charities, both Jewish and non-Jewish. This was laudable, but not unusual. His personal library and his vision for its continued growth and place within Vilna is what elevated him beyond his roles as a scholar and communal figure, and placed him in the circle of Jewish personalities who indelibly affected subsequent generations.

Vilna Builds Its Public Library

MATTITYAHU DIED ON SUNDAY NIGHT, December 13, 1885, without an heir.[1] His will, however, provided for the disposition of his library and estate. In the past, those with large libraries sold or bequeathed them to individuals or private institutions.[2] Mattityahu's appreciation for the value of his library went well beyond the individual books. During his lifetime, he opened the library to all, effectively converting his home into a study house. He saw no reason that his death should extinguish the character of his library. He elected a novel approach for the disposition of his library and left it entirely to the Vilna Jewish community at large, a fully public library and the first such library in the Jewish world.[3]

Days before his death, Mattityahu drew up his will. The will is written in Russian in Mattityahu's own hand (an indication of his fluency) and is preserved in the Lithuanian State Historical Archives. His bequest reads:

> The library belonging to me . . . , which comprises a rich collection of Jewish textbooks and books with spiritual content, I bequeath without the right of alienation to the above-mentioned merchants Ovsei Khaim Mordukh Epshtein and David Shmuil Utskovich and [Iavich] Broido, on the condition that these books be placed in two rooms on the premises that I bequeathed to them, [on Glazier Street] or at another location at their discretion and these books from the library will be open and used only there on location for all of those who desire them for reading or prayer, under the supervision of a librarian to whom [the trustees] are obligated to pay a salary.[4]

According to the terms of his will, Mattityahu's library was to be accessible to anyone and everyone "who desires them for reading or prayer," and it stipulates that the bequest is "without the right of alienation," that is, irrevocable. To fulfill all of those conditions required that the entire community would own, operate, and provide open access to the library.

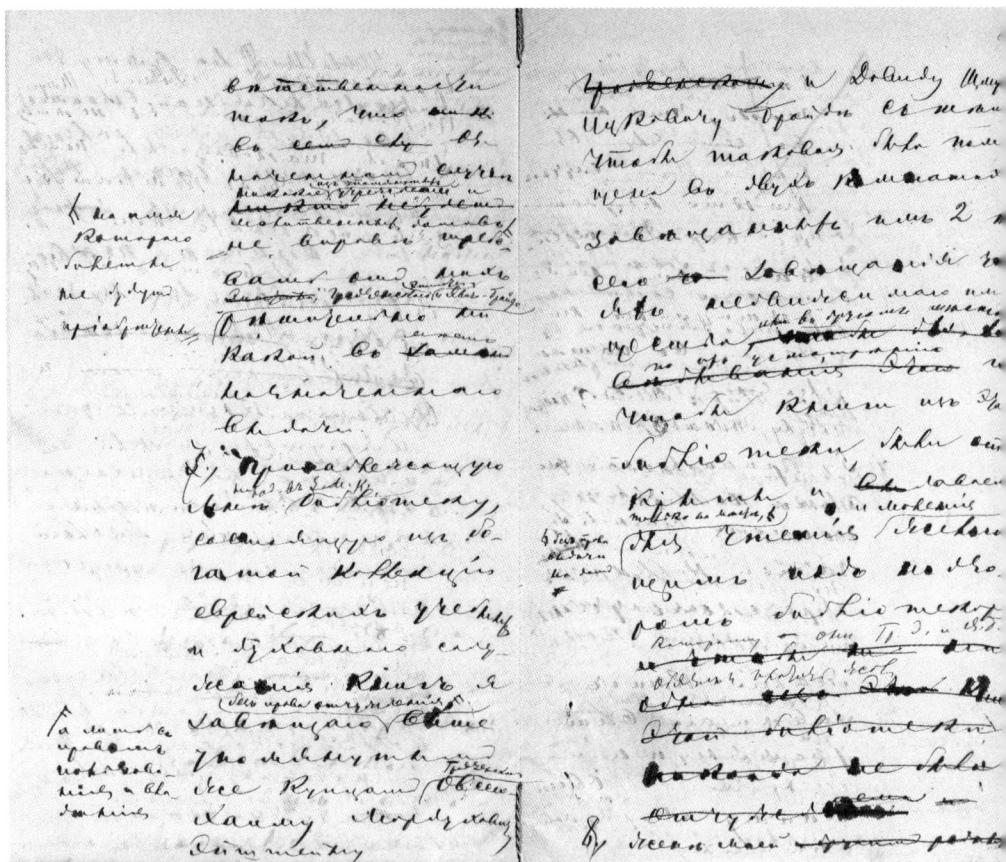

2. Mattityahu's last will and testament in his own hand.
Lithuanian State Historical Archive, f. 450, ap. 7, b. 125.

But Mattityahu also intended that his library would remain relevant, and another portion of his will designated funds for the formation of an endowment for the library, which would assist in continually augmenting the collection to address the ever-changing needs of its patrons.

On his deathbed, Mattityahu explained exactly what he intended for his library: "I am sanctifying my library for the good of the public [hek-dashti kodesh la-Hashem]; my vision is that it should be modeled after the Bibliotek that I have seen in the Diaspora."[5] That is an institution which does not yet exist in the Jewish world, but like the many other beneficial contemporary ideas that he adopted and championed, despite the fact that they may have originated from the Diaspora, the modern "Bibliotek" too should be embraced by the Jews.

The "Bibliotek of the Diaspora" is a relatively new institution, the modern public library, that began in earnest in the nineteenth century in Russia and the Western world. On a most basic level, these institutions permitted unfettered access to everyone without economic or social barriers. To ensure that portions of the public would not be excluded or that restrictions on access or content would not be enacted required public control. This was accomplished by public ownership, support from public funds, and control by a governing body tasked with acting in the interests of the public without regard to those of individuals or groups — in Mattityahu's case, the whole of Jewish Vilna.[6]

The contents of Mattityahu's will were made public at his funeral and were likely read or described in R. Yitzhak Elhanan Spektor's graveside eulogy.[7] The vast majority of his estate went to charities, Jewish and non-Jewish, but the library bequest was considered the most important of those.[8] The press published descriptions of his funeral and also transcribed and translated his will into Hebrew. In addition, many obituaries prominently featured the conveyance of Mattityahu's library to the community, an act that would "provide a legacy beyond that of any actual blood descendants."[9] So critical was this bequest that the letter to the editor in the December 22, 1885, issue of the Jewish newspaper *Ha-Tsefirah* complains that the previous issue's coverage of Mattityahu's death was lacking because it "omitted [Mattityahu's] most important bequest, his large and valuable library (estimated at twenty thousand rubles), that he donated to the Vilna community for the benefit of all."[10]

The significance of his bequest notwithstanding, the completion of Mattityahu's full vision, the creation of a library for the entire Vilna community, would wait seventeen years. During that time, the library was accessible to varying degrees, but never to the degree imagined by Mattityahu, able to function like the libraries in the Diaspora. For that to occur, simply putting the books into the hands of the trustees was but a small first step. Rather, as with almost any new and novel institution, the process of turning Mattityahu's directive into a reality was a lengthy and complex one. This type of confusion and delay was common to similar projects of that time. For example, in New York, Samuel J. Tilden, the governor of New York, sought to establish a New York Public Library. When he died in 1886, Tilden directed that the majority of his estate should be used to "establish and maintain a free public library and reading room in the city of New York and to promote . . . scientific and educational objects." Despite Tilden's magnanimity and laudable intent, it would be nearly two decades before the New York Public Library would open its doors. But when it did in 1911, it served the *public*: "men, women, and children; immigrants of various nationalities and native born; Jews, Catholics, and Protestants; scholars and devourers of popular fiction; the masses and the middle class." It was, as the Strashun Library also became, "a new kind of public library, and a new kind of public institution for a new century."[11]

For seven years following Mattityahu's death, until 1892, his books "remained under lock and key" and were available to only those with special permission,[12] in spite of the fact that the trustees were in control of Mattityahu's library and that his bequest provided space and funds for operations. The continued closure led to discontent among Vilna residents. In 1886 an article in the Jewish press complained bitterly about the lack of access to the library and accused the trustees of "public theft" every day the library remained closed.[13] In 1890 another newspaper article repeated this allegation and highlighted the irony of the situation. When Mattityahu was alive, he freely gave access to his books to everyone, yet now, when the purpose of Strashun's bequest was to enable even more patrons of his library, no one was permitted to access the books.[14]

Some attributed the delay in opening the library to the public to paternalistic motives, which seemingly ran counter to Mattityahu's vision. Mattityahu had built a diverse collection, including many books espousing Haskalah philosophy. According to an anonymous newspaper article, the trustees were allegedly concerned that permitting unrestricted public access ran the risk of inducing some readers to abandon tradition.[15] Others, however, attributed the delay to more banal issues. First, Mattityahu's library was disorganized and required substantial efforts to organize it to make it suitable for public use.[16] Second, since the censorship law of 1865, the Russian authorities tightly controlled libraries and required authorization from local authorities for all lending libraries and reading rooms.[17] The trustees were mired in bureaucratic difficulties in obtaining the necessary permits.[18]

Whatever the reason for the delay, it had a profound impact on the library and likely resulted in missing out on an opportunity to acquire Moses Friedland's significant library. That library was estimated to be over ten thousand volumes, most dating to the sixteenth and seventeenth centuries; approximately three hundred manuscripts, most on vellum; two hundred books that predated 1540 (the Hebrew incunabula period); and thirty-two incunabula. According to the bibliographer Samuel Weiner, who composed a partial catalog of the collection and was familiar with the entire library, only the Bodleian's and British Museum's libraries surpassed Friedland's.[19]

Toward the end of his life, Friedland sought a home for his collection. In 1892 he identified the recipient as the Asiatic Museum in the St. Petersburg Imperial Library. His intent was publicized in the *Ha-Melits* newspaper on February 18, 1892, and was immediately met with scathing criticism. Much of the criticism centered on gifting these books not to a Jewish community or institution but instead to a Russian institution, a government that had oppressed Jews for decades and a location that Jews were unlikely to frequent. Friedland decided not to publicaly reply to any of those attacks and went ahead with this plan. After negotiating with the library and securing promises, on October 25, 1892, *Ha-Melits* announced that the donation was final, and published a Hebrew translation of the agreement between Friedland and the library.[20]

As previously discussed, when the first notice of Friedland's intent was published, Dovid Friedman wrote to Friedland and suggested that rather than donate his library to the Imperial Library, he create a new and special institution—with all the hallmarks of a modern public library— in Jerusalem to house the collection. Friedman provided a detailed description of his vision, and his program is very similar to Mattityahu's ideas, aligning with the concept of a modern public library: public control, open to all, organized, and diverse. Friedland appreciated Friedman's thoughtful suggestion but concluded that it was not viable. Friedland rejected Jerusalem as a viable place for his library, mainly because of the extremists who were inhospitable to a library that contained materials they found objectionable. Indeed, they had already forced the closure of the Montefiore Library.[21] But Friedland explained that prior to his decision he had looked closer to home and surveyed other Jewish libraries in Europe; and he mentioned two in particular, one in Warsaw and the other the Strashun Library. The Warsaw library was inoperable because of permitting issues. The Strashun Library too was ruled out, not because it failed to fulfill any of Friedland's criteria or Friedman's model in principle, but because it had yet to open. Left without any viable options, Friedland took the radical solution of gifting it to the Imperial Library.[22]

The Strashun Library trustees lost a treasure. The Strashun Library first opened in July 1892, just four months after Friedland finalized his decision. We can only speculate on what the Strashun/Friedland library would have become if the trustees had been able to move more quickly.

During the delay in opening the library, the trustees were not idle.

They appointed Samuel Strashun, a distant relative of Mattityahu, as librarian. Samuel worked at Romm Press and was known as a specialist in rabbinical commentaries (*lomdish seforim*). His first order of business was to catalog the collection. Moshe Antokolski, "a scholar and great intellectual," was selected to assist in the project.[23] Moreover, during this time, an ex libris attesting to Mattityahu's prior ownership was affixed to the books. In 1889 a catalog of Mattityahu's personal collection, *Likutei Shoshanim*, was published in Berlin.[24] The catalog contains 5,753 entries listing his Hebrew and Yiddish books, 150 manuscripts, and 63 of his own unpublished manuscripts.[25] The catalog, however, was far from complete. It did not include Mattityahu's estimated one thousand books of Judaica in languages other than Hebrew.[26] In addition, not all of the Hebrew and Yiddish books were properly counted; some items were left out entirely and others' entries are incomplete. The final work product was so disappointing that the two compilers refused to allow their names to be associated with the book. Dovid Strashun, Mattityahu's nephew, who was assisting the trustees in establishing the library, elected to go forward with the catalog in its current state and make any necessary corrections later. He hoped that the catalog, even in that condition, was sufficient to provide order to the collection and permit the library to open to the public.[27]

But that was not to be. Instead, the library remained shuttered until the summer of 1892. In July 1892, seven years after Strashun's death, the library was finally opened to the public, converting Mattityahu Strashun's personal library into the official Mattityahu Strashun Library. The library's first home was in Kahal (Jewish community council) Hall, a room on the upper floor of the Great Synagogue building.[28] Although the kahal was dissolved in 1844 by the Russian authorities, the hall continued to bear the "kahal" designation and be used for communal activities and was controlled by the Tzedakah Gedolah, the defacto kahal. The public Strashun Library's use of that space adhered to that tradition.[29]

The library's condition was still not in conformance with Mattityahu's vision of a public library that permitted unfettered access; this became obvious almost immediately, but it still required the next decade to correct. The books were available, but there was an important caveat: access was controlled by the trustees. Access restrictions applied to the space and to the books. The library was open only four hours a day, between the hours of 12 pm and 4 pm. This schedule necessarily excluded a large class of the public, day laborers and workers.[30] The books too were restricted, driven by ideology and the idea that Haskalah literature was verboten; some books were unavailable to patrons because they were deemed "an abomination, and inappropriate for the people."[31]

Financially, the library's status was far from ideal. With the library under the control of the trustees, and not the community, the Tzedakah Gedolah required rent for the use of Kahal Hall. Those fees consumed all the funds that otherwise could be used to purchase books, leaving the library unable to keep its holdings current or purchase newspapers and other periodicals common to most public libraries.[32]

The nature of the trusteeship was particularly vexing. Mattityahu intended that his books become the property of the community for their intellectual benefit, and the trustees' role was temporary until that transfer was completed. The time had come to relinquish that role and fully vest the library to the community. The trustees, however, continued to act as if they, and not the community, were in control and could make decisions without accounting for the community. Although Strashun's intent was clear—that the library was to be public and not private property—fulfillment of his directive remained uncertain.

Clarification of the rightful ownership of public institutions was an issue within the Vilna Jewish community. This was especially so when claims to property were seen as proxies for larger symbolic claims. An earlier incident, with a number of similarities to the later issue with the Strashun Library, provides a frame of reference and a better understanding of the legal precedent of this quandary. In this parallel case, claims of individual ownership competed with claims of communal ownership in the absence of a clear heir. This dispute arose regarding the establishment of the Gaon's Kloyz.[33] But this was no mere dispute regarding property rights; at stake was the legacy of the Vilna Gaon, arguably the primogenitor of the Strashun Library.

The earliest records reveal the Gaon's living quarters were in an apartment in a larger complex of buildings originally known as "Fatel House," named for the philanthropist Michael ben Fatel, and subsequently Reb Leib-Layzer's hoyf.[34] The complex, which was designated for the use of the poor and for important rabbis, was located next to the Shulhoyf. During his time, thirty-three other families lived in the building.[35] By 1767 one of his wealthy relatives,[36] Elijah Pesseles, purchased part of a building in the Shulhoyf, where the Gaon had studied from time to time, and allowed him and his followers to use it on the condition that it be used solely as a *bet midrash*, a house of study and prayer. The Gaon and a select group of students routinely studied there and were permitted to hold an informal *minyan* (prayer group); the assembly was known as the "Minyan Ha-Gaon." According to the terms of the donation, Hasidim were barred from studying in the building.[37]

The Gaon continued to live and study in his home in Reb Leib Layzer's hoyf. But there was significant tension between the Gaon and the occupants of the complex. Repeatedly, the Gaon complained that his study was being disturbed by the smells emanating from the house of his neighbor, a candlemaker. Eventually, in 1772, the Gaon filed suit, and the Bet Din ordered the neighbor either to mitigate the smell or to cease making candles. Nonetheless, the neighbor's odors continued, and the Gaon decided that his only choice was to move if he were to have peace of mind. Thus, in 1785 a building in the Slutzki Courtyard was purchased, and the Gaon moved out of the building in Reb Leib Layzer's hoyf. The new building in the Slutzki Courtyard was sufficiently large to accommodate the Gaon's students and not require that the Gaon regularly travel to the Minyan Ha-Gaon building. In 1795 the Gaon's name was officially recorded as the owner of the new building.[38] Also in 1795, a fund was established from the proceeds of real estate properties for the upkeep of the building and to provide a stipend to those who studied there. One of the Gaon's students, Sa'adia of Shklov,[39] as opposed to one of the Gaon's family, was appointed to oversee the fund.[40] The intent was to convert the new building, in the Slutzki Courtyard, to an official prayer and study house, a kloyz, with the condition that the Gaon continue to live there.

The Gaon died on October 9, 1797, before any change to the legal status of the Slutzki building. With his passing his family and students clashed regarding which group owned the Slutzki building and by extension were the full legal heirs to his legacy.

Less than one week after the Gaon's thirty-day mourning period ended, his family took action. At their behest, the Vilna Jewish community board significantly altered the composition of the board controlling the Gaon's Minyan, removing Sa'adia and filling seats with members of the Gaon's family or their supporters. The minyan, the building, and the fund associated with it were now entirely under the control of the family.[41]

The family then set their sights on the Slutzki building. The Gaon's students and minyan assumed that any ownership interests the Gaon and his family held had been extinguished when he expressed his intention to cede the building to the community and transform it into a kloyz. They proceeded on the basis of that assumption and moved to fulfill the Gaon's intention. Indeed, they questioned whether the Gaon, in his individual capacity, ever purchased the Slutzki building as a private home. Rather, they argued that the building was purchased from the general fund for the upkeep and maintenance of the building, solely for the purpose of maintaining a quasi-public study house; and the building was not part of the Gaon's estate. The Gaon may have lived there, but that was only a concession to him. Thus, the intervention of the Gaon's death was the only reason the building's transfer was not otherwise finalized and was, for all intents and purposes, communal property.[42]

Elijah's sons saw things very differently.

The family maintained that the students' claims were baseless and the community did not own the building. Rather, the Gaon had purchased the Slutzki building with his own funds and personally executed the transaction,[43] and consequently the building should be included in the Gaon's estate.[44] The family maintained that the Gaon did not donate the building to the public; he merely encumbered the building with a very limited easement that, subject to certain conditions, permitted public access. Irrespective of the Gaon's alleged intentions, intent alone was insufficient to transfer property rights. Accordingly, the building remained in his sons' control; and to the extent that the community wished to incorporate the Slutzki property into the planned kloyz, it needed to purchase the property outright from the sons. The family argued that the students had the rights to a building for study and prayer, but not specifically to the Slutzki building.

Without a clear directive, the matter was litigated in the Jewish rabbinical court. Neither side could produce conclusive evidence supporting their respective positions. The court held that if the Gaon's children took an oath which attested to their position that their father had purchased the Slutzki building outright with his own funds, and without formally encumbering the building, it would escheat to the family and not the community. But the court also held that even if the sons were the legal owners, they still were required to permit the Minyan ha-Gra to use the space for study. The sons agreed, and the matter was settled in their favor.[45]

The court's decision, however, failed to fully settle which party was the sole heir to the Gaon, and is illustrative of the complexity of heirship exacerbated when commingled with the issue of communal ownership. Indeed, the decision seemingly conferred elements of heirship on both parties. The family owned the building, but it had to be maintained as a study hall for the minyan. This rendered the property, for all intents and purposes, worthless. Apparently, neither party was satisfied, and they returned to court. In the final settlement, the students purchased the Slutzki building and were given control of the fund and the building in the Shulhoyf. Rather than remain in the Slutzki building, the students moved their study location back to the building in the Shulhoyf, and in 1801, formally established the Gaon's Kloyz in that building. Nonetheless, the court's final decision clarified only the logistical issues related to the building and minyan. But the decision did not definitively declare one party or the other heir to the Gaon.[46]

The dispute over the physical location of the Gaon's scholarship, and its future, was merely one example of identifying the "true" heir to his larger legacy. Beyond the Slutzki building, the Gaon's family refused to recognize the students as legitimate heirs to the Gaon's intellectual legacy, despite the students' long-standing intellectual connection to the Gaon. The family claimed that only they had the right to publish any of the Gaon's manuscripts or any scholarship that could be attributed to the Gaon. During the Gaon's lifetime, his scholarly output was confined to copious marginalia and lectures among his select group of students. After the Gaon's death, his sons and his students disagreed on who held the rights to the Gaon's intellectual property, his spiritual legacy, and who held the publication rights to his manuscripts. Here too the family prevailed, and the court determined that all books with content attributable to the Gaon must first obtain the family's permission.

The difficulty in determining the heir to the Gaon, arguably the "property" of all of Vilna, presaged controversies regarding Vilna's other communal intellectual property.[47]

The Strashun Library finally opened to the Vilna public in 1892, ostensibly confirming its title to Mattityahu's library. Mattityahu's bequest was clear, that his library should fully transfer to the community "without the right of alienation." But even after the opening, Mattityahu's will had never been amended to substitute the community for the trustees. This remained the state of affairs until the issue was forced in the late 1890s. By then, Joshua Hayim Epstein was the only trustee who remained.[48] Epstein held a tight grip on the library, and his intentions regarding ceding control and clear title to the community were ambiguous. There were rumors that the collection was to be transferred to the private home of Epstein's son, Mordechai, potentially cementing the Epstein family's control of the library.[49] Even if the library was not moved into his son's house, Joshua was elderly; and with the imminent prospect of his dying without unambiguously declaring the community's ownership, his son might still contest the community's title to the library and seek a declaration that he remain a trustee. Either of these possibilities would continue to restrict full community access as determined by the community and for all intents and purposes convert Mattityahu's library back into a private one.[50] This created the potential for another messy and, ultimately, unsatisfactory outcome (at least from the perspective of the Vilna community). Rather than the Gaon remaining just the spiritual inspiration for the Strashun Library, the prospect that his legacy would include the issue of private versus communal ownership loomed large. Consequently, a group turned its focus on ensuring that *ma'aseh avot siman labanim* (the actions of the founders are precursors for their descendants) was limited to the beneficial aspects of the Gaon's legacy.[51]

The final resolution of the issue of the ownership of the Strashun Library was brought to a close indirectly through the generosity of another Vilna bibliophile and friend of Mattityahu, Samuel Joseph Fuenn, and the leadership of the Vilna proto-Zionist organization Hovevei Tzion. The latter's role in securing Mattityahu's legacy was in spite of Mattityahu's opposition to Zionist ideology and its spread in Vilna. Yet the Zionists, and no other group, fought to ensure the fulfillment of Mattityahu's final bequest, demonstrating the ability of diverse and even opposing groups to set aside their private views for the sake of the Vilna community and its continued intellectual growth.[52]

Fuenn was a colleague of, and shared many of the same qualities as, Mattityahu.[53] He was steeped in traditional and Enlightenment literature, and was one of Vilna's leading scholars. He read at least eight languages, wrote on a wide array of topics, and accumulated an impressive library. His most lasting book, *Kiryah Ne'emanah*, documented the history of Vilna and its personalities.[54] Mattityahu had a keen interest in the topic, and when Fuenn asked for assistance, he contributed a substantial amount of material that was included in the book.[55]

Posthumously, Fuenn provided the raw materials to return Mattityahu's favor. Upon Samuel's death in 1891, Fuenn's son, Benjamin, a physician, inherited his father's substantial estate and library.[56] Samuel's intent was that those be used for the benefit of the community. Benjamin was among the leaders of the Vilna Jewish community, sitting on many boards, and an active member in Hovevei Tzion. After the founding of the Zionist movement in 1897, the members of Vilna's Hovevei Tzion redirected their focus from external projects, funding missions to Palestine and the like, and turned their attention inward, toward assisting their own community.[57] In furtherance of that aim, Benjamin placed a substantial portion of his own and his father's estate into a living trust. Benjamin designated two leading members of Hovevei Tzion, Isaac Leib Goldberg and Aryeh Neuschul, to act as trustees. Their first order of business was securing the community's intellectual property, Mattityahu's library, and converting it into a public institution.[58]

The first attempts to address the communal ownership of the Strashun Library served to highlight the need for a change to the status quo that still limited full public access at no cost. At that time, the library was open for only four hours during the day, when many were unable to use it. At the request of Hovevei Tzion, Epstein agreed to add evening hours, but on the condition that Hovevei Tzion pay for the additional costs associated with the extended hours.[59] Even these extended hours still were insufficient to provide access for all segments of the community. The library was still closed on the Sabbath. The closure was not an issue for the older people seeking traditional rabbinic religious literature; they could avail themselves of the libraries in the batei midrash. But for those patrons — workers and shopkeepers — who had leisure time only on the Sabbath and wanted to read works of Jewish history and Haskalah literature, "the door of the Strashun Library, the only place where they could sate their desires, remained locked."[60]

To fully complete the transfer of the library to the community, the efforts of members of Hovevei Tzion were focused not only on Epstein, but also on the community — in this instance represented by the Tzedakah Gedolah — which must agree as well to assume responsibility for the library. Until then the community had affirmatively not agreed to any responsibilities; on the contrary, the library was paying rent to the Tzedakah Gedolah for Kahal Hall. The rental payments were so substantial that they consumed all the funds which otherwise would have been used to purchase additional books — as some pointed out, a perverse situation for an ostensibly communal library.[61] For the successful resolution of the issue of ownership of the library, Epstein must agree to cede trusteeship to the community, and the community must agree to accept the responsibility of the library.

On 20 Heshvan, October 24, 1899, their efforts paid off, and Epstein agreed to unambiguously cede control of Mattityahu's library and property to the Vilna community for the purposes of erecting and maintaining a communal library. The library came under the auspices of the Tzedakah Gedolah, of which Mattityahu had been a member.[62] A special board (other than the trustees) was established on behalf of the library, and the board adopted a number of resolutions regarding the library's future and the community's ownership and ensuring its status as a public institution, including constructing an independent building for the library that will remain the property of the community in perpetuity. The library was to be accessible to all, free of charge, seven days a week and on all Jewish holidays. The library would be closed on only the High Holidays.[63] The community became the sole legal owner of the library. Taken together, these conditions ensured that everyone in the community, irrespective of economic, occupational, educational, or any other communal status, would have full access to the library and that the community's interests and not those of an individual or private institution would dictate the library's operation, creating the first Jewish public library.[64]

The community also received a plot of land from Mattityahu's estate that was earmarked for the library's upkeep. In addition, money from Fuenn's estate was provided to fund the construction of a building for the library, and his library was incorporated into the Strashun Library. The Shulhoyf contained an arcade of butcher shops that fronted the Great Synagogue, and there had been complaints for years that these stores were inconsistent with the unique Shulhoyf neighborhood. A suggestion was made that those shops be demolished and the Strashun Library be erected in that space.[65]

Mattityahu's library was now destined for its public home. The agreement made appropriate provisions to ensure that Mattityahu's contributions — not just financial but also intellectual — were not lost. His personal library was to be kept intact and assigned a special place, preserving in perpetuity the distinctive composition of his library, reflective of his and his city's intellectual heritage.[66]

Unlike some of the earlier aspects of the disposition of Mattityahu's library and the public Strashun Library that proceeded slowly, once the agreement was reached in the fall of 1899, the Strashun Library building was completed in short order. The building was finished by Passover, April 15, 1901, and later that year the library moved in to its new home.[67] The impressive stone building with its distinctive arched windows was designed by the Lithuanian architect Konstantin Koroedov.[68]

The library building fronted Jews' Street and was situated to the right

3. Exterior of the Strashun Library facing Jews Street. The Great Synagogue is visible in the background. Vilna Gaon State Jewish Museum.

of the main entrance of the Shulhoyf and opposite the Gaon's Kloyz, directly in front of the Great Synagogue, its imposing edifice partially blocked by the library building.[69] The library occupied the second floor of the building, but had its own entrance from the Shulhoyf. The library's location—within the Shulhoyf—was demonstrative of its centrality to the Vilna public.[70]

The Strashun Library building was officially opened on April 27, 1902, the fourth of the intermediate days of Passover, with great fanfare.[71] Vilna's hazan sang Psalm 20, "Mizmor Shir Hanukat ha-Bayit" ("Song for the Dedication of the House"), and the prayer "Mah Tovu," said upon entering a synagogue, an implicit comparison of the library to a temple. Echoing the contents of the Strashun Library, speeches in Yiddish, Hebrew, and Russian were given by a diverse group of communal leaders: the official preacher, the rabbi of Vilna, the government rabbi, and Neuschul, who was among those from Hovevei Tzion who led the effort to transfer the library to the community, among others. Leaving no doubt as to the identity of the Strashun Library's owners, emblazoned on the side of the building facing Jews Street, on the second story, was "Bet Otzar ha-

Sefarim asher le-Adat Vilna 1900–1901"; the portraits of Mattityahu and
Fuenn—Mattityahu's colleague and kindred spirit, who was instrumental in finalizing the library—hung on the wall. Almost immediately after
its opening, however, the government closed the library because it lacked
the proper permits. Obtaining the necessary permits for the library was a
challenge from the outset. Ironically, this was in part because of Mattityahu's directive that the library be fully accessible to the entire community.

The censorship law of 1865 required all lending libraries and reading
rooms to obtain permission from the authorities. The terms of Mattityahu's will forbade lending books, but his intent was that the library
would permit full access to the books, clearly qualifying as a reading
room. Jewish libraries were at an even greater disadvantage than those
of the general public. All the library's books were scrutinized to ensure
that they were in keeping with the interests and ideals of the empire. The
authorities published lists of approved books, without a single Yiddish
book listed. Jews were also less versed in the nuances of the application
process, which required providing the authorities with the library's by-
laws that described the proposed library's operations and resources.[72]

When the trustees sought approval in 1886, they were denied a permit.[73] The denial may have been because the library lacked an inventory

of its holdings, and it could not be effectively reviewed to ensure that it contained only "acceptable" books. That may explain why, in the late 1880s, the trustees elected to focus on a creating a catalog. After the completion of the catalog, Dovid Strashun, who was managing the library project, petitioned the government for a permit.[74] Apparently that effort was unsuccessful. The library's move in 1892 to Kahal Hall in the Great Synagogue may have been precipitated by more than aligning with the communal nature of the space. Because reading rooms and lending libraries required a permit, the use of Kahal Hall potentially obviated the need for authorization. The Jewish community treated Mattityahu's library as simply a collection of books, rather than a public reading room, located within the spiritual center of Vilna, the Great Synagogue, for the use of its parishioners, which did not require a permit.

Whether or not the move to Kahal Hall was driven by concerns regarding permits, when the library finally moved into its new separate building in 1901, it did so without applying for permission from the local authorities. Instead, as before, the Jews deemed the Strashun Library as an appendage of the Great Synagogue. But right before the official opening ceremonies, an anonymous complaint was filed with the authorities that the library was unpermitted. The ceremonies went forward, but the library was almost immediately closed by the authorities, and they initiated a review of the library's legal status.

The government did not accept the interpretation that the library was part of the Great Synagogue. Nonetheless, after a review of the library's history and contents, on September 20, 1902, the second day of Rosh Hashanah, Vilna's governor-general Victor von Wahl signed the authorization for the Strashun Library. No politically sensitive books were found in the library, but it could not purchase or hold any books in Polish.[75] That von Wahl granted permission was far from a foregone conclusion. Not three months earlier, von Wahl had overseen the beatings of Jewish May Day demonstrators. In retaliation, a few days later, Hirsh Lekert, a Jew and member of the Bund, attempted to assassinate von Wahl. Lekert was executed on May 28.[76] Nonetheless, somehow those events did not sufficiently prejudice von Wahl's decision regarding the Strashun Library.

Completing the full and total transfer of Strashun's library to the Vilna Jewish community was not the final step in crossing the abyss from private to public. The Strashun Library was intended as a public library, a model that was being implemented in many other countries, which was central to and served the entire public.[77] Though Mattityahu's collection was substantial both in terms of size and breadth, it was still the product of one man's idea of a library. For this reason, one of Vilna's leading scholars and historians, Hillel Noah Steinschneider,[78] pleaded with the public to donate books and ensure the completeness of the library, and thus enable it to fulfill its mission of serving the entire community. He acknowledged that Mattityahu had amassed a very impressive private collection, but that for a public library, his collection alone was insufficient because "it is lacking in books for [a] public" whose interests did not align with Mattityahu's.[79] That is, a public library is not simply one that is accessible to all, but also contains materials with broad relevance that provide value to all. Consequently, the library's composition must reflect the entirety of its audience and not a single collector. Although the Strashun Library did not acquire Friedland's library, Steinschneider's plea was successful, as numerous Vilna scholars donated their collections to the library.[80]

Those involved in ensuring that the Strashun Library became the property of the public also participated in expanding the library's holdings. Samuel Fuenn's library became part of the Strashun Library, a contribution to the conversion and expansion of Mattityahu's private library into a public institution, complementing his close friend Mattityahu's intellectual legacy.[81]

The Epsteins, who had initially fought efforts to clarify the community's ownership, were among the donors. Joshua Hayim's son, R. Mordechai Epstein was a member of the Strashun Library board. He was a scholar in his own right and a book collector. And in 1924, his collection of approximately one thousand rabbinic books was donated to the Strashun Library.[82]

Many of Vilna's intellectual aristocracy—adherents of the Vilna Haskalah—donated their libraries. These included: the Talmudic scholar Dov Ber Ratner (1852–1917), best known for his critical editions and commentary on the Jewish chronological work *Seder Olam* and the Jerusalem Talmud; Jacob Benjacob, whose library included books from his father, Isaac, the first modern Hebrew bibliographer; Haim Leib Markon, the editor of the Vilna newspaper *Ha-Karmel*, and Judah Bahak, another editor of *Ha-Karmel* and of the first Haskalah journal, *Pirkhei Tsafon*, in which Mattityahu published one of his earliest articles; and the well-known Haskalah writer Kalman Shulman.[83] Recognizing the communal nature of the Strashun Library, donations came from all sources. Publishers and authors also contributed materials. In 1928 the library of Vilna University began donating its Hebrew, Yiddish, and Judaica books to the Strashun

5. Khaykl Lunski in the Strashun Library.

Library. By 1935 the library had received three thousand books from the university alone.[84] Eventually, the donations proved so substantial that many remained in their boxes and completely filled all the available storage space, and were piled along the walls, blocking some of the windows.[85] The Strashun Library not only accepted donations, it also returned them in kind and sent some number of duplicate books to the Hebrew University Library in Jerusalem.[86]

Arguably the most important contribution to the Strashun Library's continued growth and relevance was the appointment, in 1895, of Khaykl Lunski (1881–1943) as librarian. Lunski shared duties with Isaac Strashun, who at fifteen had become librarian after his father, Samuel, fell ill in 1894 (he died in 1895).[87] Nonetheless, Lunski would be the driving force behind the library ballooning from Strashun's 5,739 items to over 50,000 in 1940, and simultaneously maintaining the remarkable diversity of its collection.

Lunski was the embodiment of everything great about the library he helmed and its founder. Born in Slonim, Lithuania, in 1881, he received a traditional Orthodox education. In 1892 he came to Vilna to study. He was poor and took a job as the *shamesh* (beadle) in the Old Synagogue that was located in the Shulhoyf. Lunski was a voracious reader and began to read Haskalah literature. In the mold of the nineteenth-century Vilna maskilim, he maintained an Orthodox lifestyle, but he also was active in many secular intellectual and cultural institutions and wrote on related topics.

Lunski was a scholar in his own right and published a number of articles and books.[88] Like Mattityahu's, many of Lunski's articles were devoted to Vilna's history. Lunski's intimacy with Jewish Vilna was nearly legendary. Israel Klausner, himself an expert on Jewish Vilna and the author of a half-dozen books on its history, writes that Lunski knew "every one of its street and alleys, every one of its synagogues and batei midrash, every house on the Jewish streets, and every basement and balcony" in Vilna.[89]

The Strashun Library was his passion. He was at the library every day, including Shabbat and holidays. He regularly worked ten- to fifteen-hour days; and when he returned home, he would spend hours compiling a catalog of the library.[90] Lunski loved books; an autodidact, he eventually became one of the world's leading experts on Hebrew books and manuscripts. He received letters from all over the world requesting his assistance. Although an expert himself, he almost always deferred to others and minimized his own scholarship. Moreover, anyone who came to the library could expect that Lunski would greet them with a smile and assist them with whatever their needs were. Although the larger Strashun Library lacked a catalog (only Mattityahu's personal library was cataloged in *Likutei Shoshanim*), Lunski became a living one, able to locate any book in the library's collection almost instantaneously.[91] Lunski's creation embodied the best of the Vilna community's heterogeneity and intellectualism.[92] Appropriately, he has been called "The Guardian of the Jerusalem of Lithuania."[93]

In Lunski's zeal to ensure the completeness of the Strashun Library holdings, he went so far as to risk his life. Hirsz Abramowicz was conducting research at the Strashun Library for a series of articles regarding the Kishinev pogrom of 1903. Lunski had ready all the relevant Jewish articles and books that had any information, even the smallest bits. But Lunski was not satisfied with providing Hirsz information from just the Jewish press; a patron of the Strashun Library deserved all of the material that could be had. Thus, Lunski collected and secreted illegal publications related to the pogrom — a capital crime.[94]

One story is telling of both Lunski's personality and intellectual prowess and the diversity of the Strashun Library's holdings. Abraham Karpinowitz (1913–2005) was born and lived in Vilna until 1937, and wrote richly detailed stories about his hometown. In one, a reporter for one of the Yiddish newspapers, Siomke Kagan, was friendly with a former prostitute, Tamar, and wanted to establish a school to teach about love and sexual education. After writing a lengthy article about this plan, he went to seek out materials for his courses. First, he tried the bookstores, but came up empty-handed. He realized he was looking in the wrong places, and "it dawned on him that Khaykl Lunsky, the librarian at the Strashun Library, could help him." He went to the Strashun Library, and Lunski "went over to a side cupboard in the library and took out a thin little book. The pamphlet precisely spelled out all the fine points for correctly having sex with a woman as well as what to do to please the man. Khaykl Lunsky stroked the pamphlet, reprinted from an old manuscript which had to be a good few hundred years old." There was no author listed, and the book, *Ahavah Bata'anugim* (*Pleasures of Love*), was written in Hebrew. Siomke asked if Lunski would translate it into Yiddish, but Lunski declined with a smile. Although Siomke attempted to convince Lunski of the value of the having such a book available for the larger public, "with steadfast patience, Khaykl Lunsky heard Siomke out. Then he put the pamphlet back into the cupboard amongst the other rare religious books."[95]

The story is fictional, and the book *Ahavah Bata'anugim* likely is imagined.[96] Nevertheless, much of the story aligns with fact. If there ever was such a religious book, even on such an esoteric topic, the Strashun Library would be the obvious place for it. Despite the book's rarity, Lunski would immediately know of it; and that he would take Siomke's request seriously and listen patiently all ring true.

Abramowicz's conclusion to his profile of Lunski captures his unique personality, one that expresses the best of what influenced him and what he reciprocated: Vilna, Mattityahu, and the Strashun Library. "Lunski was one of the last representatives of a generation of autodidacts who lived on the cusp between declining circles of Orthodox scholars who were followers of the Haskalah and modern times. And if there were any righteous men in that generation, Reb Khaykl Lunski—a pure, just man and a historian of great scholarly strength—was among them."[97]

The diversity of the Strashun Library's holdings and its librarian—his erudition and welcoming attitude—contributed to its heavy usage by the entire Vilna community and far beyond. The Strashun Library's main reading room could seat up to one hundred patrons at a time. The library was open seven days a week (although on the Shabbat, the patrons were prohibited from writing) and became the central meeting place for the residents of Vilna.[98] Its patrons were representative of Strashun's commitment to both traditional and modern ideas and ideals, and Vilna's heterogeneity.[99] From the establishment of the library, descriptions of the library's patrons consistently emphasize that diversity as a unique aspect of the library, in many instances using nearly the same verbiage. Ben-Zion Dinur was in Vilna soon after the Strashun Library opened and proclaimed that "there is no other Jewish community with [as much] Jewish unity as in Vilna, and especially so in the institution of Jewish unity, the Strashun Library." His first visit to the library left a "lasting impression," where inside there "were long simple tables, [. . .] and chairs and benches one next to another, where a large crowd was sitting; in total silence, not a sound was heard. Rabbis and old Talmudic scholars studying responsa and Jewish legal texts, and next to them the younger generation, nearly all pale faced, were swallowing Haskalah literature with gusto."[100]

Likewise, in 1918 Lunski wrote that the library is a place of respite for "rabbis, preachers, teachers, maskilim, writers and regular people, shopkeepers and those who lost everything, and householders."[101] According to one visitor in 1930, he found the Strashun Library "now, as it was in the

good days of the past, a diverse set of readers, that one cannot find anywhere else: a Jewish *lamdan* [scholar] sways over a difficult passage in [a
traditional commentary], next to him sit young girls, students from the
gymnasium, who style their hair in the modern fashion."[102]

Indeed, from when the Strashun Library first opened, women too were
counted among its patrons.[103] In 1935 Lunski estimated that they accounted
for 25 percent of the library's readers.[104] A 1938 visitor's description of the
reading room emphasized this aspect of the reading room's heterogeneity and that the reading room was not just "venerable long-bearded men,
wearing hats, studying talmudic texts, elbow to elbow with bareheaded
young men," but "even young women, bare-armed sometimes on warm
days, studying *their* texts."[105] One observer saw the diversity of the library
represented even in the portraits that hung on the wall.[106] The portrait of
Y. L. Peretz,[107] who is counted among the troika of founders and masters
of modern Yiddish literature, was displayed next to that of Mattityahu

6. Strashun Library bookshelves. Moses Vorobeichic, *Yidishe Gas in Vilna*, 1931. Courtesy of the Lithuanian National Library, Judaica Research Center.

and "meant that they were comparable to one another . . . that these two personalities from different generations and who held different ideological positions, 'met in the same hotel' (*mizdamnim le-pundak ehad*)."[108]

When dignitaries came to Vilna, the Strashun Library was a landmark on their itinerary.[109] In anticipation of the Zionist leader Theodor Herzl's visit in 1903, the library commissioned a special guest book, Sefer ha-Zahav, the "Golden Book," to inscribe the names and comments of the visitors. Herzl would be the first to sign. But either for safety concerns or because the Russian government refused permission, Herzl never reached the Shulhoyf or the Strashun Library.[110] The "Golden Book" was lost during the Holocaust, but in 1939 Lunski published a short article about the book and transcribed some of the entries. As Lunski explained, "The inscriptions in the 'Golden Book' of the Strashun Library number in the hundreds in a variety of languages, Hebrew, Yiddish, Russian, French, Polish, and English. There are also many group signatures of guests, communal activists, and delegates attending various conferences in Vilna, as well as tourists (Jews and non-Jews), scholars, professors, teachers in gymnasia, representatives of organizations, etc., all of them express themselves with ecstasy and enthusiasm in favor of the collected intellectual treasures of the Library."[111] Even the handful of entries from Strashun Library's "Golden Book" that are preserved reflect the diversity of its visitors and their impressions of the significance of the library to Vilna. Many saw the two as inseparable: "To be in Vilna without visiting the Strashun Library is like not being in Vilna at all."[112] A similar sentiment is expressed in another entry, that "the Strashun Library left [the visitor] the same impression as from the city of Vilna, uniquely Jewish."[113] Baron David Gunzburg, the philosopher Hermann Cohen,[114] and the scions of Yiddish literature Mendele Mokher-Seforim (Sholem Yankev Abramovitsh)[115] and Sholem Aleichem (Shalom Rabinovitz) all signed the book.[116] Sholem Aleichem exclaimed, "I have never seen such a Jewish treasure house as this library, neither in real life nor even in a dream, during which fantasy seizes the author and carries him on wings far, far away from reality."[117] In addition, the Hebrew poet Hayim Nahman Bialik,[118] R. David Friedman (who proposed a similar institution for Friedland's books),[119] and staunch traditionalists R. Hayim Ozer Grodzenski[120] and R. Israel Meir Kagan (Hafetz Hayim)[121] all visited and signed the book.

The historian Simon Dubnow visited in the spring of 1903 and wrote that the library "contained substantial holdings, in terms of numbers and subjects and upon which a Bayit Ne'emanah (a True House) of our literature can be built, in our languages [Hebrew and Yiddish] and all languages, Hebraica and Judaica[.] It is particularly fitting that Vilna, our communities' elder statesman, should be the place that a Hebrew and Jewish library will become a spiritual center for all those seeking knowledge."[122]

Within a year after the library opened, its reading room's one hundred seats proved insufficient for the numbers of patrons. The library was so busy that on many days one had to wait for a seat to open up. The cloak-room was converted into a seating area, and the walls were covered with people leaning against the wall and reading, waiting for a seat.[123] Prior to World War I, the library served close to 52,000 patrons a year, or almost 150 daily, as compared to the Kovno community library, which averaged 58 people per day.[124] A 1925 article reported that 300 patrons visited the Strashun Library daily and 100,000 yearly.[125] Lunski's 1935 article on the library reports a slightly lower number, with 230 patrons daily, comprising 75 percent men and 25 percent women, of which 40 percent were religious students, 20 percent writers and teachers, 25 percent general students, and 15 percent workers. A broad division of the types of books used by patrons was 50 percent rabbinic, 25 percent Haskalah literature

7. Interior of the Strashun Library with its diverse patrons, some bareheaded, others with beards, and on the right, two women. The librarian, Isaac Strashun, is in the foreground. Mattityahu's portrait is visible on the far wall.

in Hebrew, 20 percent Jewish literature (50 percent belles lettres, 20 percent academic books, and 30 percent newspapers and journals), and 5 percent Judaica.[126]

Lunski highlights some of the important scholarly works that were produced using the Strashun Library. Among those are key twentieth-century histories, Ze'ev Yavetz's *History of the Jews*[127] and Simon Dubnow's *Divrei Yemei Yisrael*. During the infamous Beilis trial in 1913, the rabbi of Moscow, Rabbi Jacob Mazah, requested two books from the Strashun Library, which were cited in the decision and reported on in the newspapers.[128] A Polish university student wrote his dissertation at the library on the first Yiddish Bible dictionary and concordance, which were among the first three Yiddish books and the first published in Poland, *Mirkeves ha-Mishne*. This rare book, published in 1534–35 in Krakow, was among Mattityahu's books and is foundational for the study of Yiddish, which this student used to his advantage.[129] Finally, the founder of modern scientific Talmud study, Jacob Nahum Epstein, also frequented the library.[130]

The Strashun Library served as more than just a place of books; it provided a space for other communal needs. Groups and organizations held meetings in the library, including what eventually became some of Vilna's leading institutions and associations. During challenging times, the Strashun Library's reading room was an oasis of calm and provided some sense of normalcy for the displaced. In Lunski's history of Vilna during World War I, he proudly notes the role that the library played, and that it did so for everyone.[131]

The library ultimately became the largest public Judaic library in Eastern Europe.[132] By 1940 Mattityahu's library had expanded to almost ten times its original size to 50,172 books.[133] The Strashun Library remained especially strong in rabbinics and responsa, but the collection as a whole was incredibly diverse. Sometime after 1918 Lunski began drafting what he intended as the master subject index of a catalog of the Strashun Library holdings. He lists at least twenty-two separate categories, a number containing subcategories, a sampling of which includes Hebrew grammar, homiletics, history, letters, math, geography, anthropology, eulogies, ethics, bibliographies, philosophy, Zionism, Kabbalah, medicine, poems, songs, and German, Russian, English, and French language primers.[134] Books from nearly every Western language were represented, including German, Russian, Latin, French, Italian, English, Polish, Spanish, Lithuanian, Hungarian, and one book in Arabic.[135]

On the one hand, the Strashun Library was recognized as one of the greatest cultural institutions in Eastern Europe; and on the other hand, like so many public institutions, it struggled to raise sufficient funds throughout the early part of the twentieth century, consistently hampered in its ability to maintain and build its collections, and at times forced to reduce public access.[136] It would not be funding that led to its demise, however, but rather the Nazis and their nefarious campaign to appropriate Jewish cultural treasures.

Jewish Books and the
Ravages of World War II

ALFRED ROSENBERG, A BALTIC-BORN Nazi intellectual and Adolph Hitler's racist ideologue, was a man of grand but dark ambitions. He envisioned a network of institutions of higher learning, across the German Reich, as study centers of Nazism.[1] The Institute for Research on the Jewish Question in Frankfurt (IEJ) would concentrate on Jews and would contain the greatest collection of Jewish and Jewish-related items. Rosenberg's dream required amassing Jewish cultural property, and he elected to do so by outright theft. He created an organization whose mission was to loot and pillage Jewish cultural artifacts for the institute's collections.[2]

Germany was a signatory to the 1907 Hague Conventions that codified the legal regimen which governed spoils of war. According to the treaty, armies were permitted to seize property that had a military purpose, such as ammunition, arms, and supplies. But the treaty outlawed the looting of cultural property. Indeed, after World War I, Germany was required to repatriate illegally looted cultural property, and to the extent that was no longer possible, pay reparations or restitution in kind for destroyed or damaged property. Yet Germany failed to honor its commitments to the treaty.[3]

In 1938 the mayor of Frankfurt lobbied Rosenberg to place his Jewish institute in Frankfurt. As an incentive, the mayor offered Rosenberg the over 550,000 volumes of the city's extensive collection of Judaic literature contained in the Frankfurt City Library at the former Rothschild Palace, among the most significant Judaica holdings in the world. In 1928 the Rothschilds had gifted the Rothschild Palace and its associated library to the city of Frankfurt, which became part of Frankfurt's municipal library system—with the name of its founders removed.[4] In April 1939 the agreement between Frankfurt and the Nazis was reached, and the first illegal transfer of the Frankfurt municipal library, of what would ultimately number millions of volumes of priceless Judaica, to Rosenberg and his institute in Frankfurt was launched.[5] Rosenberg converted the library into IEJ's library and formally opened in March 1943.[6]

On July 1, 1940, Rosenberg petitioned Hitler for his consent to establish an organization to loot and plunder items that would form the foundation of his institute. Hitler's reply was almost immediate. On July 5, 1940, Rosenberg received the Führer's formal blessing to unleash throughout the German territories a program of limitless looting and plunder of valuable property for use at the Frankfurt institute. Rosenberg formed a special unit, Einsatzstab Reichsleiter Rosenberg (ERR), to implement the program.[7] Rosenberg was discerning regarding his mandate and did not suck up everything that crossed his path. Rather, true to the language of Hitler's order, Rosenberg targeted "valuable property" to implement his goal of looting sufficiently valuable Jewish religious and cultural property to build his institute.[8]

Almost immediately, beginning with the Western European countries, the task force began plundering the great Jewish libraries of Europe.[9] One month after the Nazis occupied France, they carried away fourteen hundred crates of books from the Alliance Israélite Universelle's collection, which included three hundred manuscripts and a number of fragments from the Cairo Genizah.[10] Rosenberg also seized a number of libraries throughout Western Europe belonging to the Rothschilds, totaling approximately twenty-eight thousand volumes.[11] Indeed, in the spring of 1941, Rosenberg boasted that the institute's Frankfurt library "is already the largest in the world dealing with Judaism," and that "in the coming years it will be enlarged in a most decisive way."[12]

The ERR was so successful in the pursuit of its mission that the institute was unable to cope with the massive numbers of items the ERR returned to Frankfurt; and the IEJ building itself, at 68 Bockenheimer Street, also formerly a Rothschild palace, was used to accommodate the looted property. There, nearly all remained in their crates, uncataloged, never making it into the institute's library. This delay in moving the materials to the city library proved auspicious and spared those books from the fate of most of Frankfurt's library, which was destroyed during the American bombing campaigns. Instead, once Frankfurt was threatened, the crated books were moved to safer locations outside the city. Thus, nearly all of the plundered materials sent to Frankfurt remained in deep storage and protected from the ravages of war. Rosenberg's IEJ acted as an ark for this plundered property, saving the most important European Jewish treasures, the last symbols of the greatness of a no-longer-extant population that otherwise likely would have gone the way of millions of Jews and been lost forever.

On August 23, 1939, the Soviet Union and Germany signed the Molotov-Ribbentrop Pact. Pursuant to its terms, Lithuania was declared within the Soviet orbit of control.[13] The Soviet army briefly occupied Vilna, but on October 28, 1939, Lithuania was declared independent with Vilna its capital.[14] Vilna enjoyed its autonomy for a little over eight months, until June 17, 1940, when the Soviets reoccupied Vilna.[15] However brief its independence, that status created a tiny sliver of Eastern European land which provided the final opportunity to escape the Holocaust.

The Germans invaded Poland on September 1, 1939. Immediately, the Jews bore the wrath of the Nazis; and with the Soviets in the East, Polish Jews were trapped between the Soviets in the East and the Nazis in the West. The southern border with Romania was closed. Lithuania was the only remaining exit point from Poland.[16] "Vilna fever" infected the Jews of Poland, and they began pouring into Vilna in the thousands.[17] The number of monthly refugees reached its height in late 1939; and in May 1940, a month before the Soviet occupation of Vilna, over ten thousand refugees had reached Vilna.[18] With Vilna's swelling population, the Strashun Library was now busier than ever; and with the Polish refugees came a new type of patron to inhabit the Strashun Library reading room: "Hasidim, wearing their long silk robes, white socks and fur hats."[19] A few thousand refugees escaped, many through the efforts of the Dutch and Japanese consuls.

On June 15, 1940, the day after the Nazis entered Paris, Lithuania was annexed by the Soviets. The Soviet occupation would last a little more than twelve months and bring considerable change to the Strashun Library.[20] On August 3, 1940, Lithuania officially became the sixteenth republic of the USSR; and on November 1, 1940, all of Vilna's major libraries, including the Strashun Library, were nationalized. The Strashun Library was renamed Public Library Number Four.[21]

The Soviets immediately shuttered all of Vilna's Jewish libraries and conducted a comprehensive review of their contents, removing from circulation any books deemed objectionable to the government.[22] Nearly all of the Strashun Library's Hebraica, essentially its entire rabbinic collection, fell into this category, leaving only Yiddish books. Limiting access to a single category affected the diversity of the library's patrons but not its numbers. Because the Yiddish collection comprised mainly secular books, the Orthodox were no longer seen in the Strashun Library's reading room. Overall, however, the number of visitors to the reading room rose significantly during this period.[23] The Soviet's review of the Strashun Library produced one positive outcome, a precise inventory of the library's holdings. That September 30, 1940, accounting shows that as of that day, the Strashun Library held 50,172 volumes, in thirteen different languages.[24]

The Soviets also nationalized another major library and research center in Vilna, the Yiddish Scientific Institute (Yidisher Visnshaftlekher Institut; YIVO), and renamed it the Institute for Jewish Culture with the intent that it would absorb the other Vilna Jewish cultural institutions under a single roof.[25] The Soviets' goal was for the eventual consolidation of all Jewish libraries, including the Strashun Library. Lunski was alarmed that merging the Strashun Library with others would destroy the library's unique character and ultimate value to Vilna's Jewish community. He drafted an urgent plea for all Jews to take up the cause of the Strashun Library and not imperil its irreplaceable heritage.[26]

Lunski was particularly horrified regarding the lack of outrage within the community — the Strashun Library was not simply a library but the "National Library" of the Jews. The library was more than just books. The Strashun Library's thousands of books contained the very essence of the Jews: their heritage, ethics, spiritual life, music, literature, and political and Hebrew philology. The Strashun Library was nothing less than "the repository of the soul of the Jews from all times and generations."[27] Ultimately, the Nazi invasion put a stop to any Soviet consolidation of Vilna's intellectual institutions; and for the time being, the Strashun Library remained in its building in the Shulhoyf.[28]

Some Vilna Jews put their faith in the city's special spiritual history to protect them. They thought "that [the] Jerusalem of Lithuania would avoid the persecutions because, [. . .] in Vilna, are the graves of the Ger Tsedek[29] and the Vilna Gaon."[30] That was not to be. Like the Jerusalem of old, Vilna fell prey to its enemies; and its temple, the Strashun Library, would be razed to its foundation. The Nazis' designs on the Strashun Library were of an entirely different sort than the Soviets'. The Soviet plan for the Strashun Library was to include it in a larger consolidation of intellectual institutions in order to advance scholarship for the benefit of all its citizens, including Jews. The Nazis, however, sought to plunder the library to further their racial and genocidal goals, and turn the books against their owners and use them as tools of antisemitic "scholarship."[31]

In what must be one of history's most ironic twists of fate, when the Nazis unleashed their ideologically driven, programmatic, and organized looting, on a scale and scope unlike anything before, that same program saved many of European Jewry's most prized cultural materials. Most, if not all, would otherwise have been obliterated by the ravages of war, including the Allies' extensive bombing campaigns, the Nazis' destruction of Jewish cities and ghettos, and the Soviet offensive. The nearly inconceivable twist of fate is illustrative of many of the difficult issues attached to the wartime rescue of cultural materials. In this instance, those seeking to turn back the effects of the Nazis resorted to a variety of tactics, some of which proved sadly to be more harmful than beneficial.

War brings total upheaval to daily life, the rule of law, and the function of society, calling into question nearly all existing conventions. In this case, even if the Jews wanted to resist the Nazis' looting and preserve the Strashun Library books, the question of how best to do so was entirely uncertain. Because looters are known to place self-interest above all, blithely destroying cultural objects without regard for their value, whether historical, sentimental, or financial, the obvious course of action to rescue the books was to keep as many of them out of the Nazis' reach as possible. Proceeding under that assumption involved Jews and non-Jews smuggling books out of the Strashun Library, under the eyes of the watchful Nazi guards, under penalty of death, and secreting the books in the ghetto. Tragically, many of those books did not survive the destruction of the Jewish ghetto. But many of the books that found their way into the Nazis' machine of plunder and were sent to Germany survived the war intact. The Strashun Library episode illustrates how even the purest motivations of those Jews and non-Jews who risked their lives cannot inoculate against contrary results.

The Jews of Vilna recognized that their rescue attempts might be for naught. Yet at the same time, they refused to sit on their hands and simply watch their priceless material culture vanish before their eyes. Their quandary was succinctly articulated by Herman Kruk, one of the Jewish actors in this episode, who expressed his frustration as to the uncertainty of his actions. He admitted there was the potential that, no matter how altruistic their actions, in hindsight they might prove "gravediggers" rather than "saviors" of the Strashun Library.[32] Nonetheless, they decided that something needed to be done, and Kruk and others participated in hiding books in the ghetto. Unfortunately, Kruk proved especially prescient. The Jews' own actions—keeping materials in the ghetto—resulted in consigning many books to their grave. Nearly all of the books sent by the Nazis to Germany, however, survived.

Much of the information regarding the Strashun Library during this period is contained in recently unearthed archives in Lithuania and the Ukraine, and the personal diaries of two of the main characters involved, Herman Kruk and Zelig Kalmanovitch. Both Kruk and Kalmanovitch kept diaries and recorded their experiences under the Nazis, and then hid those diaries in the ghetto for later recovery. The Nazis then sent Kruk to concentration camps in Estonia, where he continued to write his diaries. On September 17, 1944, Kruk buried his last cache of diaries in the Lagedi Camp. The next day, one day before the Soviets liberated the camp, Kruk and most of the remaining Jews were shot and their bodies burnt. Kalmanovitch too was sent to a concentration camp in Estonia, where he died in 1944.

Szmerke Kaczerginski was among the workers whom the Nazis conscripted to assist in the plunder of the Jewish books. At the request of ERR, in 1944, he produced a handful of reports on the overall progress of looting. Kaczerginski survived the Holocaust and returned to Vilna, where he recovered many items that had been hidden. Among those were the diaries and reports of Kruk and Kalmanovitch. Subsequently, Kaczerginski and one of his former colleagues from YIVO, Abraham Sutzkever, smuggled those documents out of the USSR to the safety of YIVO in New York City, where they currently reside in the eponymous Sutzkever and Kaczerginski Collections.[33]

Operation Barbarossa, the campaign to blitzkrieg the Baltics and the Ukraine, began on June 22, 1941. The next day Vilna found itself the target of a terrible aerial bombardment. Two days later, on Wednesday, June 25, 1941, the Nazis entered Vilna. One week later two specialists, Dr. Johannes Pohl and Dr. Herbert Gotthard, of the Rosenberg detail arrived in Vilna and began surveying its Jewish cultural materials.[34] The Jewish materials took precedence over the Lithuanian state materials.[35] Pohl held a keen interest in Jews and Judaica and was the director of the Frankfurt IEJ's Hebraica collection. He had written a book on the Talmud, regularly wrote for the antisemitic magazine *Der Stürmer*, and advocated for a course of study, Jewish Studies without Jews.[36] Gotthard, a librarian, taught Oriental and biblical studies at Berlin University. The Strashun Library, as Vilna's oldest and perhaps most distinguished library, was identified as one of the first targets for this campaign.[37]

8. R. Yisrael Meir Kagan's *Mishnah Berurah*, Petrokav, 1912, with the stamp of Rosenberg's Institut zur Erforschung der Judenfrage (Institute for Research on the Jewish Question). From the collections of the Hebraic Section, African and Middle Eastern Division, Library of Congress, Washington, DC.

The looting of the Strashun Library occurred in two phases, beginning within the library's building and continuing later at the University of Vilna. The cataloging and selection of library materials in situ began almost as soon as the Nazis seized Vilna. In a particularly cruel fashion, the Nazis conscripted Jews to assist in the identification of the most valuable cultural materials for plunder at Vilna's most important institutions. Three of Vilna's scholars and keepers of its literary and cultural treasures were arrested: Noah Pryłucki, the director of YIVO and professor of Yiddish at Vilna University; Elijah Jacob Goldschmidt, a teacher, writer, journalist, and director of the An-sky Museum (which contained Jewish ethnographic artifacts and a library) in Vilna;[38] and Lunski. Daily they were transported from the jail to their respective institutions. Lunski prepared the list of important Strashun Library books, including its incunabula and manuscripts, to be sent back to Germany.[39] Needless to say, Lunski was "distraught" that "he [was] supposed to help remove the treasures from 'his' Strashun Library that he protected for 45 years!"[40] Isaac Strashun, Mattityahu's nephew and the director of the Strashun Library since 1894, was unable to bear the raiding of the Strashun Library and committed suicide, hanging himself with his *tefilin* straps.[41] In August 1941 the list of important books was completed, and Gotthard left Vilna.

Eight crates of the Strashun Library's valuable books, manuscripts, and its five incunabula were sent to Germany.[42] Ultimately, Rosenberg's institute never received many of these, the rarest Strashun Library items. Instead Rosenberg was preempted by the German army, which confiscated the best items for its own Judaica library.[43] Pohl appealed through official channels to transfer the looted property to the IEJ, but there is no evidence that he met with any success.[44] On August 18, 1941, the Gestapo shot Pryłucki; and Goldschmidt, after enduring beatings, died in prison.[45]

Lunski and others refused to passively participate in the pillage of the Strashun Library.[46] While Gotthard and his minions were still in Vilna, Jews and non-Jews risked their lives to steal and hide books from the Nazis. Firsthand accounts suggest that, at the very least, three thousand books and manuscripts from the Strashun Library were hidden throughout the Jewish ghetto.

For example, Lunski hid all the Strashun Library incunabula while he was compiling lists of rare materials for Gotthard. But he was unable to keep their location secret: Lunski remained imprisoned until he revealed the books' whereabouts. In early September 1941, days before the Germans herded the Jews into what would become Vilna Ghetto No. 2, the old Jewish Quarter, Lunski revealed the artifacts' location and was freed, and Gotthard snatched up the Strashun Library incunabula.[47] Others' efforts proved more successful.

In one instance, another Vilna Jewish library—the only one functioning in the ghetto—came to the aid of the Strashun Library. The Mefitsei Haskalah (the Society for the Promotion of Enlightenment) had opened its library in Vilna in 1910.[48] Because of the efforts of its librarian, Fayvush Krasner, by 1939 the library was the largest in Vilna in terms of number of volumes and the number of books in circulation. Its collection focused on popular literature, and most of its books were in foreign languages; and consequently, "from the standpoint of the book collection's significance as a Jewish library, Mefitsei Haskalah ranked far from the top."[49] Within two months of the Nazi occupation, the library lost nearly 20 percent of its holdings, because the Nazis confiscated fifteen hundred volumes and readers removed thousands of other books. Ultimately, Krasner was executed.[50]

On September 6, 1941, Vilna's Jews were herded into two ghettos: approximately thirty thousand Jews went into the larger one, Ghetto No. 1, and eleven thousand went into the smaller one, Ghetto No. 2. Before the war, only six thousand people lived in the combined ghetto area. The

Strashun Library, the Shulhoyf, and a few adjacent blocks made up Ghetto No. 2. Ghetto No. 1 was larger and located where the Mefitsei Haskalah Library was at 6 Strashun Street, the same street named in Mattityahu's honor. On September 8, 1941, the Judenrat (the Jewish ghetto administration) appointed a new librarian, Herman Kruk, the former director of the Grosser Library in Warsaw, to helm the former Mefitsei Haskalah Library, now the Ghetto Library.[51] In addition to his role in the Vilna Ghetto Library, Kruk was instrumental in saving parts of the Strashun Library and other Vilna libraries.

The winter of 1941–42 proved particularly harsh, and the Ghetto Library's operations did not begin in earnest until May 1942. In the interim, other uses for the building were devised. An underground bunker, a *malina*, was dug in the basement and served as one of the many hiding places in the ghetto for books and other cultural items. During that time period, the Strashun Library was undergoing the book selection process, and that provided the opportunity to smuggle and hide books in the ghetto. A significant number of Strashun Library books were hidden in the Ghetto Library malina.[52]

Almost immediately after establishing the ghettos, the Nazis began killing the Jews in Ghetto No. 2, who were mostly the elderly and those unable to work. They were taken to Ponar, a forest at the edge of Vilna, and machine-gunned, their bodies left in large pits. By October 21, 1941, Ghetto No. 2 had been cleared of its residents. Jews, however, continued to sneak into Ghetto No. 2 and salvage what they could, and additional books from the Strashun Library were collected. The beadle of the Great Synagogue also took part in the smuggling effort. Somehow, he found room in his house to hide a few thousand books.[53] That ended in late December 1941, when the Germans sealed the Strashun Library.[54]

On January 2, 1942, the locks on the Strashun Library door were broken, and the Jews seized on the opportunity of unfettered access to the library. A group of Jewish municipal workers who were tasked with collecting the property of those massacred in Ponar, assisted by a Polish Christian and with the participation of Herman Kruk, removed as many valuable books as possible.[55] Kruk's diary and archival documents show that approximately three thousand books, twenty manuscripts from the Strashun Library, and a portrait of Mattityahu were secreted in the Ghetto Library building.[56]

Gotthard's initial survey of the Vilna Jewish materials revealed an overwhelming number of materials and repositories. Unlike in Western

Europe where the Nazis seized entire significant Jewish libraries, looting Vilna required a new approach and a much more significant effort than previously anticipated.[57] The books would first be sorted, and based on certain criteria, only a limited number would be sent to Germany.

Dr. Pohl, who was designated to oversee an expanded looting operation, was well equipped to complete the task.

In February 1942, Pohl arrived from Germany with three experts.[58] He established a central collection and sorting location outside the ghetto — at the Vilna University Library building at 3 University Street — for all the Jewish materials in Vilna, including the Strashun Library. Pohl demanded that the Judenrat provide him with twelve Jews to assist in moving the Strashun Library, and to help with the eventual sorting and selection process once the books arrived at Vilna University.[59] Pohl then appointed three Jewish scholars, Zelig Kalmanovitch,[60] Herman Kruk, and Lunski, to oversee the move of the Strashun Library and subsequent selection.

Pohl's reports to his superiors show that an estimated twenty-five thousand books were moved to 3 University Street. Many manuscripts and rare books were divided between a vault at the Strashun Library and a special cabinet at 3 University.[61] According to a report from 1944 by Kaczerginski, before the transfer, many of the Strashun Library books were carted off by the surrounding population.[62] Books from other libraries, the Gaon's Kloyz and the Glaziers' Synagogue, were also sent to Vilna University for a determination of their fate.[63]

The workers were to remove duplicates, and the remainder was destined for Germany.[64] The team was provided with a spacious area for their work. But a portion of that space was occupied by the university's Marxist-Leninist book collection, established by the Soviets, and Kruk intended to move this to make room for the Jewish books. The university librarian, Ona Šimaite, requested that Kruk, to the best of his abilities, protect the Marxist-Leninist collection, and in exchange, she agreed to smuggle out and hide Jewish books.[65] Šimaite continued to assist Jews in the ghetto and smuggled in food and clothing in addition to books.[66] She also hid a Jewish teenage girl and was subsequently denounced and arrested by the Gestapo. Nonetheless, Šimaite refused to give up the girl, and she was eventually deported to the Dachau Concentration Camp. She survived the war, however, and lived for a few years in Israel, ultimately making her home in Paris.[67] Today, a plaque is displayed in the Vilna University courtyard honoring her as a "rescuer of Jews," and in 2015 a street was named in her honor.

Rather than consigning the duplicate Strashun Library books to the paper mills, as was the Nazis' normal course of action for unwanted materials, incredibly, Kruk convinced the Germans to release some duplicates from the Strashun Library (which prior to the war were estimated at fifteen thousand) to the Ghetto Library, although the exact number of those that were at the university collection point is unknown. Moreover, under the watchful eyes of the Germans, Kruk and others hid books elsewhere in the university building so that even if the residents were deported and killed, "we will remain victorious" because at least a part of the great Strashun Library would be safe.[68] The selection process continued until at least May 1942; and as late as April 1943, some number of Strashun Library books remained in the university building.[69] In July 1943, a final survey of the work at the Strashun collection point was ordered, which enabled a few final items to be smuggled into the ghetto.[70] On September 23–24, 1943, the Nazis liquidated Vilna's Ghetto No. 1, and for all intents and purposes Vilna was *Judenfrei* and *Judenrein* (free and cleansed of Jews).

By September 1944, when the Red Army reentered Vilna, the Germans had shipped at least twenty-three thousand books from the Strashun Library to Frankfurt, in addition to the contents of the eight crates that were looted by the German army and sent to Berlin. When the books arrived in Frankfurt, they joined the thousands of others awaiting processing and remained unpacked until after the end of World War II.[71]

By 1945 the Strashun Library had been nearly entirely destroyed; only a small side room remained standing, still containing a single metal book cabinet open and bereft of its precious treasures.[72] In 1945 the Yiddish poet and author Chaim Grade returned to Vilna. He described the remnants of the Strashun Library building, which had previously shone forth as a beacon of light and the lifeblood of Vilna, as now "an entire row of shattered windows" that "casts an enormous black shadow, like a black covered cloth hung over the mirror in a house where there has been a death."[73] In the 1950s the Soviets dynamited the remaining buildings in the Shulhoyf, erasing the last vestiges of the Strashun Library building.[74] Today, the Shulhoyf, the former center of Jewish Vilna, is silent; its conglomerate of buildings is now an empty field. The awe-inspiring Great Synagogue with its impressive interior has been replaced with a low-slung, one-story school in the drab gray style associated with Soviet architecture.[75] All that remains of this formerly magnificent testament to the intellectual power of the Vilna Jewish community is a sign across the street, in English, Russian, and Lithuanian, offering a brief description and a photo of the Great

Synagogue, conveying nothing of what it represented. The sign does not mention the Strashun Library. Strashun's name has also been removed from its honorific place in the former Jewish area, where Ghetto No. 1 once stood. Strashun Street has reverted to its prior name, Zemaitijos. A small plaque at the end of the street reads, in Lithuanian, "This street was previously named after the Jewish scholar, philanthropist, and bibliographer M. Strashun (1817–1885), whose name was attached to the collection of one of the largest Judaica libraries in Europe." The former Mefitsei Haskalah Library building still stands, of course now on Zemaitijos Street, although only a shell remains. A plaque at the end of Jews Street indicates the former house of the Vilna Gaon; a few feet away is a bust of the Gaon. The bust itself is disappointing. Without the legend, one would mistake it for Karl Marx with a yarmulke. Needless to say, none of the depictions of the Gaon look even remotely like the sculpture.[76]

But not everything is gone. Fragments remain, but locating an actual remnant of the Vilna Jewish community requires vigilance. Walking down a street that was formerly part of the Jewish Quarter, one can spy on the side of one building five small Hebrew letters that peek out from under the plaster. In their current state, they appear random, their order spells nothing; their only contemporary meaning: once there were Jews here.

Yet not all was lost. Despite the destruction of Vilna's buildings, the deportation and murder of its inhabitants, and the exile of the Strashun Library, most of the Vilna-owned Strashun Library survived the ravages of war. The possibility remained that this collection could help preserve and perpetuate pre–World War II Vilna and its former owners' special history and play a role in the ongoing development of Jewish culture.

Lost and Found in
a German Book Depot

In April 1945, after defeating the Nazis at the Battle of the Bulge, the United States Third Army, led by Lt. Gen. George Patton, began its sprint eastward. Patton and his men ultimately reached Czechoslovakia, the farthest point east reached by any of the American forces, and in the process, on May 5, 1945, liberated Mauthausen-Gusen, the last concentration camp freed by the Allies. One month earlier, on April 8, 1945, the Third Army's Fifth Infantry Division, led by Lt. Robert Schoenfeld, a Jewish refugee from the Nazi atrocities, came upon, in a castle in Hungen, Germany (approximately thirty miles north of Frankfurt), a massive repository of Jewish manuscripts, books, and other cultural treasures that had fallen victim to Rosenberg's ERR looting operation.[1] The Jewish materials alone were estimated to be between one million and 2.5 million items.[2]

The next day the American newspapers breathlessly reported this incredible find, and in particular, Schoenfeld's role in the discovery. His personal history led some to characterize the discovery not only as valuable because of the priceless nature of the materials, but also as symbolic of a larger victory. For example, a headline in the April 9, 1945, edition of the *Brooklyn New York Eagle* read, "Boro Lieutenant's Discovery of Manuscripts, Paintings Avenges His Flight from Vienna."[3] The article also traced Schoenfeld's unlikely path, beginning with his birth in Lviv, Ukraine (then Lemberg, Poland), to Austria, and by way of America, back to Europe and finally to Hungen and his discovery of the Nazis' cache of Jewish property.

One year after Schoenfeld's birth in 1913, his family left Lviv (formerly Lemberg) and moved to Vienna.[4] There Schoenfeld received his law degree. In 1938, after the *Anschluss*—the German annexation of Austria—and with it the persecution of Austrian Jews, transport of thousands to concentration camps, and seizure of their assets, the Schoenfelds feared that Robert was at risk from the Germans and decided that he should leave Austria for America. He arrived in the United States in 1939, and over the course of the next year, the rest of his family would join him at 1696 East 21st Street, Brooklyn, New York. According to his mother, Robert swore that he would never return to Europe. Yet he was unable to keep that vow. He became a United States citizen, and in 1943, Robert was inducted into the US Army. Because of his linguistic skills—he spoke six languages—he found himself in an intelligence unit. In 1944, after receiving his commission, he went to Europe, setting in motion the series of events that led to his unit's eventual discovery of the cache at Hungen. Consequently, the press reported Schoenfeld's find not only as a measure of "personal vengeance," but "also [as] vengeance for his people." That these Jewish treasures, which Rosenberg had intended to manipulate to support the Nazis' philosophy[5] that treated Jews as *Untermenschen*, were now under the control of a Jew "was also the vengeance of [Schoenfeld's] people."[6]

In 1947 a *New Yorker* reporter and a firsthand observer described the Hungen cache as "the most insulting of all" of Rosenberg's repositories. Therein "priceless illuminated parchment Torahs were found cut into covers for Nazi stenographers' typewriters or made into shoes."[7] This description is confirmed by Leslie Poste, a second lieutenant and a libraries and archives specialist, who prepared one of the earliest reports regarding the recovered materials in Frankfurt and subsequently went on to write his doctoral dissertation on post–World War II libraries. He explains that in the Germans' haste to remove materials from Frankfurt to Hungen, "hundreds of thousands of volumes were literally flung" into the buildings with "scant attention being given to protecting the materials from the elements or theft. Thousands of books, for instance, were found heaped in one small brickyard."[8]

The Hungen discovery of looted Jewish cultural artifacts was among over one thousand such discoveries made by the Americans.[9] Rosenberg's IEJ in Frankfurt and its associated library was the destination for most of the looted Jewish books.[10] Ultimately, the IEJ collection became the largest Jewish library in all of Europe.[11] Unlike the Frankfurt Municipal Library that was selected by the ERR because it was a preexisting library, the Hungen repository was selected for its physical attributes. That location was established in 1943 only after the Nazis, fearing for the safety of the Frankfurt facility because of sustained Allied bombing, began moving books to the castle's cellars.[12] Indeed, during December 1943 the IEJ library at the Frankfurt Municipal Library building suffered bomb damage, although many incunabula and manuscripts had already been moved farther east to safety in a castle in Mitwitz, Germany.[13] Nonetheless, the Frankfurt library's extensive collection of fragments and related catalogs of Cairo *genizah* materials were lost.[14]

In March 1944, the IEJ building at 66 Bokenheimer Street suffered a direct hit, but much of the material survived in the basement.[15] When the Americans arrived there in 1945, they discovered over one hundred thousand books.[16] Many of these had suffered significant damage after languishing on the damp ground floor of the building. In an effort to dry out the books, some were hung on clotheslines, and newspapers were inserted between the pages in others, while worm-eaten and moldy books went to the Sachsenhausen hospital for disinfection.[17]

The recovered Jewish materials fell under the control of the Monuments, Fine Arts, and Archives (MFA&A) Division of the US military, and its staff, known as the Monuments Men, who were depicted in the 2014 movie of the same name.[18] In April 1943 with the Allies landing in Italy, President Franklin D. Roosevelt approved the creation of a commission with a mandate to protect and salvage "Artistic and Historic Monuments." Led by Associate Justice Owen J. Roberts, the commission became known as the Roberts Commission.[19] Based out of the National Gallery of Art in Washington, DC, the commission's members included top American art experts, academics, and curators.

The Americans discovered an estimated fourteen hundred sites containing looted property from all the German-occupied countries; it was unreasonable to maintain each site separately.[20] Major Mason Hammond, a professor of classics at Harvard, proposed a collection-point concept —the same management theory used by the Nazis in Vilna—to more effectively and efficiently process the looted property.[21] Ultimately, seven such collection points would operate throughout the entire American occupation zone.[22] In June 1945 the army described its progress of the past three months and the role of the MFA&A officers who "have been able to pass into the mystery of the most recent and probably most fabulous of chapters in the history of art: the mass evacuation of hundreds of thousands of works of art by the Germans into countless temporary repositories scattered over their country [. . .] and the first steps to assemble the most important holdings into central collection points for immediate protection and eventual inventory have been initiated." This was all accomplished "by only a handful of six experts." Moreover, the press release emphasized the complex nature of these operations and explained that "this is no 'pansy' job—it is probably the only function in the Army that has continually combined staff with field operations." The MFA&A "officers consider it necessary to follow close on the heels of the combat troops when some special target is endangered: one officer was killed in action early in April."[23] In late 1945 the Rothschild building was converted into a collection point for all the Jewish books and archival material recovered within the American zone.[24] The other two collection points were placed under the control of the local *Länder*, German military governments established by Gen. Dwight D. Eisenhower, and not the US Army. The Rothschild building, however, containing mostly Jewish looted property, was placed under the direct control of the army and its Office of Military Government for Germany (US) (OMGUS).[25]

In 1945 a German Jewish reporter for *Haaretz*, Robert Weltsch, visited the Rothschild building and described the state of the Jewish books. Weltsch, echoing Flanner's description of the Hungen repository, criticized the disarray and the Nazis as indiscriminate collectors of Jewish books: "The 'Hebrew book' category includes all books with Hebrew characters, from Tanakh and Talmud and Rambam and *She'elot u-Teshuvot* to Mapu and Sholem Aleichem and Yiddish folk calendars."[26] His critique of the Nazis' poor curatorial skills notwithstanding, the broad definition of what constitutes a Jewish book is nearly identical to descriptions of the Strashun Library's collection.

The Rothschild facility quickly proved inadequate as a collection point, and the inventorying and cataloging there moved at a glacial pace, as books continued to arrive.[27] By July 1945 the building had already received an estimated 130,000 volumes, of which only thirty thousand were cataloged; and they were anticipating the arrival of close to two million additional items. If cataloging continued at that pace, cataloging the additional two million items would require over twenty years.[28] The structure itself was in a state of disrepair, and in December 1945 it had to be closed because of a lack of coal to adequately heat the building.[29] Instead, in September 1945, OMGUS designated another collection point across the Main River in Offenbach at a large five-story building, formerly owned by the chemical and pharmaceutical company I. G. Farben.[30] Much as with the discovery of the Hungen cache, the conversion of the I. G. Farben building into a repository for the restoration of Jewish property was a tiny measure of justice for the Jews: I. G. Farben had willingly partnered with the Nazis and actively participated in implementing the "Final Solution." Farben knowingly benefited from the slave labor at the Auschwitz concentration camp, and created and manufactured Zyklon B, used to gas Jews and others. At the Nuremberg trials, Farben's collusion with the Nazis was established as so great that "it is no exaggeration to assert that the corporation made possible the war crimes and crimes against humanity perpetrated by Nazi Germany."[31]

In late February 1946, Captain Seymour J. Pomrenze was appointed as the first director of the Offenbach collection point; and on February 26, 1946, the I. G. Farben building was officially rechristened the Offenbach Arrival Depot (OAD).[32] Pomrenze was well suited for the project to shepherd the massive collection, identification, and restitution of Jewish books at the OAD. He was proficient in Hebrew, German, and Yiddish, and prior to his military service, he had served as an archivist at the United States National Archives. Like Schoenfeld, Pomrenze had served in the OSS; and in the months before arriving at the OAD, Pomrenze was surveying archival materials in other parts of Germany. Perhaps most important for the task at hand, Pomrenze possessed considerable military administrative experience.[33]

Pomrenze and his successors created detailed monthly reports describing the activities at the OAD that permit reconstruction of many of the events during its operation. The reports contain discussions of mundane matters, such as the amount of coal and gas used, in addition to the number and type of materials received, lists of important visitors, significant accomplishments, and descriptions of the collections and their disposition. These reports, now declassified, are available at the National Archives and online.[34]

When Pomrenze first arrived at the OAD, he found it staffed by just six Germans, personnel clearly inadequate to handle the 1.5 million items at the depot. Pomrenze moved quickly to remedy the insufficient staffing levels, and by the end of the month, there were 167 Germans on his staff.[35] Moreover, Pomrenze developed an organizational structure and implemented a process and workflow for the efficient uncrating, identification, inventorying, sorting, and restitution of the property at the OAD. Pomrenze established sorting areas on two separate floors, and unopened crates remained on the ground floor. In Vilna and other cities, the Nazis conscripted Jews into sorting books; now it was the Germans who were pressed into the task of sorting and classifying Jewish books. They unboxed and reviewed the crates' contents to first determine whether the material could easily be identified as belonging to or originating from one nation or was otherwise unidentified. Each country was assigned its own area, and unidentifiable items were kept separate, awaiting a decision from the US government on their fate. To the extent possible, items were boxed, crated, and prepared for shipment.[36]

The number of libraries that were identified was incredible. For example, by March 22, 1946, the staff had identified 67 institutional libraries and 257 private libraries from Germany. In addition, the staff had completed the transfer of the items at the IEJ to the I. G. Farben building.

Ultimately, Pomrenze's mission was the restitution of as many identifiable objects as possible. By the end of March, having made great progress, he reported that, of the 1.8 million items at the OAD, he had shipped an estimated 242,840 items to their rightful owners.[37] Pomrenze explained that there was "no record of any items having been restituted by predecessor agencies [from] July 1945 to 1 March 1946."[38]

When cataloging began, many important Jewish libraries from across Europe were discovered nearly intact. For example, in March, the OAD staff identified and returned three significant Jewish Dutch libraries: the Bibliotheca Rosenthaliana from Amsterdam received 194 crates of books, the Ets Hayim (Jewish Portuguese Seminary) received 109 such crates, and the Spinoza library received 15.[39]

Hidden among the millions of books at the OAD, close to twenty-five thousand books from the Strashun Library sat undisturbed, so substantial a number that it merited its own special holding area.[40] Because the over two hundred crates were all marked with the same stamp, "MSV," the German sorters knew that they formed a single collection. Nevertheless, months would pass before anyone realized that these books were all from the famed Strashun Library of Vilna and were now at the OAD. Instead, the German sorters misidentified the "MSV" books and associated them with a single person and not the Strashun Library, a public institution.

The Germans' confusion was likely attributable to a misinterpretation of the meaning of the acronym "MSV."[41]

The monthly report includes two entries related to Strashun books, that of a personal collection, "Straszun, M. Vilna," and of a commercial collection, "Strashon, Mattew (Bookdealer)." Some of the books in the crates were (originally) those of "Straszuna, M. Vilna." Indeed, those books from the Strashun Library that originated from Mattityahu's personal library carried the personal ex libris and are likely those that the German sorters associated with "Straszuna, M. Vilna." Nevertheless, the sorters reasonably assumed that all the books from "MSV," which included over two hundred crates amounting to tens of thousands of books, were unlikely solely from a *personal* library and that the "MSV" must refer to someone else in addition to Straszuna. If not a personal library, then what? Perhaps it was that of a bookseller — the V standing for the German *Verkäufer*, or "seller." That identification seemed to the German sorters to be a realistic conclusion; it fitted with both the size of the collection and the assignment to an individual and not an institution — but commercial and not personal. Neither, however, properly attributed the entire collection to a single institution, the Strashun Library. The correct decryption of "MSV," however, was not to transform Mattityahu Strashun from a banker into a *Verkäufer*, a bookseller, but instead to indicate the geographic origin and the nature of the books — "MSV" equals "Mattityahu Strashun, Vilna." That is, the "MSV" marking was correct; all of those books originated in Vilna, some originally from Mattityahu's library, but subsequently all were treated the same and were the property of the uppercase "V," Vilna's Jewish community, that of the collective Mattityahu Strashun Vilna Public Library. But it would be months before anyone realized the significance of the MSV collection, and the books remained assigned to the fictive bookseller.

In May 1946 Captain Isaac Bencowitz replaced Pomrenze as the director of the OAD.[42] Bencowitz refined Pomrenze's methodology and provided a narrative and schematic of the modified workflow. The books' journey began on the top floor, where they were unboxed, and worked their way down until ideally reaching the bottom floor, where the books were reboxed and shipped to their owners. Bencowitz's most important innovation was the creation of a catalog of ex libris contained in the books at the OAD, which vastly sped up the identification process, leading Pomrenze to refer to the new system as the "Bencowitz sorting system."[43] Bencowitz, after sampling books within the depot, photographed and reproduced as many ex libris as possible, and assigned numbers to each. Thus, sorters could mechanically compare the stamps with Bencowitz's catalog and quickly move through the crates.[44]

The number of stamps provides evidence of the reach of the Nazis' looting operation. Bencowitz's catalog contains 4,015 stamps: two-thirds are of Jewish provenance, and the majority are sourced from Eastern European libraries. Vilna alone had 213 separate stamps.[45] Strashun's personal stamp and that of the larger library appear in the catalog.[46] Presumably because the Strashun Library books were already on the ground floor and not on the sorting floors, the implementation of a photographic catalog system did not immediately result in a reevaluation of the "MSV" collection. That would occur not at the OAD, but rather across the Atlantic Ocean, thanks to a scholar in New York City.

On July 9, 1946, Max Weinreich, then the director of the YIVO Institute —one of Vilna's preeminent cultural institutions that had been reconstituted in New York[47]—wrote to Bencowitz and correctly stated that the Strashun Library was at the OAD. Weinreich had just received a copy of the May 1946 report that included the map of the OAD building, wherein the "MSV" and "Matthew Straszuna Library" room appears on the first floor.[48] Similarly, the YIVO books were identified as being in the room adjacent to the Strashun Library. Weinreich also alluded to a relationship regarding YIVO's ownership of the Strashun Library. Weinreich wrote, "I should also like to call your [Bencowitz's] attention to some important facts concerning the ownership of the Matthew Strashun Library of Vilna which quite appropriately has been placed by you in the immediate vicinity of YIVO collections; but this may be reserved for a future letter."[49] Weinreich's allusion to information "concerning the ownership of the Matthew Strashun Library of Vilna" and that the Strashun Library may be related in some manner to YIVO collections is surprising. Although YIVO was headquartered in Vilna before World War II, it was a private institution; and since 1899, ownership of the Strashun Library had been fully vested to the Vilna Jewish community and not to any single organization or individual.[50]

Numerous pre–World War II histories of the Strashun Library confirm its communal status. Among those histories is that of Khaykl Lunski, the Strashun Library's librarian, from 1895 until the Strashun Library's last days in Vilna. His history fails to mention what would have been a seismic transformation of the Strashun Library's ownership, from that of public property to the private property of YIVO. Similarly, diaries written

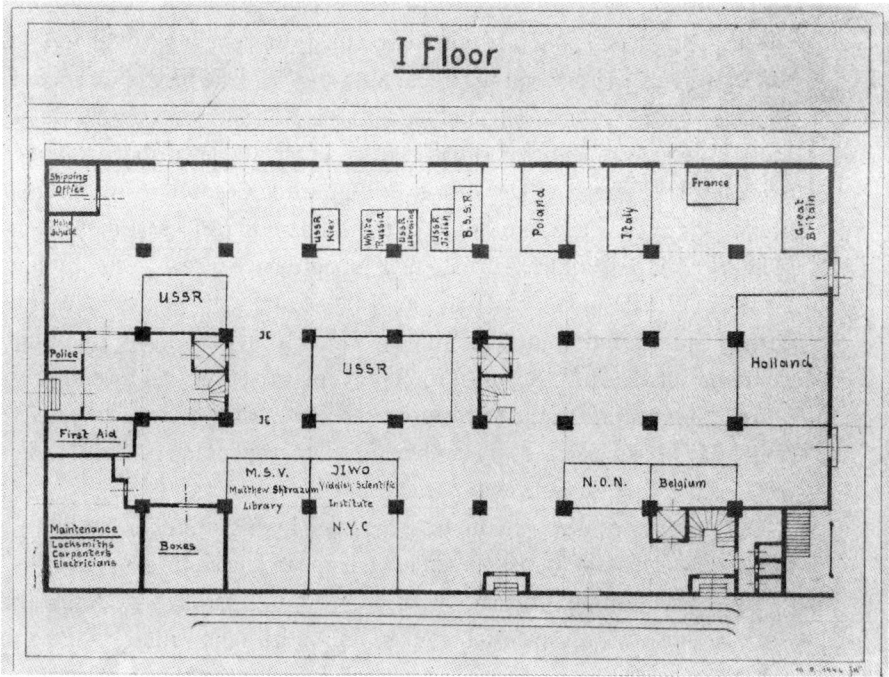

I Floor

Shipping Office · Main Depot · USSR · Police · First Aid · USSR Kiev · White Russia · USSR Lithuania · USSR Vilna · B.S.S.R. · Poland · Italy · France · Great Britain · Holland · M.S.V. Matthew Shtrazun Library · JIWO Yiddish Scientific Institute N.Y.C. · N.O.N. · Belgium · Maintenance Locksmiths Carpenters Electricians · Boxes

9. The diagram of the first floor of the Offenbach Depot that showed the Strashun Library books in proximity to the YIVO materials. Monthly Report, May 1946. National Archives, College Park, MD.

during the Nazi occupation from 1942 to 1944, by those who participated in the removal and sorting of the Strashun Library, fail to indicate that yivo had any role, responsibility, or oversight of the Strashun Library. This is so, even though the Strashun Library and the Nazis' plunder receive extensive treatment throughout their diaries.[51] An examination of the history of yivo and its library, from its establishment until July 1946, yields the same result: no evidence of any formal or informal relationship between yivo and the Strashun Library and certainly no claim to ownership of the library.

In 1891 the Russian Jewish historian Simon Dubnow issued a call to action and demanded that Jews begin to preserve and study the Eastern European Yiddish-speaking Jewish experience; otherwise they risked irrelevance at best and a total loss of Jewish identity at worst.[52] Historically, Yiddish and Yiddish culture was viewed with disdain by Jewish scholars, who considered it the language of the uneducated and women.[53]

This position stood in stark contrast to the realities of Jewish life. Yiddish was the language spoken by over two-thirds of Jews worldwide with a thousand-year history. Rather than shunning Yiddish, or worse, encouraging Jews to abandon their Yiddish heritage, Dubnow embraced Yiddish. Indeed, he viewed Jewish Yiddish culture as placing Jews above the need for political or geographic sovereignty. Rather, Jews could maintain their unique identity while remaining in the Diaspora.[54] Successfully accomplishing this goal indicates that such "people have attained the highest stage of cultural-historical individualization and may be considered indestructible if under subsequent conditions [they] intensely [maintain their] national will."[55] Sustaining Yiddish culture first and foremost requires preservation of the historical record. That record cannot simply be limited to books. Instead, the collection of documentary evidence, *zamlen*, by collectors, *zamlers*, was paramount.[56]

Dubnow's appeal was taken up in earnest by his students, "becoming the credo of three generations of East European Jewish intellectuals."[57]

YIVO was founded in 1925[58] by a handful of Dubnow's students and other Eastern European intellectuals, its institutional mission being to foster the study and preservation of Yiddish culture, channeled through the collection of ephemera and other historical documentary records. It was arguably the culmination of Dubnow's vision.[59] In short order, YIVO was christened a "temple" for "a virtual cult of documentary collection."[60]

Many of YIVO's founders were Vilnaites, but Vilna was not necessarily the obvious location for YIVO's headquarters. Indeed, the YIVO research arm was composed of four sections, and only one, the philological section, was in Vilna.[61] Citing a number of factors, some argued that Berlin was the best location for YIVO's headquarters.[62] Yet by 1928 Vilna had become the de facto location for the headquarters. The selection of Vilna was tacit, rather than explicit, and occurred with YIVO's embarkation on a building campaign for its headquarters in Vilna.

Continuing the Vilna Jewish community's unusual recognition of the value of nontraditional material aspects for nurturing intellectual ideals, the design of YIVO's headquarters was an integral part of its philosophy and mission. In the fall of 1928, YIVO selected a site for its new headquarters, 18 Wiwulski Street. The address was not in the Shulhoyf or even nearby; instead, it was deliberately located in a "remote" neighborhood that was "a fifteen-minute walk from the antiquated Jewish quarter . . . with its only close Jewish neighbor the playing field of the Maccabi sports club."[63] The location—and its distance from old Jewish

Vilna — was interpreted as a symbolic message: "YIVO was no seedy relic of the past; it belonged to the future,"[64] and signaled that it was the "'upstart' boldly staking its claim [as the future of Jewish culture]," which was "in contrast to the Strashun, the dignified aristocrat tucked away in the Shulhoyf."[65]

That is not to say that YIVO viewed itself as antithetical to Vilna's history.[66] To the contrary, YIVO too embraced Vilna's intellectual heritage. YIVO was simply an articulation of "the old constancy" of Vilna's inhabitants' "love for Torah and wisdom," while YIVO's "very function [was to act] as 'a bridge from the past to the future.'"[67] YIVO was, to all intents and purposes, "the contemporary version of the yeshivas and kloyzn for which Vilna had long been renowned."[68]

The embrace of modernity extended to the architecture of YIVO's headquarters, which had many radical differences from other Jewish institutions. Its aesthetics were particularly unusual, and the building's grounds were beautifully landscaped; one observer remarked that she "had never seen a Jewish institution in so verdant a setting."[69] The interior was no less impressive, with "parquet floors, glass display cases, [and] well-equipped workrooms."[70] The lobby was among its most awe-inspiring features, with a grand staircase and on the top landing an outsized colored map of the world marked with the numerous worldwide branches of YIVO — emphasizing its vast reach and impact well beyond Vilna and extending around the globe.[71] When YIVO celebrated its thirteenth anniversary with its first commemorative book, the lobby and map were selected for the cover.[72] In one respect it was more modern than even the New York Public Library: it had "built-in tubular fluorescent lamps" at every seat in its reading room.[73]

The building's most significant feature was its capacity to safely store and access the books and archival materials of the institute. This is no surprise considering that YIVO's core mission was gathering and preserving the material culture of Eastern European Jewry. The storage cellar was specifically included to protect the priceless items housed in the building. Max Weinreich, one of the founders of YIVO and in whose house the institute was first stored, highlighted the facility's "fireproof storage for [the] YIVO collection." Similarly, the American section of YIVO described the building as "a fireproof treasure for Jewish creativity in all lands and of all times."[74] This was not an empty boast. By 1938 the YIVO building held forty thousand books and ten thousand newspaper issues and could legitimately boast that it was "the richest of all Jewish collections of this type."[75] YIVO's Yiddish holdings eventually surpassed those of the Strashun Library, which had previously held the title to the largest collection of Yiddish treasures.[76] The size of YIVO's holdings did not hinder its accessibility.[77] Unlike the Strashun Library, which dealt with the size of its collection in an ad hoc manner and relied on a single individual, Lunski, who was impressively capable of locating the library's books, YIVO addressed size scientifically; and its library became the first European Jewish library to implement the Dewey Decimal Classification.[78]

The YIVO building, just like the Strashun Library, became a must-visit destination in Vilna. The building was so popular that it was forced to set special visiting hours to accommodate the crowds.[79] It was not simply a matter of visiting an important Vilna cultural institution; YIVO, with its branches all over the world, was a worldwide movement and naturally attracted people from the many areas it touched.

The year 1939 brought irreparable change to YIVO and its library. In August its director and arguably its most important personality, Max Weinreich, left Vilna for a conference in Copenhagen, and unbeknownst to him, was never to return.[80] Instead, from Copenhagen, Weinreich traveled to America for what was intended to be a few months' residence, but where he would reside for the rest of his life. When the Soviets occupied Vilna on September 19, 1939, YIVO's ability to operate in Vilna was called into question. The Soviets were openly hostile to many Jewish organizations, including YIVO, suspecting them of anticommunist views. Indeed, when the Soviets reoccupied Vilna in June 1940, they permanently shuttered YIVO.

During their 1939 occupation, the Soviets did not close YIVO, but dealt it a devastating blow. One of its most important leaders, Zalmen Reyzen, was arrested. He was a journalist and editor of the daily newspaper *Unzer Tog*, and some speculate that an article that was critical of the Molotov-Ribbentrop Pact, which appeared in his newspaper, led to his arrest.[81] He never returned, and was shot by the Russians in 1941.[82]

Vilna became an increasingly precarious location for YIVO. Communications between the Vilna branch and its other worldwide branches suffered, with long delays in delivery contributing to uncertainty about the effect of the occupation on the day-to-day operations in Vilna.[83] In mid-October the Soviets unexpectedly withdrew from Vilna and recognized Lithuania as an independent state with Vilna as its capital. By June 1940, when the Soviets occupied Vilna and stopped immigration, more than fourteen thousand Polish Jews had immigrated to Vilna.[84] Most sought to use Vilna as an escape route from Europe.[85] But these refugees, mostly Yiddish speakers, created a renaissance of Yiddish culture in Vilna.

The Soviets' return to Vilna on June 15, 1940, marked the beginning of the end of YIVO's presence in Vilna. Like the other Vilna Jewish educational and cultural institutions, YIVO was nationalized and its library shuttered until its collections could be reviewed and undergo "purification and reorganization" to remove any anti-Soviet materials.[86] Unlike the Strashun Library, YIVO was never reopened before the invasion of the Nazis and was accessible under very limited circumstances, reducing the number of patrons to a minuscule figure. The Soviets, however, added approximately twenty thousand volumes to the library, including thousands of volumes of Jewish Soviet literature. After the annexation of Lithuania, in January 1941, the Soviets established the Academy of Sciences of the Lithuanian Soviet Socialist Republic, and YIVO was absorbed into the academy.[87] YIVO became the Institute for Jewish Culture, a sister institute to the Institute for Polish Culture and three corresponding Lithuanian scientific institutions.[88] To signal the new academic interest in Jewish culture, the Soviets established the long-awaited chair of Yiddish at the Vilna University.[89]

On June 22, 1941, the Nazis conquered Lithuania, and Vilna again changed hands. Like the Strashun Library, YIVO, with its substantial holdings, quickly became a target of Rosenberg and his minions in the ERR. Indeed, YIVO was considered among the most important scientific or research institutions in the Baltics.[90] Unlike the Strashun Library, where the selection process began in February, the course of sorting and selection at YIVO did not begin in earnest until March 1942, when the Germans established a second collection and sorting site at YIVO headquarters.[91] Prior to March, the YIVO building had been requisitioned by the German army, and the library and archives were in complete disarray; according to one estimate, twenty-four thousand of YIVO's books had already been destroyed.[92] The wall map of YIVO's worldwide branches was torn down and replaced by a painted German eagle accompanied by the inscription: *Deutschland wird leben und deshalb wird Deutschland siegen* (Germany will live, and thus Germany will be victorious).[93] Like the Strashun Library collection site, the YIVO collection spot received many other Vilna libraries and private collections, including Lunski's, in addition to those of the towns surrounding Vilna.[94] The YIVO collection point did not receive the Strashun Library. Those books remained at the Vilna University collection point.

Just as with the Strashun Library, some courageous workers at the
YIVO building risked their lives to rescue its irreplaceable cultural treasures.[95] Because the YIVO building was outside the ghetto, the Jews smuggled the materials *into* the ghetto when they returned from work. YIVO
was established to preserve the archival materials of Eastern European
Jewry and relied upon individuals, its *zamlers*, to send materials to YIVO
for its collection and preservation. Now, within the walls of the YIVO
building, individuals continued to play the role of *zamlers*, only this time
rather than sending items to YIVO, they were removing them from the
building to preserve them. After reaching the ghetto, the documents and
books were hidden in underground bunkers, within attics, and even in
the walls of the Strashun Library building, anywhere that there was hope
they would survive the Nazi atrocities. Unlike the Strashun Library smuggling, which consisted almost entirely of books, many of the smuggled
materials from the YIVO building consisted of documents and ephemera.
When the Jews returned to the ghetto, they would secrete the documents
under their clothes, and the Jewish ghetto police generally let them pass
unmolested. Because of the smugglers' choice of contraband, the police
coined the term the "Paper Brigade" to describe the smugglers.[96]

From March 1942, when the YIVO collection site opened, until September 1943, when the Nazis liquidated the Jewish ghetto, the Paper Brigade
removed[97] thousands of books and tens of thousands of archival materials
from the YIVO building into the ghetto.[98] Despite the heroic efforts of the
Paper Brigade, the ERR sent an untold number of YIVO materials to Germany. But a considerable number of YIVO's materials—at one point up to
70 percent—were consigned to paper mills for pulp.[99] Like the Strashun
Library, YIVO books and archival materials were discovered by the Americans after the war.

The recovery of the YIVO materials provided hope to those who had
survived the Holocaust, especially those who hailed from Vilna, that
some of the pre–World War II glory of YIVO's library and archives might
be restored. The majority of world Jewry was no longer on the European
continent; now the United States was home to most Jews. YIVO too had
reconstituted its headquarters in New York City. For all intents and purposes, no longer was Yiddish culture's capital Vilna; now New York was
its heart. If YIVO's Vilna archives and library could be transferred from
the OAD to New York, YIVO could reestablish itself in its new home, bridg-
ing its past and future.

As part of his effort to find the YIVO collection after the war, Weinreich's identification of the Strashun Library books meant that the fate of the first Jewish public library during the Holocaust was known—close to 50 percent of the Strashun Public Library survived intact and was within the American zone. Yet that identification would carry far more serious consequences for the Strashun Library than had the previous erroneous association of it with a fictive bookseller. Instead, the result of the correct identification converted Vilna's communal property into that of a private institution, as YIVO claimed ownership of the Strashun Library. To date, that transfer in title has never been acknowledged. Instead, the Strashun Library, one of the few collections that survived the Holocaust despite all odds and found its way to the OAD in the most unbelievable fashion—because of the actions of the Nazis—remains in private hands.

‖‖

CHAPTER SIX

A Transatlantic Crossing

FOUR YEARS AFTER VILNA WAS RAZED to the ground, and two years after the war ended, a substantial portion of the Strashun Library was still intact. The hundreds of crates marked "MSV," and kept segregated from the millions of other books at the OAD, presented an almost unfathomable possibility—that Jewish Vilna might survive beyond Vilna, even after its people were wiped off the face of the earth, and be refashioned in some small way from the Strashun Library. To do so, however, required that the books in those crates be treated as a discrete collection.

The possibility of fulfilling the dream of rescuing the Strashun Library remained when, on June 18, 1947, it left the OAD. Upon its departure, the Strashun Library books were recorded on the receipt of transfer as a single library, "M. S. V. [. . .] 25,362 books."[1] Nonetheless, the opportunity to capitalize on the value of the Strashun Library and have it remain as one was not to be. Rather, the Strashun Library would languish in obscurity for decades; and then, when its existence was finally divulged, the Strashun Library was no longer treated as an entity in and of itself. Instead, it was absorbed into a larger collection that was made up of a hodgepodge of items from Vilna, part of YIVO's "Vilna Collection." The Strashun Library books came to seen as just some of tens of thousands of items that originated from Vilna, leaving the public unable to appreciate what the surviving Strashun Library could have stood for. The books counted as mere relics of the past, paper tombstones among innumerable other ignominies the Jewish people suffered because of the Holocaust.

The US Army's discovery, in April 1945, of a huge cache of Jewish books and manuscripts from Rosenberg's IEJ was widely reported in the American press. When word reached YIVO in New York, the institution wasted no time in seeking the US government's assistance to determine whether any part of its library and archive was among the recovered items of Jewish property, and if so, to begin the process of transferring it to New York.[2]

The day before V-E Day, on May 7, 1945, a delegation from YIVO, consisting of Sol Liptzin,[3] a Yiddish writer, critic, and humorist who had immigrated to the United States from Poland in 1909 and served as secretary of the Academic Council of YIVO, and Weinreich[4] met with officials at the State Department. YIVO requested that the government provide its assistance to determine whether any of YIVO's property was in Germany and protect it from further looting.[5]

The YIVO delegation was not the only group concerned with protecting the looted Jewish property. In April 1945, when the Americans discovered the Hungen cache, "the remaining [German] staff pleaded with the incoming Americans to protect the treasures."[6] But by August 1945, the Americans were struggling with how to address rampant looting, especially of art. Some advocated a public relations campaign; others, however, argued that "any general 'pollyanna' publicity on causal looting from public collections would only call attention to the possibility [of looting] without having any preventative effect."[7]

The government acted swiftly on YIVO's appeal, and its request was forwarded from Washington, DC, to Germany. Gen. Lucius D. Clay, the deputy governor of the American zone and the supreme commander of OMGUS, ordered a survey of the discovered books and manuscripts to ascertain their provenance and quantity.[8] From June 19 to 21, MFA&A officer 1st Lt. J. H. Buchman, with the assistance of a Jewish captain, Abraham Aaroni, examined the looted materials under American control and preliminarily identified the provenance of some of those materials.[9] Aaroni was a friend of YIVO, and on June 20, 1945, before the survey was even completed (and likely without authorization), he cabled his wife, Cecilia, that one hundred thousand items were identified as the property of three libraries, among them YIVO, and "informing her to tell Shlomo Noble, a Yiddish linguist at YIVO" of the find.[10] Aaroni promised to do everything in his power to ensure that YIVO property in Germany was transferred to New York and continued his efforts, as did others in theater who similarly discovered YIVO materials.

Late in July 1945 the State Department confirmed that YIVO materials had been identified within the American zone.[11] That confirmation, however, was limited to the existence of YIVO property and took no position regarding any rights YIVO may have had to the other discovered property. For the time being, that remained an open question.[12]

On September 19, 1945, Weinreich received word from Col. Saul Kagan, a Vilna native, that he too had come upon a substantial quantity of YIVO

Vilna materials, an estimated "20,000 volumes from the YIVO collection." Kagan had discovered these in the Rothschild building, where many of the ERR materials were held and where he was stationed. He also was aware of another "7,000 crates of books" in Hungen, and that there may have been even more, because "who knows what else will be discovered there." Kagan also made clear to all the personnel stationed at the Rothschild building "that everything the Germans brought from Vilna probably [*varshaynlekh*] belongs to YIVO." Kagan "explained to [them] that many personal libraries, old books, and manuscripts were donated to YIVO," and apparently that would explain why they should ignore any indications on the books of private ownership and that they should treat those as belonging to YIVO. He provided Weinreich with detailed instructions on how best to proceed and have those items transferred to New York.[13]

In November 1945, Weinreich received word from Koppel Pinson, another son of Vilna and YIVO sympathizer then in Germany, that he too had discovered identifiable YIVO books in Frankfurt.[14] Weinreich requested Pinson's assistance to send YIVO property at the OAD to New York. Weinreich's trust in Pinson was so absolute that he was appointed YIVO's official representative at the OAD.[15]

Paralleling Pinson's and Kagan's personal efforts on behalf of YIVO in Frankfurt, Weinreich continued his negotiations with the State Department in Washington.[16] Rather than rely on Pinson and Kagan in Germany, Weinreich decided to open a direct line of communication with US officials in Germany. In early March 1946, with the establishment of the OAD and Pomrenze's appointment as its director, Weinreich wrote directly to Pomrenze. Like Pinson and Kagan, Weinreich's outreach to Pomrenze was not solely because of his position at the OAD, but also because of a personal connection with YIVO. In Weinreich's first letter to Pomrenze, written in Yiddish,[17] Weinreich begins by invoking Pomrenze's brother, Chaim, who as Weinreich emphasizes "is a very close friend of YIVO's and is an active member of its board of directors and executive office"; consequently, YIVO was "certainly pleased that we have in you [Seymour] a friend of YIVO's."[18] Weinreich then provides details regarding YIVO and requests Pomrenze's assistance in transferring property at the OAD to New York. On March 19, 1946, Weinreich wrote:

We know that the YIVO library, together with other Jewish European libraries, is now under your authority. The YIVO library was, as you know, one of the largest and most important Jewish libraries in the entire world. In 1939, on the eve of the war, the library owned eighty-five thousand volumes, only twenty thousand of which were cataloged. By chance, in the year 1938–39, when YIVO suddenly began to grow, books streamed in by the thousands, among them mounds of rare items, but we had no money to hire a larger staff that would stamp and catalog them. We were expecting a larger subsidy from the Joint by the end of the year that would make it possible to appoint a few more workers to move the cataloging forward. But then the war broke out.

Theoretically, one could argue that other libraries which were brought to Frankfurt also had a large number of uncataloged books. In truth, however, that was not the case for such fundamental collections as the Rosenthaliana in Amsterdam[19] or the École Rabbinique in Paris. In those institutions, there were completed, long closed, and in a certain sense congealed collections, to which were added a few hundred books a year. It is no exaggeration to say that the only Jewish library in Europe that grew in the years leading up to the War at a tempestuous pace was the YIVO library.

Therefore, it must be seen to that we receive, along with our stamped and numbered books, the other sixty-five thousand as well. They must be packed together with the identified YIVO volumes, so that at the point of dispatch all the crates head off to New York together.

You surely know that the YIVO library is an immensely significant Jewish cultural treasure, and by ensuring that this library is protected and sent back to its owners, you will have done a hugely important thing in saving whatever has survived of this rich Jewish cultural possession. I am certain that you will not decline to take upon yourself such a responsibility.[20]

Weinreich does not count the Strashun Library among YIVO's property. Nor does he mention the Strashun Library, either to assert a claim or to request information regarding its whereabouts. In addition, by Weinreich's count, YIVO's library held eighty-five thousand volumes before it was looted by the Nazis. That number, however, is likely exaggerated. Indeed, even Weinreich concedes that prior to 1938, the YIVO library was considerably smaller. Weinreich does not attribute the library's growth to the absorption of the fifty-thousand-volume Strashun Library. Instead, he attributes YIVO library's growth to anonymous "books that streamed in by the thousands."[21] A more realistic estimate of YIVO library's 1939 holdings is closer to forty thousand volumes.[22]

Moreover, to the extent that the Strashun Library books were included in the eighty-five thousand, Weinreich had all the more reason to call them out. According to Weinreich, YIVO was uniquely disadvantaged in its quest to return its property because much of it was unmarked and therefore independently unidentifiable. A substantial portion of the fifty thousand Strashun Library books were marked with the Strashun Library's ex libris. If YIVO's library comprised the Strashun Library books, searching for books with that ex libris provided an easy way to identify the majority of the nearly fifty thousand Strashun Library books of the YIVO/Strashun Library. To the contrary, according to Weinreich, only twenty thousand books could be identified as belonging to YIVO. Consequently, if the Strashun Library was YIVO property, the absence of any mention of the Strashun Library in Weinreich's letter is striking.

Weinreich similarly omitted the Strashun Library from a critical document that described, in detail, YIVO's prewar property. In 1946 the Commission on European Jewish Cultural Reconstruction published a detailed survey of important Jewish cultural institutions and collections under Axis control, the "Tentative List of Jewish Cultural Treasures in Axis-Occupied Countries," to assist "the agencies of the United Nations and Jewish communal leadership to identify and to ascertain the present location of those treasures which had been looted by the Nazis and to evaluate the complex problems of restoration and reparation."[23] Indeed, the "Tentative List" provided such a detailed record of the looted Jewish property that some feared the list would do more harm than good: it would apprise the Soviets and other Eastern European countries of the looted property, and they would then agitate for its restitution to the respective countries rather than to the Jews.[24]

Weinreich, a member of the commission, was among those who assisted in drafting the list.[25] Weinreich placed complete trust in the "Tentative List's" description of the YIVO property; and even at the earliest stages in the process of compiling the list, Weinreich invoked it as an authentic rendition of YIVO's 1939 holdings.[26] Later, Weinreich would claim two other collections because "they are mentioned as belonging to YIVO in the 'Tentative List.'"[27]

On March 22, 1946, Weinreich again wrote Pomrenze and requested the restitution of the YIVO collection as it appears "in the 'Tentative List of Jewish Cultural Treasures in Axis-Occupied Countries,' published by the Conference on Jewish Relations in *Jewish Social Studies* (1946, VIII, 1)."[28]

The YIVO entry describing its library and archive holdings in 1939 appears at number 246 in the "Tentative List."[29]

Yiddisher Visenshaftlecher Institut (YIVO)
in VILNA (Yiddish Scientific Institute)

At the outbreak of the war the headquarters of the Yiddish Scientific Institute were transferred to New York City.

In 1939: 85,000 vols., of which only 20,000 were cataloged. 75,000 handwritten documents and mss.; over 100,000 items of Jewish folklore. The library was outstanding for Jewish history and included Judaica in all languages.

The archives included documentary material of the former rabbinical school in Vilna, of several liquidated Jewish communities in the district of Poznan, scores of pinkassim; the collection of over 2,000 books on folklore and ethnology of the late folklorist Judah Leib Cahan, besides Cahan's own manuscript archives (contained material for six volumes and only one volume was published): the manuscript of Alfred Landau's Yiddish dictionary, compiled over a period of sixty years; thousands of documents relating to Jewish history in Eastern and Central Europe; the collection of 600 life-histories of Jewish youth (over 70,000 handwritten pages); many manuscripts of a religious character; over thirty manuscripts of *Toldot Yeshu*; thousands of letters of Yiddish and Hebrew authors and many of their manuscripts; a great part of the archives of Simon Dubnow; very large collections on the history of the Jewish labor movement in Eastern Europe and America; the archives of J. Dinesohn; a great part of the archives of Rabbi E. Gutmacher from Grodziec; material on the history of Jewish colonization in Argentina and on Jews in the Ukraine during the pogroms of 1918–1919.

The press division contained over 14,000 volumes of Jewish periodicals in many languages; over 400 current periodicals were received regularly.

The Esther Rachel Kaminski Theater Museum, founded in 1927, contained tens of thousands of objects concerning the history of the Jewish theater.

The Art Museum of the YIVO, founded in 1935, contained a good collection of paintings and etchings, by Marc Chagall, Mane Katz, etc.; figures by Ryback.

The entry is highly specific regarding the YIVO library and its archive, containing information regarding the different divisions and private and institutional donations. Yet the half-page description omits any mention of the Strashun Library or any connection therein. To the contrary, the Strashun Library is a separate entry, number 248, that *immediately follows* the YIVO entry. By comparison, the Strashun Library's entry is notable for its brevity.

Biblioteka im. M. Straszuna in VILNA (M. Straszun Library)

In 1937: 35,000 vols.;[30] 150 mss.; 5 incunables; many rare prints. Included the collections of Straszun, Fin, Markon, Baer Ratner, M. Epstein. This library of the Jewish Community was very valuable for all branches of rabbinic literature and Jewish scholarship.

The Strashun Library is correctly identified as the "library of the Jewish Community" and not that of any individual or private institution.

YIVO's claim to the Strashun Library first surfaced in the summer of 1946, at least a year after YIVO engaged the government regarding YIVO property in Frankfurt. The belated interest in the Strashun Library is consistent with the distinct and independent status that it and the YIVO library enjoyed prior to World War II. Moreover, on many occasions during 1945–1946, when the question of transferring YIVO property to New York appeared settled and would have closed the chapter regarding YIVO property, YIVO made no effort to assert its rights to the Strashun Library.[31]

As noted earlier, in July 1946 Weinreich received the May 1946 OAD monthly report, which included the map of the OAD building, with two adjacent areas on the first floor separately marked "JIWO Yiddish Scientific Institute N.Y.C," and "M.S.V. Matthew Straszuna Library." In addition, the report identified two other collections, the archives and library of Simon Dubnow and the Vilna Teachers Institute collection. On July 9, 1946, Weinreich wrote to Bencowitz, the director at the OAD, regarding the Strashun and the two other collections. Weinreich provides a detailed history of how and when the Dubnow archives and Vilna Teachers Institute library were incorporated into YIVO's collection, provides an affidavit from Dubnow's daughter confirming Weinreich's discussion of her father's property, and cites the "Tentative List" as the final confirmation of YIVO's ownership. After Weinreich's lengthy discussion regarding the other two collections, he wrote: "I should also like to call your [Bencowitz's] attention to some important facts concerning the ownership of the

Matthew Strashun Library of Vilna, which quite appropriately has been placed by you in the immediate vicinity of YIVO collections; but this may be reserved for a future letter."[32] Weinreich would delay about providing those details until February 1947—by then Bencowitz was already in America and a new director had replaced him.

Bencowitz did not respond to Weinreich's July 1946 letter. Yet he did not even wait for the "important facts" that Weinreich promised in a future letter, and soon after receipt of the July letter, acted upon his petition and proceeded to include the Strashun Library within YIVO property.[33] Bencowitz's novel treatment of the Strashun Library was never explicitly acknowledged, and attention was never paid to this redefinition of the Strashun Library's primary holders. He elected to mislabel the Strashun Library in the monthly reports, and hid the library's existence by effectively applying a YIVO stamp to the crates holding Strashun Library books and giving YIVO what it did not otherwise own. In the subsequent OAD monthly reports, the YIVO library was now listed as "YIVO and Associated Libraries" and assigned 76,042 items. The identity of the "associated libraries" is left unstated, even though the term was previously entirely unknown. Unacknowledged is that the Strashun Library was subsumed within the "associated libraries" and represented a significant contribution, approximately 25 percent of the 76,402 items.[34]

Bencowitz's strategy was so successful that even Weinreich remained unaware of the significance of the newly minted "YIVO and Associated Libraries." Only in early 1947, when Bencowitz returned to United States, was the mystery of the "associated libraries" solved. He provided Weinreich with all the details, including the meaning of "associated libraries," and that for all intents and purposes converted the Strashun Library into YIVO property.[35]

Weinreich may have learned that the Strashun Library was included in the YIVO inventory at the OAD, although there is no indication he provided that information to the State Department or any government officials in the United States. The MFA&A under the authority of OMGUS was the agency in Germany responsible for the protection, sorting, and identification of looted property at the OAD.[36] The State Department had no presence or direct responsibilities at the OAD and had no reason, or basis, to question the sufficiency of the contents of the "YIVO and Associated Libraries" as they appeared in the monthly reports. Instead, the State Department limited its involvement in the YIVO matter to the issue of the legal status of YIVO in New York vis-à-vis YIVO in Vilna. On this issue, the State Department confirmed that the New York organization was "YIVO." From the State Department's perspective there were "no doubts about [YIVO's] rights to the property; it was just a matter of formulating in writing the organizational continuity of YIVO from Vilna to New York," to finalize the department's approval of the shipment to New York.[37] YIVO provided the State Department with three affidavits, two from Weinreich and one from its executive secretary, Julius Uveeler, all concentrated on the current legal status of YIVO in New York and the transfer of the Vilna YIVO's operations and property to the United States. The affidavits provide dates of relevant board meetings, resolutions, and other details regarding the alleged transfer of the Vilna property to New York.[38]

The State Department required that the claim by YIVO in New York be fully compliant with all applicable laws, including the nuances of corporate law. Moral entitlement was insufficient; legally recognizable title to the property at the OAD was the only acceptable means for restitution. On the other side of the Atlantic, in Germany at the OAD, an entirely different opinion of YIVO's entitlement was in effect, albeit unstated. According to Bencowitz at the OAD, "associate libraries" of YIVO—libraries that prior to the war had little to no legal or formal connections with it—qualified as YIVO's property, a policy that underscored the less rigorous and alternative legal criteria in operation in Frankfurt.

The two mutually exclusive procedures and bases for YIVO's claim to the Strashun Library could safely coexist so long as "associated libraries" was absent in negotiations with the State Department, which remained entirely unaware of the fundamental conflict with its colleagues in Europe regarding the constitution of YIVO property or the extrajudicial bases for awarding the Strashun Library to YIVO. The very term "associated libraries" potentially implied less than full legal entitlement. Weinreich recognized that any mention of the "associated libraries" to the State Department risked scrutiny of YIVO's title to the Strashun Library, and potentially the loss of close to one-third of the property at the OAD marked for YIVO.[39] Thus, "associated libraries" was assiduously avoided in all the extant communications with the State Department.

In early February 1947, YIVO was on the verge of finalizing the transfer of its library and the Strashun Library to New York; and that required direct coordination between the State Department and the OAD, potentially setting up a clash between the two legal interpretations and the discovery of the true meaning of "associated libraries." By February 14 YIVO submitted to the State Department the required testimony establishing the New

York YIVO's rights to the OAD property, and the State Department was ready to recognize YIVO in New York as the "YIVO."[40] To effectuate that decision, the State Department would issue an injunction informing the army and the director at the OAD, Joseph Horne (he assumed the role after Bencowitz's departure), that from the department's perspective the books could be transferred to New York. The State Department asked Weinreich to draft the approval letter for Director Horne at the OAD.

Weinreich recognized that "since [in] our correspondence with the State Department starting in 1942 the term 'associated libraries' was not used, [he] could not ask the State Department to include it."[41] Weinreich struggled to ensure that the Strashun Library was included in the State Department's injunction without needlessly calling attention to its inclusion. To avoid the risk of possible review by the State Department, Weinreich's draft did not use the term "associated libraries," nor did it explicitly mention the Strashun Library in the items approved for shipment to the United States. Rather, in Weinreich's draft, the YIVO property was simply referred to as an "estimated 76,482," items. As Weinreich later explained, using the lump sum aligned with Bencowitz's attribution of 76,482 items to YIVO because of its entitlement to "associated libraries" (i.e., the Strashun Library) as reflected in the total count provided in the monthly reports, without invoking the term "associated libraries," and this satisfied both Horne and the State Department.[42]

In February 1947, when Horne was first installed as the director of the OAD, he apparently was unaware of the provenance of YIVO's "associated libraries," and that Bencowitz had unilaterally converted the Strashun Library into YIVO's property. Although the Strashun Library was altered in the monthly reports, physically the books themselves remained unchanged. They all still contained the Strashun Library ex libris and were likely still in crates marked with "MSV" and not "YIVO." In addition, until Bencowitz's censorship, earlier monthly reports correctly had separated the Strashun Library from the YIVO materials. Taken together, if the "YIVO and Associated Libraries" books were inspected and examined, their provenance would be easily discernible—they were Strashun Library and not YIVO library books—calling into question YIVO's entitlement.[43] Anticipating that scenario, in February 1947, Weinreich finally drafted the "important facts concerning the ownership of the Matthew Strashun Library of Vilna," which he had promised Bencowitz in July 1946.[44]

After the State Department's approval, Weinreich requested permission to travel to Frankfurt to accept and guide the YIVO materials to New

York, and presumably smooth out any issues regarding YIVO's title to the Strashun Library. But Pomrenze was ultimately selected for that mission, and he was the recipient of Weinreich's version of the nature of the "associated libraries."[45] Because the Strashun Library, as an associated library, was neither fully owned by nor entirely unrelated to YIVO, Weinreich's explanation needed to fall somewhere in between those two extremes. On February 14, 1947, Weinreich wrote in Yiddish to Pomrenze and described for the first time the two libraries' unique relationship:

> I would like to give you a short summary of the history of [the Strashun] library and its relationship with YIVO, a relationship that began long before Offenbach. Mattityahu Strashun was a wealthy and very learned man, who bequeathed his collection to the Great Charity Fund of Vilna [*Vilner tsdoke gedoyle*] prior to his passing. From the time of his death in 1885, the library grew through new bequests: the collections of Dov Ber Ratner, Arye Neuschul, Dr. Joseph Regensburg, and others were acquired. In 1919, the Great Charity Fund, as well as the Strashun Library, was transferred to the authority of the newly organized Jewish community. The first chairman of the community was Dr. Zemach Shabad, one of the founders of YIVO; and various others affiliated with YIVO were also members of the community administration and thus, necessarily, trustees of the Strashun Library. For a certain period, I myself was also a member of the community presidium.
>
> With the passage of time, the Strashun Library grew not only in its size but also in its interests. From a purely traditional scholarly library, it evolved into a Jewish library for all branches of both old and modern Jewish culture. When YIVO was founded in 1925, it too sought to assemble a broad collection. In this way, one could say that both libraries were generally Jewish in content, though their *emphases* were different: for Strashun, there was *more* of an emphasis on traditional scholarly literature, for us, *more* on modern literature.
>
> During the entire period from 1925 to 1939, relations between the two libraries were perfectly cordial. It should suffice to cite the fact that, even though neither of the libraries would lend books to be taken out of its building, there was, nevertheless, an agreement between YIVO and Strashun that the books of both collections could be consulted in either building.
>
> After the outbreak of the War, a plan was hatched to create in Vilna, in YIVO, a central Jewish library that would house all of the indepen-

dent libraries of a scholarly bent. It would comprise Strashun, Mefitsei Haskolah's scholarly department, and others; my own private library of more than six thousand volumes was also included in that super-collection. No one had any doubt that the center should be at YIVO, because all of the other institutions were simply book repositories, while YIVO included not only a large library, but also a great research apparatus and scholarly publishing house. The process of unifying the libraries was at such an advanced stage that the Germans considered the Strashun Collection to be a part of YIVO library; in fact, our men, with Z. Kalmanovitch at the head, worked like a slave gang to sort and pack up all of the books for the Germans.

As you can see, the relationship between the two libraries is of long standing, and with the years it has grown even more intimate. No living heirs of an independent Strashun Library remain; the last trustee of Strashun, Rabbi Isaac Rubinstein, passed away not long ago in New York.

It may be that I have gone into too much detail here, but I wanted to give you a sense of YIVO's associated libraries and of the influential position YIVO assumed in the period leading up to the Holocaust.[46]

Weinreich immediately admits that the two libraries' respective emphases and missions were distinct and remained so. In his telling, the basis for YIVO's claim to the Strashun Library is predicated on YIVO's long-standing relationship with the Strashun Library, a relationship that intensified over time, ending in a planned full consolidation of the two into a "superlibrary" that would be helmed by YIVO. The lack of explicit intent to merge the Strashun Library into YIVO notwithstanding, evidence to that effect could be inferred from the Nazis' treatment of the two libraries as under the responsibility of YIVO. The Nazis' selection of Zalman Kalmanovitch, a member of YIVO's board of directors, to lead the selection and looting of the Strashun Library, is evidence of the maturity of the merger plan and YIVO's role in the superlibrary. Thus, with the intended merger nearly complete, the Strashun Library qualifies as an "associated library" of YIVO.

Even accepting that an "associated library" should be transferred to New York, and the articulated relationship—an intended yet unfulfilled merger—qualified for the "associated library" treatment, the creation of a single combined superlibrary in 1939 is not reflected in the archival record. The only such plan originated with the Soviets in 1940, when they sought to impose the consolidation and amalgamation of all of Vilna's research institutions, Jewish and non-Jewish, into a single research institution. That proposal was vehemently opposed by, among others, Lunski, the Strashun Library librarian, as contrary to the essence of the library.[47] Like Weinreich's superlibrary, the Soviet plan was never fully realized, and none of the books from the Strashun Library were moved into YIVO or a central Soviet institution. To the contrary, YIVO was the sole Jewish institution that the Soviets succeeded in incorporating into the central state institute before the Nazis' arrival.[48]

With the Soviet's planned consolidation never realized, the Germans never labored under that fiction. The Germans did not treat the Strashun Library and the YIVO collection as one, and specifically separated both libraries. Although Kalmanovitch was associated with YIVO and was responsible for the sorting and selection at both libraries, his coequal was Herman Kruk, a Bundist, the head librarian of the Ghetto Library and a refugee from Warsaw, with no connection to YIVO. There is no indication that their dual tasking was related to the near consolidation of the Strashun and YIVO libraries. Rather, as Kruk explains in his diary, they were conscripted because of their expertise in Jewish books and familiarity with the libraries.[49]

To the extent that the Nazis contemplated combining the two libraries, for purposes of looting and plunder, the Nazis preferred to consolidate YIVO's collection with the Strashun Library and not the other way around. In early 1942 the Strashun Library was moved to a university building to undergo selection for shipment to Frankfurt. The Nazis intended to convert the university building into a central collection point for the sorting and selection of all Jewish books from Vilna's libraries, including YIVO. The plan was abandoned for logistical reasons, however, among them that the size of YIVO collection made it impractical to move to the Strashun Library collection point.[50] With the option of moving the YIVO materials to the Strashun Library collection point no longer viable, the Nazis were forced to leave the YIVO collection in place and designate its building as a second collection site. This second site became the main collection site not only for Vilna libraries but also for hundreds of other libraries—private, communal, and public—from areas surrounding Vilna. Nevertheless, as Abraham Sutzkever records in his diary, the Strashun Library remained the one exception to the consolidation of libraries at the YIVO building.[51] Consequently, there was no communal residence while the libraries remained in Vilna; the Strashun Library underwent sorting and selection at 3 University, and the YIVO library underwent sorting and selection in its building.[52]

Weinreich's representations regarding the pre-1939 "long-standing" relationship between the two libraries, and specifically their planned combination or treatment by the Nazis, is unsupportable. Rather, the extant record shows that YIVO had no significant relationship with the Strashun Library; and their only coresidency occurred after the war, when the two libraries, along with thousands of other libraries, were under the same roof at the OAD. Weinreich's narrative essentially backdated the timing of the Soviet's planned consolidation to 1939 and misattributed the plan to the Jewish community.

More fundamentally, Weinreich fails to acknowledge that, beyond that the two libraries' distinct foci, the very character of each was entirely dissimilar. Weinreich never states that the Strashun Library was a public library, the most critical distinction between it and the YIVO library. Instead, Weinreich elides significant parts of the Strashun Library's history and omits critical facts that would demonstrate the impossibility of YIVO's claim to a public institution. Mattityahu's bequest is described as transferring his library to the Tzedakah Gedolah, leaving unstated any communal ownership interest. To the extent that the Tzedakah Gedolah was involved with the library, it was in its capacity as the de facto kahal and thus acted on behalf of the community. Weinreich then skips key events in the history of the Strashun Library. He neglects to mention that by 1899, any ambiguity regarding the public's ownership had been put to rest or that communal ownership was cemented when the library moved into its own building, which was paid for by the community (via the Tzedakah Gedolah) and located in the Shulhoyf with other communal buildings. Weinreich, however, jumps from 1885 to 1919, and only then mentions for the first time the Vilna Jewish community. Yet even then he undermines the community's role by emphasizing individual members of the administration. Of course, since 1899 the trustees had been stripped of any independent powers and the identities of the members, whether or not they subsequently became affiliated with YIVO when it was founded in 1925, are irrelevant. Finally, Weinreich combines the Strashun Library with the Mefitsei Haskalah and his private library under a single category, "independent libraries of a scholarly bent," which would be combined into a superlibrary. Combining otherwise independent libraries alters the legal status of each library. But for the consolidation of the Strashun Library into a superlibrary to take place, not only must it lose its independence, but it also must be converted from communal property to private property — impossible without the consent of the community.

Weinreich's letter's factual representations would prove critical to YIVO's claim to the Strashun Library. Although the letter was written to Pomrenze, it was partially translated from the original Yiddish and sent directly to Captain Horne, the director of the OAD. In turn, Horne included the translation in his correspondence with his superiors regarding the legitimacy of YIVO's ownership of the Strashun Library, and received their approval to release the Strashun Library to YIVO.[53]

Yet Weinreich's efforts were nearly undone just before YIVO received final governmental approval. This was not because anyone discovered the issues with his version of the libraries' relationship, or because of the inconsistent treatment of YIVO property between the State Department and Bencowitz. This time, his seven-month delay in providing the historical underpinnings of the Strashun Library's relationship with the YIVO library proved problematic.

In 1938 Lucy Schildkret (later Dawidowicz) went to Vilna to study at YIVO. She became close to many of the leaders of YIVO and remained in Vilna until August of 1939, when the American Embassy recommended that she leave Europe. When she returned to the United States, she continued her involvement with YIVO. Since 1944, Dawidowicz was aware of and had participated in YIVO's endeavors regarding the transfer of YIVO's Vilna library to New York. She drafted letters on Weinreich's behalf and on occasion contacted the government directly, and until she left the United States, was aware of the details and progress of the negotiations.[54] In the summer of 1946, she decided to return to Europe as part of the Joint Distribution Committee (JDC) to assist Displaced Persons (DPS). She left for Europe in August 1946 and initially focused her efforts on DPS. She worked to provide educational materials; for example, a bulletin for Hanukkah with songs, history, and stories.[55] But by early February her focus had shifted. On Tuesday, February 4, 1947, she reached the OAD. There she was to select books and other items from the OAD for a loan program to DPS throughout Germany. The program limited the loan to books that were cataloged as heirless, books at the OAD for whom the status of the owner was indeterminate. Dawidowicz's first task was to first examine the books and then set aside those that were heirless to loan to the DPS.

Prior to arriving at the OAD, she recognized the possibility that the JDC mission might be compromised if she continued to involve herself in YIVO's efforts; and she made a commitment "to stay within the limits of [her] JDC [role], separating [herself] and the JDC from the affairs of YIVO's library."[56] That promise proved impossible to keep.

Initially, Dawidowicz thought she could accomplish her mission to identify books for the loan program within four days, but that estimate proved far too optimistic; and she remained at the OAD for over five months. During that time, her mission fundamentally changed, and rather than selecting books for DPs, she was redirected to the identification of YIVO and Strashun property. Had her work been confined to that assignment, her role would likely have merited only a footnote in the story of the Strashun Library. Rather, she used the opportunity to much greater effect.

Dawidowicz sought Horne's approval for the restitution of the YIVO materials and Strashun Library books to YIVO in New York. These direct negotiations proved critical to securing the Strashun Library for YIVO, at the very least reducing the time until the YIVO materials and the Strashun Library left the OAD, and likely confirming YIVO's title to the Strashun Library. But she was operating alone, without Weinreich's or YIVO's awareness, and she was similarly unaware of the status of Weinreich's concurrent negotiations in the United States with the State Department. Indeed, Weinreich learned of the true import of Bencowitz's "associated libraries" only in January, long after Dawidowicz's departure for Europe. Thus, she provided Horne with an entirely different version of YIVO's relationship with the Strashun Library and how the otherwise independent library was removed from communal ownership and transferred to the YIVO organization.

During her first week at the OAD, she focused on the identification of books for the JDC loan program; and by the weekend of February 9, she traveled to Munich to discuss the details of the JDC loan. When she returned to the OAD on Tuesday, February 11, within "a matter of days" she came upon books from the YIVO and Strashun Library collections. The find had a profound effect on her, invoking a feeling "akin to holiness, that [she] was touching something sacred." These were not simply books; she recognized that these books were more than just books, she was "holding in [her] hands the remains, as it were, of the civilization of the Eastern Jews."[57] No longer could she confine herself to the JDC mission, and all of "her good intentions not to entangle [her] JDC work with the affairs of the YIVO library collapsed."[58]

With Bencowitz's conflation of YIVO and the Strashun Library already in operation at the OAD, Dawidowicz was able to move to solidify his characterization of the relationship between YIVO and the Strashun Library. And "with a tingle of triumph," she immediately notified Horne of her find and discussed YIVO's claim to the Strashun Library.[59] On Friday, February 14, Horne communicated to her "that a decision about the disposition of YIVO library was imminent and that YIVO's chances were good for the return of its property and the remains also of the Strashun."[60] That same day she cabled Weinreich in New York the news that "chances fairly good to get also Strashun," and requested that he send "copies of all papers" supporting YIVO's claim posthaste.[61] In *three days* she accomplished what had taken Weinreich nearly two years.[62]

Her conversations with Horne occurred in early February 1947 and predated Weinreich's letter to Pomrenze regarding the nature of the Strashun Library's "long-standing relationship" with YIVO. Dawidowicz offered an entirely different narrative supporting YIVO's claim to the Strashun Library.

> Many books which I could identify came from the Strashun Library. They reminded me of a strange story Weinreich had told me back in 1940, when we had begun to work at YIVO in New York. Soon after the Soviet occupation of eastern Poland, when the Russians had given Vilna over to the control of Lithuanians, Kalmanovitch had cabled Weinreich, then in Copenhagen, and the New York YIVO, proposing that they get the YIVO library out of Vilna. It was an idea born of desperation. The trustees of the Strashun Library, also fearing for the safety of their library, asked the Vilna YIVO to ship their library, too, and to become responsible for its security. On that basis, I told Horne, the remains of the Strashun Library ought to be considered as YIVO property, since Strashun no longer had any owners or heirs.[63]

In Dawidowicz's telling, YIVO's claim to the Strashun Library materialized only after Lithuanian independence in October 1939, and while Weinreich was still in Copenhagen before he left for America in March 1940. During that timeframe Kalmanovitch, a member of the YIVO board, fearing the worst, contacted the New York YIVO and requested that they assist in removing the YIVO library. The linchpin of this narrative was that when YIVO acceded to the Strashun Library trustees' request to piggyback on YIVO's attempted shipment of its library to New York, that created in YIVO an ownership interest in the Strashun Library. Dawidowicz does not mention that the Strashun Library was an "associate library" of YIVO (or use that term at all), that the two libraries had a "long-standing relation-

118

THE LOST LIBRARY

ship," or that they had intended a merger to create a superlibrary which was nearly complete. Rather, the first significant interaction between the two libraries occurred out of desperation in late 1939–June 1940, and only then were the two libraries thrown together. This was an entirely different narrative regarding YIVO's relationship with the Strashun Library than Weinreich provided to the State Department in the United States. Yet her narrative shares the same defect of Weinreich's: there is no mention that the Strashun Library was a public library and that the trustees likely had no power to convert the public's assets into YIVO's private property. Dawidowicz's account, however, was not created out of thin air. Although she was unaware of Weinreich's February 14, 1947, superlibrary account of the bond between the YIVO and Strashun libraries, an earlier affidavit from Weinreich, attested to on March 13, 1946, provided the kernel for Dawidowicz's chronicle of events related to the Strashun Library.[64] Like Weinreich's later affidavit of February 1947, the purpose of the March 1946 affidavit was to convince the State Department that YIVO in New York was legally the same entity that it had previously been in Vilna; and the affidavit addressed the nuances of that transfer of power and not the specific contents of YIVO.[65] Rather, for purposes of confirming the shift of power to New York, Weinreich briefly touches on an unsuccessful attempt by the New York YIVO to assist in moving YIVO's collection out of Vilna to New York.[66] Because that affidavit was drafted long before Weinreich was aware that the Strashun Library was at the OAD, the Strashun Library is absent from his testimony. Apparently, the March 1946 affidavit proved sufficient, and the State Department agreed in principle to approve YIVO's request, establishing YIVO's claim to the OAD property. In March 1946, Dawidowicz was still acting as Weinreich's secretary, and as late as March 22, 1946, was drafting letters on his behalf.[67] Because the aborted 1940 shipment of the YIVO library was among the items that tipped the scales in YIVO New York's favor, Dawidowicz simply expanded the property that was intended for transport to New York to include the Strashun Library. As YIVO attempted to act on the State Department's approval, however, intervening events halted the process, delaying the conclusion of the transfer of YIVO property until 1947.

The two main obstacles to consummating the State Department's approval was the US Army's unwillingness to recognize an exception or change to the existing law of restitution without the agreement of the other Allies (which was not forthcoming), which precluded a resolution of the YIVO claim. Moreover, in March, other Jewish groups began serious negotiations with the army to create a global restitution policy for all heirless Jewish property and stayed a decision on the YIVO property.[68]

Whatever the reason was that Dawidowicz invoked the shipment as forming the necessary relationship between the two libraries, as Kalman Weiser has demonstrated, archival evidence—including YIVO's board meeting minutes from Vilna in 1939—contradicts critical elements of her account: that the request originated with YIVO in Vilna, and specifically Kalmanovitch, and that those in Vilna agreed to the removal of the YIVO library to New York. To the contrary, it was Amopteyl, the American branch of YIVO, that advocated transferring the YIVO library to New York, and YIVO in Vilna vigorously and vocally fought for the library to remain in Vilna and never acceded to Amopteyl's plan.[69] Indeed, Weinreich's own contemporaneous correspondence indicates that YIVO in Vilna did not resolve to remove its library to New York in 1939.[70]

Those in Vilna, and Weinreich in Copenhagen, thought they were not only safe but that some of the developments in 1939-1940 augured well for YIVO in Vilna. Not only did those in Vilna challenge any transfer of the YIVO collection, they also refused to acknowledge any shift in the centrality of Vilna as YIVO's headquarters. Even after Weinreich accepted Amopteyl's offer to travel to New York in March 1946, he assumed that trip was a visit and intended to return to Vilna at the end of the summer of 1946. In New York, however, they saw things differently. They appreciated that Jewish Vilna was on the brink of destruction and that there was one last opportunity to save what they could before it was all lost. Yet Weinreich's, Uveeler's, and Dawidowicz's accounts of YIVO in Vilna in 1939-1940 are versions that superimpose Amopteyl's views on those in Vilna. Indeed, in hindsight, Amopteyl was right to worry about Vilna remaining the headquarters of YIVO; but that cannot alter history as it occurred, that YIVO in Vilna never attempted to remove its library to New York.[71] Yet Dawidowicz, based on Weinreich's representations in the 1946 affidavit and his "strange story"[72] from 1940, turned opposition into acquiescence. Without the Vilna YIVO agreeing to ship its library, the Strashun Library trustees had no reason to approach the otherwise unrelated YIVO to share space or otherwise—casting doubt on Dawidowicz's narrative.

Yet both Uveeler and Weinreich's version was correct in one significant aspect. Whether or not those in Vilna appreciated the peril they were in, with Weinreich in America and the ability of Amopteyl to a large degree to dictate to the Vilna YIVO, YIVO's center of gravity had irrevocably shifted to the United States. With or without a formal transfer of operations, a de facto one had already occurred. Indeed, the selection of Vilna as the headquarters occurred in almost the same fashion, without the need for a formal resolution.[73]

Evidence suggests that Dawidowicz's misrepresentation of the record was likely deliberate. On February 15, 1947, she wrote Weinreich a long letter detailing her progress at the OAD and explaining how Horne's willingness to include the Strashun Library with the YIVO property was because she had "built up in his mind some real and fictive connections between Strashun and YIVO."[74] Because at the time she drafted this letter, the only connection she had discussed with Horne was the request by the Strashun Library trustees for space on the YIVO shipment, her reference to a "fictive connection" most likely refers to the shipment story.

Dawidowicz recognized the extraordinary risk she took in recording such sensitive details. In a handwritten note on the top of the document, preserved in her archives, she wrote to her future husband, Szymon Dawidowicz, that she wished him to keep it safe. "I don't dare keep it in Germany," she confessed.[75] The original letter to Weinreich included a typed message that similarly indicates her concern regarding anyone else reading it. On the top of that version she explained that rather than mail it in Germany as was her practice, "Am having this letter mailed in Paris to rush it and avoid any possibility of censorship."[76]

Dawidowicz's confidence in obtaining Horne's agreement regarding YIVO's entitlement to its and the Strashun Library was also partly because of her ability to manipulate him. She described Horne as a "very weak and an emotional person," and as "too scared to be dishonest and too intelligent to want to take a risk. He is afraid of his job, because life was never so good for him back home."[77] Moreover, her "personal relationship with Horne has given me knowledge not only of him, but also of the Depot to the extent that no other person presently in Germany has." She was not entirely comfortable with these advantages and admitted that "sometimes I think it sort of unfair to capitalize on it," but that in the end, "business is business, and I [am] far more interested in the disposition of the Jewish books than in the disposition of Horne."[78]

On February 14, 1947, Dawidowicz first cabled Weinreich with news of her "positive" discussions with Horne about the holdings of the Strashun Library. Dawidowicz had no knowledge of Weinreich's negotiations regarding the YIVO/Strashun Library in Washington since January 1947, and so Weinreich was both shocked and worried that Dawidowicz had revealed to Horne the inclusion of the Strashun Library in the "associated libraries" moniker. Weinreich feared that her revelation would undo that carefully constructed edifice begun with Bencowitz, and now fleshed out with the State Department, regarding YIVO's "associated libraries" and its relationship to the Strashun Library. To fully explain the complex series of events and nuanced historical narratives, Weinreich sent Dawidowicz a letter written in Yiddish and marked "Strictly Confidential," for reasons she "will well understand." Although the letter would take longer to arrive than a telegram, Weinreich preferred providing a complete picture of YIVO's actions to secure its library and the Strashun Library as opposed to the brevity inherent in the latter form of communication. Weinreich also enclosed his February 14, 1947, letter to Pomrenze detailing the alleged history of the relationship between the two "associated" libraries, which was "enhanced over time" and demonstrated that the Strashun Library was an "associated library" of YIVO.

> From the telegram we sent you yesterday in response to your telegraphic message to us, you could only discern our shock to a limited extent. Our first thought was to immediately telegraphically communicate to you the most important facts. But after the two people occupied with this matter were consulted, we decided that it would be better if we would write out all the details and send them over by airmail. It would take a couple more days, but that way you would have the full picture.
>
> [. . .]
>
> Into this situation, your telegram dropped like a bombshell. You might have guessed that our first instinct was to cancel our earlier negotiations, to explain to Mr. Pomrenze what had happened, and to lay the entire matter on your shoulders. But once we calmed down, we realized that we could not do that, or at least that it is still too early to do sond these are the reasons:
>
> 1) We do not know how strong the connections are that you so unexpectedly established in Frankfurt.
>
> 2) All things being equal, it would be much better for YIVO to receive its property through a direct injunction issued by the State Department than through an administrative act in Frankfurt.
>
> 3) If we tell Mr. Pomrenze that we can save him a trip, he will, obviously, not object. However, if, Heaven forbid, something falls apart on your end, it would be much harder to fix things in Washington, and it would also be more difficult to prevail upon Mr. Pom-

renze to suddenly change his plans, drop everything, and travel abroad.

4) The point about the Strashun Collection is also terribly important. From the attached copy of our letter to S. Pomrenze you will see that the Strashun Collection may and should be considered a part of YIVO library. However, we reckon (at least, prior to having heard the details of your intervention) that when S. Pomrenze arrives here with an injunction from the State Department, he will be able to accomplish the task much faster and more smoothly.

[. . .]

We expect from you a telegraphic confirmation of your receipt of this letter. If, in your reply telegram, you can also say something about the substance of the matter, that would certainly be welcome. If not, write us an answer at length posthaste.

Even though we are all working toward the same goal, still, we wish to sincerely thank you for your efforts. The true thank-you will come when our entire Vilna Library will, God willing, sit on the shelves in New York.[79]

Ultimately, Weinreich was fortunate to find a strong ally in Dawidowicz to continue the consolidation of the libraries. Although Weinreich was unaware, by the next day Dawidowicz had already written her "answer at length." She explained that her confidence regarding the transference of the property at the OAD was, in part, because she had provided Horne with fabricated links establishing a relationship between the Strashun Library and YIVO. In addition to her successful discussion with Horne regarding the Strashun Library, she also allayed Weinreich's repeated concerns that the Soviets would claim the libraries, because "so far, no one from the Soviet Union has put in for anything," the sole exception being "some Polish major who wants all Polish publications (anything published in Poland) to be returned there." But after Horne requested Dawidowicz's input regarding a Polish option, she "helped him maintain the opinion he already had, that there is no hope for renewed Jewish cultural life in Poland. There may be a Jewish community there, but he feels that no one will ever make use of the material." Similarly, Horne was "opposed to sending anything to Palestine on the grounds of security." Finally, Horne agreed with the Library of Congress's opposition to any plan "that would split up the collection of unidentified" heirless Jewish property from library collections because "the best use for the most scholars would be attained by keeping all the books together." Horne's preference for keeping heirless libraries intact was likewise "a good argument for YIVO with its present library, its YIVO collection in Offenbach and the balance."[80] In reference to both YIVO's library and its "collection in Offenbach," the latter most likely referred to the Strashun Library. That is, aside from Dawidowicz's "fictive" connections between YIVO and the Strashun Library, the Library of Congress's opinion (with which Horne was also in agreement) was for a preference to keep libraries intact, another reason that YIVO had a good chance to receive the Strashun Library.

Nine days later, Weinreich wrote again (in Yiddish) to Dawidowicz. He suggested that if they worked in tandem, Weinreich in the United States and Dawidowicz at the OAD, final approval was imminent. Weinreich's ideal version of events was that first "the State Department [will] order that our library (YIVO and Associated Libraries, including the Strashun, approximately 76,000 books) be released to us, and after you have won over Mr. Horne, there will be no difficulty for us to receive our property in Offenbach."[81]

Weinreich concluded his letter with a heretofore unmentioned detail regarding the advanced stage of the establishment of the (nonexistent) superlibrary. Previously, Weinreich had indicated that the Nazis' assignment of members of YIVO to sort and select books from the Strashun Library demonstrated that the merger was nearly complete. Now Weinreich went one step further and asserted that "the books from the Strashun Library were already in YIVO's building, 18 Vivulski St., when the Germans took it for transport." That is, the book sorting project was not simply overseen by YIVO personnel, but the Strashun Library books were physically resident in YIVO's building.[82] This later narrative of cohabitation does not appear to have been raised with the government in 1947. More important, according to those actually involved in the sorting in 1942–1943, Kalmanovitch and Kruk, the Strashun Library books were never moved to YIVO and were sent directly from 3 University. Decades later, in 2001, YIVO would revive this version of events to explain the relationship between the libraries.[83]

Dawidowicz quickly fulfilled her part of the mission. A little over two weeks later, on March 15, 1947, Dawidowicz cabled Weinreich that YIVO's claim to "Strashun . . . [was] assured . . . [and that] congratulations do not seem premature."[84]

Two days after Dawidowicz's cable to Weinreich, Horne sent his superiors a memo marked "confidential" regarding YIVO property and the

Strashun Library. Horne relates the history of YIVO from its founding and the details regarding its library and the property at the OAD. Horne was confident of the legality of YIVO's title to its library and that of two of its "associated libraries," the Dubnow archives and the library of the Jewish Teachers' College. Horne recognized, however, that the Strashun Library's relationship with YIVO was of a more complex character than that of the other two "associated libraries."

> The question of the disposition of the Strashun Library, however, is not so simple. The Vilna collection was simply lumped together in the reports as "YIVO and Associated Libraries," but in the case of the Strashun the term is misleading. The Strashun Library was the private collection of Matthew Strashun. After his death, it was greatly enlarged by the absorption of other small libraries. It is not known at this time whether or not the entire collection is at the Depot. The total here is about 4,500[85] volumes.

Horne continues and provides Weinreich's three examples of YIVO and Strashun Libraries' prewar relationship.

> The working connection between YIVO and the Strashun Library appears to have been very close. Inter-library loans and exchanges were made. However, the strongest evidence we have of the Strashun-YIVO relationship is the fact that the Germans considered them as parts of the same Library. It was packed and shipped by the Germans with this understanding. Also, the Vilna Libraries were under the supervision of a board of scholars, which was made up in large part of the members of the Board of Directors of YIVO.[86]

Horne considered the superlibrary theory and the Nazis' subsequent treatment of the two libraries "the strongest evidence we have of the Strashun-YIVO relationship."[87] Yet there is no evidence that Horne was ever aware that the Strashun Library had been a public library, and that irrespective of whatever relationship it may have shared with YIVO, that cannot displace the public's ownership interest in the Strashun Library.

By the end of May 1947, with Weinreich securing the State Department's approval and Dawidowicz accomplishing the same with the army, Pomrenze was ready to leave for Germany and shepherd the YIVO shipment from the OAD to New York.[88] Nevertheless, YIVO's account of the relationship between YIVO and the Strashun Library metamorphosed yet again.

On June 5, 1947, Uveeler provided "a full description of YIVO's Associated Libraries."[89] Uveeler's "full description" includes a claim to twelve different libraries, the Strashun Library among them. Uveeler begins with a history of the Strashun Library almost identical to that of Weinreich, but then veers off into virgin "historical" territory.

> The Straszun Library, founded in the middle of the 19th century by the wealthy and learned Mathias Straszun, was originally devoted to rabbinic literature. Later it developed into a collection for all branches of Jewish scholarship, though still with particular stress on rabbinics. On the other hand, YIVO from its very beginning, that is, since 1925, was interested in all branches of Jewish knowledge, but paid particular attention to its more modern and secular aspects. This, from the very outset, led to friendly cooperation between both libraries and to several working agreements which brought them ever closer as time went on. The Straszun Library was administered by a committee appointed by the Jewish Community Council, many members of which were among the directors of YIVO. When war conditions made the removal of cultural treasures from Vilna imperative and it was learned that YIVO was about to ship its treasures to New York, the Community Council committee in direct charge of the Straszun collection, headed by Chief Rabbi Izaak Rubinsztejn, a YIVO sponsor for many years, approached the YIVO Executive Board with a request for a legal merger. This request was granted in October 1939, and a written agreement to that effect was drawn up and duly signed. Rabbi Rubinsztejn died in New York in 1946. All other members of the pre-war Vilna Jewish Community Council perished during the war at the hands of the Germans.[90]

In Uveeler's mash-up of Weinreich's and Dawidowicz's narratives, the Strashun Library trustees approached an institution with a preexisting connection to the Strashun Library. Uveeler also clarifies that the Strashun Library trustees' request to piggyback on the YIVO shipment was not a request to share space but more than that, according to his version—a full legal transfer of the Strashun Library to YIVO, signed and sealed by all the parties. All of those involved on the Strashun Library side, however, were dead by June 1947, leaving only Uveeler's affidavit to attest to the merger. Uveeler's deft combination narrative, however, does not cure the fundamental flaws in Weinreich's and Dawidowicz's histo-

ries: that both are unsupported by documentary evidence, and the trustees had no power to convert the Strashun Library into private property.

On Sunday, June 15, 1947, Pomrenze arrived in Offenbach, not as its director, but this time on behalf of YIVO.[91] By 5 pm Tuesday, June 17, 1947, 420
crates containing 79,204 items left the OAD to board the USS *Pioneer* and
arrive less than three weeks later, on July 1, in New York.

The entire number of 79,204 items is not solely attributable to books;
rather, books occupy approximately 40 percent of the shipment, and
the rest were documents and ephemera. There were 34,204 books in
270 crates. A copy of the handwritten inventory of the YIVO shipment
is preserved in the National Archives in College Park, Maryland, listing
each crate and its corresponding number of books. The books, unlike the
archival materials, were individually counted and inventoried, permitting an exact accounting of the total number of Strashun Library books
that were shipped to New York. According to the document, 205 crates
containing 23,709 Strashun Library books were on their way to America.
Nearly half of the pre–World War II Strashun Library survived the greatest Jewish tragedy in human history. The YIVO library did not fare as well.
Of the estimated 40,000 volumes in YIVO's library, only 8,842 YIVO books,
in 61 crates, were accounted for. The Strashun Library books constituted
nearly half of *all* the 420 crates of both books and archival materials, 75
percent of all the books, and almost three times more books than YIVO.[92]

*It must be realized that, at the
present moment, the various Jewish
institutions here . . . are interested in
staking "claims" to Jewish materials
recovered in Germany. Each of the
principal Jewish libraries, for example,
sees in the present situation a unique
opportunity of enlarging its holdings
without expense.*

THEODOR GASTER, head of
the Hebraic Section, Library of
Congress, December 30, 1945

CHAPTER SEVEN

Ex Libris and Obscurity
in Postwar America

IN LATE SUMMER 1947, THE 209 CRATES containing 23,709 Strashun Library books were finally off the European continent and safely ensconced at YIVO in New York City.[1] Lucy Dawidowicz appreciated the fragility of YIVO's claim and that the suspect nature of her and others' tactics did not create an ironclad title to the libraries. Accordingly, she took steps to mitigate any risk of later challenges to YIVO's right to the Strashun Library.

On June 17, 1947, her last day at Offenbach and the day the 420 crates were shipped, Dawidowicz emphasized the need for discretion once the Strashun Library books arrived in New York. She asked Weinreich, "Who will work on the books? REMEMBER you can have only such people whom you trust implicitly to look the stuff over. This is extremely important for everyone concerned."[2] Dawidowicz then suggested a creative solution to cure any lingering question regarding ownership of the Strashun Library books.[3]

Bencowitz again, this time indirectly, provided the means to unilaterally cement YIVO's title to the Strashun Library. Now, Bencowitz's 1946 photographic catalog of ex libris, and not creative verbiage, was the key to Dawidowicz's strategy. The catalog reproduced prewar ex libris, including many from YIVO, that were held sufficient to establish ownership and a right to restitution.[4] Thus, Dawidowicz told Weinreich to "get a couple of stamps made [in New York] and start stamping." Toward that aim, she

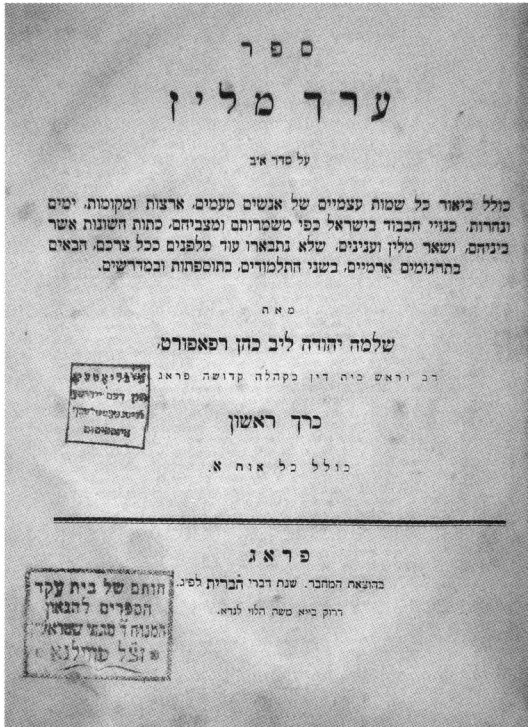

ס פ ר

ע ר ך מ ל י ן

על סדר א״ב

כולל ביאור כל שמות עצמיים של אנשים מעטים. ארצות ומקומות. ימים
ונהרות. כנויי הכבוד בישראל כפי משרותם ומצביהם. כתות השונות אשר
ביניהם. ושאר מלין וענינים. שלא נתבארו עוד מלפנים בכל צרכם. הבאים
בתרגומים ארמיים. בשני התלמודים. בתוספתות ובמדרשים.

מ א ת

שלמה יהודה ליב כהן רפאפורט,

רב וראש בית דין בקהלה קדושה פראג

כרך ראשון

כולל כל אות א.

פ ר א ג

בהוצאת המחבר. שנת דברי הברית לפ״ק.
רחוק ביא משה הלוי לגרא.

10. Shlomo Yehuda
Rapoport, *Erekh Milin*,
Prague, 1857, with the
Mattityahu Strashun
and YIVO library
ex libris. Private
collection of
the author.

"enclosed copies of YIVO ex libris which Bencowitz had made up during
his time."[5] That is, her instruction was effectively to backdate YIVO's
ownership of the Strashun Library to 1939. Copying the pre–World War II
YIVO stamp and applying it to the Strashun Library books gave the books
the imprimatur indicating that these books were held in the YIVO Library
prior to the Nazis' expropriation and looting of the Strashun Library, a
brilliant revision of the material history of each Strashun book.

YIVO, despite its various accounts that seemingly confirmed its ownership of the Strashun Library, and notwithstanding the imprimatur of
its prewar ex libris, remained incredibly guarded regarding the Strashun
Library and did not disclose that it was at YIVO in New York or that the library had survived the Holocaust for an astonishing sixteen years.[6] YIVO
may have engaged in highly questionable methods to acquire the Strashun
Library, but the rescue of such an important Jewish cultural treasure as
the Strashun Library books arguably trumped any legal considerations.
Thus, YIVO's subsequent failure to divulge that it held the residuum of a
preeminent Vilna institution is even more difficult to understand.

Setting aside the failure to acknowledge the Strashun Library, when the time came to unveil the library to the world, YIVO's treatment of the books blunted the very meaning of the Strashun Library, effectively consigning the library to history rather than contemporary relevance.

Rather than treating the Strashun Library as a unique vestige of Vilna history, all of the 23,709 books were subsumed within YIVO's Vilna Collection, lumped together with the 40,000 or 50,000 books that originated from prewar Vilna and were now at YIVO in New York. The Strashun Library books were simply books among many, whose only connection was their geographic source. The Strashun Library, however, was not merely a large Vilna library of 50,000 volumes; instead, its true value lay in the library as a whole and its 50,000 heterogeneous books, each reflective of the public it served and its role in fostering Vilna as a virtual study house. So long as the surviving books would persist in their original state, as a singular discrete unit, the possibility remained that those books would stand in lieu of the Vilna Jewish public that was no longer. But the bitter irony of YIVO's conduct toward the Strashun Library books was that their value was reduced to their numbers, inflating YIVO's holdings of Vilna books but not preserving the integrity of a special Vilna treasure.

YIVO recognized the individual value of many of the Strashun Library books. Though the history of its acquisition was obscured, the Strashun Library was among the treasures in YIVO's New York library and was critical to YIVO reestablishing itself as a significant force within the American Jewish consciousness as a guardian of the memory and history of Vilna and European Jewry.[7] Thus, YIVO was keen to publicize that it held Strashun Library books, but without disclosing the tortured history of the Strashun Library.

To accomplish these seemingly mutually exclusive objectives, YIVO deployed another version of Bencowitz's tactic of retitling YIVO holdings to obfuscate its composition. YIVO abandoned counting the Strashun Library within its "associated libraries" and offered a different umbrella term, the "Vilna Collection," to include, without acknowledgment, any of the books from the Strashun Library.[8] In so doing, YIVO repeatedly and openly discussed and highlighted the Strashun Library's *contents* without mentioning (and in drawing attention away from) their source — and even as the Strashun Library provenance was arguably as important as the books it had comprised. Indeed, many, if not all, of those books were not unique to YIVO and were available in other libraries with substantial Jewish holdings. Broadcasting its storied history would have added to the books' prestige and their unique nature. The absence of any independent reason for not doing so leads to the conclusion that the omission served to cloud and avoid mentioning the Strashun Library as the source.

Early histories of the YIVO library celebrate its journey from Vilna and arrival in New York, yet the Strashun Library is absent, its very existence expunged entirely. As early as 1950, YIVO had the opportunity to disclose at the very least that the famed Strashun Library, in a nearly miraculous turn of events, had survived the Holocaust, if not that it was in New York at the YIVO library. Page four of the February 1950 issue of the *News of YIVO* reproduces a photograph, "The Reading Room of the Strashun Library." The caption accompanying the photo states: "A scene in the reading room of the famous library in Vilna, which in its last period became closely connected with Yivo."[9] The caption acknowledges that during the Strashun Library's "last period [it] became closely connected with Yivo," alluding to the history of the two libraries that Weinreich provided in 1947, and which was relied on by Horne and the MFA&A to release the Strashun Library to YIVO. Nevertheless, the caption fails to mention perhaps the most significant fact of the two libraries' relationship, that it was the cornerstone of YIVO's successful claim to the Strashun Library and that a substantial portion of that library was in New York at YIVO and had not been destroyed.

Likewise, the March 1951 issue of the *News* featured a cover article entitled "YIVO LIBRARY IS BACK AT HOME," which described the history of the establishment of its library, its fate during the Holocaust, and its journey from Vilna to New York.[10] The Strashun Library is not mentioned by name. Instead, YIVO's dogged requests in 1946–1947 to include the Strashun Library, which comprised triple the number of books that YIVO had, transformed into an appeal by YIVO to the American authorities for "the transfer of the *Vilna collection* from Offenbach to New York."[11] The makeup of what is termed the Vilna Collection remains unexplored. Nonetheless, the next issue characterized the March article as "a comprehensive account of the return to YIVO library of a large part of the former Vilna collection," sustaining the generalization of the Vilna Collection sans the Strashun Library.[12]

Yet the March article is not without merit. It fills a gap in the Strashun Library's narrative: why Bencowitz acted on YIVO's behalf and converted the Strashun Library into YIVO's property. Unlike Pomrenze, when Bencowitz arrived at the OAD, he was entirely unaware of YIVO, let alone its books. Nonetheless, he acted unilaterally on Weinreich's July 1946 letter that mentioned the Strashun Library books and merely alluded to some relationship with YIVO (left unexplained until February 1947). In this account, Koppel Pinson, who in December 1946 was among the first to identify YIVO materials in Germany, was a key figure. By July 1946 Pinson was the "cultural director of the Joint Distribution Committee in Europe, [and] instructed [Bencowitz] in these matters. Thus 300 crates of materials were selected and set aside" as the property of YIVO and its associated libraries.[13] Indeed, during that same time period Bencowitz and Pinson teamed and smuggled rare books and manuscripts out of the OAD for the benefit of the Hebrew University Library.[14]

Similarly, issue 46, published in 1952, features an article regarding censored Jewish texts and highlights seventeen such books in YIVO's collection. The books' source is identified generically as the "Vilna Collection," even as fourteen of the books are easily identifiable as originally from Mattityahu's personal library.[15] A few years later YIVO gave up referring to the Strashun Library as the "Vilna Collection" entirely and just merged it with its own the "Vilna YIVO Library."[16]

In 1963 YIVO finally acknowledged the distinct existence of the Strashun Library and that it was in New York at YIVO.[17] Like much of the Strashun Library's saga and its transfer to YIVO in New York, even this late telling elides significant facts and fails to provide a complete account of the communal Strashun Library's absorption into the collection of YIVO, a private organization, or even acknowledge the public nature of the Strashun Library. In addition, the article repeats many unsupportable facts that YIVO had previously provided to the government in 1946 and 1947.

> The [YIVO Vilna] collection has a dramatic history. It derives from the Vilna YIVO Library and in part from the famous Strashun Library in that city. It was at great expenditure of time and effort by YIVO that this collection was brought to New York after the war. The history of rescue of this collection was told in detail in the *News of YIVO*, no. 40, and well bears a brief recapitulation here. When the Germans entered Vilna, the YIVO office in New York became apprehensive lest the Germans remove YIVO treasure to Germany, particularly the library, which had by then become enriched through the addition of the Strashun Library (in the beginning of the war the latter had amalgamated with YIVO Library). The New York office of YIVO notified the State Department of this possibility and requested the right of reclamation after a victo-

rious conclusion of the war. In June 1945, a large part of YIVO Library was found in Germany. Strenuous efforts were then made to take this precious find out of Germany. YIVO was immensely aided in this by Seymour J. Pomrenze, then a major in the armed forces of the U.S.A. With the aid of the State Department and the Library of Congress, the recovered YIVO property reached New York at last.

The collection contained some 40,000 books and 38,000 files of the archive. Included among the books is a large number of rabbinica, some of it from the former Strashun Library.

[. . .]

The collection of rabbinica consists of about 12,000 volumes. To facilitate its use, it is divided into several divisions, such as rare editions and editions from the 16th century, Bible, Talmud, codes, commentaries, responsa, homiletics, mysticism, liturgy, philosophy, history, Hasidim, Kara[i]tica, and the like.

As described here, the rabbinical collection "has a dramatic history," yet YIVO elected to wait nearly sixteen years before disclosing it. Rather than acknowledging that this is the *first* (partially) complete telling of that history, the article asserts that "the history was told *in detail* in the *News of YIVO*, no. 40" (italics mine), and that what follows in 1963 is merely "a brief recapitulation" of those earlier articles. Issue number 40's detailed history, however, omitted the Strashun Library altogether. Regarding why the "famous Strashun Library" from Vilna was now at YIVO repeats the counterfactual narrative that "when the Germans entered Vilna" the YIVO library was "enriched through the addition of the Strashun Library (in the beginning of the war the latter had amalgamated with YIVO library)." The article's lack of specificity remains in stark contrast to YIVO's public descriptions of its own transfers and origins.[18]

The article implies that the recovery of the Strashun Library was always part of YIVO's "strenuous efforts" to transfer YIVO property to New York; specifically, that "when the Germans entered Vilna," YIVO's New York office notified the State Department of the prospect that "YIVO treasures [. . .] particularly the Library," by then "enriched" by the Strashun Library, which collectively formed the YIVO library, had been removed to Germany, and that "in June 1945, a large part of YIVO Library was found in Germany." In reality, YIVO referenced the Strashun Library only in July 1946, and finally explained to the government the libraries' relationship (one that evolved over time) in February 1947.

The article similarly deletes other relevant background. In addition to YIVO's "strenuous efforts" for the government's declaration of YIVO's "right of reclamation," it was "immensely aided in this by Seymour J. Pomrenze, then major in the armed forces of the U.S.A." Pomrenze's relevance is to the time when he was a major, but that occurred *after* he left his position as director of the OAD.[19] There is no mention whatsoever of Pomrenze's most relevant position, director of the OAD. Pomrenze's involvement began almost immediately with his appointment as director, when Weinreich, at the behest of Seymour's brother Chaim, a member of the YIVO's board of directors and executive committee, contacted Pomrenze. Indeed, Pomrenze's responsibility for the OAD was an important aspect of the entire restitution episode, and likely a large part of his credibility during the January–April 1947 negotiations with the State Department that led to its approval for the transfer of YIVO property to New York.[20]

Finally, the article describes the YIVO/Strashun Library that was sent to New York as consisting of "some 40,000 books [...]. Included among the books is a large number of rabbinica, *some* of it from the former Strashun Library" (italics mine). The shipment to New York in July 1947 contained 34,204 books, of which *most*—23,709—were from the Strashun Library.[21]

Critically, other than the article's vague allusion to an "amalgamation" of the two libraries in Vilna, no further details regarding the role of the "amalgamation" in the inclusion of the Strashun Library in the shipment to New York, or what precipitated the "amalgamation" of a public, communal library with that of a private institution's library, is addressed. That would have to wait for Dawidowicz's memoir and her version of the historic record.[22]

Dawidowicz's retelling in 1989, presumably long after any risk to the Strashun collection remained, still studiously avoided providing an accurate account of the Strashun Library's journey. Dawidowicz's actions —her call to backdate the stamps and employ only trusted persons to uncrate the books—arguably enabled YIVO's decades-long secrecy associated with the Strashun Library and its complete history to remain secret. Indeed, her 1989 alternative narrative fits within YIVO's long history of refusing to acknowledge the true history of how a private institution whose mission was the preservation and study of Yiddish and Eastern European Jewish culture received a public library, the first of its kind, whose emphasis was rabbinic literature. Nevertheless, without YIVO's publicly providing the specific reason that it had received the Strashun Library, Dawidowicz's published version—the alleged shipment and the Strashun

Library trustees' plea to share space with YIVO—became *the* version for YIVO's claim to the Strashun Library and its residence in New York.[23]

YIVO's reticence to discuss the full details of the Strashun Library transfer is not due to lack of opportunity—in fact, YIVO has strategically shared and mostly hidden this problematic history. In 2001 YIVO mounted an exhibition, "Mattityahu (Mathias) Strashun (1817–1885): Scholar, Leader, and Book Collector," that showcased books "drawn from the holdings of YIVO Library, Strashun Collection, and YIVO Archives." The exhibition's companion volume contains a preface and "A Brief History of the Strashun Library," by YIVO head librarian Aviva Astrinsky, and an article by Mordechai Zalkin, a noted scholar of Vilna's Jewish history.[24] Only Astrinsky's portions discuss the Strashun Library's journey from Vilna to New York, wherein she describes the Strashun Library's provenance in broad strokes. Critically, she never directly addresses YIVO's claim to the Strashun Library.

In the preface, the connection point between the two libraries is placed at "the YIVO building in Vilna, located outside the ghetto, [that] was converted into a processing center for ransacked Jewish libraries and archives from Vilna and the surrounding areas. This is where almost all of the Strashun books were crated and shipped by rail to Germany. In 1947, with the help of the American Army, YIVO in New York managed to recover some of the confiscated materials, including a substantial part of the Strashun Library."[25] This passage does not specifically state that the comingling of the Strashun Library and YIVO collection at the YIVO building is the basis for which "YIVO in New York managed to recover [. . .] a substantial part of the Strashun Library." Yet the impression is that the two events appear connected to one another, implying that the time the Strashun Library spent in the YIVO building is related to the eventual transfer of the library to New York. Indeed, in February 1947, Weinreich had told the same story as part of the libraries' history to justify YIVO's title to the Strashun Library.[26] But as previously discussed, the archival record does not support that the Strashun Library was moved to the YIVO building. On the contrary, as noted earlier, the Nazis contemplated moving the YIVO collection to the old ghetto, 3 University, the location of the Strashun Library selection and shipping operation.

Astrinsky's essay discusses the ERR's activities in Vilna and states that the Strashun Library and YIVO were looted. But beyond their suffering the same fate, no other relationship is mentioned. The Strashun Library's journey from the OAD is reduced to explaining that the libraries "were rescued from the ruins of Europe and brought back to YIVO in New York in 1947,"[27] leaving untold even a "brief history" of the transformation in character and ownership of the Strashun Library books.

Likewise, in April 2013 the executive director of YIVO, Jonathan Brent, visited Vilna, and in a subsequent article discussed his trip and the larger history of YIVO and its pre–World War II property. Brent's description of the Strashun Library continued to perpetuate an unsupported account of its relationship to YIVO prior to 1947. He states that "according to oral accounts from that confused time, [the Strashun Library] was put into the safekeeping of the YIVO Institute." Brent does not identify the sources of any of those "oral accounts" and makes no reference to published accounts, such as Dawidowicz or those that appear in the *News of the YIVO*. Perhaps he is referring to Weinreich's superlibrary history, but that too is documented in letters and other archival materials, leaving unanswered the identity of the "oral accounts." Nonetheless, once the Strashun Library was transferred to "the safekeeping of the YIVO Institute," and after the Nazi invasion, the Strashun Library "as well as the rest of YIVO's holdings, were divided into three parts. . . . The Germans looted one part, taking it to Frankfurt." The Frankfurt portion was "discovered after the war by the U.S. Army. This material was eventually shipped to the United States, where it became the core of the library and archive of the reconstituted YIVO Institute, which had relocated to New York in 1940." No further details or explanation is provided on how "safekeeping" was transformed into the Strashun Library books' becoming "the core of the library and archive of the reconstituted YIVO Institute, which had relocated to New York in 1940."[28] Consequently, as one scholar noted as late as 2016, "the full story of the transfer of non-YIVO Vilna materials to the New York City YIVO has not yet been told."[29]

In the end, YIVO continues to maintain its version of history. On Sunday, January 22, 2017, YIVO held a one-day conference, "The History and Future of the Strashun Library," and again elided how the Strashun Library ended up in New York, and squandered another opportunity to potentially correct the record and broadcast the larger significance of the Strashun Library's residence at YIVO. The conference program's preface provides a short history of the Strashun Library, starting with Mattityahu and his library and concluding with YIVO's current efforts regarding the books. The relevant page chronicling the critical time period from 1941 to 1947, when the Strashun Library books came to YIVO, omits any discussion on how and why that occurred and fails to address the full impact of the surviving portion of the Strashun Library. Instead, the Strashun Library's history is that "under the Nazi occupation [of Vilna], the Strashun Library as well as YIVO's library, were taken over, and Jewish intellectuals, among them YIVO associates, were forced to select and crate hundreds of thousands of Jewish books and manuscripts to be shipped to Frankfurt-am-Main" for the IEJ.[30] The history continues with the stale narrative that the books were discovered by the Americans, and that "about 40,000 books from the Strashun Library, YIVO and other Vilna libraries were brought to YIVO in New York in 1947."[31] In addition to the inflated total number of books—less than thirty thousand were transferred to YIVO in 1947—the Strashun Library books are lumped together with the other two sources, without any acknowledgment that the Strashun Library books comprised close to twenty-four thousand books, suggesting that only a small number survived, and thereby reducing their value to mere books rather than half of YIVO's 1940 holdings. Were YIVO to mention the total number of Strashun Library books, the public would finally grasp how much of "the Great Strashun public library in Vilna —a highly regarded place for scholarship and study and a Jewish cultural center"[32] was still extant, as a library rather than stray books, and consequently how it might be possible to revive some of its pre–World War II glory, enabling Jews in the twenty-first century—today's public—to reconnect with a cultural icon and a significant piece of Vilna's history that was otherwise thought to be destroyed.[33]

In 1947, when YIVO received the Strashun Library books, the opportunity presented itself to preserve a unique totem that contained within it a true-to-life portrait of the nature of Jewish Vilna. Those wishing for a tangible representation of prewar Vilna had only to view the collection of Strashun Library books salvaged from the ashes of the Holocaust. The Strashun Library—the library and not the individual books—collectively demonstrated the breadth of the city's intellectual interests and its capability for those to coexist under a single roof, evidencing Vilna's larger symbolism as a study house. All that was required was to leave the books as they had arrived, in their own crates which were individually identifiable, and maintain them as a special collection—something as simple as providing separate shelf space and creating the YIVO Vilna Collection and Strashun Library. YIVO missed that opportunity when it instead elected to camouflage the Strashun Library books, effectively burying their significance forever.

In the intervening years, the Strashun Library books were swallowed up in YIVO's larger collection of miscellaneous Vilna materials, the YIVO Vilna Collection. But the Strashun Library was more than simply a large library with a substantial number of books. Vilna held at least three other libraries that were of comparable size. The Strashun Library differed from those fundamentally because of its status as a public library; its collection specifically reflected its owners' — the entirety of Vilna's — interests. To the outside observer, however, the YIVO Vilna Collection was simply an assemblage of books based on geography, not unlike a private library comprising books that relate to a particular topic or that were printed in a particular city or country. The public Strashun Library was converted into its individual parts, simply enlarging YIVO's Vilna holdings, the books' identity lost among thousands of other books and treated as lifeless relics.

Today, YIVO itself is no longer a stand-alone institute and instead is housed with four other research institutions within the Center for Jewish History in New York City. Nonetheless, for the first time, YIVO separately recognized the Strashun Library, naming a room in its honor. Yet that room operates in name only, for the Strashun Library books are housed elsewhere in the building, subsumed either within the center's rare book room or in YIVO's stacks. Instead, the "Strashun Library" room is used primarily for presentations.[34] In the end, YIVO may have saved the Strashun Library books, but YIVO failed to save the Strashun Library.

The story of YIVO building its collections of Vilna materials with the Strashun Library books, and its willingness to engage in questionable tactics, is but one such example among numerous others. Lisa Leff has noted in her insightful analysis on the subject that many individuals and organizations, including libraries, used similar tactics based on similar perspectives on post–World War II Jewish property.[35] YIVO's expansive viewpoint of what it was heir to, and therefore rescuer and preserver of, was common thinking among Judaica librarians, especially in America. They "had come to think of their libraries as saviors and preservers of a European Jewish patrimony that had barely escaped total destruction."[36] Indeed, "ultimately archivists and librarians everywhere, and particularly those working with Judaica, recognize that such ambiguities are in fact part of the normal functioning of their institutions."[37]

YIVO resorted to questionable means to secure the Strashun Library and other collections. But one cannot divorce those means from the context in which they occurred. Contemporaneously, black-and-white definitions of property ownership were sparse.[38] Postwar restitution of heirless Jewish property was fraught with uncertainty. The property at the OAD included Jewish property the Nazis had seized to create an institute for the academic study of the—hoped for—exterminated Jewish people. Looting Jewish property was *the* goal of the Nazis; however, application of the existing international restitution law excluded Jews—the very target of the Nazi program. Instead, the law recognized only nation-states as legitimate recipients of restituted property. European countries, some of which collaborated and participated in the genocide of their Jewish populations, and others that promulgated inhospitable antisemitic laws—making them poor candidates for repopulation of their decimated Jewish communities—were in line to receive the recovered Jewish property. The most egregious result of the law was in regard to German Jewish property. Because the Nazis began their looting with their nation's Jewish population, German Jewish property was represented in the largest amounts at the OAD. But pursuant to the restitution laws, Germany would be entitled to that Jewish property, permitting the German people to reap the rewards of their own illegal behavior.[39]

Property that originated in Lithuania and Poland, such as that of YIVO and the Strashun Library, was at risk of falling into Soviet control, an equally inappropriate result. In Eastern Europe, some Jews had been murdered after they returned to their homes; how would books be treated? Under existing law, the Soviets might lodge a successful claim to that property, imperiling its survival or, at the very least, public access. Indeed, by July 1946 the Polish and Soviet governments had already received Jewish property.[40] According to a contemporaneous report, the state of Jewish books in Poland was that "in Lodz fish is wrapped for sale in Gemorah [Talmud] sheets."[41]

To address the shortcomings of the existing law, in lieu of Jewish nationhood, Jewish organizations and institutions proposed that for purposes of restitution they should be recognized as proxies for the exterminated Jews. But without a modification to the existing laws, the Americans, who controlled the OAD, were unwilling to grant Jewish bodies nation-state status. Only after protracted negotiations, and without the consent of the other Allies, did the US government agree to revise the existing law, after which a single Jewish organization, JCR (later JRSO), was acknowledged as a legitimate destination for Jewish property. That new law, Military Law 59, was agreed on in principle in December 1946 and finalized in July 1947. The legal ambiguity prior to, and during the process of enacting, Military Law 59 was demonstrative of the elasticity and evolution of property rights in postwar Europe. This legal vacuum led some to seek extrajudicial remedies.[42]

Once Weinreich discovered the Strashun Library books, he and others took extraordinary steps to remove the collection from Europe and bring it to the safety of the United States. At that time, the very real possibility remained that the Soviets would claim the property. Despite its great value, and a general recognition that the return of heirless Jewish property to the Soviet Union or Soviet satellite states would consign the property to obscurity at best and destruction at worst, modification to the law had yet to occur. This might lead to the repatriation of the Strashun Library to Lithuania or Poland. The property was heirless because the Jewish people were victims of one of the worst crimes against humanity, and despite the extraordinary series of events that saved the Strashun Library from otherwise certain destruction, now the law would relegate it to oblivion or worse. Indeed, not until after the Strashun Library was sent to New York would the law officially be modified, even as the Soviets continued to assert that they were entitled to property which originated in Eastern Europe.

From the moment that heirless Jewish assets were discovered in 1945, Weinreich was thwarted time and again from recovering YIVO materials because the United States asserted its intention to apply existing law to Jewish property. When Weinreich learned of the existence of the Strashun Library in July 1946, despite repeated assurances and seemingly final approval from the government, the YIVO property still remained at risk of Soviet repatriation. In March 1946, the State Department approved the shipment of YIVO materials, but that was undone by the army because the War Department's current position was that "the archives, books and other library materials will be restituted to the countries of origin by the Director of the Offenbach Archival Depot in accordance with procedures set forth in Title 18, Military Government Regulations."[43]

The facts on the ground at the OAD validated Weinreich's concerns. In the middle of May, Weinreich learned that the Soviets had requested a visit to the OAD, making the urgency of action all the more apparent.[44] Weinreich's reports were accurate. Bencowitz received the Soviet's request on May 13.[45] Less than a week later, Weinreich received a letter which indicated that Eisenhower had questioned any deviation from the law until Jewish groups could finalize an acceptable proposal to modify the law.[46] Now, perversely, the delay of the Jewish groups might result in YIVO's losing what was unassailably an irreplaceable Jewish cultural treasure.[47] Not three weeks after Weinreich raised the issue of the Strashun Library to Bencowitz, Pinson, who was still in Europe, reported that the Strashun Library specifically was at risk of repatriation to Lithuania and suggested that the books must be smuggled out immediately.[48] Likewise, in August 1946 Weinreich received reports that the Soviets had just received over one thousand crates from the OAD. The situation became particularly acute when Bencowitz officially left the OAD in December and his replacement had yet to arrive. The materials at the OAD effectively were left without anyone from the United States watching over them. That vacuum was even more distressing because of concurrent reports of Polish and Russian officers in the area, making for the real possibility that they would unilaterally assert their "legal" rights and act before anyone could stop them, notwithstanding the ongoing negotiations between the United States and the Soviet Union about modifying the law.[49]

Recognizing that under certain circumstances, otherwise illegal actions are justifiable and permitted, theft for rescuing archival materials that otherwise would be destroyed provides one justification and defense. Under those conditions, theft is converted into salvage or rescue.

In Leff's discussion of the unilateral decision of individuals to "rescue" in post–World War II Europe, she explains that "archives, books, and other such cultural treasures have long been associated with nations and with sovereignty, and the association became particularly powerful in the twentieth century."[50] This association has been identified by Jacques Derrida, who explains that the "only meaning" of "archive" is from the Greek *arkheion*, which referred to the residence of the *archon*, or the commanding ruler. Because of the ruler's publicly recognized authority, the ruler's private home was not only a private residence, but also the house where official documents of public importance were domiciled. When those documents are confined to a form of "house arrest" and "where they dwell permanently, marks the institutional passage from private to public," it is then the task of the sovereign, explains Derrida, to guard what the sovereign was entrusted with. For nations with functioning governments, cultural treasures such as archives are preserved at the seat of state and are protected with the tools provided by statehood.

Applying Derrida's definition of an archive and the role of the sovereign to use the "tools [that] are provided by statehood" to protect and preserve records of national importance confirms the unique position of heirless Jewish property after World War II. In the immediate aftermath of the Holocaust, Jews were deprived of any sovereign to stand guard over these cultural treasures, necessitating that an alternative protectorate step in.

The Strashun Library is but one example of permissive vigilantism in pursuit of the Jewish historic record. Individuals and institutions willingly engaged in similar lawless behavior. Libraries with obvious stolen materials include Hebrew Union College, New York Public Library, Yeshiva University, Harvard University, the Jewish Theological Seminary, and Brandeis University.[51] Librarians who purchased obviously stolen materials justified their actions by applying "the methodology of wartime rescue and their sense of their own role within it [that] functioned to support their decisions to acquire these materials."[52]

Many institutions have disclosed their historical collection methods and begun a necessary dialogue regarding the complexities of the confluence of war, lawlessness, looting, and the responses of institutions tasked with preservation of the historical and cultural record.[53] The complete history of the Strashun Library, and specifically the methods that resulted in transferring it to New York in the late 1940s and the fate of many of its books in the years that followed, have yet to be reckoned with.

Another Port of Call

OVER THE COURSE OF THE LATTER HALF of the twentieth century, and into the twenty-first, the storied history of the acquisition of the Strashun Library remained undisclosed. Early on, however, YIVO's claim to ownership of the Strashun Library was complicated by the emergence of an apparent heir, Tzvi Harkavy (1926–1979), to the Strashun collection. In this instance, an inherent issue regarding heirship to Eastern European Jewry rose to the surface, and two diametrically opposed views on the proper determination of heirship were brought into direct conflict. The dispute with Harkavy went beyond Harkavy as a relative of Strashun; it went to the core issue of heirship to the legacy of Eastern European Jewry — the Diaspora or Israel.

In the late 1950s, Tzvi Harkavy, a great-nephew of Mattityahu Strashun,[1] an officer in the Haganah, a prodigious writer who contributed to and wrote fifty-seven books and over six hundred articles in at least six different languages,[2] one of the closest confidants of the Lubavitcher Rebbe, a Zionist leader, and the director of the Central Rabbinical Library at Hechal Shlomo in Jerusalem, discovered that his ancestor's Vilna library had miraculously survived the Holocaust and was now housed in New York.[3]

Harkavy's path to discovery began with a manuscript of Mattityahu's father, Samuel. In Harkavy's mind, the Strashun Library's landlord and custodian, YIVO, a secular Yiddish organization in New York, lacked any obvious connection to the Strashun Library, a diverse home of religious texts. Instead, Harkavy imagined Jerusalem as the Strashun Library's rightful postwar home, where it would reside at a library whose collections and patrons better reflected the Strashun Library's core holdings, rabbinics. According to Harkavy, the library he oversaw was the just the type of institution to propound the life mission of the Strashun Library.

This particular chapter of the Strashun Library's history has been alluded to only by historians, in part because Harkavy was not forthcoming with details.[4] Moreover, the history was complicated by the multiple parties involved, concurrent proceedings that occurred on two continents halfway around the world, and the erratic timeline. Beyond mining archives and newspaper accounts, this portion of the history of the Strashun Library's books is also told in their ex libris.

The Harkavy episode begins with his wife, Dina. In October 1955, Dina traveled to the United States.[5] At that time, YIVO had yet to publicize that it held a substantial portion of the Strashun Library. The undefined Vilna Collection was public knowledge, but there is no indication that Dina or Tzvi was aware that it comprised almost entirely books from the Strashun Library. Nonetheless, somehow Tzvi learned that YIVO had a manuscript of Samuel Strashun's commentary on Maimonides.[6] Dina visited YIVO and was granted permission to copy and publish the manuscript.[7] Yet the manuscript was not the only Strashun-related item found at YIVO, as apparently the larger collection of Strashun Library books and their survival and residence at YIVO was also discovered by the Harkavys.

Now Weinreich and Dawidowicz's worst fears were realized. The repercussions came quickly. News of the discovery appeared in a November 1955 newspaper article that attempted to address the obvious question: "How did the Strashun Library end up in New York?"[8] The article's answer was that by rights the Strashun Library should never have gone to YIVO in New York, and the only reason it did was attributable to a mix-up in book stamps. According to the article, the Strashun Library's trip to New York began when the Soviets occupied Vilna in the fall of 1940. The communist government permitted YIVO to maintain its operations, but not the Strashun Library. The Strashun Library was placed under the authority of YIVO. While under the auspices of YIVO, the Strashun books were incorrectly marked with YIVO's ex libris. During the Nazi occupation, the Nazis looted those libraries and sent books from both to Frankfurt. After the Americans recovered the books, all of the materials marked "YIVO" were sent to New York, including the erroneously marked Strashun Library books. Because of the mistake in markings, the Strashun Library's books were regarded as YIVO's, where they continued to reside.[9] Not only was YIVO's secret ownership of the Strashun Library uncovered, but that ownership was also understood to be the product of an error.

The underlying basis for the Strashun Library's journey to YIVO in New York, according to this anonymous writer, is close to but diverges from Weinreich's superlibrary narrative. According to Weinreich's story, in 1939, at the suggestion of scholarly Jewish institutions, it was decided that they would consolidate all the Jewish libraries and research institutions into a single organization under the auspices of YIVO. As previously discussed, Weinreich's narrative differs from the extant evidence, and in 1939 the Strashun Library books were never merged with or moved to YIVO. This newspaper account differs from the earlier narrative; according to the article, the Soviets are identified as the culprits for a planned superlibrary. Yet another critical element is mistakenly inserted into this new story of how the Strashun Library went to YIVO, the story of the ex libris. YIVO's ex libris in the Strashun Library books were likely the deliberate work of YIVO in New York, based on Dawidowicz's suggestion and not the Soviets'—and specifically intended to backdate YIVO's ownership of the Strashun Library books and avoid any challenges to YIVO's title to the books.[10]

Because the superlibrary narrative originated with Weinreich, other than YIVO and the State and War Departments no one outside those circles was aware of this unsupported historical account. The most likely source for this fourth narrative is someone at or affiliated with YIVO. Whatever the source of the ex libris narrative that appeared in the newspaper article, the ex libris were decidedly not an indication of ownership. Rather, according to the article, YIVO did not have any independent right to the Strashun Library books; their receipt was solely the result of an error.

Harkavy admitted that he was "well-known to be a man that sought controversy."[11] His role in the Strashun Library incident reinforced that moniker. By January 1956, less than three months after the article discussing the Strashun Library books, Harkavy had already initiated legal proceedings, as a descendent of Mattityahu, to remove the Strashun Library books from YIVO to Israel. Harkavy repeatedly publicized his opinion that YIVO held the library illegally.[12]

The discovery of the Strashun Library and the contention that YIVO lacked title to it prompted two parties to jointly demand that YIVO send the library to Israel: the Association of Jews from Vilna and Tzvi Harkavy.[13] This union may have been formed for strategic reasons, to anticipate a line of argument against either plaintiff's stand-alone claim to the library. In 1939 the Strashun Library remained the property of the Vilna Jewish community, but with that community no longer extant, at least in Vilna, the first issue that needed to be resolved was whether there were any legitimate living heirs to that community. The association could argue that it was the only heir to the community and that the pre–World War II Vilna Jewish populace was now represented by the association. But to the extent that the association's argument was rejected and there was no legally cognizable community, then Harkavy could step in as an heir to the Strashun family. Pursuant to the terms of Mattityahu's bequest— that the library was required to be held in perpetuity by the community —if that condition is no longer met, then the library would revert to the Strashun family. Thus, if Harkavy could establish that he was the legal heir to Mattityahu, he would be entitled to the library.

To the extent that both of those arguments were rejected, then there would be no living heir at all; and legally no individual or institution would be entitled to the Strashun Library, leaving only policy or pragmatic factors to decide the case. To address that situation, Harkavy appealed to a third Israeli party, the Ministry of Religion, and it also joined the fight to remove the Strashun Library books to Israel.

Just as when in 1946 YIVO appealed to the government agencies responsible for the distribution of the books at the OAD, Harkavy sought the Israeli Ministry of Religion's intervention regarding the removal of the Strashun Library from New York to Israel.[14] In the summer of 1956, Zerach Warhaftig, the deputy minister of religion, agreed to sign a letter requesting the removal of the Strashun Library books to Israel.[15]

Since 1947 Israeli libraries and institutions had been receiving heirless books from Europe that had been recovered by the Allies. By 1956 the Ministry of Religion was the government agency responsible for heirless Holocaust-related religious books.[16] The ministry, like many other institutions within Israel, believed that Israel—and not the Diaspora—was the correct destination for all heirless Jewish property from the OAD, and was keen on receiving the Strashun Library. The Israeli view was driven by the Zionist philosophy that Israel was *the* heir to any such property and now personified no-longer-extant European Jewry.[17]

YIVO, however, disputed the Israeli viewpoint. Instead, the United States and specifically YIVO fulfilled the role of heir. No longer was YIVO simply a private institution, and a center for research and preservation of Yiddish and Eastern European Jewish culture and history. Now, reconstituted in America, the new home of the vast majority of Jews, YIVO became a "national institution" for *all* "Jewish research," and modified its English name "from the Yiddish Scientific Institute to the YIVO Institute for Jewish Research."[18]

An Israeli institution, Hechal Shlomo held similar ambitions. Hechal Shlomo's mission was no less than to become the representative of—and reign supreme over—worldwide Jewry; it would "be a beacon of light which will cast its rays of Torah on all the communities of Israel and throughout the Diaspora."[19] Not content to merely assert that Hechal Shlomo would operate in that capacity, in early internal documents, board meetings, and on letterhead it referred to itself with that title, "the Supreme Centre for World Jewry."[20] Indeed, a draft of a pamphlet, signed by the two chief rabbis of Israel, providing an update on progress regarding the creation of Hechal Shlomo and its intended mission, initially read that its goal was to act as the "supreme spiritual center"—in lowercase. That was deleted and revised to read "the Supreme Religious Centre for World Jewry," converting the descriptive phrase into the formal title.[21] Consequently, Hechal Shlomo established itself as a single self-contained institution that incorporated all aspects of religious Judaism—the Jerusalem religious courts, the chief rabbinate, a museum, an office of religious outreach, a committee to determine questions of Jewish law, a synagogue, and a library. Rather than an "institute," it was a *hechal*, an all-encompassing temple.

Like a temple, Hechal Shlomo took pride in its physical structure "with its imposing modern design and beautiful architecture," which itself was "a valuable contribution towards providing dignity and honour of religion[;] if no other activity would have been undertaken it would have still served a most useful purpose . . . [in that] the beauty and dignity of the building have influenced the activities undertaken by its institutions."[22]

Hechal Shlomo was so certain of its centrality to religious Jewry that it expected that "every Synagogue and Community will become associated with the Centre in Jerusalem either by donating a large sum" as a one-time fee "or by subscribing an annual affiliation fee" to fund one of the rooms or courts.[23] That is, Hechal Shlomo unilaterally levied what was for all intents and purposes a tax on Jews worldwide for the support of the institution.

Originally, the chief rabbinate was to be housed in a special build-ing; however, that plan was abandoned in favor of consolidation within the larger Hechal Shlomo institution.[24] Yet Hechal Shlomo assiduously avoided any impression that it was synonymous with and limited to the office of the chief rabbis. This created some tension between the chief rabbinate and the administration of Hechal Shlomo. For example, there was considerable internal debate on whether to include any mention of the "chief rabbinate" in the title of the institution and on official corre-spondence. In part, the concern was that inclusion of the chief rabbin-ate might give the erroneous impression that the institution was a state agency and that its mission was limited to that of the chief rabbi—serv-ing just Israel. Ultimately, after three board meetings, and four different proposals, a compromise was reached that the official title would be-come "Hechal Shlomo" on the top line in large letters, and underneath, in smaller type, "The Seat of the Chief Rabbinate of Israel."[25]

In addition, Hechal Shlomo vigilantly guarded against the percep-tion that it was linked with any other institutions or entities. For ex-ample, an article appeared in the *Jerusalem Post* that referred to Hechal Shlomo as the "central building of the Mizrachi organization."[26] The ex-ecutive of Hechal Shlomo quickly wrote to the *Post's* editor and expressed "amaze[ment]" that the [*Post's*] correspondent . . . should in her article last Friday" erroneously conflate Hechal Shlomo with the Mizrachi. The executive stressed the multifaceted nature of Hechal Shlomo's mission and that it "has no connections or affiliations official or unofficial with Mizrachi or any other party" and that "various activities and functions of Hechal Shlomo are available to every Jew and its doors open to all."[27]

Indeed, within three years Hechal Shlomo asserted that it was "the first point of interest for every visitor of Israel, and . . . over a million and a quarter people have been given guided tours of the building."[28] By then, according to Hechal Shlomo, its dominance was a foregone conclusion; it "no longer hears the question: 'Will Hechal Shlomo really become a world religious center?' Its position as such has been [so] firmly established [that] communities, organizations and individuals in Israel and throughout the world [. . .] turn for advice, help and guidance [to] Hechal Shlomo."[29]

Like the Hechal Shlomo institution, its library, the Central Rabbinical Li-brary, imagined itself to be the religious library for all of world Jewry, the heir and progeny of European Jewry. The library's first acquisitions were heirless books that originated in multiple libraries in Europe.[30] This particular point was emphasized in a Hechal Shlomo promotional brochure, proclaiming that the library was a veritable "'intergathering of exiles,' for among its rich collection are to be found many invaluable tomes, that were rescued from the ruins of the Jewish communities of Europe."[31] Even prior to the opening of the library, at a February 1958 Hechal Shlomo board meeting, the minister of religion expressed his hope that the "library would become the largest library in Israel for Jewish religious legal texts"; and it was well on its way to accomplishing that goal, with "only one library in Israel with larger holdings of legal texts, the Rambam Library in Tel Aviv." Once it became number one, the Central Rabbinical Library would draw a diverse group of experts in Jewish law, including "*talmidei hakhamim*, academics, and intellectuals."[32]

The library was officially opened to the public on July 6, 1958, with Harkavy as its director.[33] In his first report to the Hechal Shlomo administration, Harkavy described the library's history and its current inventory, twenty-five thousand volumes, and alluded to his efforts to obtain additional books "from within Israel and abroad, with more information forthcoming in a special report."[34] Hechal Shlomo was already working in tandem with the Ministry of Religion in its quest to rescue additional heirless Jewish books that remained in Europe. To that end, in the summer of 1958, the ministry was planning a trip to Hungary and Czechoslovakia. Recognizing that the Central Rabbinical Library might benefit from that mission, Hechal Shlomo agreed to split the costs of the mission with the ministry.[35]

After Harkavy was appointed director of the Central Rabbinical Library, in theory he had a much bigger organization behind him to achieve his goal of relocating the remains of the Strashun Library. In accordance with the Hechal Shlomo's self-anointed status as the institution that represented all of religious Jews worldwide, now he had the weight of the World Centre for Religious Jewry. In addition, the very philosophy driving Hechal Shlomo's vision of itself was its representation and replacement of the destroyed European Jewish communities, which was channeled through its library's acquisition of heirless Jewish books. What better books than those from the Strashun Library, which represented one of the greatest pre–World War II Jewish cities?

In November 1958, Harkavy was sent abroad on behalf of the Central Rabbinical Library. He spent over two months traveling throughout

Western Europe and the United States visiting libraries with large Judaica holdings and meeting with librarians, publishers, and associations that supported Hechal Shlomo.[36] These included representatives of the French National Library, the British Museum, the Royal Library of Copenhagen, the Rosenthaliana and Ets Hayim Libraries in Amsterdam, and the Jewish Theological Seminary, Library of Congress, and Yeshiva University in America. He succeeded in obtaining assurances from at least five American publishers that they would send copies of their books, the commitment from Yeshiva University to transfer doubles of rabbinic books to the Central Rabbinical Library, and an agreement from New York University that it would provide microfilm copies of certain Hebrew manuscripts. All those agreements were significant accomplishments, but they were not the main purpose of his trip. Rather, as Harkavy explained soon after embarking on it, transferring the Strashun Library books posthaste to the Central Rabbinical Library was his main goal. He took great umbrage at the books' current location because it was antithetical to their history, as he asked rhetorically, "What do Yiddishists in New York have to do with a rabbinic library that Mattityahu Strashun bequeathed to the Vilna community for the use of its scholars?"[37]

On November 25, 1958, in his capacity as the director of the Central Rabbinical Library, he reached a settlement with YIVO regarding the Strashun Library books. YIVO did not cede ownership of the Strashun Library. Instead, pursuant to the terms of the agreement, YIVO would "gift" to the Central Rabbinical Library, in Jerusalem, all duplicates of rabbinic books that bore the stamp of the Strashun Library. The record is unclear whether the settlement agreement was entirely worked out while Harkavy was in the United States or there had been communication between Harkavy or others in Israel and YIVO before Harkavy's arrival in November. June 1956 meeting minutes of the Ministry of Religion indicate that deputy minister of religion agreed to sign a letter requesting the transfer of the Strashun Library books. But the author could not locate any materials that confirm that such a letter was sent. (As previously discussed, correspondence related to YIVO's library is preserved at its archive but this author was denied access to that record group, RG 100, on the grounds that the entire archive is closed to researchers. Nonetheless, since 2008, at least six other researchers have relied upon documents contained in that archive.) YIVO's portion of the Strashun Library's rabbinic section's catalog, however, was in process and required completion before duplicate copies could be assessed. The parties estimated the catalog's completion date at three months thence.[38] The catalog was being compiled by the bibliographer Hayyim Lieberman, who had a long history with the Strashun Library. His involvement with cataloging its books in small measure enabled him to assist where he previously could not. In the late 1930s, he had collaborated with Lunski on a complete bibliography of Vilna and Horodna prints prior to 1836, when the Russian government closed the Hebrew presses. Lieberman and Lunski corresponded regarding the project, and in August 1939 Lieberman had completed the bibliography. But during the Nazi invasion of Poland, Lieberman's library was destroyed in a fire, and he lost his books and the bibliography.[39] Now Lieberman was tasked with cataloging the Strashun Library books.

The settlement appeared to resolve any issues regarding ownership or location for the Strashun Library books, now split between YIVO in New York and Hechal Shlomo in Israel, but soon afterward the settlement was nearly undone. Harkavy's claim initiated in 1955 remained undecided until, in early 1959, the Jerusalem court finally issued its ruling and declared that Harkavy was the sole heir to Mattityahu Strashun.[40] The rationale for this decision remains opaque. The court's opinion remains under seal because it relates to a personal rather than a commercial case.[41]

Mattityahu had five siblings, two brothers and three sisters. His sister Serna Itta married Joseph Betzalel Harkavy, Tzvi's great-grandfather.[42] After Mattityahu's death, however, his two brothers' sons, Eliyahu and Dovid Strashun, were declared heirs.[43] Serna Itta was excluded. Nevertheless, according to one report, Harkavy established his rights to Mattityahu's estate through "the testimony of Dr. Israel Klausner, the deputy director of the Zionist Archive and historian of Vilna Jewry, and Nahum Sanpiri,[44] the secretary of the Association of Jews from Vilna in Israel."[45] Because the Association of Jews from Vilna was involved (and remained so at least until 1962) in the effort to remove the Strashun Library from YIVO, Sanpiri's testimony is arguably tainted by a conflict of interest. Klausner, however, having written dozens of books and articles on the history of Vilna, visited the Strashun Library, and been involved in an effort to catalog its collection, was certainly an expert on the history of the city and did not have a personal stake in the outcome of the case.[46] Nevertheless, because Tzvi was descended from Mattityahu's sister, who was not an heir, the relevance of even Klausner's testimony regarding Tzvi's genealogy, beyond establishing that Harkavy was related to Strashun, remains unknown.

Fundamentally, Harkavy's relationship to Mattityahu seems wholly irrelevant. Regarding Mattityahu's personal books, he signed those away when he died. He gave them to neither his sister's nor his brothers' children; his will specifically excludes "his sister and other relatives."[47] Those books were bequeathed to the community, without recourse and in perpetuity. Beyond establishing that Harkavy was an heir, he should also have been required to establish that Mattityahu's entire bequest was invalid. Otherwise, the entire collection of Strashun Library books remained communal property and not that of the Strashun family. Moreover, the books at YIVO comprised both Mattityahu's and those of the larger public Strashun Library. The Strashuns/Harkavys never owned any of the books from the larger collection. Even if Mattityahu himself arose from the dead, he would have no claim to any books from the larger library. Instead, the court's decision regarding Harkavy's ownership of the Strashun Library books is perhaps best understood as predicated upon a larger policy reason than established legal principles.

Irrespective of the soundness of the court's opinion, in Israel it was the law; Harkavy was the sole owner of the Strashun Library books. The Strashun Library books would go to only the Central Rabbinical Library if Harkavy agreed, effectively rendering the settlement with YIVO a nullity. Nonetheless, Harkavy, from the outset of his campaign for the Strashun Library books at YIVO, committed to donating his share to the Central Rabbinical Library. After the ruling in his favor, he intended to fulfill that promise, leaving unchanged the books' destination. Although in principle Harkavy agreed to send the books to Hechal Shlomo unbound by the November 1958 agreement, he negotiated new terms and conditions with Hechal Shlomo; and a final settlement was agreed upon by all the parties on September 29, 1960.[48]

In many ways, Harkavy's conditions were a reset to the original conditions attached to Mattityahu's gift. When the Strashun Library was inaugurated in 1902 and Mattityahu's personal library lost its possessive — going from Mattityahu Strashun's Library to the Strashun Library — the trustees sought to ensure that his contribution to the Strashun Library, which built the foundation that enabled the library's success, was not lost in the process; and his personal library was cataloged separately and kept in a special room in the new Strashun Library building. In addition, keeping his library intact permitted the patrons of the Strashun Library to appreciate the multifaceted nature of the collection.

Likewise, the new agreement between Harkavy and Hechal Shlomo stipulated that all the books from the Strashun Library were to be kept separate from the rest of the Hechal Shlomo library, in their own specially designated area, separately cataloged, and specially marked. The books were to be re-bound, and continue to maintain their specific material culture — book markings. The new covers were to be embossed with the appropriate (and uncontested) provenance, either "from the library of R. Mattityahu Strashun z"l," or "from the remains of the R. Mattityahu Strashun Library z"l from Vilna," depending on the history of the respective book.[49] This convention inverts the aphorism "Don't judge a book by its cover." Harkavy's approach to the Strashun Library books was antithetical to YIVO's, which combined, without distinction, the books within YIVO's larger Vilna Collection.

Not all of Harkavy's demands were agreed upon. Harkavy requested that Mattityahu's portrait hang in the library, just as it had in the Strashun Library in Vilna. The final agreement omits that condition, leaving the books rather than physical likeness of Mattityahu as his legacy.[50]

With these new terms, these books could potentially continue to perpetuate not only the legacy of Mattityahu and the Strashun Library, but also a small piece of Jewish Vilna. In addition, these books, admittedly only a small number within the larger Central Rabbinical Library, might also fulfill the sweeping vision of Hechal Shlomo to preserve the legacy of European Jewry.

From the November 1958 settlement and the arrival of the Strashun Library books in Israel in October 1960, another notch was added to the Strashun Library's journey. In addition to archival and contemporaneous records, evidence of this convoluted history can be adduced from the ex libris that are imprinted on the Strashun Library books that were sent from YIVO to Israel. Those books include at least four ex libris: the Strashun Library, YIVO, and two recording donations to Hechal Shlomo, one memorializing YIVO's donation of the book to the Central Rabbinical Library at Hechal Shlomo, and a stamp memorializing Tzvi Harkavy's donation of the book to the Central Rabbinical Library at Hechal Shlomo. The donation ex libris, however, are mutually exclusive regarding post–World War II ownership of the books. Harkavy's ex libris reads, in Hebrew:

A remnant of
the Gaon Rebi Matittyahu Strashun Z"l's Library from Vilna.
A gift to the Central Rabbinical Library in Israel

at the Hechal Shlomo in Jerusalem
From, haRav Dr. Tzvi Harkavy the sole heir to R"ᴍs
[Rabbi Mattityahu Strashun]
Jerusalem, Tishrei [September–October] 1960.[51]

Whereas the ʏɪᴠᴏ ex libris states, in Yiddish:

A gift for
"Hechal Shlomo"
in Jerusalem from *Yidisher Visnshaftlekher Institut* — ʏɪᴠᴏ in New York
Spring 1960.

With no indication of partnership, these two stamps are in conflict regarding the donor.

The conflicting donor ex libris are a result of ʏɪᴠᴏ's claim to the Strashun Library books, Harkavy's unrelenting campaign regarding his genealogical status, and geographical issues both logistical and philosophical. When Harkavy executed the November 1958 settlement as a representative of the Central Rabbinical Library, it did not affect his independent suit for a declaration of rightful inheritance. It was sometime in early 1959, after Harkavy returned to Israel, that the Rabbinical Court of Jerusalem concluded that Harkavy was the rightful heir to the Strashun Library.[52] That was the state of things in Israel; but on the other side of the Atlantic, at ʏɪᴠᴏ, there had been no change to the status of the Strashun Library books since they had arrived in 1947, and there is no indication that any American court accepted the Jerusalem court's decision, or that anyone at ʏɪᴠᴏ was even aware of it. ʏɪᴠᴏ still maintained that it owned all of its Strashun Library books, a claim that was cemented with the ʏɪᴠᴏ pre-World War II ex libris. Consequently, when the books were shipped in spring 1960, ʏɪᴠᴏ placed its dedication ex libris in Yiddish, which emphasized the Diaspora roots of the institution, on the Strashun Library books.

Harkavy, however, was free to ignore all of ʏɪᴠᴏ's ex libris. With the court's declaration of his title, ʏɪᴠᴏ's rights to the Strashun Library were retroactively extinguished, effectively erasing ʏɪᴠᴏ's ex libris. From Harkavy's perspective, with the court's declaration and Israel as the new home of the Jewish people, the Strashun Library began with Mattityahu, was transferred to the Vilna community, and then returned to Mattityahu's family. Irrespective of the books' stamps peacocking ʏɪᴠᴏ's gift and ownership, the court held him the master of the Strashun Library's

11. Ex libris of Harkavy and YIVO donations. Private collection of the author.

destiny. Harkavy, however, was on the other side of the world and unable to enforce the court's judgment until the books reached Israeli soil.[53] But when they did arrive, Harkavy placed his own stamp on the books, adding the fourth ex libris in Hebrew, the new Jewish lingua franca—one that declared his ownership, and his belief that Israel was home to these books and spiritual heir of Eastern European Jewry.

The cataloging of the Vilna Collection's rabbinical books was completed in July 1960, a year and a half after the signing of the settlement agreement. The first shipment of Strashun Library books arrived in early October 1960 and contained 383 books from the Strashun Library, of which forty-eight were from Mattityahu's personal library, and at least twenty of which included his marginalia.[54] When the books arrived at the Central Rabbinical Library, they were greeted with great fanfare, even as YIVO had yet to publicize that it held the Strashun Library books. The Central

Rabbinical Library held a ceremony coinciding with the seventy-fifth anniversary of Mattityahu's death, on 6 Tevet, 5721 (December 25, 1960), to celebrate the opening of the Strashun Library collection to the public.[55] The ceremony was attended by two hundred and fifty people—among them one of the two witnesses who had testified on Harkavy's behalf, Israel Klausner—and included an exhibition of books and items related to Mattityahu and the Strashun Library. A particularly moving portion of the ceremony was the affixing of a *mezuzah* that originally adorned the Strashun Library and had been rescued by a Holocaust survivor, Kalman Farber.[56] The YIVO settlement was among the items displayed. According to an anonymous article written by Harkavy, during the exhibition the issue of transferring the remaining Strashun Library books at YIVO was repeatedly discussed, because YIVO "did not have title or a legal right" to the books. Instead, he asserted that the fight to transfer the books was far from over and that the issue would be raised at the next Zionist Congress.[57]

In total, YIVO sent two shipments, the second arriving in February 1962, to the Central Rabbinical Library, amounting to approximately five hundred duplicate rabbinic books—from among the 23,709 Strashun Library books YIVO had received from the OAD.[58] A little over a year later, in June 1963, YIVO finally disclosed publicly that it held thousands of books from the Strashun Library.

Harkavy and the Association of Vilna Jews refused to accept that approximately 98 percent of the Strashun Library books were still in New York. As late as the mid-1970s, there were reports of continuing efforts for the immediate transfer of the remaining books to Jerusalem.[59] Yet despite Harkavy's intention to keep pressing the issue of the Strashun Library, there is no indication that he met with any success. Not only did Harkavy fail in his quest, but another attempt, by Simon Federbusch, also met with disappointment. Federbusch's attempt bears mention, if for nothing else, because his explanation regarding why he elected to join the fray is notable for its tantalizingly close alignment with the history of YIVO's acquisition of the Strashun Library books, and provides a heretofore unacknowledged detail regarding that acquisition.

Federbusch presided over the World Jewish Congress (WJC) Committee on the Recovery of Jewish Cultural Property.[60] From at least June 1945, a few months after the discovery of the Jewish materials from Rosenberg's IEJ, the committee actively sought restitution of heirless Jewish property, and specifically to lead the Jewish efforts in that regard. This created tension between the WJC and other Jewish groups that claimed supremacy over the process.[61] Ultimately, Federbusch and the WJC coordinated with the other organizations; and when in 1946 a single entity, the Jewish Cultural Reconstruction (JCR), was agreed upon by the Jewish groups, including YIVO, and recognized by the US government, Federbusch was appointed one of its three vice presidents.[62]

In 1965 Federbusch published a short biographical sketch of Samuel and Mattityahu Strashun and mentioned Harkavy's ongoing efforts to remove the Strashun Library books from YIVO to Jerusalem.[63] Federbusch was also involved in those efforts, but he discloses that this was not his first attempt to ensure that the books went to Israel and not YIVO. He alludes to an episode that occurred in 1946 when the Strashun and YIVO books were still at the OAD. According to Federbusch, there was some discussion about where to send the Strashun Library books, and he "demanded that the [Strashun Library] books be sent to Israel and not YIVO, because the core of that collection was rabbinic and an Israeli institution was a more suitable home." The sole reason he was unsuccessful was "because before he could act, and without his knowledge, a young Jewish officer in the American Army, who did not know how to read Hebrew, nevertheless was responsible for the books plundered by the Nazis, and he had family ties with a YIVO executive" and transferred the books to YIVO in New York.[64] Although Federbusch does not identify the army officer, he most likely is referring to Pomrenze.[65]

Federbusch provides but the barest of details, not even naming the key person. A November 11, 1946, letter from Salo Baron to Jerome Michael fills in some of the gaps. At that time, Baron was the chairman of the JCR, and it was in the midst of intense negotiations with the Americans on a final agreement regarding the treatment of heirless Jewish books at the OAD. In the working draft, YIVO in New York received a place for the YIVO property at the OAD. That property would be treated as identifiable and not subject to whatever the ultimate terms are that govern heirless property. Instead, the YIVO property would be sent to New York. Weinreich had repeatedly expressed concerns that the YIVO property would be classified as heirless, with the likely outcome that the property would be distributed to multiple organizations and institutions, as was proposed in the draft document.[66]

In his letter Baron raises a "matter [that] is a little more ticklish and may get us into some difficulty." That ticklish issue was Federbusch's accusation of firsthand knowledge of a scheme to send to YIVO books that did not belong to it. The alleged method: "When Pomrenze while in Offenbach put labels on books allegedly belonging to YIVO which really had not been theirs." That collection of misidentified books was "perhaps 70,000 volumes, [that] reputed[ly] [. . .] include[d] some of the rarest items in Offenbach." Baron shared Federbusch's suspicions, so he therefore proposed to Michael that he modify the draft proposal to address these suspicions. The agreement should require that any books sent to YIVO be examined by independent inspectors. Baron emphasized that these proposed inspections must occur "before these volumes are incorporated in YIVO"; otherwise, they presumably would be difficult, if not impossible, to identify and remove if necessary.[67] Nothing came of Baron's proposed language. Instead, in 1946 Bencowitz misidentified the Strashun Library materials in the monthly reports; and in 1947 Pomrenze, on behalf of YIVO, transferred the YIVO materials to New York, without any independent inspection of those materials, where they were subsequently stamped with the YIVO prewar ex libris and assimilated into the YIVO Vilna Collection.

The otherwise seemingly heirless Strashun Library's legal status after World War II is not straightforward, and deciding its disposition went beyond the application of estate or international law. Neither was a good fit. International law likely required the return of the library to some Eastern European country that was under Soviet control, effectively consigning the books to oblivion. Likewise, applying the laws of inheritance was an exercise in futility. The legal basis for the rabbinical court's declaration of Harkavy's heirship to Mattityahu appears tenuous at best. Likewise, YIVO's claim to the Strashun Library—certainly from the extant documentation—is questionable. The very notion that heirship to the Strashun Library is possible to establish seems contrary to the legal status of the institution. The Strashun Library belonged to everyone and no one. It was entirely owned by the Jewish community of Vilna. That is, the communal nature of the library came about not because it received public funds, like many otherwise private institutions, or because the public was permitted to use the library, as was the case with the Gaon's Kloyz. Instead, every Jew in Vilna, collectively, held title to the "public" Strashun Library.

The battle between YIVO and Hechal Shlomo is perhaps better understood as a function of both institutions, in keeping with their missions, transforming the ownership of the Strashun Library books into symbolic ownership of Vilna's legacy. Indeed, the mission and message that they both articulated is eerily, but unsurprisingly, analogous. They both sought to cast a wider net and obtain an outsized role within post-Holocaust Jewry.[68]

And yet neither institution was true to Mattityahu's or the Strashun Library's mission. Pursuant to the terms of the settlement, YIVO was required to send duplicate rabbinic books from the Strashun Library to the Central Rabbinical Library. The Strashun Library's origins lay with Harkavy's ancestor, Mattityahu, who refused to restrict his library to traditional rabbinic books. He recognized that artificial literary limitations resulted in immature and stunted scholarship and, instead, built a diverse library. The Strashun Library built upon that foundation and continued to incorporate books from all fields and languages. In contradistinction to that intellectual heritage, now a single subject, rabbinic books, was amputated from the body of the Strashun Library and sent to Hechal Shlomo's Central Rabbinical Library, an institution and library that similarly had a single focus. The integrity of the Strashun Library collection at YIVO was lost when the books fell prey to that institution's quest to enlarge its library, and at Hechal Shlomo when the books were restricted by their contents.

Harkavy left his own black mark on the Strashun Library books with his donation ex libris. He insisted that the books be emblazoned with an ex libris recording his alleged largess in ceding his personal rights in the Strashun Library, those that Mattityahu had unambiguously transferred to the Vilna public in perpetuity; and perhaps even more egregious, he applied the stamp to Vilna's Strashun Library books, which were never owned by an individual, Strashun relative or otherwise.

The full nature of the Strashun Library and Vilna's past are not reflected in the missions of either organization. Each laid claim to but one aspect of Judaism; the two institutions were situated in different parts of the world, communicated in different languages, and saw only themselves, exclusive of all others, as representing true modern Jewish expression. Vilna's ethos, however, was rooted in the melding of all aspects of Judaism into an idea that was greater than any of its individual parts. That ethos was best articulated in the Strashun Library's holdings, which comprised books that were religious and secular, old and new, Hebrew and Yiddish, and its readers, who similarly included Bundists, Yiddishists, rabbis, maskilim, men and women. These all readily came together under a single roof to drink in Judaism's intellectual heritage. The Strashun Library was truly a temple for the ingathering of the exiles. With the destruction of Vilna, the tragic reality is that there was no true heir, no *single* institution, country, or individual that alone proved to be the new Vilna.

Nonetheless, not all is lost. The extant Strashun Library books, liberated from the confines of any one particular entity, can endure as an expression of Vilna's unique and otherwise irreplaceable part in Jewish history.

In a perverse twist of fate, that possibility remains.

*I would not be surprised in the
least if in the present freakish times
they would regress to the old decrees
to burn the Talmud or eradicate all
"superstitious" books from Jewish
libraries . . . The pillars of our four-
thousand-year-old culture are strong
enough to endure the oppression
of any inquisition, no matter what
form it takes. The "soul of the people
[Volksgeist]" is exalted and undying;
being here, in the great Strashun
Library, I feel the radiant spark of
this soul.*

s. ANSKY, *The Golden Book*

Postscript

ARTISTIC ILLUSTRATIONS IN HEBREW BOOKS are among my bibliographical interests. Among Mattityahu's five incunabula is Immanuel
of Rome's (ca. 1261–1328) *Sefer ha-Mahbarot* (Book of Collected Writings),
completed on Monday, October 30, 1491.[1] It is the first Hebrew book of secular poetry (although it also contains religious themes as well), comprising twenty-eight chapters of poetry and prose, of which the final chapter
was likely influenced by Dante's *Inferno*.[2] Because of the erotic nature of
some of the poems, the book was allegedly banned by some rabbis. *Sefer
ha-Mahbarot* contains illustrations of the zodiac symbols and is the first
Hebrew book to incorporate those symbols. Subsequently, these symbols
became commonplace in many Jewish books.

Sefer ha-Mahbarot was published by the greatest of the early printers of Hebrew books, Gershom Soncino. He published over one hundred
books across southern Europe and the Ottoman Empire and is the only
Hebrew printer of the incunabula period who printed into the seventeenth century.

Although in some instances, such as the *Sefer ha-Mahbarot*, illustrations appear within Hebrew books, the most common form of artistic
illustration appears on the title pages and frontispieces.[3] At times these

images take on unexpected forms: pagan gods, Christian themes, and nudes all are represented on Hebrew title pages, but most are biblical figures: Moses, Aaron, David, Solomon, nearly always paired, the accepted heraldic figures.[4]

R. Jacob Moelin (ca. 1365–1427), also known as Maharil (Morenu ha-Rav Jacob ha-Levi), was a leading legal scholar of his generation. His responsa, *She'elot u-Teshuvot Maharil*, printed in Hanau in 1610, is the first frontispiece to include the paired of biblical figures.[5] That frontispiece depicts Moses on the left side of the page, and he holds the tablets in one hand and in the other hand he grasps his staff. Aaron is depicted wearing the garments of the high priest: the tunic, bells, and breastplate, and he is carrying incense. Both images include obviously Christian elements. Moses has horns and Aaron is wearing a bishop's miter, and the incense is contained in a censer.[6] Nonetheless, the non-Jewish imagery was copied in other Hebrew books; and there are many examples throughout the seventeenth century and beyond, across Europe and the Middle East.

In most of the books illustrations of biblical figures are unrelated to their content or titles, or the names of their authors. Hebrew printers did not explain why certain images were included on title pages; the assumption is that it was simply for aesthetic purposes. The first Hebrew book to employ an illustrated title page that is a reference to its title is R. Aaron ben Hayim Perachia's responsa, *Perah Mateh Aaron* (*The Flowering of Aaron's Staff*), published in Amsterdam in 1703. This book's biblical pairing depicts Aaron twice, on both sides of the page, and unusually Moses is entirely absent. The Aaron on the left is the standard depiction (with the Christological elements), but the one on the right is distinct from its predecessors, with Aaron holding a budding almond branch—*perah mateh Aaron*—a reference to the story of Aaron's vanquishing those who challenged his priesthood when his staff grew almonds (Numbers 17: 1–8). Of course, the book's illustrative deviations are understandable, because the "second" Aaron and his unique "staff" are not merely aesthetic, but are illustrative of the title of the book.[7]

I own Mattityahu's copy of *Perah Mateh Aaron*. Mattityahu's library was richest in responsa literature, and it is no surprise that he would own this book. But Mattityahu's copy is unique. This copy's end pages are the final uncut pages of an exceedingly rare polemical pamphlet by R. Joel Sirkes, written in Yiddish and Hebrew, *Re'ah Neho'ah* (*A Pleasing Smell*).[8] This pamphlet was published in Fürth, Germany, in 1724, and only one complete copy exists today.[9] Aside from the end pages, Mattityahu did

12. Title page of R. Aaron ben Hayim Perachia's *Perah Mateh Aaron*, Amsterdam, 1703, with the double Aaron illustration. The image on the left shows Aaron with a bishop's mitre and censer, and the image on the right depicts Aaron with a flowering staff. Private collection of the author.

not own a copy, either complete or incomplete. Sirkes was a cantor, *hazzan*, and his pamphlet is a response to an anonymous diatribe, *Shelosha Tzo'akim ve-ainan Ne'anin (Three Screeds without an Answer)*, which accuses cantors of misunderstanding the prayers and being interested only in musicality at the expense of the prayers' meaning.[10] *Re'ah Neho'ah*'s first eight folios are in Yiddish and the final four are in Hebrew. The final four are particularly rare. For example, the copy in the National Library of Israel, which previously belonged to the well-regarded bibliophile and book collector Israel Mehlman, is missing these pages.[11] The end pages in Mattityahu's copy are those Hebrew pages.

These end pages also tell us of the journey of the book. Because these are uncut printer's sheets, we can reasonably assume that Mattityahu's book was bound in the proximity of *Re'ah Neho'ah*'s printer, in Fürth, and around the same time as the book was published in 1724. How it arrived in Mattityahu's collection is unknown.

This book was not among the books that were sent to Israel to Hechal Shlomo. Instead, YIVO deaccessioned the book (at some indeterminate time), and I purchased it from a bookdealer in the United States in the 2000s. The book was bound in leather with wood covers; on one side the leather hangs limply where the cover is broken, and only half remains. Did this occur when the book was shipped to Frankfurt or perhaps on its trip across the Atlantic? Although we will likely never know, we can place the location of one element in the book: YIVO's stamp, its pre–World War II ex libris — that was applied in New York and not Vilna.

In 1947 YIVO received 23,783 Strashun Library books. How many of those, however, remain in New York is unclear. Approximately 500 went to Hechal Shlomo in the early 1960s. A certain number have been exchanged for other books, and some have been offered for sale by private bookdealers, as I learned from personal experience. And in one instance, they were sold at auction.

YIVO was significantly affected by the economic downturn of 2008. In 2009 it faced a budget shortfall of "hundreds of thousands of dollars." To close the deficit, YIVO decided to sell duplicate books from its own collection and the Strashun collection at auction.[12] On Thursday, September 9, 2009, the Strashun books, including some from Mattityahu's personal library, underwent another selection; this time, caught between the auctioneer's hammer and the bidders' hand waving, they were sold to the highest bidder.[13]

13. End page of *Perah Mateh Aaron* with the uncut sheets from R. Joel Sirkes's *Re'ah Neho'ah*, Fürth, 1724. Private collection of the author.

Fewer than fifty Strashun books were included in the 2009 auction.[14] While the number was small, the historical value of these books was not. Indeed, YIVO itself thought them significant enough that they were among the small number reproduced in the companion volume to the 2001 YIVO exhibition on the Strashun Library, as well as a 2005 YIVO publication that highlights "significant treasures" from its collections.[15]

One might conclude that, while the sale was unfortunate, YIVO was compelled to sell these specific books because they were the only ones that were sufficiently valuable to make a dent in the deficit. But an examination of these books' historical prices paid at auction indicate that these are far from the most expensive books; none has sold for more than a few thousand dollars. This auction was no different. The auction returned $28,000, not accounting for any commissions owed to the auction house. The $28,000 includes books from both the Strashun Library and the larger YIVO library.[16] Indeed, the catalog did not distinguish between the two sources and lacked any description of the books' incredible post-Holocaust journey or even the underlying historic nature of Mattityahu's and the Strashun Library's books. Of course, decisions cannot be judged by their outcomes, and deaccession of books and other property from libraries and museums is itself a complex topic. Nonetheless, had the description of the books reflected their true historical value, they might have realized higher prices.

The very criteria applied in selecting Strashun Library books for auction appears fundamentally flawed. These books were allegedly "duplicates." A Strashun Library book is of a unique character; its value is not simply in its contents. Instead, these books carry with them a special history; and if there was another copy of the same book in YIVO's collection, that one could have been selected as the duplicate. A book from the Strashun Library by its very nature should never be treated as a duplicate of another. Beyond the historical importance of the Strashun Library books held in the YIVO collection since 1947, some contained their own unique aspects, marginalia, or other ephemera such as the *Perah Mateh Aaron*. But apparently, the books were never photographed, digitized, or otherwise preserved before they were auctioned.[17]

When the Strashun Library books left the OAD, Lucy Dawidowicz appreciated that the books were more valuable than their contents, that she "had in fact saved a few remnants of Vilna, even if they were just books, mere pieces of paper, the tatters and shards of a civilization." Indeed, her involvement allowed her to "lay to rest those ghosts of Vilna that had haunted [her] since 1939," when she escaped from Vilna. Now she "had realized the obsessive fantasies of rescue which had tormented [her] for years."[18]

Max Weinreich, in 1965, explained that YIVO's mission in post–World War II America was to ensure that "the spirit of Jewish Eastern Europe . . . live on in future generations of Jews everywhere. YIVO has a great research task in this regard, because it is a scholarly tool of the Jewish collective. It is no exaggeration to say that the fate of world Jewry depends upon the extent which Jews [everywhere . . .] will absorb the spirit of Vilna."[19] The preservation and conservation of Strashun Library books, "a scholarly tool of the Jewish collective"—the Vilna public—provided an opportunity for YIVO to transmit and imbue the current generation of Jews with the "spirit of Vilna." In 2009, however, a number of the books were converted into a banal asset, a tool for financial gain.

The Strashun Library books at the Hechal Shlomo suffered a far worse fate. When the books arrived at Hechal Shlomo, they were re-bound and the covers embossed with the books' provenance. But that process also destroyed any ephemera that were on the end pages. In addition, during the binding process some books' margins were trimmed to conform with the cover sizes, resulting in the loss of text. In the early 2000s, contrary to the explicit provisions of Harkavy's gift, *all* the Strashun Library books were sold. Indeed, the Central Rabbinical Library no longer exists, and its holdings were entirely gutted—crated up and sold en masse to book-dealers without regard for their contents. Here, there was no selection, no attempt to identify and save the most valuable books, or at the very least, donate them to a similar institution that would keep the collection intact, preserving a modicum of Vilna's history. Rather than an ingathering of the Diaspora, Hechal Shlomo dispersed the books, consigning them to their own diaspora. The self-proclaimed center for all religious Judaism dispersed "the remnant of the Strashun Library," and with it one of the last testaments to Jewish Vilna.

Captain Bencowitz, who was instrumental in the transfer of the Strashun Library from the OAD to New York, described his feelings and what was at stake in the restitution of the property at the OAD:

[Entering] the loose document room to take a look at the things there and [I] find it impossible to tear myself away from the fascinating piles of letters, folders, and little personal bundles. [. . .] [I]n the sorting room, I would come to a box of books which the sorters had brought together, like scattered sheep into one fold — books from a library which had been in some distant town in Poland or an extinct Yeshiva. There was something sad and mournful about these volumes . . . as if they were whispering a tale of yearning and hope long since obliterated.

I would pick up a badly worn Talmud with hundreds of names of the many generations of students and scholars. Where were they now? Or, rather, where were their ashes? In what incinerator were they destroyed? I would find myself straightening out these books and arranging them in the boxes with a personal sense of tenderness as if they had belonged to someone dear to me, someone recently deceased.

[. . .] How dear all these tokens of love and gentle care must have been to someone and now they were so useless, destined to be burned, buried, or thrown away. All these things made my blood boil . . . How difficult it is to look at the contents of the depot with the detachment of someone evaluating property or with the impersonal viewpoint of scholarly evaluation.[20]

The Strashun Library books were among the books that Bencowitz was mourning and that he refused to stand by and let molder in the depot or be subjected to a potentially perverse restitution law. It is a sad irony that despite his good intentions, the remnant was not treated in the way he had hoped.

The restitution of Jewish cultural property, especially previously public property, in the immediate aftermath of the Holocaust was the first in modern history to wrestle with heirless property and questions of non-nation-state restitution. The Holocaust was a particularly complex case, especially with the commingling of emotional and legal issues. The Strashun Library was but one of the hundreds of examples testifying to these challenges.[21] And the lingering question remains: What should have occurred to the Strashun Library after it was discovered at the OAD? Of course, answering that question decades later under conditions that are entirely dissimilar from those in 1947 is a nigh impossible task. Yet the question remains a compelling one because, unfortunately, similar circumstances — acts of genocide and the inability to identify heirs, coupled with the risk of restituting property to the persons and countries that committed the atrocities — remain all too common.

Today in the United States, the issue of restitution of looted cultural and personal Jewish property remains unsettled and is a live controversy, although generally the focus of these discussions is limited to the restitution of art and not books.[22] Nevertheless, "in the United States and elsewhere, [we] pay scant attention to the issues that arise when prevention fails. Specifically, those laws neglect to provide adequate guidelines for cultural property litigation and enforcement."[23]

In the 1980s this lacuna was first identified in a case that arose regarding the auctioning of Hebrew books smuggled out of Germany in 1940, the first case in the US courts specifically to address heirless Holocaust books. Nonetheless, the result of that case still left unanswered the question of guidelines or legal bases for deciding disputes regarding heirless Holocaust books.[24]

The Hochschule für Wissenschaft des Judentums (The Institute for Jewish Studies), founded in Berlin in 1872, held one of the greatest pre-Holocaust libraries in Europe. The Hochschule was not aligned with any religious movement or faction and sought to remain independent and serve simply as an institute that was focused on academic study. Over time, the Hochschule built an impressive Judaica library. According to the entry in the "Tentative List," it held a "comprehensive library of scientific and rabbinic literature," numbering 58,590 volumes, 115 manuscripts, and "some incunables."[25]

The Hochschule began suffering the effects of Nazism almost immediately after Hitler rose to power in 1933. Yet it continued to limp along, until it was closed by the Nazis on July 19, 1942. Attempts to transfer the Hochschule library from Germany to Great Britain were unsuccessful. The Hochschule was never reconstituted. With its closure, the library was confiscated by the Nazis. In this instance, this was not carried out by Rosenberg and his ERR. The ERR was not the only Nazi organization that sought to build Judaica collections through looting to serve Nazi ideological purposes. The Reich Security Main Office (RHSA), under the control of Heinrich Himmler, also created its own section that would amass Jewish cultural property.[26] That institution established a library in Berlin, and was especially active in plundering Jewish books. During Kristallnacht alone, some three hundred thousand books were plundered by the RHSA. By 1943 the library was estimated to hold two to three million, although that estimate includes both Jewish books and books from additional "objectionable" libraries identified as Marxist and Freemason.[27] The RHSA likely accumulated more books than the ERR. The vast majority of books from the Hochschule seized by the RHSA remained in Berlin. In 1943, when Berlin was no longer considered safe from Allied attack, the RHSA library was moved to other locations that provided greater protection. Yet the Hochschule books were not removed soon enough, and nearly all of its books were destroyed when the RHSA library was bombed. In the main, only its periodical collection was spared.[28]

Not all was lost: a small number of books survived in Berlin. When the Soviets first arrived, they left the RHSA library open and the library's books were looted again, this time by individuals, mainly bookdealers.[29] The Americans eventually took control and sent what remained of the library to the OAD. Over time, an unknown number of books from the Hochschule were sent to Great Britain, and sixty-eight went to the Hebrew University.[30]

Not all of the Hochschule's books were seized by the RHSA. In 1939 Alexander Guttmann, a professor at the Hochschule, succeeded in obtaining a visa sponsored by Hebrew Union College in Cincinnati (HUC) to emigrate to the United States. Heinrich Veit Simon, the grandson of the Hochschule's founder and son of its previous chairman, approached Guttmann and asked that he act as a courier and smuggle rare items from the library. Guttmann agreed, although if he were caught he almost certainly would be put to death. Guttmann himself was permitted to take only inexpensive books from his library, and to ensure compliance all of his property was thoroughly examined by the Gestapo. Guttmann, however, succeeded in avoiding detection.[31]

Guttmann initially hid the books under a pile of garbage and created a false inventory of his library. After the Gestapo had inspected part of the boxes containing Guttmann's nonvaluable books, at the end of the day they placed the inspected boxes in a sealed room. But the Gestapo neglected to account for the outside door that was next to a balcony. Guttmann climbed out onto the balcony and entered the room through a terrace door. He placed the Hochschule items in the boxes that had already been inspected, thereby evading discovery.[32]

Guttmann arrived in the United States in 1940 and taught at HUC over the next forty years. During that time, he never disclosed that he had the Hochschule items. Not until 1984 did the public learn that items from the Hochschule had survived and were in the United States. Yet concurrent with this amazing discovery was the prospect that those rare items would almost immediately be lost again.

In April 1984 Sotheby's announced that its upcoming auction, to be held on June 26, 1984, would feature sixty-two lots of important and rare

Judaica, including twelve incunabula.[33] This was no idle boast. The auction included two illuminated manuscripts, a fifteenth-century illuminated Bible, and a fourteenth-century *mahzor* (prayer book), in addition to many early Hebrew books. In what was subsequently revealed as a gross understatement, Sotheby's asserted that some of the "lots had not been viewed by the public in nearly 45 years." The auction catalog did not identify the consignor of what was likely fifty-seven of the sixty-two lots that were originally from the Hochschule.[34] Nonetheless, Guttmann's name came to light when a number of groups and individuals sought to stop the auction.

The Guttmann case raised issues similar to those of the Strashun Library books after the Holocaust. First, who was the party with the right to stop the auction? The Hochschule was no longer, and there was no transfer of ownership and no clear heir with an ownership interest in the auction items. Nonetheless, a number of groups attempted to step in on behalf of the no-longer-extant Hochschule and stop the sale of the items before they were swallowed up again and lost to the public. HUC saw itself as a possible stand-in for the Hochschule. Some of the Hochschule's surviving former students and teachers, like Guttmann, had ended up at HUC. HUC had sponsored Guttmann's visa and even paid Guttmann's moving and shipping costs, including for his library (and although it was unknown at the time that it encompassed Hochschule materials). Thus, HUC asserted that it should have standing to challenge the sale.[35]

The Central Conference of American Rabbis (CCAR) also claimed an interest in the property. It pointed to the significant number of Reform rabbis in the CCAR, including its president, who had either attended or been ordained by the Hochschule. The Jewish Restitution Successor Organization, which was created in 1947 with responsibility for the disbursement of heirless property in the American zone, joined in as well.[36]

The second issue was Guttmann's claim itself. According to him, he was entitled to the books for two reasons: (1) Veit Simon had agreed to give Guttmann those items as a condition of smuggling out the library materials, and (2) simply because he risked his life (and his wife's and baby's) acting as a courier. The first argument is straightforward, although no one involved was alive to corroborate it, besides Guttmann. The second reason is slightly more complex, but arguably supported by existing legal precedents.[37]

Despite the uproar, and even before the scheduled auction, the Jewish Theological Seminary (JTS) negotiated a private sale for the two manuscripts.[38] Ivan Boesky, who would later go to prison for two years for insider trading, purchased the manuscripts for $900,000 ($25,000 less than the high estimate) and loaned them to JTS. JTS's position was in stark contrast to that of HUC, whose president, Dr. Alfred Gottschalk, said that his institution would not even bid on the items because they were tainted.[39]

Ludwig Jesselson, a refugee from Nazi Germany, had amassed his own impressive collection of Judaica.[40] He was determined that the Hochschule items remain public property and not be transferred into private hands. Jesselson enlisted New York State Attorney General Robert Abrams to stop the auction. After discussing the matter, both Jesselson and Abrams "agreed that all the books were the undisputed 'patrimony of the Jewish people,' and should remain under the aegis of the Jewish community at large. [. . . Otherwise] these Jewish communal treasures were at risk [of] disappearing from the public sphere, perhaps forever."[41] Abrams had his office file suit charging Sotheby's with "persistent fraud and illegality" for misrepresentations regarding provenance.

Abrams was especially passionate about the case; and while initially the case was brought on behalf of the citizens of New York, he amended the case to include himself as a co-plaintiff. Beyond challenging the legality of Guttmann's ownership, Abrams asserted that "these manuscripts belong to, and are part of, the cultural heritage of the Jews. Their sale into private hands is both legally and morally improper."[42]

Prior to the auction, the attorney general sought to enjoin the sale. But that was not to be, and on June 26 the sale went forward and everything was sold, raising $1.45 million, well in excess of the high estimates, with Sotheby's receiving $220,000 in commissions.[43]

After the auction, the attorney general continued to press the case and sought to nullify the sales. In late August, the court ordered Sotheby's to withhold the proceeds from the auction.[44] But the books and manuscripts had already been sent to their respective purchasers.

This case was described as "'perhaps the most complicated and morally fraught example' of art-restitution cases."[45] Guttmann's daughter characterized her father as a "hero," whose only crime was that "he [. . .] save[d] these manuscripts from certain destruction. He is a dedicated loving educator who has only the best interests of his students and fellow man at heart."[46] Others viewed him as a wartime profiteer valuing money over his own Jewish heritage. Whatever one's assessment of Guttmann's character, the legality of his ownership was also subject to interpretation. With seemingly valid arguments on both sides, the Guttmann case provided an opportunity to articulate a legal construct for recovered Holocaust assets. But that did not occur, and for over a year the case would remain contested.

In July 1985 the parties had reached a tentative settlement that was approved by the court on August 14, 1985. Pursuant to its terms, JTS was required to return the two manuscripts, and Boesky was refunded his money. Jesselson paid the $900,000, and one manuscript was sent to what is now the National Library of Israel and the other to Yeshiva University Library. Recognizing that those institutions are effectively acting as custodians and that those manuscripts are the "patrimony of the Jewish people, prior to sending the manuscripts to those institutions, the manuscripts were required to be exhibited publicly for three months at JTS, HUCA, and New York Public Library." All other manuscripts and books that were not otherwise in libraries were returned to Sotheby's, and the purchasers were refunded their money. A special committee distributed those books to Jewish libraries.[47] Other books could voluntarily be returned for a refund. Sotheby's was required to disgorge any remaining proceeds, estimated at $850,000, and distribute that money to six different Jewish institutions in the United States, England, and Israel, for the purchase of rare books and manuscripts.[48]

The aftermath of the Hochschule auction produced mixed results. The settlement left Guttmann with $900,000 for the two manuscripts, but he was stripped of his teaching privileges and remained a pariah at HUC for the rest of his life.[49] JTS did not receive either manuscript, but over the course of time Boesky provided the institution with many other rare books and manuscripts. Boesky, however, remained the legal owner of those items. When he divorced in 1994, the items were subject to the divorce settlement and sold—by Sotheby's.[50] Because of the Guttmann sale and other sales, in 1985 the New York City Department of Consumer Affairs, which licenses all auction houses, began a comprehensive assessment of auction practices.[51] Sotheby's reexamined its policies governing assessing provenance.[52] Nonetheless, questions regarding the provenance of property allegedly misappropriated during or after the Holocaust continue to dog Sotheby's (and other auction houses). Today, public access to the two manuscripts is essentially unfettered; both are available in high-quality images online.[53]

A more recent and still unresolved example of restitution of Jewish property relates to the Chabad Lubavitch library and archive. Unlike the Guttmann case, which involved a private individual, this case involves a nation-state and raises additional issues related to post-Holocaust assets. Part of the library and archive of the Chabad Lubavitch was nationalized by the Soviets shortly after its creation, and another portion was looted by the Nazis and subsequently recovered by the Soviets, and both are now held in the Russian State Library and other state institutions.[54] Chabad has requested the return of its property, but negotiations and litigation applying international and US laws thus far have proven fruitless.[55] This issue has significantly affected other important cultural objects. The Russian government has refused to lend American museums and galleries Chabad's art and other cultural artifacts, fearing that they might be seized by the American authorities; and American institutions have threatened to take similar action regarding loans to Russian institutions, further impeding the public's access to these materials.[56]

American and other international libraries, museums, and galleries, including Jewish institutions, have recently begun identifying objects in their collections that were sourced from other countries or individuals. But the return of these objects is not a certainty. The response from the institutions is inconsistent; some items have been returned, while in other cases the institutions have resisted all efforts to wrest the property from their collections.[57]

An ambitious project was recently completed to remedy one instance of looted Holocaust books. Dr. Aron Freimann was the curator of the Frankfurt Library; and in 1933, a year before he was dismissed from his post as curator, he published a catalog of the library.[58] He was among the most significant Hebrew bibliographers; and among his other many articles and books, he published a seminal work on Hebrew printing, *Thesaurus Hebraicae Saeculi XV* (Berlin: Marx, 1924–31).

He also amassed his own impressive library. The first iteration of his private library he sold to Hebrew Union College in 1920. At the time, of Hebrew Union College's sixty-four incunabula, twenty-eight came from Freimann. After selling his books to the college, he then proceeded to build another impressive collection.[59] That collection was looted by the Nazis. In 2016 nearly all of the Freimann collection was reassembled, digitized, and made available online.[60]

The Strashun Library could also serve as a catalyst for the necessary and long overdue analysis of these thorny issues, and its storied history might serve as a guide for those discussions. But without a complete accounting of the acquisition of the Strashun Library books, the library's place in that dialogue is absent.

Throughout the Strashun Library's history, it has at times been saved through the most unlikely of circumstances and actors: from the Zionists in Vilna, who ensured the fulfillment of Mattityahu's bequest, despite his anti-Zionist position, to the Nazis bent on nothing less than the complete erasure of Jews from the world. And in the late 1980s, another chapter in the Strashun Library's history was discovered that was also nearly unimaginable.

During World War II, most of the European continent suffered destruction on an unparalleled scale. Without a doubt, the Nazi campaign of looting and plundering Jewish treasures protected them from certain destruction. Indeed, the Nazis were especially good caretakers. Toward the end of World War II, when the Jewish books in Frankfurt came within the zone of Allied bombing, the Nazis transported the books to salt mines and the deep basements of castles. While preparing to make their final stand, facing the likely prospect of their own demise, the Nazis allocated precious resources to ensure the longevity of Jewish cultural property. The Nazis were similarly diverting resources for another Jewish project, sending as many Jews as possible to concentration camps and their death.

Jewish efforts at preservation oftentimes proved less effective than the Nazis'. In the Vilna Ghetto, members of the Paper Brigade and others risked their lives to keep as many books as possible from being destroyed or going to Frankfurt. Yet for the most part their efforts were for naught. When the ghetto was destroyed in the fall of 1944, many of books suffered the same fate.[61]

After the Holocaust, two members of the Paper Brigade, Abraham Sutzkever and Szmerke Kaczerginski, returned to Vilna. They dug up materials they had hidden in deep bunkers and hiding places across the now destroyed Vilna Ghetto. They discovered that the Strashun Library books had yet again narrowly escaped destruction. The three thousand Strashun Library books that had been courageously stolen from the hands of the Nazis by Kruk and others were taken to the 6 Strashun Street book hiding place. That was discovered by the Germans, who threw everything they found in a bonfire in the courtyard. Yet the Strashun Library books had been moved earlier to the bunker next door at 8 Strashun Street. That bunker survived intact and was where Sutzkever and Kaczerginski recovered thousands of books, including many rarities.[62] On July 26, 1944, two weeks after the Soviets liberated the ghetto, Kaczerginski and Sutzkever founded the Jewish Museum, which would later be formally recognized by government authorities. By the fall of 1945, the museum held an estimated twenty-five thousand Hebrew and Yiddish books.[63] In another postwar twist of fate, the museum found space in a prison in the basement of the former ghetto library. The prison where the Gestapo had tortured and killed Jews was now resurrected as a place that was to ensure the life of Judaism, using the very property the Nazis had sought to destroy. Yet this tiny ray of light was short lived. Within two years, Sutzkever and Kaczerginski recognized that the museum was untenable under the Soviets and again began a smuggling operation, this time to move the Jewish property, including some of the recovered Strashun Library books, out of the former Jewish ghetto and to the YIVO building in New York.[64] Even after Sutzkever and Kaczerginski fled with rare materials, the museum continued to operate and its holdings grew.

The Soviet Union was among the countries that voted for the partition of Palestine, ushering in the establishment of the State of Israel. Nonetheless, within a year, the Soviets began suspecting Zionists, and by extension all Jewish cultural institutions, of promoting anti-Soviet activities and being enemies of the state. Soon after, Lithuanian authorities began espousing similar antisemitic propaganda; and the Lithuanian Council of Ministers (the executive branch of the government, which was effectively controlled by the Communist Party of the Soviet Union and Lithuania) officially closed the museum in the summer of 1949.[65] Now the Lithuanian Communists filled the shoes of the Nazis and plundered and looted the museum of its Jewish materials, including over thirty-eight thousand books.[66]

In a situation akin to what transpired during the Nazi regime, the materials were moved to their own collection point, a former Roman Catholic church and monastery, which came to be known as the Book Chamber of the Lithuanian SSR. The Book Chamber held books of local importance, of which the seized Jewish books made up but a small number. Unlike the non-Jewish materials, which were mostly properly attended to, the Jewish books were summarily dumped into the chamber's storage facility in the adjacent monastery. There, the Strashun Library books that had survived in Vilna, with tens of thousands of other Jewish books, were heaped into massive piles and left undisturbed for decades.

Early in their residence in the chamber, they were all nearly lost to the vicissitudes of the Stalin years. Until Stalin's death in 1953, Jewish materials were considered anti-Soviet, and many were destroyed. Like Ona Šimaite, the non-Jewish Lithuanian librarian who during World

War II had assisted Jews in saving books at great risk, now, a decade later, another non-Jewish librarian, Antanas Ulpis, the director of the Book Chamber, risked his career and probably freedom, defied Stalin's order, and preserved the books. After Stalin's reign, he directed a small cadre of his library colleagues and some Jewish volunteers to secretly catalog the books, but kept that information within the group, and moved them to the church building, thereby ensuring the preservation of the Strashun Library books once again.[67]

During the next half century, while the other Strashun Library books crisscrossed oceans and were transferred from hand to hand, within the Book Chamber, the Strashun Library books went into hibernation, buried within their lair. Unfortunately, because of neglect many books fell into disrepair. Nevertheless, with the fall of the Soviet Union, Lithuanian independence, and its eventual incorporation into the European Union, the Strashun Library books were slowly brought out of their slumber.[68]

Much as was the case in 1945, the public learned from an article of the existence of these books in Lithuania that were assumed to be lost forever; and almost immediately YIVO moved to recover the property. In 1988 a scholar living in Vilna, Emmanuel Zingeris, published an article in the Yiddish Soviet communist magazine *Sovetish Heymland* (*Soviet Homeland*), describing the history of Vilna's Jewish libraries.[69] He mentioned that approximately twenty thousand Hebrew and Yiddish books were in the Book Chamber. The rediscovery of the Strashun Library books once again brought to fore the indeterminate heirship of Holocaust assets and began yet another chapter in the Strashun Library's history.

When the cache of books was disclosed, the provenance of the books was indeterminate. The books and items in the Book Chamber were in total disarray, and the first task was to identify the past owners of the books. To address the situation, the then director of the Book Chamber, Algimantas Lukošiunas (Ulpis died in 1981), established the Mattityahu Strashun Judaica Department to catalog the books. Eventually, the staff discovered books belonging to YIVO, Strashun, or other institutions such as the Telshe Yeshiva, formerly from Lithuania and relocated to Cleveland, Ohio. They also discovered that archival materials were among those books, some marked with the YIVO stamp.[70]

For the remaining years of Soviet control of Lithuania, government officials indicated that any transfer of the discovered materials to the United States was unlikely. In 1989, with the support of the government, a Jewish museum was reestablished in Vilna with Emmanuel Zingeris as its director. Zingeris unilaterally declared that these materials were the Lithuanian cultural heritage. This designation was adopted by government officials, and it continued to be the position of the Lithuanian government after independence. They refused to honor the ownership markings and took the position that as national treasures the books were not subject to restitution. This was despite the fact that during the Soviet period they were at best tolerated, if not slated for destruction, and deemed antithetical to the accepted ideology, kept in a state of disrepair, and inaccessible to the very people of that nation.

Despite the intransigence of the Lithuanian government, YIVO refused to give up. Thus began a nearly fifteen-year negotiation that would span six directors of YIVO and six Lithuanian presidents to address the disposition of the Jewish books.[71]

In 1997 a group of American librarians visited the Book Chamber and produced a comprehensive report regarding the inventory and condition of the books. According to that report, 74,225 books had been cataloged and approximately 13,000 remained uncataloged, of which 2,000 were classified as rare.[72] The librarians were able to identify the provenance of some of the books, and Strashun Library books were among the two "most prominent examples" of identifiable books. Yet these books were still categorized as YIVO's because they continued to be defined as encompassing "materials from . . . YIVO's 'associated libraries' (as outlined in correspondence between representatives of YIVO and the Library of Congress shortly after World War II)."[73] Consequently, the position of YIVO vis-à-vis its alleged historic relationship with the Strashun Library remained unchanged—although which version of that history, Weinreich's, Dawidowicz's or Uveeler's, is not clear.[74]

The report also documented the history of the books and prior negotiations and agreements (which mostly related to archival materials and not books), with each side accusing the other of failing to fulfill its responsibilities.[75] A number of recommendations were made, but the issue of the ownership of the books remained unresolved. In 2014 YIVO reached the decision that challenging ownership was futile and instead, as its director Jonathan Brent articulated, YIVO's "job is to preserve materials for future generations and make them available to scholars worldwide who can make sense of these materials."[76] A different plan for the Strashun Library books was envisioned. This plan reached back to the backdrop of Vilna's intellectual heritage and married contemporary technologies with the historic Strashun Library's books: the books would undergo state-of-the-art digitization and be posted on the internet — a solution that sought "to create an electronic bridge over a troubled stream."[77]

Beyond the limited issue of where the Strashun Library books would reside, in Lithuania other steps were taken to preserve the memory of the Strashun Library. On May 22, 2017, the Lithuanian National Library established the Judaica Research Center. The center's reading room was named in honor of Khakyl Lunski, and the center's inaugural exhibition was "The People and Books of the Strashun Library," curated by the director of the center, Lara Lempert (Lempertienė). Since she had begin working at the library in 1995, Lempertienė had led the effort to identify and catalog Mattityahu's books. The exhibition displayed Mattityahu's personal books, a handful that had originally belonged to his father, Samuel, and some of the public Strashun Library holdings. Among Mattityahu's books was his copy of *Kiryah Ne'emanah* with his extensive marginalia — the additional notes that he alluded to in his lengthy addendum that was published posthumously in the second 1902 edition, one that was later incorporated into Kaczerginski and Sutzkever's Jewish Museum; a rare 1512 book *Midrash Tehilim*, printed in the Ottoman Empire; and the journal *Pirhei Tsafon*, wherein Mattityahu published his first articles with his marginalia. Documents related to the Strashun Library were also exhibited, among them Mattityahu's original will attesting to his bequest, a Nazi document recording Lunski's imprisonment, his handwritten lists of books in the Strashun Library, part of his unfinished catalog of the library, and two documents about the library during World War II — a November 1939 letter from the Jewish community confirming that the Strashun Library was a public institution, and an official Lithuanian document from 1940 that records the continued communal ownership of the Strashun Library.

The National Library petitioned for the inclusion of Strashun Library books in UNESCO's "Memory of the World" program. That program recognized that "collections worldwide have suffered a variety of fates. Looting and dispersal [. . .], destruction, inadequate housing and funding" were among the reasons cited; the aim now was "to counter that history" and to "preserve and protect for all, and with due recognition of cultural mores and practicalities, [those looted items, which] should be permanently accessible to all without hindrance."[78] In 2017 the Strashun Library books in Lithuania were placed on the UNESCO list.

Not only were the Strashun Library books in Lithuania to undergo digitization, but also YIVO, as part of a larger project to digitize much of its collection of materials related to Vilna, acceded to applying the same program to the remainder of its portion of the Strashun Library books. The first category of books for digitization consists of those which originally belonged to Mattityahu. After an extensive process, YIVO has identified approximately 2,000 of Mattityahu's books in its collection.[79] And 1,404 books, 211 issues of periodicals, and three manuscripts from Mattityahu's personal collection are among the thousands of Strashun Library items that are preserved in Lithuania.[80] At the completion of the project nearly 3,500 of Mattityahu's 5,735 books will be (re)gifted to the public, ensuring that anyone and everyone seeking to benefit from his intellectual treasure and its universal message can do so once again. To complete the reconstruction of Mattityahu's library, books that were either destroyed or dispersed with the closure of Hechal Shlomo will be replaced with digital copies from other libraries. It is to be hoped the project can continue and be applied to all of the recovered Strashun Library books and not just those owned by Mattityahu. In this instance, rather requiring the Strashun Library to revert to private hands, it would become an evolved version of the first Jewish public library. No longer just for the Vilna Jewish public, it would now be the property of the entire world.

Notes

Introduction

1. Asher ben Jehiel, *She'elot u-Teshuvot Besamim Rosh*, ed. Saul Berlin (Berlin: Hevrat Hinukh Ne'arim, 1793).

2. Moshe Samet, "'Besamim Rosh shel Shaul Berlin," *Kiryat Sefer* 48 (1973) 509-23; Eliezer Brodt and Dan Rabinowitz, "Benefits of the Internet: Besamim Rosh and Its History," *Seforim Blog*, April 26, 2010, http://seforim.blogspot.com/2010/04/benefits-of-internet-besamim-rosh-and.html.

3. For other examples of forgeries in the responsa literature, see *Kuntres Ha'teshuvot Ha'hadash: Otsar Bibliographie Le'safrut Ha'she'alot Ve'ha'teshuvot Me'reshit Ha'defus ve'ad Shenat TSh"S*, ed. Shmuel Glick, vol. 4 (Jerusalem: Machon Schocken, 2010), index, "teshuvot *mezvyafot*."

4. Moshe Pelli, *The Age of Haskalah: Studies in Hebrew Literature of the Enlightenment in Germany* (Lanham, MD: University Press of America, 2006), 171–89. For a discussion regarding the precursor to Saul's iteration of Haskalah, see David Sorkin, "The Early Haskalah," *New Perspectives on the Haskalah*, ed. Shmuel Feiner and David Sorkin (London: Littman Library of Jewish Civilization, 2001), 9–26.

5. Raphael Mahler, *Divrei Yemei Yisrael: Dorot Aharonim*, vol. 2 (Merhavyah: Ha'kibutz Ha'artzi Ha'shomer Ha'tzair, 1954), 79.

6. Pelli, *Age of Haskalah*, 184–89.

7. Asher ben Jehiel, *She'elot Teshuvot Besamim Rosh*, ed. Saul Berlin (Krakow: Fischer and Deutscher, 1881).

8. For changing views toward suicide during the Enlightenment, see Michael Cholbi, "Suicide," *The Stanford Encyclopedia of Philosophy* (Summer 2016 ed.), ed. Edward N. Zalta, https://plato.stanford.edu/archives/sum2016/entries/suicide. Contemporaneous with Saul, some early Hasidim also adopted nonnormative positions regarding suicide. Zvi Mark, "Madness, Melancholy and Suicide in Early Hasidim," *Kabbalah: Journal for the Study of Jewish Mystical Texts* 12 (2004), 27–44.

9. Shlomo Zalman Hanau, *Binyan Shlomo* (Frankfurt: Matis Andre, 1708).

10. Sorkin incorrectly asserts that Hanau began challenging his predecessors only in his second book, *Sha'arei Torah*, published ten years after *Binyan Shlomo*, in 1718. Sorkin, "Early Haskalah," 11.

11. The page was reprinted in *Zeitschrift für Hebräische Bibliographie* 8 (1904), 93–94.

12. Edward Breuer, *The Limits of Enlightenment: Jews, Germans and the Eighteenth-Century Study of Scripture* (Cambridge: Harvard University Press, 1996), 132–36.

13. Shmuel Feiner, "Towards a Historical Definition of the Haskalah," *New Perspectives on the Haskalah*, 184–219.

1. Vilna: The Study House

1. Chroniclers of Vilna Jewish history struggle with the spelling and name that is most appropriate for the city. I have elected to follow Israel Cohen's usage in his 1943 book *Vilna*. Israel Cohen, *Vilna* (Philadelphia: Jewish Publication Society, 1943), xxii. Cohen's selection of "Vilna" was based on its currency among Jewish circles in the 1940s, and not what was accepted by Lithuanians or the international community. "Vilna" remains the most common form of the name of the city within Jewish circles. Thus, I too use "Vilna" throughout the book. Regarding the variant spellings of "Vilna" in Hebrew characters, see Dovid Katz, "Vilne, Vilno, Vilna (Vilnah)," in *Virtual Yiddish Mini-Museum of Old Jewish Vilna* 16, http://defendinghistory.com/keepsakes-of-old-jewish-vilna-16 (Yiddish).

2. Regarding Napoleon's occupation of Vilna, see Laimonas Briedis, *Vilnius: City of Strangers* (Vilnius: Baltos Lankos, 2012), 81–123.

3. Cohen, *Vilna*, 104–5. Jews in Vilna generally remained loyal to the tsar. Ibid., 262–63, 501–6. But Jews also showed compassion for the retreating French. Briedis, *Vilnius*, 108–110. Jews in Lithuania were conflicted regarding Napoleon. R. Shneur Zalman of Lyady, the founder of the Chabad movement, was opposed to Napoleon because he was perceived as creating circumstances that encouraged Jews to relax their religious practices. Hillel Levin, "'Should Napoleon Be Victorious . . .': Politics and Spirituality in Early Modern Jewish Messianism," *Jerusalem Studies in Jewish Thought* 16–17 (2001), 65–83. But Jews generally held favorable views of Napoleon, including some who saw him as the potential Messiah. Simon Schwarzfuchs, *Napoleon, the Jews and the Sanhedrin* (London: Routledge and Kegan Paul, 1979), 164–78; Binyamin Shlomo Hamburger, *Meshihei ha-Sheker u-Mitnagdehem* (Bnei Brak, Israel: Makhon Moreshet Ashkenaz, 2009), 480–518; Barukh Mevorakh, ed., *Napolyon ve-Tekufato: Reshumot ve-Eduyot Ivryot shel Bene ha-Dor* (Jerusalem: Bialik Institute, 1968).

4. Briedis, *Vilnius*, 11–12.

5. Ibid. (quoting Renate Lachmann, *Memory and Literature: Intertextuality in Russian Modernism*, trans. Roy Sellars and Anthony Wall (Minneapolis: University of Minnesota Press, 1997), 164.

6. Czeslaw Milosz and Tomas Venclova, "A Dialogue about Wilno," in Tomas Venclova, *Forms of Hope* (New York: Sheep Meadow Press, 1999), 7. Czeslaw Milosz, *A Year of the Hunter*, trans. Madeline G. Levine (New York: Farrar, Straus and Giroux, 1994), 4.

7. Briedis, *Vilnius*, 43.

8. Giedrė Mickūnaitė, *Making a Great Ruler: Grand Duke Vytautas of Lithuania* (Budapest: Central European Press, 2006), 54.

9. Briedis, *Vilnius*, 43.

10. Ibid., 29.

11. Age Meyer Benedictsen, *Lithuania, "The Awakening of a Nation": A Study of the Past and Present of the Lithuanian People* (Copenhagen: Egmont H. Petersens, 1924), 174–77 (quoted in Broides, *Vilnius*, 149).

12. There are many treatments of Jewish Vilna. Mordechai Zalkin, "Vilnius," in *YIVO Encyclopedia of Jews in Eastern Europe*, ed. Gershon David Hundert (New

Haven, CT: YIVO Institute, 2008), cols. 1970–77; Israel Klausner, *Toldot ha-Kehillah ha-Ivrit be-Vilna* ([Vilna]: 1938); Israel Klausner, *Korot Beit ha-Almin ha-Yashan be-Vilna* ([Vilna]: Yotse le-Or be-Hishtatfut ha-Kehillah ha-Ivrit, 1935); Israel Klausner, "Vilna," in *Yahadut Lita* (Tel Aviv: Ha-Agudah le-Ezrah Hadadit le-Yotzei Lita be-Yisrael, 1967), vol. 3, 257–71; Cohen, *Vilna*.

13. Cohen, *Vilna*, "The Foundation of the Community," supp. notes, 481–82.

14. Ibid., 29–30; Shmuel Arthur Cygielman, *The Jews of Poland and Lithuania until 1648 (5408): Prolegomena and Annotated Sources* (Jerusalem: Zalman Shazar, 1991), 381–83.

15. To the Jews of Vilna, the term "ghetto" did not evoke a cloistered and backward existence. Instead, some "writers referred to the Jewish quarter as a ghetto with a sense of affirmation." Cecile E. Kuznitz, "On the Jewish Street: Yiddish Culture and the Urban Landscape in Interwar Vilna," in *Yiddish Language and Culture: Then and Now*, ed. Leonard Jay Greenspoon (Omaha, NE: Creighton University Press, 1998), 74–75. Regarding the history of Jewish ghettos, see Benjamin C. I. Ravid, "The Venetian Ghetto in Historical Perspective," in *The Autobiography of a Seventeenth-Century Venetian Rabbi: Leon Modena's "Life of Judah,"* trans. and ed. Mark R. Cohen (Princeton: Princeton University Press, 1988), 279–83.

16. Portions of German Street (today, Vokiečiu) were also included in the ghetto. For a description of the Jewish Quarter and its streets, from its inception until the mid-twentieth century, see Klausner, *Toldot ha-Kehillah ha-Ivrit be-Vilna*, 55–85; Kuznitz, "On the Jewish Street," 67. A depiction of Leib-Leizer's courtyard appears in Chaim Grade, *Di Kloyz un di Gas* (New York: Schulsinger Brothers, 1974).

17. David Frick, "Jews and Others in Seventeenth-Century Wilno: Life in the Neighborhood," *Jewish Studies Quarterly* 21, no. 1 (2005), 13. Despite the stated limitations on Jewish residential space, those boundaries were never honored. Ibid., 14–15. In 1783 the Jewish Quarter was officially abolished, and with limited exceptions Jews were officially permitted to reside in the entire city. Cohen-Mushlin, *Synagogues in Lithuania N-Z*, 240.

18. Jacob Elbaum, *Openness and Insularity: Late Sixteenth Century Jewish Literature in Poland and Ashkenaz* [Hebrew] (Jerusalem: Magnes Press, 1990); Gershon David Hundert, *Jews in Poland-Lithuania in the Eighteenth Century: A Genealogy of Modernity* (Berkeley: University of California Press, 2004).

19. Cohen-Mushlin, *Synagogues in Lithuania N-Z*, 240.

20. Eliyahu Stern, *The Genius: Elijah of Vilna and the Making of Modern Judaism* (New Haven, CT: Yale University Press, 2013), 18–23, 27–30. Biographies of the Gaon began appearing in the mid-nineteenth century and continue to the present. See Yeshayahu Vinograd, *Thesaurus of the Books of the Vilna Gaon: Detailed and Annotated Bibliography of Books by and about the Gaon and Hasid R. Eliahu b. R. Shlomo Zalman of Vilna* (Jerusalem: Kerem Eliahu, 2003), 176–87, 229–30. The first biography was written by Yehoshua Heschel Levine, *Sefer Aliyot Eliyahu: Toldot ha-Adam ha-Gadol be-Anakim . . . Gaon me-Vilna* (Vilna, 1856). Levine never met the Gaon, but he solicited information from many of the Gaon's students and contemporaries. In addition, Levine includes a bibliography of the Gaon's writings, *Aliyat Kir*. For a biography of Levine, see Eliezer Katzman, "Le-Demut ha-Gaon R' Yehoshua Heschel Levine

ZTs"L," *Yeshurun* 5 (1999), 742–83, and *Yeshurun* 6 (1999), 700–27. The reception of *Aliyot Eliyahu* was uneven, and some took a dim view of the accuracy of Levine's portrayal of the Gaon. See ibid., 702–12. For recent treatments, in addition to Stern, see Gil S. Perl, *The Pillar of Volozhin: Rabbi Naftali Zvi Yehuda Berlin and the World of Nineteenth-Century Lithuanian Scholarship* (Boston: Academic Studies Press, 2013); Shaul Stampfer, "The Image of the Ga'on," in *Ha-GRA u-Bet Midrasho*, eds. Moshe Halamish et al. (Ramat Gan: Bar-Ilan University Press, 2003); Immanuel Etkes, *The Gaon of Vilna: The Man and His Image*, trans. Jeffery M. Green (Berkeley: University of California Press, 2002); Dov Eliakh, *Ha-Gaon: Le-Toldot Hayav u-Beirur Mishnato shel Morenu ve-Rabbenu HaGR"A Ha-Gaon Rebi Eliyahu me-Vilna ZTsUK"L*, 3 vols. (Jerusalem: Moreshet Hayeshivot, 2002). For antecedents to the title "gaon" and its application to Elijah, see Stern, *Genius*, 146–56. The Vilna Gaon was neither the only well-regarded rabbinic personality in Vilna nor the first. From the early seventeenth century, Vilna was "a preeminent center for rabbinical studies, and numerous scholars were born or served in Vilna." *Encyclopaedia Judaica*, s.v. "Vilna," vol. 16, col. 140. Regarding the use of the honorific "gaon," see Ya'akov Shmeul Speigel, *Amudim be-Toldot ha-Sefer ha-Ivri: Be-Sha'arei ha-Defus* (Jerusalem, 2014), 141–49.

21. The Gaon left his self-imposed seclusion in 1760. Eventually, the Gaon's advice was sought to resolve major controversies that roiled the Jewish world. These included the question of choosing the next chief rabbi of Vilna and the ultimate decision to abolish the post, and the Emden-Eybeschuetz controversy. Stampfer, *Families*, 325–26 (discussing the Gaon and Emden-Eybeschuetz). Stern, however, questions whether the Gaon took sides in the debate over the Vilna chief rabbinate. Stern, *Genius*, 187n76.

22. Etkes, *The Gaon*, 73–95; and see generally, Allan Nadler, *The Faith of Mithnagdim: Rabbinic Responses to Hasidic Rapture* (Baltimore: Johns Hopkins University Press, 1997).

23. Mordecai Wilensky, *Hasidim u-Mitnaggedim: Le-Toldot ha-Pulmus Shebenayhem be-Shenat 5532–5575* (Jerusalem: Mossad Bialik, 1990).

24. Šarūnas Liekis and Antony Polonsky, "Introduction," in *Polin: Studies in Polish Jewry*, ed. Šarūnas Liekis, Antony Polonsky, and ChaeRan Freeze (Oxford: Littman Library of Jewish Civilization, 2013), 10. The exact geographic borders of those displaying this peculiar personality is inexact, but the particular dialect of Yiddish is helpful in defining the general area of the Litvaks. Katz, *Words on Fire*, 145–54.

25. Freeze, *Everyday Jewish Life*, 9.

26. Allan Nadler, "Litvak," in *YIVO Encyclopedia of Jews in Eastern Europe*, 2011, accessed April 30, 2017, http://www.yivoencyclopedia.org/article.aspx/Litvak. For other characteristics attributed to Litvaks in Jewish folklore, see Katz, *Lithuanian Jewish Culture*, 63, 80, 89.

27. Dov Levin, *The Litvaks: A Short History of the Jews in Lithuania*, trans. Adam Teller (Jerusalem: Yad Vashem, 2000), 10.

28. Gil S. Perl, *Rabbi Naftali Zvi Yehuda Berlin and the World of Nineteenth-Century Lithuanian Torah Scholarship* (Brighton, MA: Academic Studies Press, 2012), 127–37.

29. Perl, *Rabbi Naftali Zvi Yehuda Berlin*, 42–49; Stefan Schreiner, "The Vilner

Gaon as a Biblical Scholar (A Reappraisal)," in *The Gaon of Vilna and the Annals of Jewish Literature*, comp. Izraelis Lempertas and ed. Larisa Lempertienė (Vilnius: Vilnius University, 1998) 128–36.

30. Jay M. Harris, *How Do We Know This? Midrash and the Fragmentation of Modern Judaism* (Albany: State University of New York Press, 1995), 235–39.

31. Etkes, *The Gaon*, 11–15.

32. Vinograd, *Thesaurus of the Books of the Vilna Gaon*, 1–173.

33. Stern, *Genius*, 29.

34. Etkes, *The Gaon*, 37–38. Etkes, however, questions whether the Gaon can truly be identified as a precursor of the Haskalah movement, and specifically, as an advocate for the combination of secular with traditional studies. Our discussion does not take a position on whether the Gaon's views were correctly understood (or objectively assessed). Instead, we are solely interested in how subsequent generations of Vilna scholars viewed the Gaon and his advocacy of secular studies. The sources provided by Etkes confirm that many Vilna scholars, and especially those of the Haskalah, perceived the Gaon as the initiator of incorporating secular study into religious learning. Eliakh portrays the Gaon as vocally against the movement. Eliakh, *Ha-Gaon*, vol. 2, 594–639.

35. Etkes, *The Gaon*, 15–16.

36. Lawrence H. Schiffman, "The Vilna Gaon's Methods for the Textual Criticism of Rabbinic Literature," in Lampertas, *The Gaon of Vilna*, 116–27; Speigel, *Hagahot u-Maghim*, 423–72; Stern, *Genius*, 62.

37. Stern, *Genius*, 34–36, 165. The Gaon was central to Jewish Vilna and remained its most important historical figure. His various residences, places of worship and study, and his grave site were all quasi-sacred among the Vilna Jews. See Leyzer Ran, *Jerusalem of Lithuania: Illustrated and Documented* (New York: Vilno Album Committee, 1974), vol. 1, 117–20. Shaul Stampfer, *Families, Rabbis and Education: Traditional Jewish Society in Nineteenth-Century Eastern Europe* (Oxford: Littman Library of Jewish Civilization, 2010), 324–41. In 1825, a few decades after the Gaon's death, his portrait (albeit imagined, since the Gaon never sat for his portrait) was drawn by Polish painter Józef Hilary Glowacki, and was then (in different iterations) mass produced and in high demand across the European continent. Stern, *Genius*, 145–46. The Gaon's portrait was displayed not only in Jewish homes, but also in Jewish communal institutions. For example, in a 1918 photograph of the Vilna Jewish Central Committee, the Glowacki portrait of the Gaon hangs behind the committee. Ran, *Jerusalem of Lithuania*, vol. 1, 133.

38. Perl, *Rabbi Naftali Zvi Yehuda Berlin*, 127–37; cf. Stampfer, "The Image of the Ga'on," 41–61; Etkes, *The Gaon*, 9.

39. Levin, *Aliyot Eliyahu*, 70.

40. Norman Lamm, *Torah Lishmah: Study of Torah for Torah's Sake in the Work of Rabbi Hayyim Volozhin and His Contemporaries* (New York: Ktav, 1989).

41. Etkes, *The Gaon*, 177–202.

42. Shaul Stampfer, *Ha-Yeshiva ha-Litait be-Heithavusta* (Jerusalem: Merkaz Zalman Shazar, 2005), 44–49, Etkes, *The Gaon*, 202–8.

43. Stampfer, *Ha-Yeshiva*, 57–58; Etkes, *The Gaon*, 226–27.

44. Ibid., 269n122.

45. Mordechai Zalkin, "Ir shel Torah—Torah ve-Limudeha be-Merhav ha-Ironi ha-Lita'i be-Me'ah ha-Teshah-esreih," in *Yeshivot u-Batei Midrashot*, ed. Immanuel Etkes (Jerusalem: Merkaz Zalman Shazar, 2007), 146–59.

46. Yaakov Barit, *Toldot Ya'aqov* (Vilna: 1883), 6.

47. See, generally, Israel Zinberg, *A History of Jewish Literature*, vol. 11: *The Haskalah Movement in Russia*, trans. and ed. Bernard Martin (Cincinnati: Hebrew Union College Press, 1978), 3–169.

48. Freeze, *Everyday Jewish Life*, 11–29.

49. Cohen, *Vilna*, 266–68.

50. A number of scientific and medical books were translated by Vilna scholars or printed in Vilna. Mordechai Zalkin, "Scientific Literature and Cultural Transformation in Nineteenth-Century East European Society," *Aleph*, no. 5 (2005), 255–57, 260–62, 265–72.

51. Katz, *Words on Fire*, 228–29.

52. Lara Lempertienė, "The Transformations in the Culture of Reading amongst Lithuanian Jews in the Second Half of the Nineteenth Century—First Half of the Twentieth Century," *Straipsniai*, http://www.zurnalai.vu.lt/knygotyra/article /download/10016/7873.

53. Cohen, *Vilna*, 316; Shmuel Feiner, "Nineteenth-Century Jewish Historiography: The Second Track," in *Studies in Contemporary Jewry*, vol. 10: *Reshaping the Past: Jewish History and the Historians* (Oxford: Oxford University Press, 1994), 36–39.

54. Michael Stanislawski, *For Whom Do I Toil?: Judah Leib Gordon and the Crisis of Russian Jewry* (New York: Oxford University Press, 1988).

55. Cohen, *Vilna*, 313–14.

56. Ibid., 317–18; Olga Litvak, *Haskalah: The Romantic Movement* (New Brunswick, NJ: Rutgers University Press, 2012), 136–46.

57. Cohen, *Vilna*, 324–25; Katz, *Words on Fire*, 205.

58. Cohen, *Vilna*, 325; Katz, *Words on Fire*, 199–200.

59. Dovid Katz, *The Kingdom of the Seven Litvaks* (Vilnius: International Cultural Program Center, 2009), 32–33.

60. Cohen, *Vilna*, 270–71.

61. Only one other press in Zhitomir was permitted to operate. Susanne Marten-Finnis, *Vilna as a Centre of the Modern Jewish Press, 1840–1928: Aspirations, Challenges, and Progress* (Oxford: Peter Lang, 2004), 25.

62. The press had published three earlier editions, but the 1880 edition was its most significant.

63. The Gaon's comments were first included in the Vienna, 1806, edition. But the comments do not appear on every tractate, and the manuscript used was not in the Gaon's hand. Speigel, *Hagahot u-Magihim*, 430–44.

64. The Romm Press was founded in 1789 in Grodno and moved to Vilna in 1799. From 1871 on, the press was known as the "Widow and Brothers Romm." Hayim Liberman, *Ohel Rochel* (New York: Empire Press, 1980), 217. Shmuel Feigensohn was the editor of the Romm Press for many years and wrote a history of the press, which

first appeared in part in the journal *Ha-Sefer* 1 (1954), 27–33; *Ha-Sefer* 2–3 (1955), 46–57. The complete article appears in Shmuel Feigensohn, *Jewish Lithuania*, vol. 1, 270–302; Hayim bar-Daayan, "Introduction," *Jewish Lithuania*, 268–69. In 1920 Mathus Rapoport became the manager and part owner of the press. He remained in that position until July 7, 1941, three weeks after the Nazis occupied Vilna, when they shot him. The Nazis sold the Romm Press printing plates to be melted down and used for armaments. Joshua Starr, "Jewish Cultural Property under Nazi Control," *Jewish Social Studies* 12, no. 1 (1950), 39. See also David E. Fishman, *Book Smugglers*, 71; "Bericht vom dem Arbeitsergebnis der juedischen Arbeitsgruppe beim Einsatzstab RR Wilna," February 18–June 8, 1942, Lithuanian Central State Archive, f. 633, op. 1, del. 5 (listing Romm plates among the items captured by the Nazis). Regarding the Vilna Shas, see Michael Stanislawski, "The 'Vilna Shas' and East European Jewry," ed. S. Mintz and Goldstein, *Printing the Talmud* (New York: Yeshiva University Museum, 2005), 97–102.

65. Stanislawski, "The 'Vilna Shas,'" 97–102.

66. Zinberg, *The Haskalah Movement in Russia*, 29.

67. Joshua Mondshein, "Kitvei Yad ve-Hakhanah le-Defus be-Bet ha-Almanah ve-ha-Ahim Romm," *Alei Sefer* 6–7 (1979), 187–97; *Alei Sefer* 8 (1980), 124–36 (discussing publications of the Romm Press); see also Pinhas Kohn, "A History of the Romm Printing House in Vilna" [Hebrew], *Kiryat Sefer* 12 (1935), 109–14; Zeev Gries, "Romm Family," in *YIVO Encyclopedia of Jews in Eastern Europe*, accessed May 1, 2017, http://www.yivoencyclopedia.org/article.aspx/Romm_Family.

68. Katz, *Words on Fire*, 194–96.

69. Jonathan D. Sarna, "Jewish Culture Comes to America," *Jewish Studies* 42 (2003–2004), 52. In 1862 Alexander II rescinded the restrictions on Hebrew printing, and three rival presses opened in Vilna, yet the Romm remained the leading press. This was in part attributable to its investment in new technologies that enabled it to print more books faster and cheaper. Chaim Freidberg, *Toldot ha-Defus ha-Ivri be-Polin* (Tel Aviv: Gutenberg, 1950), 129.

70. Cohen, *Vilna*, 323.

71. Carol Diament, "The First Hebrew Newspaper and Its Significance," *Hebrew Studies* 25 (1984), 104–25; Lempertienė, "Transformations in the Culture of Reading," 40.

72. For examples, see Zinberg, *The Haskalah Movement in Russia*, 36–38, 57–58, 79–83.

73. Olga Litvak, *Haskalah* (New Brunswick, NJ: Rutgers University Press, 2012), 130–33; Levin, *The Litvaks*, 27–28.

74. Litvak, *Haskalah*, 131–47.

75. Cohen, *Vilna*, 337; Briedus, *Vilnius*, 149.

76. Briedus, *Vilnius*, 138.

77. Jozefas Frankas, *Atsiminimai apie Vilniu*, trans. Genovitė Druckutė (Vilnius: Mintis, 2001), 49–52 (quoted in Briedus, *Vilnius*, 87).

78. Joshua D. Zimmerman, *Poles, Jews, and the Politics of Nationality: The Bund and the Polish Socialist Party in Late Tsarist Russia, 1892–1914* (Madison: University of Wisconsin Press, 2004); Cohen, *Vilna*, 342–57.

79. Marten-Finnis, *Vilna as a Centre*, 51–58.

80. See Zinberg, *The Haskalah Movement in Russia*, 35–38 (discussing Levinzohn); Feiner, "Introduction," *Me-Haskalah Lohmet*, 32–33 (discussing Fuenn).

81. Katz, *Kingdom*, 37.

82. Katz, *Seven Litvaks*, 37–38.

83. Ibid., 38.

84. Zalkin, "Wilno," 227.

85. Cohen, *Vilna*, 346–48.

86. Levin, *The Litvaks*, 10.

87. Israel Klausner, *Vilna, Yerushalayim d'Lita: Dorot ha-Ahronim 1881–1939* (Lohame ha-Geta'ot, Israel: Lohame, 1988), 445–566 (discussing Vilna's associations, groups, and guilds); Ran, *Jerusalem of Lithuania*, vol. 1, 185–219, provides photos of many of these groups. For a photo of the Karaite community, see ibid., 46. Dov Liftz, "Ha-Kara'im be-Lita," in Klausner, *Yahadut Lita*, vol. 1, 138–50. Their inclusion in the community is particularly striking as some questioned the Karaites' Jewish bona-fides. Indeed, the Nazis treated the Karaites as a unique group. Warren Green, "The Fate of the Crimean Jewish Communities: Ashkenazim, Krimchaks and Karaites," *Jewish Social Studies* 46, no. 2 (Spring 1984), 169–76. Philip Friedman, "The Karaites under Nazi Rule," in *On the Track of Tyranny*, ed. Max Beloff (Freeport, NY: Books for Libraries Press, 1971), 97–123. Tapani Harviainen, "The Karaites in Contemporary Lithuania and the Former USSR," in *Karaite Judaism*, ed. Meira Polliack (Leiden: Brill, 2003), 827–54.

88. Kuznitz, "On the Jewish Street," 72.

89. Ibid., 72–73.

90. Cohen, *Vilna*, 104.

91. For a photo of the entrance, see Ran, *Jerusalem of Lithuania*, vol. 1, 64. Maps of the courtyard appear in Cohen, *Vilna*, illustration no. 2; Ran, *Jerusalem of Lithuania*, vol. 1, 105; Cohen-Mushlin, *Synagogues in Lithuania N-Z*, 283. The map's depiction of the Strashun Library, however, "is misleading." See ibid., 341n1.

92. Cohen, *Vilna*, 105.

93. Carol Herselle Krinsky, *Synagogues of Europe: Architecture, History, Meaning* (New York: Architectural History Foundation and Massachusetts Institute of Technology, 1985), 223, listing assumed dates of building.

94. Cohen-Mushlin, *Synagogues in Lithuania N-Z*, 284.

95. Cohen, *Vilna*, 105; Krinsky, *Synagogues*, 225, and fig. 93.

96. Cohen-Mushlin, *Synagogues in Lithuania N-Z*, 286; Krinsky, *Synagogues*, 225.

97. Cohen-Mushlin, *Synagogues in Lithuania N-Z*, 285; Krinsky, *Synagogues*, 224–25. Krinsky reverses the number of column types and counts only four Tuscan columns (ibid., 225, fig. 93), apparently based on a description of the columns in a 1786 rendering by Francizsek Smuglewicz of the Great Synagogue. Smuglewicz's rendering, however, "shows a structure which differs from that captured on the photographs from the first half of the 20th century." Accordingly, "one may suppose that Smuglewicz's drawing . . . does not produce a precise depiction of its 18th-century appearance." Cohen-Mushlin, *Synagogues in Lithuania N-Z*, 286. The design of the *bimah* "is sometimes attributed to the most popular Vilnius architect of the

18th century, Johann Christoph Glaubitz (ca. 1700–67)." Cohen-Mushlin, *Synagogues in Lithuania N-Z*, 286.

98. Krinsky, *Synagogues*, 225; Cohen, *Vilna*, 106. For photographs of the ark, see Ran, *Jerusalem of Lithuania*, vol. 1, 109; Cohen, *Vilna*, illustration n8, opposite p. 175; Cohen-Mushlin, *Synagogues in Lithuania, N-Z*, 284–90. The iron doors survived the Holocaust and are now displayed in the Vilna Gaon Jewish State Museum. Ibid., 285.

99. Reproduced in Cohen-Mushlin, *Synagogues in Lithuania N-Z*, 288.

100. Cohen, *Vilna*, 105.

101. Broides, *Vilnius*, 184.

102. In 1635 a mob of Christians looted the Great Synagogue, and in 1640, the tailors' guild donated an iron door for the prayer hall entrance. Cohen-Mushlin, *Synagogues in Lithuania N-Z*, 284.

103. Elchanan Reiner, "Hon, Ma'amad Hevrati, u-Talmud Torah: Ha-Kloyz ba-Hevrah ha-Yahudit Be-Mizrah Europa be-Meot ha-Sheva Esrei le-Shemonah Esrei," *Zion* 58, no. 3 (1993): 287–328. The etymology of the term *kloyz* traces its roots to the Latin *clusa*: cloister. Cohen, *Vilna*, 108. Although the Gaon's Kloyz was incorporated three years after his death, there is evidence that he studied there during his lifetime and that it was used by his students. See Shlomo Zalman Hevlin, "Pinkas Kloyz Ha Gr"a be-Vilna," *Yeshurun* 16 (2005): 746–60; cf. Cohen, *Vilna*, 111–12. Klausner, *The Jewish Community*, 78–79 (who question whether the Gaon ever studied in the kloyz).

104. Cohen-Mushlin, *Synagogues in Lithuania N-Z*, 297–302; Krinsky, *Synagogues of Europe*, 223; Klausner, *The Jewish Community*, 80 (describing the interior of the kloyz). Marc Chagall painted the only known color depiction, reproduced in Cohen-Mushlin, *Synagogues in Lithuania N-Z*, 301 and fig. 66.

105. Ran, *Jerusalem of Lithuania*, vol. 1, 111 (photograph of the chair). The chair survived the Holocaust and now resides at the Spertus Institute in Chicago. Cohen-Mushlin, *Synagogues in Lithuania N-Z*, 301.

106. Lunski, *Me-ha-Ghetto Vilna'i: Tipushim u-Tzlalim* (Vilna: Agudat-ha-Soferim veha-Zhurnalistim ha-Ivrim be-Vilna, 1921), 53–54. For a description of a visit to the Gaon's Kloyz just before the Holocaust, see Asher Katzman, "Zikhronot me'Hakloyz' shel ha-Gaon me-Vilna ZTsUK"L," *Yeshurun* 6 (1999): 685–90.

107. Lunksi, *Me-ha-Ghetto Vilna*, 53.

108. Kuznitz, *The Making of Modern Jewish Culture*, 134.

109. Y. Rubin, "Unzer Vilne," in *Unzer Tog* 9 (quoted and translated in Kuznitz, *The Making of Modern Jewish Culture*, 134).

110. Dovid Eynhorn, "Yerushalim d'lite," in *Vilne: A Zamelbukh Gevidmet Der Shtot Vilne*, ed. Yefim Yeshurin (New York: Vilner Brentsh 367 Arbeter-Ring, 1935), 788 (quoted in Kuznitz, "On the Jewish Street," 83).

111. Kuznitz, *The Making of Modern Jewish Culture*, 135.

112. Hillel Noah Maggid-Steinschneider, *Ir Vilna* (Vilna: Almanah ve-Ahim Romm, 1900), ix.

113. Kuznitz, "On the Jewish Street," 66.

114. Dov Schidorsky, "The Emergence of Jewish Public Libraries in Nineteenth-Century Palestine," *Libri* 32, no. 1 (1982), 1.

115. Earlier Jewish libraries were at best sponsored by the Jewish community, but

they were not truly communal property. Jeffrey Veidlinger, *Jewish Public Culture in the Late Russian Empire* (Bloomington: Indiana University Press, 2009), 24–39. For other examples of Jewish libraries and the distinction between the modern definition of public libraries, see Schidorsky, "Emergence of Jewish Public Libraries," 1–40. Other historical examples appear in Zeev Gries, *The Book in the Jewish World 1700–1900* (Oxford: Littman Library of Jewish Civilization, 2010), 66–67; Colette Sirat, *Hebrew Manuscripts of the Middle Ages*, ed. and trans. Nicholas de Lange (Cambridge: Cambridge University Press, 2002), 257–58. For book lists inventorying the collections of private and semipublic libraries, see Nehemya Allony, *Ha-Sifri'ah ha-Yehudit bimei ha-Benayim: Reshimot Sefarim me-Genizat Kahir*, ed. Miriam Frankel and Haggai Ben-Shammai (Jerusalem: Machon Ben Tzvi le-Heker Kehilot Yisra'el be-Mizrach, 2006); S. D. Goitein, *A Mediterranean Society: The Jewish Communities of the World as Portrayed in the Documents of the Cairo Geniza* (Berkeley: University of California Press, 1993), vol. 2, 206, 248.

116. Veidlinger, *Jewish Public Culture*, 24–66.

117. Gries, *The Book*, 66.

118. Veidlinger, *Jewish Public Culture*, 25–26.

119. For biographical information, see David Assaf, "Introduction," in *Journey to a Nineteenth-Century Shtetl: The Memoirs of Yekhezkel Kotik*, ed. David Assaf (Detroit: Wayne State University Press, 2002), 95n127.

120. Avraham Hirsch Kotik, "Dos Bukh un Der Leyzer," in *Der Fraynd*, July 8, 1911 (translated in Veidlinger, *Jewish Public Culture*, 28).

121. Only a partial catalog of Friedland's library has been published. Samuel Weiner, *Kohelet Moshe Aryeh Leyb Friedland: Rehimat Kol ha-Sefarim ha-Ivrim Nidpasim be-Kitve-Yad, ha-Nimtsa'im be-Asefat-Friedland be-Otsar Muzeom ha-Aziaici shel ha-Akademia le-Mada'im be-St. Peterburg* (Petropolis: Commission for the Imperial Academy of Sciences, 1893–1902), vols. 1–7.

122. David Karlin to Moses Aryeh Löeb, 25 Kislev, 5640 [November 19, 1880], in Abraham Isaac Katz, "Moshe Aryeh Leib Friedland ve-Sifri'ato ha-Meforsemet," *Perakim* (New York: n.p., 1963), 19–21. The dates provided in Katz's article are in error. Friedman wrote Friedland in 1890 and not 1880, and Friedland's response was in 1892. See Eitam Henkin, "Me-Hibbat Tzion le-Anti-Tzionut: Temurot be-Orthodoksiah ha-Mizrah Europit — Ha-Rav Dovid Friedman me-Karlin (1915–1928) ke-Mikreh Mivhan" (Phd diss., University of Tel Aviv, Tel Aviv, 2013), 22n60.

123. Moses Aryeh Löeb Friedland to David Karlin, 5 Nissan, 5642 [March 25, 1882], in Katz, "Friedland's Library," 19–22.

124. A. Yudels, "In der Alter Strashun Bibliotek," *Literarishe Bletter*, December 17, 1926, 850; Cohen-Mushlin, *Synagogues in Lithuania N-Z*, 289.

2. Mattityahu Strashun: The Book Collector

1. Maggid-Steinschneider, *Ir Vilna*, 250; Tzvi Harkavy, "Toldot ha-RaSh"Sh u-Ketavav," in Samuel Strashun, *Mekorei ha-Rambam* (Jerusalem: Hotza'ot ha-Sefarim Eretz Yisraelit, 1957), 53. See also 53n3 for additional biographical sources. Some incorrectly convert the Hebrew date to the Gregorian 1794. Zalkin, "Samuel and

Mattityahu," 3; Shor, *Likutei Shoshanim*, 15. A Russian archival document from 1813, however, indicates that Samuel was born in 1796. Genrich Agronowskii, *Jewish Pages from the Lithuanian Archives* (Kaunus: Saugi pradžia, 2017), 202.

2. Harkavy, "Toldot," 53. In the nineteenth century, "very early marriage was never common among all the Jews of eastern Europe, but they were widespread within the elite subgroup." Shaul Stampfer, *Families, Rabbis, and Education: Traditional Jewish Society in Nineteenth-Century Eastern Europe* (Oxford: The Littman Library of Jewish Civilization, 2010), 19, 183. Prior to the nineteenth century, Jews did not use surnames. Rather they were simply referred to by their given name and their father's name, i.e., Samuel ben David. Eugene M. Avrutin, "The Politics of Jewish Legibility: Documentation Practices and Reform during the Reign of Nicholas I," *Jewish Social Studies* 11, no. 2 (Winter 2005), 136–49. Within Jewish circles at times, Samuel was still referred to as Samuel Zaskevichini. Abraham Danzig, *Benat Adam* (sha'ar Orakh Hayim, no. 10). Sara predeceased him, and he eventually remarried. David Radner, "Sheni Tsanta'rot ha-Zahav," *Keneset ha-Gedolim*, vol. 1 (Warsaw: Chaim Kalter, 1890), 24.

3. David was a distiller. After his death in 1842, his three sons and daughter (Samuel's wife) inherited and continued to operate the business. Samuel also participated in the management of the business. Steinschnieder, *Ir Vilna*, 250–51; Radner, "Sheni," 23; Agranovskii, *Jewish Pages*, 203 (archival documents from 1856 refer to Samuel as a distiller).

4. Maggid-Steinschneider, *Ir Vilna*, 121–22. For a partial list of students, see 121n2.

5. Rafael Katzenellenbogen, "RaSh"Sh le-Shitato," in *Mekorei ha-Rambam le-RaSh"Sh*, ed. Tzvi Harkavy (Jerusalem: Ha-Sefarim ha-Erets Yisraelim, 1957), 64.

6. Speigel, *Hagahot u-Magihim*, 460–62.

7. Ibid., 39–157. Shua Englman, "Rabbi Samuel Strashun (HaRaShaSh) ve-Hagahotov le-Talmud Bavli" (PhD diss., Bar-Ilan University, Ramat Gan, 2008), 115–70. Regarding the various historic positions regarding amending and correcting Jewish texts, see Speigel, *Hagahot u-Magihim*.

8. Ibid., 421–22.

9. Zalkin, "Samuel and Mattityahu Strashun," 6–7.

10. Samuel Strashun, *Midrash Rabba* (Vilna: Romm Press, 1856). Additional notes were incorporated throughout Zvi Hirsch Katzenellenbogen's commentary on midrash and in a special appendix. Zvi Hirsch Katzenellenbogen, *Netivot Olam* (Vilna: Romm Press, 1859), 225–28.

11. Perl, *Pillar of Volozhin*, 45, 49.

12. For examples, see Englman, "Rabbi Samuel Strashun," 221–40.

13. Ibid., 222; Radner, "Sheni," 24.

14. Reuven Fahn, *Kitvei Re'uven Fahn: Helek Sheni: Pirkei Haskalah* (Stanislawow: Graphika, 1937), 43–47; Israel Zinberg, *History of Jewish Literature: The Berlin Haskalah*, trans. and ed. Bernard Martin (Cincinatti: Hebrew Union College Press, 1976), vol. 8, 182–84.

15. Abraham Meir Habermann, "He'arot ve-Hashlamot," in Nathan Nata Rabinovich, *Ma'amar 'al Hadpasat ha-Talmud: Toldot Hadpasat ha-Talmud*, ed. Abraham Meir Habermann (Jerusalem: Mossad Harav Kook, 1952), 239–41. According to the legend,

Ben Zeev was caught red-handed in the press on Shabbat. When he was discovered, he ran outside to the outhouse to hide, whereupon he died.

16. Englman, "Rabbi Samuel Strashun," 228-30, 231-32.

17. Ibid., 234. Shnayer Z. Leiman, "R. Moses Schick: The Hatam Sofer's Attitude toward Mendelssohn's Biur," *Tradition* 24, no. 3 (Spring 1989): 83-86; Meir Hildesheimer, "Moses Mendelssohn in Nineteenth-Century Rabbinical Literature," *Proceedings of the American Academy for Jewish Research* 55 (1988): 79-133; Peretz Sandler, *Ha-Bi'ur le-Torah shel Moses Mendelssohn ve-Si'ato Hithavuto ve-Hashpa'ato* (Jerusalem: Mekor, 1984), 194-219. According to some reports, the Gaon also read the *Biur*. Stern, *Gaon*, 70. If that is correct, Samuel's usage of the *Biur*, like that of other aspects of his scholarship, may have been based on the Gaon's intellectual program.

18. Englman, "Rabbi Samuel Strashun," 234-36.

19. Ibid., 29n148. The passage originally appeared in Rafael Katzenellenbogen, "Ha-RaSh"Sh le-Shitato," in *Mekorei ha-Rambam*, 64. Katzenellenbogen's article was reprinted without the passage in 1972 in the journal *Ha-Moriah* and in a collection of Katzenellenbogen's writings, published by his son, Ya'akov Gershon. Rafael Katzenellenbogen, "Ha-Rashash le-Shitato," *Moriah* 10-12 (1972): 98; Rafael Katzenellenbogen, "Ha-Rashash le-Shitato," in Ya'akov Gershon, *Be'er Ro'ei* (Jerusalem: Midrash Rabbi Rafael, 1981), 86. Engleman collects Samuel's citations to the *Biur*; see Engleman, "Rabbi Samuel Strashun," 237n1245.

20. Immanuel Etkes, "Teudah beYisrael—Bein Temurah le-Mesorot," in Isaac Baer Levinsohn, *Teudah beYisrael*, ed. Immanuel Etkes (Jerusalem: Merkaz Zalman Shazar, 1977), 3.

21. Etkes, *Vilna Gaon and Haskalah*, 38-39; Englman, "Rabbi Shmuel Strashun," 238.

22. Etkes, *Vilna Gaon and Haskalah*, 252-253n82. According Eliach, Poswoler's endorsement was coerced and the result of government intervention. Eliach, *HaGaon*, 3:1305-1306. Because Poswoler granted endorsements to other Haskalah works, there is little reason to question the authenticity of the endorsement to *Teudah be-Yisrael*. See David Assaf, *Untold Tales of the Hasidim: Crisis and Discontent in the History of Hasidim* (Waltham, MA: Brandeis University Press, 2012), 22-23 and nn45-46.

23. He later faced opposition from other Vilna rabbis when he attempted to print another one of his books. Zinberg, *Haskalah Movement in Russia*, 47-48.

24. Levinsohn published a second copy of his appeal in Vilna. Levinsohn, *Teudah beYisrael*, "Prenumeranten," n.p.; Zalkin, "Samuel and Mattityahu Strashun," 8. See also Zalkin, *Be-Alot ha-Shahar: Ha-Haskalah ha-Yehudit ba-Impiriah ha-Rusit be-Meah ha-Tesha Esrei* (Jerusalem: Magnes Press, 2000), 236 (examining other Haskalah books' *prenumeranten*). Berl Kagan, *Sefer Prenumeranten: Vegvayzer tsu Prenumerirte Hebreishe Sefarim un Zayere Hotmim fun 8,767 Kehilot in Ayrope un Tsafon-Afrike* (New York: Library of the Jewish Seminary and Ktav, 1975) (an encyclopedia of *prenumeranten*). Generally, subscription lists in Hebrew books are a valuable, yet underutilized, source of history. See, e.g., Shnayer Z. Leiman, "A Note on R. Bezalel Alexandrov's [*Mishkan Betzalel*] and Its *Prenumeranten*," *Seforim Blog*, November 28, 2016, http://seforim.blogspot.com/2016/11/a-note-on-r-bezalel-alexandrovs-and-its.html.

25. Zinberg, *Haskalah Movement in Russia*, 28–52.

26. Harkavy, *Le-Heker Mishpahot*, 42.

27. Freeze, *Everyday Jewish Life*, 420. The original source uses Garkavy, the Russian version of Harkavy. The Latin letter *h* is transliterated generally to the Cyrillic Г, Ge. Regarding the source of the surname, see Harkavy, *Le-Heker*, 28n3.

28. According to one scholar, Benjamin Nathans, by the end of the nineteenth century, Jewish university students likely outnumbered those studying in yeshivot. Benjamin Nathans, *Beyond the Pale: The Jewish Encounter with Late Imperial Russia* (Berkeley: University of California Press, 2004), 234. But as Nathans concedes, estimates of yeshiva enrollment are uncertain, making it difficult to accurately compare attendance at university vis-à-vis yeshiva. Ibid.

29. Lunski, "Ha-'Kloyzim' be-Vilna, Hatzer Bet ha-Kneset ve-Rehov ha-Yehudim," *Ha-Tsefirah*, July 4, 1921, 138; Cohen-Mushlin, *Synagogues in Lithuania N-Z*, 336–37. For many years, the kloyz held Samuel's copies of the Talmud containing his extensive notes and posted a "beautiful" plaque commemorating "his genealogy and good deeds." Lunksi, "Ha-Kloyzim," 138. For a description of Samuel's daily class, see Radner, "Sheni," 24.

30. Freeze, *Everyday Jewish Life*, 420; Nathans, *Beyond the Pale*, 242–43 (reproducing Harkavy's portrait and discussing him and other Jewish students at Moscow University).

31. Tzvi Hirsch Katzenellenbogen, *Netivot Olam*, 197.

32. Lithuanian National Archives, f. 380, op. 120, d. 596, 1.14–15 (quoted in Agranowskii, *Jewish Pages*, 212).

33. Agranovskii, *Vil'nius. Po sledam Litovskogo Ierusalima. Pamiatnye mesta evreiskoi istorii i kul'tury. Putivoditel'*, 373.

34. For biographical sources, see Harkavy, *Toldot*, 56n13.

35. Pludermacher, *Zikaron le-Hakham*, 13. In one of his early articles, Mattityahu discusses Johannes Buxdorf's Latin translation of R. Judah ha-Levi's *Kuzari* at length. Mattityahu Strashun, "Letter," *Pirhei Tsafon*. Mattityahu's multilingual fluency is more extensive than that of some contemporary maskilim. See Zalkin, *Be-A'lot*, 297–98.

36. Pludermacher, *Zikaron le-Hakham*, 13–14.

37. Upon their publication, Mattityahu received laudatory letters from across the Orthodox religious spectrum, including "rabbis, among them the greatest of the time, and Hasidic leaders." Ibid., 30. He corresponded with scholars as far afield as Baghdad. Harkavy, "Mattityahu Strashun 1811–1886," 346.

38. He wrote notes for additional tractates, but he died before preparing them for publication. Pludermacher, *Zikaron le-Hakham*, 31.

39. His notes on these books appeared in eight books. Pludermacher, *Shirei Minhah*, 40–41.

40. Perl, *The Pillar*, 56. Some of Mattityahu's scholarship is included in others' books. See Harkavy, "Rebi Mattityahu Strashun," *Areshet*, 427n7.

41. See, e.g., Mattityahu Strashun, *Mattat Yah*, 9, 14, 29, 34, 52, 85, 110, 144. Mattityahu was fluent in Polish. Pludermacher, *Zikaron le-Hakham*, 13 and n2.

42. Strashun, *Mattat Yah*, 46–47.

43. Ibid., 46, 56, 59. In that vein, Mattityahu took a keen interest in publishing important manuscripts and bringing to light heretofore unknown textual variants and opinions, and he joined the Society for the Mekitzei Nerdamim (Awaking the Sleeping) an organization with that mission.

44. Reading, and certainly actively participating with, Haskalah-related newspapers was considered inconsistent with ultra-Orthodox values and was grounds for expulsion from Volozhin Yeshiva. Shaul Stampfer, *The Lithuanian Yeshiva, Revised and Expanded Edition* (Jerusalem: Zalman Shazar Center for Jewish History, 2005), 176.

45. His first recorded work was his notes to his father-in-law's brother's book *Marpeh le-Am*. His notes were included in the second edition. Yehuda Betzalel Eilishberg, *Marpeh le-Am* (Vilna: R' Menaham Man br' Barukh Z"L, 1834). Despite Mattityahu's desire for anonymity, his articles were so well regarded that there were many requests for him to reveal himself. Eventually, someone elected to decipher one of Mattityahu's pseudonyms and published his name in one of the newspapers to which he was a regular contributor. Yitzhak Mikhalavski, "Ve-Hu ve-He," *Ha-Maggid*, February 15, 1866.

46. Pludermacher, *Shirei Minhah*, 39–72. For additions to Pludermacher's list, see Harkavy, "Toldot ha-RaSh"Sh," 57n15-16. A selection of Mattityahu's articles was reprinted in 1969. Mattityahu Strashun, *Rebi Mattityahu Strashun: Mivhar Ketavim* (Jerusalem: Mossad Harav Kook, 1969). Pludermacher's bibliography is not intended to be comprehensive. He only catalogs Mattityahu's articles in three journals.

47. Pludermacher, *Shirei Minhah*, entries 264–300.

48. Ibid., 78, 91, 92, 94, 199, 201.

49. There is some confusion regarding Fuenn's birth year. Some record it as 1818 and others as 1823. Feiner, "Introduction," *Me-Haskalah Lohemet*, 1; Maggid-Steinschneider, *Ir Vilna* 2, 157 and n2. In his autobiography, however, Fuenn provides that "on the night of the first of Sukkot, [5]678 or [56]79 [1817 or 1818], I saw the earthy light of life in Vilna." Samuel Joseph Fuenn, *Dor ve-Dorshav*, in Feiner, *Me-Hasklah Lohemet*, 50.

50. Samuel Joseph Fuenn, *Kiryah Ne'emanah: Korot Adat Yisra'el be-Ir Vilna YTz"V* (Vilna: Yosef Reuven bar Menaham Romm, 1860), ix–xxiv.

51. Mattityahu Strashun, "Rehovot Kiryah," in Samuel Joseph Fuenn, *Kiryah Ne'emanah: Korot Adat Yisra'el be-Ir Vilna, ve-Tziyunim le-Nefashot Ge'oneha, Hakhmeha, Sofreha u-Neveha*, ed. Hillel Noah Maggid-Steinschneider (Vilna: Yitzhak Funk, 1915), 282–98.

52. Strashun, "Rehovot Kiryah," 298. Mattityahu's personal copy of *Kiryah Ne'emanah* was entirely covered in marginalia, yet those additional notes were never published. Pludermacher, *Zikaron le-Hakham*, 21n1. Mattityahu's personal copy of *Kiryah Ne'emanah* is at the Lithuanian National Library and contains copious marginalia. The author was unable to review that copy to determine if those notes are the ones referenced by Mattityahu because it is undergoing digitization.

53. Joanna Weinberg, "Translator's Introduction," in Azariah de Rossi, *The Light of the Eyes*, trans. Joanna Weinberg (New Haven, CT: Yale University Press, 2001), xiii–xlv.

54. Leopold Zunz, "Toldot Rabbi Azariah min ha-Adumim," *Kerem Hemed* 5 (1841), 131–58.

55. Leopold Zunz, "Tosefot le-Toldot R' Azariah min ha-Adumim," *Kerem Hemed* 7 (1843), 121–22.

56. Mattityahu Strashun, "Rehovot Kiryah," 282–284n11. Weinberg appears unaware of this source.

57. Ibid.

58. Compare Marks, *Gedoylim*, 360 with Marks, *Be-Mehitzatam*, 238.

59. Agronowksi, *Jewish Pages*, 203.

60. Ratner, "Shenei," 25. After Mattityahu left his father-in-law's home, he started his own business but went bankrupt. His father-in-law provided additional funds, and Mattityahu opened a very successful clothing and silk business. His wife, Chana, ran most of the day-to-day operations, permitting Mattityahu to continue his studies without disruption. Ibid.

61. Mattityahu Strashun to Isaac Baer Levinsohn, 1838, in Dov Baer Nathanson, *Sefer ha-Zikhronot* (Warsaw: Y. Eletin Nathanson, 1878), 49. Mattityahu was twenty at the time he wrote to Levinsohn and stated that he first read *Teudah beYisrael* "six years" prior. The second part of the same letter, which appears in a collection of Levinsohn's letters, is dated 1837, indicating that Mattityahu would have been fourteen when he read *Teudah*. Isaac Ber Levinsohn, *Be'er Yitzhak: Sefer ha-Kolel Igrot Raso ve-Shov ben Yitzhak Be'er Levinsohn u-Ven Doro* (Warsaw: Y. Eletin Nathanson, 1899), 42–43. The discrepancy in dates is not addressed in either book. Nonetheless, because Mattityahu discusses Levinsohn's *Bet Yehudah*, which was published in 1838, the date on the letter in *Sefer ha-Zikhronot* is most likely correct. Mattityahu was responding to a letter that Levinsohn had sent. Levinsohn's original letter is preserved in the YIVO Archives. YIVO Archives, RG 223, folder 34a.1.

62. Mattityahu Strashun to Isaac Baer Levinsohn, 1838, in Nathanson, *Sefer ha-Zikhronot*, 49. Levinsohn's book similarly influenced many of Mattityahu's contemporaries. See Fuenn, *Dor ve-Dorshav*, 71.

63. Mattityahu Strashun to Isaac Baer Levinsohn, in Nathanson, *Sefer ha-Zikhronot*, 49. Despite Mattityahu's appreciation of Levinsohn and his scholarship, Mattitayhu had no qualms about pointing out errors in Levinsohn's conclusions. Indeed, in that letter, Mattityahu noted errors in *Bet Yehudah* and later published a lengthier list of similar errors that appear in Levinsohn's *Shorashei Levanon* (*Bet ha-Otsar*). Mattityahu Strashun, "He'arah," *Pirhei Tsafon* 2 (1844): 194–95.

64. Strashun, *Be'er Yitzhak*, 43–44. The adoption of surnames among the Jews in the Russian Empire in the nineteenth century was itself novel. Eugene M. Avrutin, "The Politics of Jewish Legibility: Documentation Practices and Reform during the Reign of Nicholas I," *Jewish Social Studies* 11, no. 2 (2005), 136–69.

65. The best-known earlier example is Menashe of Ilya. Menashe of Ilya, *Alfei Menashe* (Vilna: Ha-Meshutafim ha-Negidim, 1815), 38–39, 45–46, 72–73.

66. Mattityahu's marriage at fourteen is attested to in his letter to Levinsohn. Isaac Baer Levinsohn, *Be'er Yitzhak: Sefer ha-Kolel Igrot Raso ve-Shov ben Yitzhak Be'er Levinsohn u-Ven Doro* (Warsaw: Y. Eletin Nathanson, 1899), 42–43; Harkavy, "Toldot ha-RaSha"Sh," 56. Pludermacher incorrectly states that Mattityahu married at thir-

teen; his error is repeated by others, including Harkavy on one occasion. Pludermacher, *Zikaron le-Hakham*, 13; Harkavy, "Rebbi Mattityahu Strashun," 346n3; Shor, *Likutei Shoshanim*, 19. Members of the Haskalah predominantly married between ages thirteen and fifteen, although that was less consistent in Vilna. Mordechai Zalkin, *Be-Alot ha-Shahar*, 271.

67. Freeze, *Everyday Jewish Life*, 23.

68. Isaac Barzilay, *Shlomo Yehudah Rapoport [SHI"R] (1790–1867) and His Contemporaries: Some Aspects of Jewish Scholarship of the Nineteenth Century* (Israel: Masada Press, 1969); Nathan Cyprus, *Shlomo Yehuda Rapoport (ShI"R), 1790–1867: Torah, Haskalah ve-Hokhmat Yisrael, ve-Reshitah shel ha-Leumiut ha-Yehudit ha-Modernit*, (PhD diss., Hebrew University, 2012); Meir Hirschkovitz, *MHR"Tz Heyot: Toldot Rebi Tzvi Hirsh Heyot u-Mishnato* (Jerusalem: Mossad Harav Kook, 1972); Bruria Hutner David, *The Dual Role of Rabbi Zvi Hirsch Chajes: Traditionalist and "Maskil"* (PhD diss., Columbia University, New York, 1971). Regarding the form of their scholarship, see Ephraim Chamiel, *The Middle Way: The Emergence of Modern-Religious Trends in Nineteenth-Century Judaism Responses to Modernity in the Philosophy of Z. H. Chajes, S. R. Hirsch, and S. D. Luzzato* (Jerusalem: Karmel, 2011); Ephraim Chamiel, *"The Dual Truth": Studies on Nineteenth-Century Modern Religious Thought and Its Influence on Twentieth-Century Jewish Philosophy* (Jerusalem: Karmel, 2016).

69. Zalkin, *Be-Alot ha-Shahar*, 113–19.

70. Jewish Vilna, however, was not monolithic in its stance toward Haskalah, whether of the Berlin or Vilna type. Vilna's maskilim were treated with suspicion if not outright hostility. This was especially so in the early nineteenth century. Samuel Feiner, introduction to *Me-Hasklah Lohemet le-Hasklah Meshameret*, ed. Samuel Feiner (Jerusalem: Merkaz Dinur, 1993), 7–10; Zalkin, *Be-Alot*.

71. Letter writing was an important medium for maskilim to express their private thoughts among their compatriots without fear of retribution. Zalkin, *Be-Alot ha-Shahar*, 113.

72. Samuel Fuenn to Ohavei Maskil [July 7, 1841], in *Me-Haskalah Lohemet*, 181; Shalom Pludermacher, *Zikaron le-Hakham*, 15; Mark, *Gedoylim*, 364. (The details regarding Mattityahu's role in the school and the shift in policy are censored from the Hebrew translation of Mark's book; cf. Mark, *Be-Mihitzatam*, 240.) Zalkin, *Be-Alot ha-Shahar*, 104. Regarding attempts to establish Haskalah schools in the nineteenth century, see Mordechai Zalkin, "Megamot be-Hitpathut ha-Hinukh ha-Maskili ba-Impiriah ha-Rusit be-Reshit ha-Meah ha-Tesha-Esrei," *Tzion* 62, no. 2 (1997): 133–71. The school was coed. See ibid., 158. In the late eighteenth century, Naftali Wesseley's book *Divrei Shalom ve-Emet* argued for the reformation of the traditional Orthodox pedagogy, and the book was subject to widespread condemnation among the traditionalists. Moshe Samet, *Hadash Asur min ha-Torah: Perakim be-Toldot ha-Orthodoksyah* (Israel: Karmel, 2005), 78–83.

73. Pludermacher, *Zikaron le-Hakham*, 15; Zalkin, "Megamot be-Hitpathut ha-Hinukh," 159. Mattityahu may also have been involved in Vilna's Rabbinical Seminary. Zalkin, *Be-Alot ha-Shahar*, 288; Mordechai Zalkin, "Bet ha-Midrash le-Rabbanim be-Vilne — Bein Dimui le-Metziut," *Gal-Ed: On the History and Culture of Polish Jewry* 14 (1995), 59–72; Erich Haberer, *Jews and Revolution in Nineteenth-Century Russia* (Cam-

bridge: Cambridge University Press, 1995), 73–75. According to Samuel's grandson David Radner, Samuel also supported the rabbinical seminaries. Radner, "Shnei," 24. Harkavy alleges (without any independent evidence) that this is false. Harkavy, "Toldot," 53n5. See also Tuvia Preshel, *Ma'amarei Tuvia: Reshimot Ma'amarim* (Jerusalem: Mossad Harav Kook, 2016), 93–94. These schools were of limited effect. The general Orthodox population was vocally opposed to any notion of a government-sponsored school. Avraam Uri Kovner, "The Vil'na Rabbinical School," in Freeze, *Everyday Jewish Life*, 412.

74. Maggid-Steinschneider, *Ir Vilna* 2, 133n4.

75. [Mattityau Strashun,] ["Note"], *Ha-Maggid*, March 4, 1858, 35. Menashe's biography and the interpretation of his philosophy is the subject of considerable debate. See Moshe Samuel Shapiro, *Moshe Shemuel ve-Doro: Kovetz Ma'asot ve-Iggeroto* (New York: Son of the Author, 1964) 127–36; Zinberg, *Haskalah Movement in Russia*, 3–20; Kamenetsky, "Ha-Gaon Rebi Menashe of Ilya TZt"L," 729–81; Eliach, *Ha-Gaon*, 375, 1293–95.

76. Historical Jewish Press, March 4, 1858, p. 3, http://jpress.nli.org.il/Olive/APA/NLI/sharedpages/SharedView.Page.aspx?sk=49FFB428&href=MGD/1858/03/04&page=3.

77. The petition is quoted and translated in Zinberg, *History of Jewish Literature*, 78–79. Regarding the ban on Jewish dress in the Russian Empire, see Israel Klausner, "Ha-gezerah al tilboshot ha-yehudim, 1844–1850," *Gal-Ed* 6 (1982), 11–26; Avrutin, "The Politics," 149–55.

78. Yaakov Lifschitz, *Zikhron Ya'akov* (Kovno: Neta Halevi Lifschitz, 1924), vol. 1, 135–38, vol. 2, 24. Although Lifschitz is highly critical of those who signed the petition, he apparently ignores Mattityahu's participation. Mattityahu is not mentioned, even though Lifschitz's source is the newspaper *Haynt*, which includes Mattityahu among the signatories. Moreover, long after this issue, Lifschitz continued to speak highly of Mattityahu and was excited to visit and spend time with him. Ibid., vol. 2, 126, 193; vol. 3, 56. Tzvi Harkavy asserts (without any independent verification) that "it is impossible that a gaon and a complete believer, whose beard was untouched, with thick long peyot and long rabbinic clothing, would align with God forbid, the lowly maskil garb" issue. Instead, Mattityahu's signature was forged. Harkavy, *Leheker*, 47n79. Lifschitz too may have dismissed Mattityahu's signature as a forgery or as nonrepresentative of his beliefs.

79. Michael Stanislawski, "Kahal," in *YIVO Encyclopedia of Jews in Eastern Europe*, 2010, http://www.yivoencyclopedia.org/article.aspx/Kahal.

80. Mordechai Zalkin, "Vilnius," in *YIVO Encyclopedia of Jews in Eastern Europe*, 2010, http://www.yivoencyclopedia.org/article.aspx/Vilnius.

81. Pludermacher, *Zikaron le-Hakham*, 25. A record of his appointment is confirmed by a government report on the Jewish communal officials. Lithuanian National Archives, f. 450, op. 7, n. 125, 1–8 (quoted in Genrikh Agranovskii, *Evreiskie stranitsy litovskikh arkhivov* (Kaunas, Lithuania: VsI "Saugi Pradzia" and Green Prints Tipografiia, 2017), 213.

82. Mark, *Gedolim*, 366; Pludermacher, *Zikaron le-Hakham*, 25.

83. Mark, *Gedolim*, 369, cf. *Be-Mehizatam*, 245 (simply mentioning a reform

of the courts without explaining why or what new requirements Mattityahu imposed). Mattityahu was well versed in all aspects of math. Pludermacher, *Zikaron le-Hakham*, 13.

84. Pludermacher, *Zikaron le-Hakham*, 16; Maggid-Steinschneider, *Ir Vilna*, 285; Lithuanian National Archives, f. 937, op. 1, n. 3875, 252–71 (quoted in Agranovskii, *Evreiskie stranitsy litovskikh arkhivov*, 213).

85. Agranovskii, *Evreiskie stranitsy litovskikh arkhivov*, 207.

86. Ibid., 207–8.

87. Mordechai Aaron Günzburg, *Ha-Moriyyah* (Warsaw: Alexander Ginz, 1878), 43–44.

88. Moshe Shimon Antokolski, *Evel Kaved*, 23; Zalkin, *Be-Alot*, 64.

89. Perets Smolenskin, "Ma'asa be-Rusya," *Ha-Shahar*, August 19, 1870, 285 (quoted and translated in Zalkin, "Samuel and Mattityahu," 23).

90. Zalkin, *Be-Alot ha-Shahar*, 62–75, 240–42, 262–90. Perl notes that part of the difficulty in classifying and appreciating Samuel, among others within his circle of scholars, is that they have "yet to receive serious scholarly attention." Perl, *Pillar of Volozhin*, 240.

91. Zalkin, "Samuel and Mattityahu Strashun," 3.

92. Feiner, "Introduction," *Me-Haskalah Lohemet*, 1–47.

93. Zalkin, "Samuel and Mattityahu Strashun," 3 and n23.

94. Shor, *Likutei Shoshanim*, 10.

95. Mark, *Gedoylim*, 359–72.

96. Mark, *Be-Mihtzatam*.

97. Ibid., 237–47.

98. Ibid., 238.

99. See, for example, Zalkin, "Samuel and Mattityahu Strashun," 1–28.

100. Pludermacher, *Zikaron le-Hakham*, 15. Strashun stands in contrast to Hayyim Yosef David Azulai (HIDA), the eighteenth-century itinerant rabbi who, in his travelogue *Ma'agal Tov*, discusses his collecting extensively. Meir Benayahu, *Rebi Hayim Yosef David Azulai: Helek Rishon: Toldot Hayav* (Jerusalem: Mossad Harav Kook, 1959), 82–83. A partial list of Azulai's library was published in 1872. Samuel Schönblum, *Catalogue d'une Collection anconienne dont la plus grande partie dérive de la Bibliotheque appartenant aux célébres C. J. D. Azulai et son fils Rafael, Rabbin à Ancone* ([Lemberg]: Poremba, 1872). Likewise, the twentieth-century collector Israel Mehlman prefaces his catalog with a discussion of his bibliophilic behavior. Isaac Yudlov, *The Israel Mehlman Collection in the Jewish National and University Library: An Annotated Catalogue of the Hebrew Books and Pamphlets* (Jerusalem: Jewish National and University Library Press, 1984), introduction.

101. Maggid-Steinschneider, *Ir Vilna*, 284–85.

102. Mira Berger, "The Strashun Library in Vilna," *Hebrew Education and Culture in Europe between the Two World Wars*, ed. Tzvi Sharfstein (New York: Ogen, 1957), 511. That is not to say that Strashun's collection was the largest or the most significant personal library in Eastern Europe. For example, Raphael Nathan Rabbinovicz, a bookdealer and noted book collector, commented after visiting Strashun and reviewing his collection that while Strashun's collection was larger than Rabbinovicz's, his

collection was richer in rare and older books. Raphael Nathan Rabbinovicz, "Iggerot Dikdukei Soferim," *Yeshurun* 33 (2000): 330; Eliezer Brodt, "Tsiyunim u-Meluim le-Mador 'Netei Soferim,'" *Yeshurun* 24 (2001), 467–68.

103. Regarding the journal and its impact on the Haskalah movement, see Mordechai Zalkin, "The Periodical 'Pirhei Tsafon' and Its Role in the Social System of the Haskalah Movement in the Russian Empire," *Kesher* 35 (2007): 63–69. This article was reprinted in Strashun, *Mivhar Ketavim*, 213–28. That reprint, however, omits the date of the letter.

104. Mattityahu Strashun, "Divrei hokhma: Mikhtav al Davar R. Shem Tov Ba'al ha-Emunot," *Pirhei Tsafon* 1 (1841): 46–48; *Pirhei Tsafon* 2 (1844): 77–89. The letter was published when Mattityahu was twenty-three, but as indicated by the signature and date at the letter's conclusion, he wrote it when he was nineteen. Ibid., 89. The difference between the date of publication and date of drafting confused Pludermacher. Pludermacher, *Zikaron le-Hakham*, 76n2 (indicating that Mattityahu was twenty-three at the time he wrote the article).

105. Strashun, "Divrei Hokhma," *Pirhei Tsafon* 1 (1841): 47; *Pirhei Tsafon* 2 (1844): 78, 80, 84, 86.

106. Ibid., 80. Mattityahu owned two copies of Alashker's book. Strashun, *Likutei Shoshanim*, nos. 1425–26. Alashker's book was likely published with the 1556–57 edition of Shem Tov's *Emunot*. *Likutei Shoshanim* records Alashker's and Shem Tov's books separately. Ibid., 1077–78. But those entries might refer to the same two copies, and they were inappropriately cataloged separately. One of these copies now resides at YIVO in New York and is available in digital format: http://digital.cjh.org /webclient/DeliveryManager?pid=4425212&custom_att_2=simple_viewer&search _terms=%D7%94%D7%A9%D7%92%D7%95%D7%AA&pds_handle.

107. Strashun, "Divrei Hokhma," *Pirhei Tsafon* 2 (1844): 79.

108. Ibid., 89.

109. Raphael Nathan Nata Rabbinovicz was among Europe's most highly regarded bookdealers and was one of Mattityahu's sources for books. Raphael Nathan Nata Rabbinovicz, "Iggerot Dikdukei Soferim," *Yeshurun* 33 (2000), 331. Bookdealers' catalogs are listed among his library. Strashun, *Likutei Shoshanim*, entries nos. 4452–61. For library catalogs see Strashun, *Likutei Shoshanim*, nos. 575, 4127–4129. In addition, Mattityahu's article in *Pirhei Tsafon* references David Oppenheimer's catalog. Strashun, "Divrei Hokhama," *Pirhei Tsafon*, 1:48; *Pirhei Tsafon*, 2:82n6. Strashun purchased books from Tzvi Hirsch Katzenellenbogen's library. See Weiner, *Kohelet Moshe*, x. Regarding other well-known Hebrew book collectors and their collections, see Alexander Marx, "Some Jewish Book Collectors," in his *Studies in Jewish History and Booklore* (New York: Jewish Theological Seminary, 1944), 198–237; Cecil Roth, "Famous Jewish Book Collections and Collectors," in *Essays in Jewish Booklore* (New York: Ktav, 1971), 330–35. *Ha-Maggid*, June 18, 1891 (discussing significant Jewish book collections in Vienna). Mattityahu's library compares favorably to his contemporary collectors both in terms of size and scope, if not rarity. For example, the library of Heimann Joseph Michael (1792–1846) contained 5,400 books. The library of famed bibliographer Moritz Steinschneider (1816–1906) contained 4,500 books and three incunabula. His rarest book was Avicenna's *Canon*, which Mattityahu also

owned. Steinschneider, like Mattityahu, collected based on need rather than as a hobby. Marx, "Jewish Book Collectors," 220–30. Both of these collectors, however, held substantially greater numbers of manuscripts than Mattityahu.

110. For some examples of Vilna's bookstores, see Hagit Cohen, *At the Bookseller's Shop: The Jewish Book Trade in Eastern Europe at the End of the Nineteenth Century* (Jerusalem: Magnes Press, 2006), 48–52.

111. Antokolski, *Evel Kaved*, 11. On at least one occasion, Mattityahu visited the spa at Bad Reichenhall, Germany, and presumably he would have traveled through Warsaw, Krakow, and Vienna, homes of significant Hebrew printers and booksellers. Ze'ev Shraga Kaplan, *Edut be-Ya'akov* (Warsaw: Ha-Tzefirah, 1904), 17–18. In 1855–1856, Mattityahu traveled through Eastern Europe and Germany in order to visit some of his rabbinic contemporaries with whom he corresponded and who were similarly erudite and held more modern positions. Pludermacher, *Zikaron le-Hakham*, 17. See also Zalkin, *Be-Alot ha-Shahar*, 119–21, regarding trips taken by other maskilim for similar purposes.

112. Four out of the five were purchased between 1874 and Mattityahu's death in 1885. In 1874 the bookdealer Raphael Nathan Rabbinovicz visited Mattityahu and noted that, at that time, he owned only *Mahberet Immanuel*, Brescia, 1492. Raphael Nathan Nata Rabbinovicz, "Iggerot Dikdukei Soferim," *Yeshurun* 33 (2000), 331. The five incunabula are described in Nojus Feigelmanas, *Lietuvos Inkunabulai* (Vilnius: Vilniaus valstybinio V. Kapsuko universiteto Mokslinė biblioteka, 1975), 427, 450, 451, 458, 464–65.

113. Moshe Shalit, "Vilner Bibliotekn," *Vilne Zamlbukh* 2, no. 1 (1916): 35. The Gaon's manuscript is a commentary on *Torat Kohanim*, entry 1173, in *Likutei Shoshanim*. The manuscript was published in the 1959 edition of the *Torat Kohanim*. *Safra de-ve'Rav ve-Hu Torat Kohanim* (Jerusalem: Safra, 1959). The manuscript, however, is not in either the Gaon's hand or his son Abraham's (who otherwise published his father's notes on *midrashim*). Dovid Kamenetsky, "Ketav Yad Kodesh shel Rabbenu ha-Gra," *Yeshurun* 19 (2007): 718n36.

114. There are two sources that discuss Mattityahu's Judaica collection, and one lists it at one thousand volumes and the other at twenty-five hundred. Khaykl Lunski, *Me-ha-Ghetto ha-Vilna'i*, 54* (listing one thousand volumes); Shalit, "Vilner Bibliotekn," 35 (listing twenty-five hundred, and that there was a hand catalog of those books). Because Shalit was reporting secondhand, we have elected to follow Lunski's inventory. Additional support for Lunski's estimate is found in a 1902 official government report. In 1902, immediately after the Strashun Library opened, the government conducted a survey of its contents to ensure that there were no books which were politically or morally sensitive. According to the official report, there were 1,075 books in foreign languages. Although some of those may be attributable to the two other collections that were already in the library and subject to the government inspection, those amounted to only 569 books in total; and it is unlikely that all of those books, including some 215 from the Great Synagogue's collection, were in foreign languages—thus closely aligning with Lunski's estimate and certainly contradicting any estimate above 1,075. See Genrikh Agranovskii and Irina

Guzenberg, *Vil'nius: Po sledam Litovskogo Ierusalima: Pamiatnye mesta evreiskoi istorii i kul'tury. Putivoditel'*, 2nd ed. (Vilnius: Gos. Evreiskii muzei im. Vilenskogo Gaona, 2016), 64. For reasons that are unclear, Shor elected to follow Shalit's estimate, without mention of Lunski's estimate or the official report. Shor, *Likutei Shoshanim*, 51.

115. Strashun, *Likutei Shoshanim*, no. 1398; Shimon Iakerson, *Catalogue of Hebrew Incunabula from the Collection of the Library of the Jewish Theological Seminary of America* (New York: Jewish Theological Seminary, 2004), [210–15].

116. Strashun, *Likutei Shoshanim*, no. 1363; Iakerson, *Catalogue*, [7–9].

117. See, e.g., Pludermacher, *Shirei Minhah*, entries 9, 54, 67, 76, 96, 141. He intended to publish his own commentary on the *Arukh*. [Mattityahu Strashun], "Nerot ha-Marakha," *Ha-Karmel*, April 26, 1851.

118. Mattityahu Strashun, *Mattat Yah*, 4b.

119. Maggid-Steinschneider, *Ir Vilna*, 285. For example, he compares three editions of the *Abudraham* to support a variant reading. Strashun, *Mattat Yah*, 59n*. See also Mattityahu Strashun, "He'arot Shonot," *Ha-Levanon*, February 26, 1868 (Mattityahu discusses *Tosefot* in TB BM 70b, which references a "Targum Yerushalmi." Chajes questioned the citation. Mattityahu, however, located the *targum* in an addendum to "a rare *humash* with an Arabic translation from Sa'adia Gaon and Syriac translation printed in 1646," which was in Mattityahu's library. (See Strashun, *Likutei Shoshanim*, entry 5492.) Mattityahu Strashun, "He-Arot Shonot," *Ha-Levanon*, February 26, 1868 (noting that Zunz lacked a copy of a rare book, *Ben Porat Yosef*, and relied on secondary sources to determine its date of publication). But as Mattityahu explains, Zunz "would not have need[ed] to rely upon inference if he had the book in hand." Mattityahu, however, owned a copy. Strashun, *Likutei Shoshanim*, n719. Likewise, he references Avicenna's *Canon*. See Strashun, *Mattat Yah*, 125.

120. Alexander Marx's observation that "while a scholar may best be judged by his writings, a glance through his library will contribute materially toward a proper appreciation of his personality" is well applied to Mattityahu. Marx, *Studies*, 198.

121. Aelita Ambrulevičiūtė, *Houses That Talk: Sketches of Vokieču Street in the Nineteenth Century* (Vilnius: Auko žuvys, 2015), 125.

122. Y. L. Smolenski, "Masa be-Rusya," *Ha-Shahar*, August 19, 1872, 486 (translated in Zalkin, "Samuel and Mattityahu," 22).

123. Shor, *Likutei Shoshanim*, 24–25. Veidlinger, *Jewish Public Culture*, 30. An unidentified maskil from Navaredok (now in Belarus) sought in vain from his local sources a copy of Adam ha-Kohen Levenshon's *Shirei ha-Kodesh*. He appealed to Mattityahu, who assisted him in obtaining a copy. The maskil wrote to Mattityahu and thanked him for "permitting [the Navaredok maskil] to comfortably join the ranks of the maskilim, because he was able to converse intelligently with the wise ones and maskilim." Zalkin, *Be-Alot ha-Shahar*, 236.

124. Veidlinger, *Jewish Public Culture*, 30 (quoting and translating Reuven Brainin, *Fun Mayn Lebns-bukh* (New York: YKUF, 1946), 246).

125. Freeze, *Everyday Jewish Life*, 14–16. Israel Bartal and Chaya Naor, *Jewish Culture and Context: The Jews of Eastern Europe, 1772–1881* (Philadelphia: University of Pennsylvania Press, 2011), 63–64. Michael Stanislawski, *Tsar Nicholas I and the Jews:*

The Transformation of Jewish Society in Russia, 1825-1855 (Philadelphia: University of Pennsylvania Press, 1983), 13-34. Nicholas also encouraged the conversion of Jews to Russian Orthodoxy, although with mixed results. Freeze, *Everyday Jewish Life*, 15.

126. Pludermacher, *Zikaron le-Hakham*, 26-27; Mark, *Gedolim*, 367-68; Klausner, *Dorot Rishonim*, 348-49. However, until the full abolition of the decree in 1874, we do not have any independent corroboration that the conscription quotas could be satisfied by paying a fine.

127. Samuel Feigensohn, "Defus Romm," *Jewish Lithuania* [Hebrew], ed. Dov Lipas (Tel Aviv: Am-Hasefer, 1959), vol. 1, 184. The widow Romm was Mattityahu's niece. Harkavy, *Le-Heker Mishpahot*, 42-43n63.

128. Pludermacher, *Zikaron le-Hakham*, 30-32.

129. Ibid., 32; Duberosh ben Aleksander Torsh, *Ma'arat ha-Makhpelah, shnei Hespedim . . .* (Warsaw: n.p., 1887), 50.

130. Erez, "Ma'asim be-kol Yom: Be-Artzenu, St. Petersberg," *Ha-Melits* 90 (December 15, 1885), 1462; Eliyahu Hayyim Rabinowits to Hayyim Zelig Slonimski, *Ha-Tsefirah* 48 (December 28, 1885), 392.

131. Pludermacher, *Zikaron*, 33; David Tzvi Hoffmann, *Melamed le'Ho'il: Mahberet Sheni'ah* (Frankfort: Harmon, 1927), no. 106, 110.

132. Torsh, *Ma'arat ha-Makhpelah*, 50.

133. Pludermacher, *Zikaron le-Hakham*, 32-33.

134. Antokolski, *Evel Kaved*, 19.

135. Pludermacher, *Zikaron le-Hakham*, 36.

3. Vilna Builds Its Public Library

1. Mattityahu likely had four children. His two sons died before 1838. Strashun, "Letter," *Be'er Yitzhak*, 42. Archival documents indicate that he also had two daughters; Gita was born on May 10, 1838, and Ita on November 1, 1841. His two daughters likely also died in infancy. At the very least, after 1851, they are not listed in archival documents. Agranovskii, *Evreiskie stranitsy litovskikh arkhivov*, 204. There are conflicting accounts of the exact time of death: 7 pm, 10 pm, and just after midnight. *Ha-Melits*, December 15, 1886 (12:17 am), *Havetselet*, January 15, 1886 (10 pm), and *Ha-Maggid*, December 24, 1885 (7 pm).

2. Jews have a long history of keeping "books for their monetary value and prestige." Veidlinger, *Jewish Public Culture*, 69; Gries, *The Book*, 56. David Oppenheimer's library was the first Jewish collection posthumously sold intact—to the Bodleian Library. See Alexander Marx, "Some Notes on the History of David Oppenheimer's Library," *Revue des Études Juives* 82 [Israel Lévi Festschrift] (1926): 451-60; Charles Duschinsky, "Rabbi David Oppenheimer: Glimpses of His Life and Activity, Derived from His Manuscripts in the Bodleian Library," *Jewish Quarterly Review* 20, no. 3 (January 1930): 217-47; Alexander Marx, "The History of David Oppenheimer's Library," in *Studies in Jewish History and Booklore* (New York: Jewish Theological Seminary of America, 1944), 238-55; and more recently in Joshua Teplitsky, "Between Court Jew and Jewish Court: David Oppenheim, The Prague Rabbinate, and Eighteenth-Century Jewish Political Culture" (PhD diss., New York University, 2012); and Abra-

ham Schischa, "Rabbinic Writings from the Collection of Rabbi David Oppenheim," *Yeshurun* 31 (2014): 781-94 (Hebrew). For other significant personal Hebrew libraries and their purchasing history, see Binyamin Richler, *Hebrew Manuscripts: A Treasured Legacy* (Cleveland, OH: Ofeq Institute, 1990), 66-67.

3. Pludermacher, *Zikaron le-Hakham*, 32.

4. Lithuanian National Archive, f. 450, ap. 7, b. 125.

5. Dovid Strashun, "Kinat Dovid," in Antokolski, *Evel Kaved*, 6. There are two versions of *Kinat Dovid*, both printed in 1886, one incorporated into some versions of Antokolski's book and one printed separately with its own title page. The latter is not recorded in modern bibliographies, but a copy resides in the Chabad Library and is available online at http://www.hebrewbooks.org/24278. Mattityahu referenced those libraries in "hutz le-aretz," which we have translated as "the Diaspora." Nonetheless, the precise reference is unclear. That term may mean specifically outside the Russian Empire, perhaps referring to the public library movement in the United States that is generally considered the model for the modern public library.

6. Dov Schidorsky, "The Emergence of Jewish Public Libraries in Nineteenth-Century Palestine," *Libre* 32, no. 1 (1982): 1-3; Carol Brey-Casiano, "Public Libraries," in *Global Library and Information Science: A Textbook for Students and Educators*, ed. Ismail Abdullahi (Munich: K. G. Saur, 2009), 493-97.

7. Eliyahu Hayyim Rabinowits, "Letter," *Ha-Tsefirah* 48 (December 22, 1885): 392.

8. The general Vilna city charity fund.

9. Antokolski, *Evel Kaved*, 17.

10. *Ha-Tsefirah* 49 (December 29, 1885): 396.

11. Tom Glynn, *Reading Publics* (New York: Fordham University Press, 2015), 222-52.

12. Among those who had access during this time was Ya'akov Wallensky. During this time, Wallensky was writing his supplement to *Piskei Teshuvot* on *Yoreh De'ah*. *Piskei Teshuvot* itself is a collection of obscure and rare works discussing issues appearing in *Yoreh De'ah*. Because Wallensky's materials were even more obscure and rare, the only place he could access these was the Strashun Library. Ya'akov Wallensky, *Daltei Teshuvah* (Vilna, 1890), introduction, 5-6.

13. *Ha-Yom*, April 15, 1886.

14. *Ha-Tsefirah*, August 13, 1890.

15. Ha-Mazkir, "Mikhtavei Soferim," *Ha-Yom* 71 (April 7, 1887); Klausner, *Dorot Ahronim*, 2:534.

16. Strashun, *Likutei Shoshanim*, iii.

17. Veidlinger, *Jewish Public Culture*, 39.

18. Strashun, *Likutei Shoshanim*, iii. According to other accounts, the delay was because the trustees' business interests interfered with focusing on the establishment of the library—an issue that Mattityahu had presaged. *Ha-Melits* 33 (May 10, 1886); *Ha-Tsefirah* 173 (August 13, 1890).

19. Weiner, *Kohelet*, 1-2. In 1888, before Friedland's collection was at its peak, Weiner reportedly assessed the Strashun Library as the most important collection of Jewish books in the Russian Empire. Naftali Maskileitan, "Alon Bakhut," *Ha-Melits*, March 16, 1888.

20. The library was required to maintain his collection separately, issue a catalog, and hang his portrait.

21. Dov Schidorsky, "Sifrei 'Bet Asuf Sefarim asher le-Montefiori' u-Parshat ha-Isurim," *Alei Sefer* 9 (1981): 151–58.

22. Moses Areyeh Löeb Friedland to David Friedman, 5 Nissan, 5642 [March 25, 1882], in Katz, "Friedland's Library," 19–22. In 1896 one writer noted that the Strashun Library still lacked a permanent location, and thus Friedland's selection was proven correct. A. L. Levinski, "Be-Ir Melukha," *Ha-Melits*, March 10, 1896.

23. Lunski, "Di Strashun Bibliotek," 279; Maggid-Steinschneider, "Vilna," *Ha-Melits*, July 11, 1895.

24. The title of the catalog, *Likutei Shoshanim*, had been selected by David and is numerically equal to Mattityahu and to Strashun. *Likutei Shoshanim*, 3. Regarding numerical titles, see Menhem Mendel Zlotkin, *Shemot ha-Sefarim ha-Ivrim: Lefi Sugehim ha-Shonim, Tokhnatam u-Te'udotam* (Neuchâtel: Dalchaux et Niestelé, 1950), 92–102. According to one account, the catalog was already completed by June 1886. *Ha-Tsefirah* 39 (June 3, 1886): 3.

25. Cf. Aviva Astrinsky, "A Brief History of the Strashun Library," in *Mattityahu Strashun, 1817–1885: Scholar, Leader, and Book Collector*, ed. Yermiyahu Aharon Taub (New York: YIVO Institute, 2001), iii, who provides that his collection was comprised of only 5,739 items. Because the catalog contains a handful of books that were published after Strashun's death which were erroneously included in the catalog, Astrinsky's slightly revised number may reflect the actual number of books that were Strashun's personal books. Astrinsky, however, does not explain her deviation from the number listed in *Likutei Shoshanim*.

26. Lunski, "Di Strashun Bibliotek," 279; Lunski, *Me-ha-Ghetto Vilna'i*, 54n*.

27. Ibid., iii.

28. A small prison was also located on the same floor. Cohen-Mushlin, *Synagogues in Lithuania N-Z*, 287.

29. Contemporaneous reports confirm the location of the Strashun Library in the communal hall. See Yetser, "Vilna," *Ha-Melits* 151 (July 19, 1892); see also Lunski, "Di Strashun Bibliotek," 276; Cohen-Mushlin, *Synagogues in Lithuania N-Z*, 289. Shor, in her history, notes that there are conflicting sources regarding the Strashun Library's first home: in addition to Kahal Hall, the home of the trustee, Joshua Epstein, and Strashun's home on Glazier Street were also mentioned. For the former, she cites Klausner, and the latter, Aviva Astrinsky. Ultimately, Shor accepts Klausner's version and claims an error in Lunski's account. Shor, *Likutei Shoshanim*, 30. But an examination of these sources indicates that the other two locations are unsupported. First, Klausner is inconsistent regarding the location. Although in one instance he provides Epstein's house as the location, in another he lists Kahal Hall. Klausner, "Bet Eked Seforim be-Yerushalim de-Lita," 74. Klausner's assertion that the library was in Epstein's house misreads the cited source. He cites an 1893 article in *Ha-Melits* (he does not reference the earlier 1892 article that specifically identifies Kahal Hall), which simply states that the trustees rented space for the library and not that the library was in a private home. Indeed, Epstein's name is not mentioned at all in the

article. Shor herself quotes the relevant portion of the article from *Ha-Melits*. Astrinsky's placement of the library in "Mattityahu's home" is similarly in error; he provides no citation. Mattityahu's home was not on Glazier Street, but on German Street. Mattityahu owned two investment properties on Glazier Street. According to Lunski, immediately after Strashun's death the books were kept in one of those, but not when the library opened to the public. Lunski, "Di Strashun Bibliotek," 296.

30. DGM"R Dumutz, *Ha-Melits* 290 (January 10, 1899).

31. Abba Aresh, "Vilna," *Ha-Melits* 98 (May 12, 1893): 5. Klausner, citing an article in *Ha-Melits*, alleges that the trustee was refusing to permit access to Haskalah books, specifically Peretz Smolenskin's works. Klausner, *Yerushalim de-Lita*, 2:534, citing [Yosef Klausner], "Be-Artsenu," *Ha-Melits* 30 (February 17, 1896). The implications of this one source are difficult to assess. Even the article's author states that on a prior occasion he was given a Smolenskin book. Perhaps a more likely explanation for the denial has less to do with philosophical issues and more to do with practical ones. At that time, only Mattityahu's books were available for public use; other books that were subsequently purchased or donated were not yet cataloged or arranged in sufficient order to permit access. Ahad me-Mokirei ha-Manah Mattityahu Strashun, "Be-Artsenu," *Ha-Melits* 251 (November 28, 1895). Thus, the first request was for Smolenskin's book *Ha-toeh be-darkhei ha-Hayim*, which was the only one in Mattityahu's library available for reading. Strashun, *Likutei Shoshanim*, no. 1438. The second request was for one of Smolenskin's other books, which was not part of Mattityahu's personal library and remained uncataloged and inaccessible. Other complaints at that time were about the lack of space and limited hours. Over Orah, "Ma'asim be-Kol Yom," *Ha-Melits* 122 (June 2, 1893). The room had seats for only ten people, was open for only a few hours a day, and was closed on Friday afternoons.

32. Ehad me-Mokirei ha-Manoh, "Vilna," *Ha-Melits* 251 (November 28, 1895).

33. For prior treatments of the history of the Gaon's Kloyz, see Israel Klausner, *Toldot ha-Kehillah ha-Ivrit be-Vilna* (Vilna: ha-Kehilah ha-Ivrit be-Vilnah, 1938), 78–80; Arie Morgenstern, "Bein Banim le-Talmidim: Ha-Maavak al Moreshet ha-Gra ve-al ha-Ideologiah," *Dat* 53 (2004): 86–92. The most important contemporaneous document regarding this episode is the *Pinkas* of the Gaon's Kloyz. The extant *Pinkas* begins in 1717 and records information related to property ownership. Yet even that document does not provide a complete history of this episode. Nonetheless, we have attempted to reconstruct the history, recognizing that the discovery of new documents may require revision. During the Holocaust, the *Pinkas* was hidden in the Vilna Ghetto and survived. After the war, it was recovered; and in the late 1940s, the *Pinkas* was smuggled out of Lithuania and brought to America to YIVO in New York, where it remains today. YIVO Archives, RG 223. Until recently, only portions of the *Pinkas* were published and did not include all the relevant documents on the establishment of the Gaon's Kloyz. Now, however, the entire extant *Pinkas* as it relates to the Gaon's Kloyz has been transcribed and published. Shlomo Zalman Hevlin, "The *Pinkas* of the Gaon's Kloyz," *Yeshurun* 16 (2005): 746–60; "The 'Kloyz' of the Gaon of Vilna ZTs"L, Ketaim me-Pinkas ha-Kloyz," *Yeshurun* 6 (1999): 678–85.

34. Morgenstern, "Bein Banim le-Talmidim," 86.

35. Ibid.

36. Pesseles also supported the Gaon and his family, and per Stern, the Gaon was entirely funded by private individuals and not the Vilna community. Stern, *Genius*, 21. Stampfer, however, notes that the evidence regarding the source of the Gaon's funding is unclear and may have come from private or public funds, or a combination thereof. Stampfer, *Families*, 327-28.

37. Hevlin, "Pinkas Kloyz-HaGrA," 748 (quoting a document from May 1767); ibid., 750.

38. Morgenstern, "Bein Banim le-Talmidim," 87.

39. For biographical information, see Fuenn, *Kiryah Ne'emanah*, 167.

40. Hevlin, "Pinkas Kloyz-HaGrA," 748-49 (quoting a document dated August 1796); Morgenstern, "Bein Banim le-Talmidim," 88.

41. Hevlin, "Pinkas Kloyz-HaGrA," 750-51 (quoting a document dated 22 Heshvan 5,558 [November 11, 1778]); Klausner, *Toldot ha-Kehillah*, 79-80; Morgenstern, "Bein Banim le-Talmidim," 88.

42. See Hevlin, "Pinkas Kloyz-HaGrA," 791-94; Morgenstern, "Bein Banim le-Talmidim," 88-89.

43. Vilna real estate was very expensive, and the Gaon's ability to make such a purchase is evidence that he was among Vilna's economic elite. Stampfer, *Families, Rabbis, and Education*, 329.

44. The Gaon's son Avraham was also counted among the Gaon's leading students. Hannanel Mak, "Rabbi Avraham ben Ha-Gra ve-Heker Midrash," in *Ha-Gra u-Bet Midrasho*, ed. Moshe Halamish, Yosef Rivlin, and Refael Shohat (Ramat Gan: Bar Ilan University Press, 2003): 99-116. Nonetheless, the family's claim to the Slutzki property was based on their general status as heir to the Gaon's entire estate.

45. Hevlin, "Pinkas Kloyz Ha-Gra," 754-55; Morgenstern, "Bein Banim le-Talmidim," 89.

46. Hevlin, "Pinkas Kloyz Ha-Gra," 554-60; Morgenstern, "Bein Banim le-Talmidim," 89-91.

47. Morgenstern, "Bein Banim le-Talmidim," 92. Hevlin, "Pinkas Kloyz Ha-Gra," 760. (The documents related to the controversy regarding the Gaon's property are instructive for many other disputes that arose throughout history. "The issue arises regarding other Torah institutions and other charitable and benevolent institutions that were established by private persons. . . . Are those treated as private property for the benefit of the community . . . or are they treated as public property under the auspices of the communal representatives.")

48. Two of the three trustees had died; Yosef Grodzenski died in 1888, and Dovid Brodi died in 1897, leaving Joshua Hayim Epstein as the sole remaining trustee. Strashun, *Likutei Shoshanim*, iv (recording Grodzenski's death); Hillel Noah Steinschneider, "Be-Artsenu," *Ha-Melits* 173 (August 15, 1897) (recording Brodi's death). Nonetheless, Grodzenski may have been replaced, either by someone in his family or otherwise. In 1899 an article discussing the issues of the library explains that Brodi had died and that a third, unidentified trustee is alive, but was banned from

Russia and is now in Germany and no longer has a connection with the library. Tze-funi Ma'arivi [David Maggid], "Me-Petersberg le-Tehum ha-Moshav," *Ha-Tsefirah* 196 (September 13, 1899): 876.

49. Yehuda Afel, *Betokh Reshit Ha-Tehia: Zikhronot U-Ketavim Miyeme "Hovevei Tzion" Be-Rusya* (Tel Aviv: Gutenberg, 1936), 28–29. Klausner, however, asserts that in 1899 the Strashun Library was already operating in Epstein's home. Klausner, *Yerushalim de-Lita*, 534. As discussed above, Klausner is incorrect. The library was housed in Kahal Hall in the Great Synagogue.

50. Klausner, *Yerushalim de-Lita*, 535.

51. Another ostensibly public institution that was connected to the Strashun family was the subject of a debate regarding its public or private status. In 1875 the parishioners of the kloyz of David Strashun (1755–1842) disputed the family's ownership, but the family successfully fought off the challenge and retained title to the kloyz. But that did not end the challenges regarding the kloyz's title. By 1905 the issue had been escalated to the Russian Supreme Court for appeals, where it was brought for final resolution. Among other arguments, the parishioners denied that the Strashun name was attached to the kloyz. Cohen-Mushlin, *Synagogues in Lithuania N-Z*, 321–22.

52. Klausner, *Yerushalmi de-Lita*, vol. 2, 534–35. For more on Mattityahu's anti-Zionism and his resistance to its spread in Vilna, see Isaac Broides, *Vilna ha-Tsiyonit ve-Askaneha: Sefer Zikhronot ve-Te'udot al Pe'ulot Hovevei Tzion veha-Tzionim be-Vilna (me-shenat 1881–1924)* (Tel Aviv: Histadrut Olei Vilna veha-Galil be-Tel-Aviv, 1939), 9–14, 73–76.

53. For biographical information, see Fuenn's autobiography, "Dor ve-Dorshav," in *Me-Haskalah Lohemet*, 41–88, and Feiner's introduction, 1–47.

54. Fuenn, *Kiryah Ne'emanah*.

55. Ibid., xix.

56. Klausner, *Yerushalim de-Lita*, 534. Much of Fuenn's wealth was attributable to his third wife. After he married her in 1851, Fuenn began collecting books in earnest. Maggid-Steinschneider, "Toldot ha-Mehaber," *Kiryah Ne'emanah*, ix–x.

57. Klausner, *Yerushalim de-Lita*, 325–26.

58. Ibid., 534–35.

59. Tsfuni Maaravi [David Maggid], "Me-Peterberg le-Tehum ha-Moshav," *Ha-Tsefirah* (September 13, 1899).

60. Ibid.

61. Ehad me-Mokirei ha-Manoh ha-Gaon Rabbi Mattityahu Strashun, "Be-Artsenu, Vilna," *Ha-Melits* (November 28, 1885); Tsfuni Maaravi [David Maggid], "Me-Peterberg le-Tehum ha-Moshav," *Ha-Tsefirah* (September 13, 1899).

62. David Maggid, "[Al davar] Bet [Otsar ha-Sefarim] Ha-Ivri she-be-Vilna," *Ha-Tsefirah* 183 (August 26, 1901): 734–35; Klausner, *Yerushalim de-Lita*, 535. The responsibility for the library changed over time. Some of those changes were a consequence of governmental policies that dissolved communal boards, such as the Tzedakah Gedolah. Shor, *Likutei Shoshanim*, 40–47.

63. Lunski, "Di Strashun Bibliotek," 277; Emmanuel Galomb, "Vilna," *Ha-Melits*, October 20, 1901. According to one contemporaneous account, Yom Kippur was the

only day the library was closed. Tsfuni Maaravi [David Maggid], "Al Davar bet Otsar ha-Sefarim shebe-Vilna," *Ha-Tsefirah*, August 26, 1901.

64. David Maggid, "Bet Otsar ha-Ivri," 734–35; Lunski, "Di Strashun Bibliotek," 276–78.

65. David Maggid, "Me-Petersberg," *Ha-Tsefirah* 196 (September 13, 1899). Cohen-Mushlin, *Synagogues in Lithuania N-Z*, 289. The building was designed by Vilna's chief architect, Konstantin Koroedov, in 1896. Yet only in 1899 was a stand-alone building agreed upon, questioning the accuracy of the 1896 date. A possibility is that in 1896 there was a plan for the remodeling of the Great Synagogue including this building, perhaps for an already identified or for some later determined purpose. In 1899 that had yet to be built, and the Strashun Library claimed it.

66. Lunski, "Di Strashun Bibliotek," 277.

67. David Maggid, "Al Davar Bet Otsar ha-Sefarim," *Ha-Tsefirah*, August 26, 1901; Lunski, "Di Strashun Bibliotek," 278; Genrikh Agranovskii and Irina Guzenberg, *Vil'nius: Po sledam Litovskogo Ierusalima: Pamiatnye mesta evreiskoi istorii i kul'tury. Putivoditel'*, 2nd ed. (Vilnius: Gos. Evreiskii muzei im. Vilenskogo Gaona, 2016), 63.

68. Cohen-Mushlin, *Synagogues in Lithuania N-Z*, 289.

69. Ibid.

70. Israel Cohen, *Vilna*, 102.

71. H. Sakhavantvhon, "Vilna," *Ha-Melits* 85 (May 1, 1902): 2. Lunski's account provides April 14, 1902, as the secular date of the official ceremony. That date is based on the Russian dating system and not the Gregorian. The correct Gregorian date is April 26. This is easily shown because the fourth day of Hol ha-Mo'ed Pesach, which Lunski also refers to, was on April 26. Nonetheless, Shor uses the April 14, 1902, date without explanation. Shor, *Likutei Shoshanim*, 34. According to one account, the library opened on Rosh Hodesh 2 Adar, March 10, 1902. To the extent that the report is correct, it may be that the March date was the informal date of opening, and official opening ceremony occurred in April. Avi David [Shmuel Yaakov Yitskin], "Hazon ha-Yom," *Ha-Tsefirah* 142 (July 9, 1902) (stating that the library was first opened on Rosh Hodesh 2 Adar [March 10]).

72. Veidlinger, *Jewish Public Culture*, 39–43.

73. See Strashun, *Likutei Shoshanim*, iii.

74. Ibn-Tshar, "Vilna," *Ha-Melits*, November 19, 1888; A. A., "Vilna," *Ha-Melits*, March 13, 1889. Although the catalog was not published until the end of 1889, for the purpose of obtaining the permit, Strashun likely submitted the manuscript.

75. Agranovskii, *Vil'nius*, 63–64. Lunski states that the permit was received on "October 20, 1902 (Rosh Hashana)." Lunski, "Di Strashun Bibliotek," 278. The month is likely a result of a typographical error. That year, Rosh Hashana was on September 19–20. Furthermore, the archival documents cited in Guzenberg are dated September 20. The permit is preserved in the Lithuanian State Historical Archives, f. 600, op. 1, d. 187, and is reproduced in Layzer Ran, *Jerusalem of Lithuania*, vol. 2 (New York: Laureate Press, 1974), 346. The legend underneath the photograph also provides the September date. Shor repeats Lunski's error. Shor, *Likutei*, 35. One newspaper article alleges that the closure was because of concerns regarding the public's access to Haskalah books. Avi David, "Hazon ha-Yom," *Ha-Tsefirah* 142

(March 10, 1902). I have been unable to locate any independent evidence to support that allegation.

76. Abramowicz, *Profiles*, 132–42.

77. The New York Public Library was established in 1911.

78. For biographical information, see Mordechai Zalkin, "Introduction," in Hillel Noah Maggid-Steinschneider, *Ir Vilna: Zikhronot adat Yisrael, Toldot Hayei Gedoleha, . . .* , ed. Mordechai Zalkin, vol. 2 (Jerusalem: Magnes Press, 2003), 1–20. According to Hillel Noah's son, David Maggid, although Mattityahu and Hillel Noah were colleagues, Mattityahu did not treat Hillel Noah as an equal. David Maggid, "Vilner Maskilim mit 60–65 Yor Tsurik," *Fun Noentn Over* 1 (1937): 106–11.

79. Maggid-Steinschneider, *Ir Vilna*, 286n2.

80. Lunski, "Di Strashun Bibliotek," 280–82; Shor, *Likutei Shoshanim*, 51–65, 174–87.

81. Sakhabenzahn, "Vilna," *Ha-Melits*, May 1, 1902; Klausner, *Yerushalim de-Lita*, 535; Shor, *Likutei Shoshanim*, 33, 53–54.

82. Lunski, "Di Strashun Bibliotek," 281. Mordekhi was also a noted philanthropist and rebuilt his family's kloyz, which is but one of four pre–World War II synagogue buildings still standing in Vilna today. Cohen-Mushlin, *Synagogues in Lithuania N-Z*, 269. The building is currently abandoned, but efforts are under way to restore it.

83. Shalit, "Vilner Bibliotekn," 34.

84. Lunski, "Di Strashun Bibliotek," 282.

85. Yudels, "In der Alter Strashun Bibliotek," 849.

86. Klausner, "Batei-Eked Sefarim," 75.

87. Lunski, "Di Strashun Bibliotek," 279.

88. For a bibliography of Lunksi's publications, see Shor, *Likutei Shoshanim*, 217–21. Shor's list, however, is incomplete. See, e.g., Lunski's necrology of Ester Rubenstein, the wife of Rabbi Yitzhak Rubenstein, Vilna's chief rabbi and a longtime member of the Strashun Library's board. Khaykl Lunski, "Harabbinit Ester Rubenstein," in *Sefer Zikhron leha-Rabbinit Ester Rubenstein* (Vilna: 1926); Khaykl Lunski, "Folkstimlekha Agodes Vegn Vilner Gaon TZ"L, *Dos Yiddishe Vort*, November 1997, 33–37. These sources were provided by Sid Leiman.

89. Israel Klausner, "Khaykl Lunski HY"D," *Reshumot* 2 (1947), 60.

90. Shor, *Likutei Shoshanim*, 102.

91. Lunski, however, recognized the need for a catalog. In addition to all of Lunski's other duties, he independently cataloged nearly all of the Strashun Library books. Lunski initially offered the card catalog for a fee, but when that was rejected, he donated it. Nonetheless, this was completed ignored; and instead, in 1930, Isaac Strashun and an assistant began cataloging the collection. Klausner, "Batei-Eked Sefarim," 76–78; for other attempts at creating a catalog for the library, see Shor, *Likutei Shoshanim*, 69–75.

92. For a biography of Lunski, see Abramovitch, *Profiles*, 260–64; Shor, *Likutei Shoshanim*, 79–158. The YIVO Archives preserve many examples of Lunski's scholarly correspondence, some of which relate to the Strashun Library and were printed by Shor. YIVO Archives, RG 58, folders 2322–2324, 2336; Shor, *Likutei Shoshanim*.

93. David Shavit, *Hunger for the Printed Word: Books and Libraries in the Jewish Ghettos of Nazi-Occupied Europe* (Jefferson, NC: McFarland, 1997), 27–28; Shor, *Likutei Shoshanim*, 79.

94. Abramowicz, *Profiles*, 261–62.

95. Abraham Karpinowitz, "Tall Tamare," in *Vilna My Vilna*, trans. Helen Mintz (Syracuse, NY: Syracuse University Press, 2015), http://www.yiddishbookcenter .org/sites/default/files/downloads/PT59_tall_tamare_sm.pdf.

96. A book by the same title and on the same topic was published in 1991, allegedly from a manuscript. *Kuntres Ahavah be-Ta'anugim: Be-Inyan Darkhei ha-Zivug ve-Hahakravah bein Ish le-Ishto, ve-Derekh Gever be-Alma ve-hu Shimush le-Hatan ve-Kalah be-Ahava ve-Ahvah ve'Shalom ve-Reyut, Hetek mi-Ktav Yad Yashan le-Hakham Kadmon ve-lo Noda Shemo*, ed. Tzvi Malachi (Lod, 1991). But most likely the book is a forgery and was written by Malachi. National Library of Israel, catalog entry, accessed August 16, 2017, http://primo.nli.org.il/primo_library/libweb /action/dlDisplay.do?vid=NLI&docId=NNL_ALEPH001201719. There is no record of any such book or manuscript in any earlier bibliographies.

97. Abramowicz, *Profiles*, 264.

98. According to one account, the library had over two hundred patrons daily, but only a hundred seats, forcing patrons to share chairs and wait for over a half hour just to enter the library. Ambramowicz, *Profiles*, 262–263n*.

99. Appropriately, Strashun's portrait hung on the library's wall. A. Yudels, "In der Alter Strashun Bibliotek," *Literarishe Bletter*, December 17, 1926, 850.

100. Ben Zion Dinur, "Yerushalayim de-Lita," in Ran, *Jerusalem of Lithuania*, vol. 1, xvi; but see the English translation of Dinur's article that commingles the two groups and has both the Orthodox and younger generation studying "responsa or modern Hebrew novels." Ibid., xx. It is unclear what accounts for this discrepancy in translation. For a breakdown of the library's readership by type (i.e., students, academics and public intellectuals, workers, etc.), see Berger, "The Strashun Library," 514–15. Yudels, "In der Alter Strashun Bibliotek," 850.

101. Khaykl Lunski, "Vilner Kloyzim un der Shulhoyf," in *Vilner Zalmelbukh*, ed. Tzemach Shabad, vol. 2 (Vilna: Rosenthal, 1918), 101.

102. Yudels, "In der Alter Strashun Bibliotek," 850.

103. Dinur, "Yerushalim de-Lita," viii; see also Shor, *Likutei Shoshanim*, 164n22. (Shor challenges one author's claim that women were not admitted until the 1930s.)

104. Lunski, "Di Strashun Bibliotek," 283.

105. Lucy S. Dawidowicz, *From That Place and Time: A Memoir 1938–1947* (New York: Bantam Books, 1991), 119. She notes that not everyone was happy with the state of things and that "the old men would sometimes mutter and grumble about what the world had come to. The young people would titter." Dawidowicz's description echoes that of many other visitors from the library's opening. Shor, *Likutei Shoshanim*, 166–68. The mixing of the sexes in late nineteenth-century Jewish Eastern Europe was not unique to the Strashun Library. In the nineteenth century, coeducation at Jewish primary schools (*hederim*) "was quite common, though certainly not the standard." Nevertheless, it "was not regarded as worthy of note or reaction" or necessarily even "an ideological statement." Stampfer, *Family, Rabbis, and Edu-*

cation, 32. In late nineteenth-century Russia, literate Jewish women visited public libraries in larger numbers, as a percentage, than literate Jewish men. Veidlinger, *Jewish Public Culture*, 55–56. As a rule, men were required to cover their heads, but that was never strictly enforced. Yudels, "In der Alter Strashun Bibliotek," 850; Klausner, *Vilna, Dorot Ahronim*, 536; Abramowicz, *Profiles*, 262; Israel Ta-Shema, "Ha-Sifriah ha-Toranit ha-Merkazit le-Yisrael," *Yad Le-Koreh* 6 (1959): 252. Shor asserts that initially head coverings were required and sometime later they were dropped. Shor, *Likutei Shoshanim*, 164.

106. In addition to scholars, the portraits of wealthy donors also hung on the walls. Yudels, "In der Alter Strashun Bilbiotek," 850.

107. Katz, *Words on Fire*, 217–23.

108. H. Z. Yoni, "Irim ve-Ayarot be-Polin," *Davar*, August 15, 1930.

109. See Shor, *Likutei Shoshanim*, 174–87; see also the description of David Wolfson's Vilna visit in Klausner, "Ha-Tenuah ha-Tzionit be-Lita," in *Yahadut Lita*, vol. 1, 522. For a photo of one such visit, see Ran, *Jerusalem of Lithuania*, vol. 2, 416.

110. Maggid, "Bet Otzar," 735; Shor, *Likutei Shoshanim*, 174–75. A copy of *Likutei Shoshanim* was also bound in silver. Shor, *Likutei Shoshanim*, 360.

111. Lunski, "Sefer ha-Zahav," 46.

112. Ibid., 45.

113. Ibid., 39.

114. For biographical information, see Edgar Scott, "Hermann Cohen," in *Stanford Encyclopedia of Philosophy*, ed. Edward N. Zalta, rev. ed. (Fall 2015), accessed January 1, 2018, https://plato.stanford.edu/entries/cohen/.

115. For biographical information, see Dan Miron, "Sholem Yankev Abramovitsh," in *YIVO Encyclopedia of Jews in Eastern Europe*, accessed March 9, 2017, http://www.yivoencyclopedia.org/article.aspx/Abramovitsh_Sholem_Yankev.

116. For biographical information, see Dan Miron, "Sholem Aleichem," in *YIVO Encyclopedia of Jews in Eastern Europe*, accessed March 9, 2017, http://www.yivoency-clopedia.org/article.aspx/Sholem_Aleichem.

117. Lunski, "Sefer ha-Zahav," 39.

118. For biographical information, see Avner Holtzman, "Hayim Nahman Bialik," in *YIVO Encyclopedia of Jews in Eastern Europe*, accessed March 9, 2017, http://www.yivoencyclopedia.org/article.aspx/Bialik_Hayim_Nahman.

119. Among his Orthodox peers, Karlin at times took a more moderate position on contemporary issues. Jacob J. Schacter, "R. David Friedman: The Ban on Secular Study in Jerusalem," *Tradition* 26, no. 4 (1992), 102–5.

120. Grodzenski enjoyed a special relationship with the library. He regularly used the library and was accorded special borrowing privileges. R. Hayim Ozer Grodzenski to Khaykl Lunski, letters in a private collection, copies on file with the author. The Strashun Library also proved a barometer of his scholarship. Grodzenski was well known for his extensive knowledge of responsa. On one occasion, he was surreptitiously tested using the Strashun Library. Moshe Samuel Shapiro visited the library and, after browsing the catalog, selected an obscure responsa book, *Ma'amar Mordechai*. He identified a recondite issue that was only tangentially related to the larger question. That Saturday night, Moshe Samuel spent time with

Grodzenski and casually raised the question from the responsa book. Immediately, Grodzenski responded "that the issue is discussed in the *Ma'amar Mordechai*." Moshe Samuel Shapiro, *R' Moshe Shmuel ve-Doro: Kovetz Ma'asot ve-Iggerot* (New York: Sons of the Author and His Good Friends, 1964), 176. For biographical information, see Benjamin Brown, "Grodzenski, Hayim Ozer," in *YIVO Encyclopedia of Jews in Eastern Europe*, accessed March 9, 2017, http://www.yivoencyclopedia.org/article.aspx/Grodzenski_Hayim_Ozer.

121. "At the Strashun Library in Vilna, A Short Survey of the Library," *Der Yom*, January 31, 1936 (both Hafetz Hayim and Hermann Cohen are lauded for their simple entries); Berger, "The Strashun Library in Vilna," 519; Shor, *Likutei Shoshanim*, 169; Lunski, "Di Strashun Bibliotek," 286.

122. Lunski, "Sefer ha-Zahav," 38.

123. Yudels, "In der Alter Strashun Bibliotek," 850.

124. Veidleinger, *Jewish Public Culture*, 55.

125. Yudels, "In der Alter Strashun Bibliotek," 850.

126. Lunski, "Di Strashun Bibliotek," 283.

127. Ze'ev Yavetz, *Toldot Yisrael: Metukun al pi Mekorot ha-Rishonim* (Berlin: [Eitshkavski], 1906).

128. Lunski, "Di Strashun Bibliotek," 284.

129. Ibid., 286n*.

130. Simha Assaf, "Professor Y.N ha-Levi Epstein," in *Brisk de-Lita: Encyclopedia shel Galuyot*, ed. Eliezer Steinman (Jerusalem: Hevrat Encyclopedia shel Galuyot, 1954), 315.

131. Lunski, *Me-ha-Ghetto ha-Vilna'i*, 54. See also Veidleinger, *Jewish Public Culture*, 64, regarding the use of Jewish libraries' reading rooms; some functioned as places for quiet study, while others brought "the sociability of the tavern."

132. Abraham Joshua Heschel, "Yerushalayim de-Lita," in Ran, *Jerusalem of Lithuania*, vol. 1, xvii.

133. Lithuanian National Archives, f. 401, op. 2, d. 518, list 16.

134. Shor, *Likutei Shoshanim*, 71–72.

135. Lithuanian National Archives, f. 401, op. 2, d. 518, list 16.

136. See Shor, *Likutei Shoshanim*, 38–39, 42 (discussing a 1926 public appeal that the library undertook in which it described its financial condition as "dire and catastrophic"); ibid., 43 ("The Strashun Library underwent many difficult financial periods throughout the nineteen years of Polish rule (October 9, 1920–September 19, 1939). But it continued to be a major Vilna cultural institution.").

4. Jewish Books and the Ravages of World War II

1. The Jewish Institute was one of only two of the many institutes Rosenberg envisioned that actually were realized. Schidorsky, *Gevilim Nisraphim*, 169.

2. Michael J. Kurtz, *America and the Return of Nazi Contraband: The Recovery of Europe's Cultural Treasures* (New York: Cambridge University Press, 2006), 22–24; Dov Schidorsky, *Gevilim Nisraphim*, 165–76. Shavit suggests that Rosenberg's ERR was the "first time in history, an agency of government was created solely for looting cultural materials, including library contents." Shavit, *Hunger*, 49.

3. Kurz, *America*, 7–10. During the United States Civil War, President Lincoln issued a code of conduct for the Union Army that addressed the looting of cultural property. Ibid., 7.

4. Gallas, *Das Leichenhaus der Bücher*, 36n22.

5. Sem C. Sutter, "The Lost Jewish Libraries of Vilna and the Frankfurt Institut zur Erforschung der Judenfrage," in *Lost Libraries: The Destruction of Great Book Collections since Antiquity*, ed. James Raven (London: Palgrave Macmillan, 2004), 220–21. Because the agreement was executed after *Kristallnacht*, Rosenberg's intent was to add any books looted during that event. Ultimately, another agency received those materials. Sutter, "Lost Jewish Libraries," 221.

6. Grimsted, "Roads to Ratibor," 406.

7. Sutter, "Lost Jewish Libraries," 221. Hitler's order was issued on June 14, 1940. On September 27, 1940, Rosenberg received permission from the High Command to expand his looting operations in the occupied territories. Schidorsky, *Gevilim Nesraphim*, 176.

8. Kurtz, "Looted Art," 20 *Cardozo Law Review* 627. The ERR did not hold a monopoly on looting Jewish cultural property. There were four significant interests vying for looted assets, with Rosenberg's as "one of the most ambitious looting efforts" of the four. Another one of the four, the Reich Main Security Office, the Reichssicherheitshauptamt, "was the single greatest looter of archives and libraries from Jews" and others. Kurtz, *America*, 20–23.

Aside from Jewish libraries, other important European libraries similarly suffered Nazi pillage and looting. Sem C. Sutter, "Polish Books in Exile: Cultural Booty across Two Continents, through Two Wars," in *The Holocaust and the Book: Destruction and Preservation* (Amherst: University of Massachusetts Press, 2001), 143–62. For a survey of the history of destruction of libraries, see Matthew Fishburn, *Burning Books* (Houndmills, Basingstoke: Palgrave Macmillan, 2008); Lucien X. Polastron, *Books on Fire: The Destruction of Libraries throughout History*, trans. Jon E. Graham (Rochester, VT: Inner Traditions, 2007); Rebecca Knuth, *Burning Books and Leveling Libraries: Extremist Violence and Cultural Destruction* (Westport, CT: Praeger, 2006); *Lost Libraries: The Destruction of Great Book Collections since Antiquity*, ed. James Raven (London: Palgrave Macmillan: 2004); Rebecca Knuth, *Libricide: Regime Sponsored Destruction of Books and Libraries in the Twentieth Century* (Westport, CT: Praeger, 2003); Anders Rydell, *The Book Thieves: The Nazi Looting of Europe's Libraries and the Race to Return a Literary Inheritance*, trans. Henning Koch (New York: Viking, 2017).

9. In Western Europe, state libraries were largely left untouched, and the Jewish libraries bore the brunt of the Nazis' looting. Kurtz, *Nazi Looting*, 28. Although the looting was carried out by the Nazis, they were not alone and required additional civilian support to fully implement the looting operation. "Second-tier operatives," such as "museum directors, art dealers, and art historians," proved critical. Kurtz, *Nazi Looting*, 31.

10. Glickman, *Stolen Words*, 122.

11. Sutter, "Lost Jewish Libraries," 221–22.

12. Ibid., 220–22.

13. Ibid.

14. Although members of the Red Army remained billeted around Vilna. Masha Greenbaum, *The Jews of Lithuania: A History of a Remarkable Community, 1316-1945* (Jerusalem: Gefen, 1995), 288-89.

15. Ibid.

16. Levin, *Lesser of Two Evils*, 198-99.

17. Ibid., 199.

18. Dina Porat, *The Fall of a Sparrow: The Life and Times of Abba Kovner*, 19, 342n7; Levin, *Lesser of Two Evils*, 200, and table 9.1, "Refugees Listed with the Refugee Committee by the Vilna Kehilla."

19. Berger, "The Strashun Library of Vilna," 51. Berger must be referring to specifically Polish Hasidim because long before the influx of Polish refugees in 1939-1940, Lithuanian Hasidim were among the Strashun Library's patrons. Lunski, *Me-ha-Ghetto ha-Vilna'i*, 54. Since 1810, when the Chabad Hasidim's kloyz was sanctioned, Vilna was no longer completely hostile territory for Hasidim. The Lithuanian government did little else that directly affected the Strashun Library. Shor, *Likutei Shoshanim*, 44.

20. Berger erroneously states that the Soviet period had no effect on the Strashun Library. Berger, "Strashun Library in Vilna," 515.

21. Shor, *Likutei Shoshanim*, 45; Shavit, *Hunger*, 37-38. The Soviets entered Vilna on June 15, 1940; however, Soviet governance over Vilna officially began on August 3, 1940, when Lithuania was annexed. Shor, *Likutei Shoshanim*, 44. The process of the nationalization of Jewish institutions began in September 1940, when the cultural commissioner, Kaznits, recommended that a number of Vilna Jewish institutions be nationalized and placed under the control of the Ministry of Culture. Ibid., 45.

22. Ibid.; Shavit, *Hunger*, 37.

23. Ibid., 38. Shavit also asserts that even with nearly 90 percent of the Strashun Library's holdings unavailable, "the number of readers increased by some 1,600 to more than 4,000 readers, with a daily average of 100 readers." But a daily one-hundred-reader average is far *fewer* than before the Soviet period. In an earlier discussion, Shavit states that in the 1930s the Strashun Library saw an average of 230 visitors a day; and with only a hundred seats, half-hour waits were not uncommon. Shavit, *Hunger*, 26 (relying on Berger, "The Strashun Library in Vilna," 513).

24. "Bibliotekos M. Strašuno varde Vilniuje, Atidavimo Priémimo Aktas," Lithuanian National Archive, f. 401, op. 2, d. 518, list 16.

25. This was not the first attempt to create a central Jewish research entity in Vilna. After World War I, the Bolsheviks briefly took control of Vilna from December 1918 until April 1919, when they were driven out. The Bolsheviks sought to implement a similar plan for the consolidation of Vilna's libraries into a single entity. Klausner, *Vilna: Yerushalayim d'Lita*, 138.

26. Shor, *Likutei Shoshanim*, 46-47 (reproducing the text of Lunski's plea).

27. Ibid., 46.

28. Ibid., 44-46. The Soviets never completed reviewing the contents of YIVO Library; and throughout the Soviet occupation of 1940-41, the YIVO collections were

only accessible under very limited circumstances, which reduced the number of patrons to a minuscule number. Shavit, *Hunger*, 38–39.

29. The Ger Tsedek, Avraham ben Avraham, was a Polish noble, Valentin Potocki, who converted to Judaism, for which he was burned at the stake. His grave site was among the most revered in Vilna's old cemetery. When that cemetery was destroyed, he was among just six others that were reinterred in the new Jewish cemetery. Shnayer Leiman, "Who Is Buried in the Vilna Gaon's Tomb? A Contribution toward the Identification of the Authentic Grave of the Vilna Gaon," *Seforim Blog*, accessed August 14, 2017, http://seforim.blogspot.com/2012/09/who-is-buried-in -vilna-gaons-tomb.html.

30. Kruk, *Last Days*, 53.

31. Kurtz, *America*, 25.

32. Kruk, *Last Days*, 212. Zelig Kalmanovitch was opposed, at least in part, to smuggling and hiding books in the ghetto, and he sought to identify as many books as possible worth shipping to Frankfurt. Kaczerginski, *Khurban Vilne*, 209. David Fishman, however, questions whether Kalmanovitch was entirely opposed to smuggling and, at least in some instances, supported that course of action. David Fishman, *The Book Smugglers: Partisans, Poets, and the Race to Save Jewish Treasures from the Nazis* (Lebanon, NH: ForeEdge Press, 2017), 271n11.

33. Fishman, *Book Smugglers*, 178–83, 213–20.

34. Ibid., 29 and 263n7 (discussing whether both men arrived in July).

35. Unlike the Nazis' plunder of Western Europe, where national libraries and collections were the focus and the first to be stripped of their treasures, in the East, Jewish libraries were the first to be attacked. Grimsted, "Roads to Ratibor," 394.

36. Kruk, *Last Days*, 268, 311; Shavit, *Hunger*, 95; Fishman, *Embers*, 3.

37. Fishman, *Embers*, 3; Sutter, "Lost Jewish Libraries," 223–24 (discussing other Vilna Libraries that were targeted by the Nazis). See also Schidorsky, *Gevilim Nesraphim*, 165–201; Shor, *Likutei Shoshanim*, 189–200. The ERR received permission to operate in Eastern-occupied countries in August 1941. Grimsted, "Roads to Ratibor," 396.

38. A partial testament to Goldschmidt's numerous activities, both professional and otherwise, in the Vilna community appears in Layzer Ran's photographic collection of Vilna. Ran, *Jerusalem of Lithuania*, vol. 3, index, s.v. "Goldschmidt, Elijah Jacob, Writer, and Teacher." The S. An-sky museum was part of the Jewish Historical and Ethnographic Society. Veidlinger, *Jewish Public Culture*, 229–60. For a history of the museum, see Cecile E. Kuznitz, "An-sky's Legacy: The Vilna Historic-Ethnographic Society and the Shaping of Modern Jewish Culture," *The Worlds of S. An-sky: A Russian Jewish Intellectual at the Turn of the Century*, ed. Gabriella Safran and Steven J. Zipperstein (Redwood City, CA: Stanford University Press, 2006), 320–45; Itzik Nakhmen Gottesman, *Defining the Yiddish Nation: The Jewish Folklorists of Poland* (Detroit: Wayne State University Press, 2003), 75–78.

39. Fishman, *Embers*, 3; Weiser, "The Chair of Yiddish," 252; Sutter, "Lost Jewish Libraries," 224. A German document indicating that Lunski was imprisoned from August 2–August 8, 1941, is preserved in the Lithuanian National Archives.

40. Kruk, *Last Days*, 212.

41. Shavit, *Hunger*, 95; Shor, *Likutei Shoshanim*, 190. But according to Kalman Farber, who was in the ghetto and kept a diary, Strashun's suicide was unrelated to the Nazi's looting of the Strashun Library. Farber relates that even before Pohl arrived, on the day the Germans entered Vilna, June 22, 1941, Isaac hung himself with his pajama belt because he remembered the horrible conditions of World War I. Kalman Farber, *Olkeniki, Radin, Vilna: Me-Yomano she Ben Torah ba-Shoah u-Lefaneha* (Jerusalem: n.p., 2006), 54.

42. YIVO Archives, RG 223, Sutzkever Collection, 678.3. Fishman, *Book Smugglers*, 31 and 263n12, citing 678.2. None of the five incunabula are recorded in any catalogs of Hebrew incunabula, and none have appeared at auction, likely indicating that they are forever lost. The Strashun Library's incunabula were not alone. There were only a handful of incunabula identified at the OAD, and some speculate that the Nazis removed them just prior to the end of the war and placed them in private collections. Schidorsky, *Gevilim Nesraphim*, 283.

43. "Bericht vom dem Arbeitsergebnis der juedischen Arbeitsgruppe beim Einsatzstab RR Wilna," Lithuanian Central State Archive, f. 633, op. 1., del. 5.; Johannes Pohl, "Bericht über die Dienstreise von Riga nach Kauen und Wilna vom 30. März bis 2. April 1942," enclosure 2, "Die jüdische Gemeindebibliothek auf den Namen M. Straschun in Wilna," April 26, 1942, Central State Archive of Supreme Bodies of Power and Government Ukraine, f. 3676, op. 1, d. 128, 185.

44. Johannes Pohl, "Bericht über die Dienstreise von Riga nach Kauen und Wilna vom 30. März bis 2. April 1942," enclosure 2, "Die jüdische Gemeindebibliothek auf den Namen M. Straschun in Wilna," April 26, 1942, 2, Central State Archive of Supreme Bodies of Power and Government Ukraine, f. 3676, op. 1, d. 128, 185.

45. Fishman, *Embers*, 3.

46. Shor, *Likutei Shoshanim*, 196, citing Shalom Cholawski, *So Much Longing, So Much Charm: Nesvizh, Vilna, Rakov*, trans. Margalit Rodgers ([Israel]: S. Cholawski, 2005), 140.

47. Kruk, *The Last Days*, 108. Kruk cynically remarked that the timing of Lunski's release ensured that "Lunski, the bibliophile, chronicler of the old [medieval] Jewish ghetto in Vilna" was "to be present at the crossing of the threshold into the brand-new ghetto." Kruk records that Lunski handed over six incunabula. But Mattityahu's personal library contained only five incunabula. Kruk does not provide any of the titles. Consequently, the identity of and Kruk's source for the sixth is unknown. Finally, in alignment with the Strashun Library's holdings, an ERR document refers to the removal of only five incunabula. Fishman, *Embers*, 18, app. 1.

48. Herman Kruk, "The Library and Reading Room in the Vilna Ghetto, 6 Strashun Street," trans. Zachary M. Baker, in *The Holocaust and the Book: Destruction and Preservation*, ed. Jonathan Rose (Boston: University of Massachusetts Press, 2001), 171–72; Veidlinger, *Jewish Public Culture*, 46–48 (discussing the society's libraries throughout the Russian Empire).

49. Kruk, "The Library and Reading Room," 171–72; Dina Abramowicz, "The Library in the Vilna Ghetto," in *The Holocaust and the Book: Destruction and Preservation*, ed. Jonathan Rose (Boston: University of Massachusetts Press, 2001).

50. Kruk, "The Library and Reading Room," 172–73; Shavit, *Hunger*, 100; Sutter,

"Lost Jewish Libraries," 224. Krasner's personal library was also looted (although only the Jewish books because those in other languages were stolen by the Germans or burnt by the Lithuanians). Kruk, *Last Days*, 654-55.

51. Dina Abramowicz, "The Library in the Vilna Ghetto," 166. The Grosser Library was named in honor of the Bundist theoretician Bronislaw Grosser; it was the largest lending library in Warsaw and "contained the city's finest social science collection." Kruk became the director in 1930; and although he lacked formal education, he adopted several modern library science conventions, including "a Jewish decimal catalog system." *International Dictionary of Library Histories*, David H. Stam, ed. (Chicago: Fitzroy Dearborn, 2001), vol. 1, 181; Bernard Goldstein, *Twenty Years with the Labor Bund: A Memoir of Interwar Poland*, trans. Marvin S. Zuckerman (West Lafayette, IN: Purdue University Press, 2016), 13n5; Benjamin Harshav, *The Polyphony of Jewish Culture* (Redwood City, CA: Stanford University Press, 2007), 164-66.

52. Kruk, *Last Days*, 164-66, 281; "Inventory fun hefetzim un muzalah uartikitin, vos gefinen zikh in bezits fun Strashun-gas 6," YIVO Archives, RG 223, folder 476. Today, the library's building is the only prewar Jewish Vilna library still standing and is irregularly used for presentations. Irina Guzenberg, *Vilnius: Sites of Jewish Memory, A Concise Guide*, trans. Svetlana Shatalova, ed. Geoff Vasil (Vilnius: Pavilniai, 2013), 52 no. 66.

53. Ibid., 212.

54. Kruk, *Last Days*, 138.

55. Ibid., 155, 164-66, 196-97.

56. A January 2, 1942, inventory lists 2,464 books. "Inventory fun hefetzim un muzalah uartikitin, vos gefinen zikh in bezits fun Strashun-gas 6," YIVO Archives, RG 223, folder 476. Kruk's February 19, 1942, diary entry records that his group had secretly removed approximately three thousand books from the Strashun Library. Kruk, *Last Days*, 164-66, 212. The ghetto library functioned from September 1941 until the final liquidation of the ghetto in September 1943. Kruk's report "The Ghetto Library and Ghetto Readers, September 15, 1941—September 15, 1942" provides details regarding the creation of and a myriad of statistics on the ghetto library. Herman Kruk, "The Library and Reading Room in the Vilna Ghetto." Similarly, Kruk's assistant, Dina Abramowicz, also recorded her experiences at the library. Dina Abramowicz, "The Library in the Vilna Ghetto," *The Holocaust and the Book: Destruction and Preservation*, ed. Jonathan Rose (Boston: University of Massachusetts Press, 2001), 165-70.

57. Fishman, *Embers*, 3; Sutter, "Lost Jewish Libraries," 225-26. The Nazis targeted Vilna Jewish public as well as private libraries. Grimsted, "Roads to Ratibor," 407.

58. Fishman has Pohl arriving in February 1942. Fishman, *Embers*, 3. Shavit, however, places Pohl's arrival in January 1942. Shavit, *Hunger*, 95.

59. Kruk, *Last Days*, 212; Sutzkever and Kaczerginski provide different numbers. Sutzkever, *Vilner Ghetto*, 109; Szmerke Kaczerginski, *Partizaner geyen!* (Buenos Aires: Tsentral-Farband fun Poylishe Yiden in Argentinei, 1947), 66.

60. For biographical information, see Gennady Estraikh, "Kalmanovitch, Zelig," in *YIVO Encyclopedia of Jews in Eastern Europe*, http://www.yivoencyclopedia.org /article.aspx/Kalmanovitch_Zelig; *Encyclopaedia Judaica*, 2nd ed., s.v. "Kalmano-

vitch, Zelig" (Farmington Hills, MI: Macmillan Reference, 2007), vol. 11, 746–47. For a critique of the Kalmanovitch entry in the 2006 edition of *Encyclopaedia Judaica*, see Shnayer Leiman, "The New Encyclopaedia: Some Preliminary Observations," *Seforim Blog*, June 5, 2007, http://seforim.blogspot.com/2007/06/shnayer-leiman-new-encyclopaedia.html.

61. Johannes Pohl, "Bericht über die Dienstreise von Riga nach Kauen und Wilna vom 30. März bis 2. April 1942," April 2, 1942, Central State Archive, Ukraine, f. 3676, op. 1, d. 128; Johannes Pohl, "Bericht über Bearbeitung der Judaica und Hebraica in der Zeit v. 21–28 April 1942 in Wilna," enclosure 2, "Die jüdische Gemeindebibliothek auf den Namen M. Strashun in Wilna," April 28, 1942, Central State Archive, Ukraine, f. 3676, op. 1, d. 128. Kruk records that twenty-seven thousand books were transferred to the university building. YIVO Archive, RG 223, folder 678.3. Another ERR report from June 1942 lists a combined fifty thousand books, brochures, periodicals, and newspapers from the Strashun Library books at the building. "Bericht vom dem Arbeitsergebnis der juedischen Arbeitsgruppe beim Einsatzstab RR Wilna," February 18–June 8, 1942, Lithuanian Central State Archive, f. 633, op. 1, del. 5. In October 1942, Pohl estimated that the university collection point held forty thousand books in total, most of which were from the Strashun Library. "Bericht über die Bearbeitung der Hebraica und Judaica im JWO (Jiddisches wissenschaftliches Jnstitut in Wilna)," October 15, 1942, Central State Archive, Ukraine, f. 3676, op. 1, d. 128, 332.

62. Szmerke Kaczerginski, "Vos di daytshn hobn aroysgefirt un farnikhtet," August 14, 1944, YIVO Archive, RG 223, folder 678.3; Kruk, *Last Days*, 212.

63. "Bericht vom dem Arbeitsergebnis der juedischen Arbeitsgruppe beim Einsatzstab RR Wilna," February 18–June 8, 1942, Lithuanian Central State Archive, f. 633, op. 1., del. 5; "Bericht über die Bearbeitung der Hebraica und Judaica im JWO (Jiddisches wissenschaftliches Jnstitut in Wilna)," October 15, 1942, Central State Archive, Ukraine, f. 3676, op. 1, 332; Kruk, *Last Days*, 220.

64. Johannes Pohl, "Bericht über Bearbeitung der Judaica und Hebraica in der Zeit v. 21–28 April 1942 in Wilna," enclosure 2, "Die jüdische Gemeindebibliothek auf den Namen M. Strashun in Wilna," April 28, 1942, Central State Archive, Ukraine, f. 3676, op. 1, d. 128, 184–86.

65. Kruk, *Last Days*, 213–14.

66. Fishman, *Book Smugglers*, 201–2; Julija Šukys, *Epistolophilia: Writing the Life of Ona Šimaite* (Lincoln: University of Nebraska Press, 2012), 52–53. Phillip Friedman, *Their Brother's Keeper* (New York: Crown, 1957), 21–32; Schidorsky, *Gevilim Nesraphim*, 182; Abramowicz, "The Library in the Vilna Ghetto," 168.

67. In April 1946, she provided an account of her activities and the location of materials that she had hidden in the ghetto, some of which were recovered. Ona Šimaite, "Declaration on Documents in the Vilna Ghetto," in Fishman, *Embers*, 25.

68. Kruk, *Last Days*, 212–13; "Bericht," February 18–June 8, 1942, Lithuanian Central State Archives, f. 633, op. 1, del. 5. The building at 7 Rudnicka was formerly the Vilna Jewish Bank and was among the largest buildings in the Vilna Ghetto. A teahouse was opened there in May 1942, and the Worker's League of the Council of Brigadiers, an autonomous cultural organization, held lectures there until the last

weeks of the ghetto. Solon Beinfeld, "The Cultural Life of the Vilna Ghetto," *Simon Wiesenthal Center Annual*, vol. 1 (1984), Museum of Tolerance Online, http://motlc.wiesenthal.com/site/pp.asp?c=gvKVLcMVIuG&b=394971.

69. Fishman, *Embers*, 11n9.

70. "Taetigkeitsbericht der Gruppe Kruk, February 2, 1942–July 10, 1943," July 19, 1943, Lithuanian Central State Archive, f. 633, op. 1, del. 5.

71. According to one report of the activities between February and May 1942, eighty crates were packed and bound for Frankfurt. YIVO Archive, RG 223, folder 678.1.

72. Berger, "The Strashun Library in Vilna," 517.

73. Chaim Grade, "The Seven Little Alleys," in *My Mother's Sabbath Days: A Memoir by Chaim Grade*, trans. Channa Kleinerman Goldstein and Inna Hecker Grade (New York: Knopf, 1986), 380. Grade later penned a lengthy poem on the Strashun Library. Chaim Grade, "Der Sefarim-Otsar fun Strashun," *Di Goldene Keyt* 95/96 (1978): 210–16.

74. Irene, *In Search of the Jerusalem of Lithuania*, 86–87.

75. Cohen-Mushlin, *Synagogues in Lithuania N–Z*, 289.

76. The bust was sculpted by Mindaugus Šnipas and unveiled in 1997, and is based on an earlier bust of a generic "biblical sage." Genrikh Agranovskii and Irina Guzenberg, *Vil'nius: Po sledam Litovskogo Ierusalima. Pamiatnye mesta evreiskoi istorii i kul'tury: Putivoditel'*, 2nd ed. (Vilnius: Gos. Evreiskii muzei im. Vilenskogo Gaona, 2016), 48–49. For a discussion of the Gaon's portrait, see Rachel Schnold, "Elijah's Face: The Portrait of the Vilna Gaon in Folk Art," *The Gaon of Vilna: The Man and His Legacy*, ed. Rachel Schnold (Tel Aviv: Beth Hatefutsoth, 1998), 48–58. On rabbinic portraits generally, see Richard Cohen, *Jewish Icons: Art and Society in Modern Europe* (Berkeley: University of California Press, 1998).

5. Lost and Found in a German Book Depot

1. Lt. Robert Schoenfeld, "Report from Hungen, MII Team 430G, 5th Infantry Division to Assistant Chief of Staff," April 8, 1945, National Archives and Records Administration (hereafter NARA), RG 94, box 6779. In addition to Jewish books, the cache included over two hundred items of rare art owned by Jews. See, e.g., "Jewish Art Cache Found in Germany: Third Army Seizes Collection Used for Propaganda by Reich Government Army to Hold Treasures," *New York Times*, April 9, 1945. Another MFA&A officer in the Third Division, Captain Robert E. Posey, wrote a report on the Hungen find. Posey was later praised by the army for his actions in securing two salt mines with looted art in Salzburg. During the offensive into that area, Posey "with his eye on the bull's-eye, ignoring all other distractions, he made straight for [the looted art]" and located "two salt-mines, one of which had worked for 3,000 years with a continuous history of operations since 1300 A.D." "MFA Summary for Germany," Headquarters Twelfth Army Group, APO 655, June 19, 1945, NARA, RG 260, M1941, reel 15; Kurtz, *America*, 74; Grimsted, "Roads to Ratibor," 444n118; Sutter, "Lost Jewish Libraries," 229.

2. Leslie I. Poste, "Development of US Protection of Libraries and Archives in Europe during World War II" (PhD diss., University of Chicago, 1958), 334; Grimsted, "Roads to Ratibor," 407, 444n118; Kurtz, *America*, 139.

3. Violet Brown and Walter Crosby, "Jew Finds Hebrew Collection Nazis Stole in Lie Drive," *Brooklyn New York Eagle*, April 9, 1945. Records of the US Occupation Headquarters, World War II, RG 260, Records Concerning the Central Collection Points ("Ardelia Hall Collection"): Offenbach Archival Depot, 1946–1951, NARA, RG 260, M1957, reel 16.

4. The article also notes that, for the past five years, the American Schoenfelds have heard nothing from their Polish relatives.

5. Kurtz, *America*, 12–19; Robert G. Waite, "Returning Jewish Cultural Property: The Handling of Books Looted by the Nazis in the American Zone of Occupation, 1945 to 1952," *Libraries and Culture* 37, no. 3 (Summer 2002), 214.

6. Brown, "Jew Finds Hebrew Collection."

7. Janet Flanner, "Annals of Crime: The Beautiful Spoils," *New Yorker*, February 22, 1947, 31–36, reprinted in Janet Flanner, *Men and Monuments* (New York: Harper, [1957]), 295.

8. Leslie I. Poste, "Books Go Home from the Wars," *Library Journal* 73 (December 1, 1948), 1700.

9. According to Poste, approximately fourteen hundred such locations were identified. Poste, "Development of US Protection of Libraries," 333. Grimsted discusses and inventories many of the discoveries of book archives not only by the Americans but also by the other Allies. Grimsted, "Roads to Ratibor." Elisabeth Gallas, "Preserving East European Jewish Culture — Lucy Dawidowicz and the Salvage of Books after the Holocaust," *Simon Dubnow Institute Yearbook* 11 (2012), 79 ("After the German surrender in May 1945, [the Americans] found several hundred repositories where the Germans had hidden their booty and German museum and library collections in salt mines, castles, and cellars.").

10. Waite, "Returning Jewish Cultural Property," 214.

11. Grimsted, "Roads to Ratibor," 406; Leslie Poste, "The Development of US Protection of Libraries," 326.

12. Grimsted, "Roads to Ratibor," 406–407, see also n118 (detailing the shipments to Hungen); Pamela Spence Richards, "Aryan Librarianship," *Journal of Library History (1974–1987)* 19, no. 2 (Spring 1984), 249–50. In total, there were six storage sites in Hungen.

13. Sutter, "Lost Jewish Libraries," 229.

14. S. D. Goitein, *A Mediterranean Society: The Jewish Communities of the World as Portrayed in the Documents of the Cairo Geniza*, vol. 1 (1996; repr., Berkeley: University of California Press, 1999), 5.

15. Grimsted, "Roads to Ratibor," 407 (citing a March 27, 1944, report to Rosenberg, "Betr: Brand der Hohen Schule, Aussenstelle Frankfurt a. M. infolge Luftangriffes am 22. Marz 1944—Verhalten der Verwaltungsorgane").

16. Poste, "Development of US Protection of Libraries," 336; Gallas, *Das Leichenhaus der Bücher*, 37.

17. Ibid. These methods to save the water-damaged and moldy books in 1945 were eerily repeated in 1966 when the Jewish Theological Seminary's (JTS) library suffered a massive fire. Because of the water used to fight the fire, many of the surviv-

ing books suffered severe water damage and mold. Several methods were attempted, including repurposing state-of-the-art freeze-drying machines used to make cereal to dry the rarest books. Ultimately, the most effective method was the same used in 1945—volunteers placed towels between the pages to dry the books. The volunteers referred to this method as "interleafing." Barry D. Cytron, *Fire!: The Library Is Burning* (Minneapolis: Lerner Publications, 1988), 19–39.

18. The movie depicts only the MFA&A's exploits as they relate to art and ignores Jewish books entirely. Sally McGrane, "What Became of the Jewish Books?" *New Yorker*, February 28, 2014. The gendered pronoun is misleading—women also served on the MFA&A. See Tom Mashberg, "Not All Monuments Men Were Men," *New York Times*, January 29, 2014, AR19.

19. Dana Herman, "Hashavat Avedah: A History of Jewish Cultural Reconstruction, Inc." (PhD diss, McGill University, Montreal, 2008), 108. Similar organizations were established by others aligned with the Allies.

20. Poste, "Development of US Protection of Libraries," 333.

21. Kurtz, *America*, 88.

22. Ibid.

23. NARA, RG 260, M1941, reel 7.

24. Gallas, *Das Leichenhaus der Bücher*, 36.

25. Kurtz, *America*, 92.

26. Robert Wetsch, "Besuch in Frankfurt," *Mitteilungsblatt des Irgun Olej Merkaz Europa*, January 11, 1946, 10. Quoted in Gallas, *Das Leichenhaus der Bücher*, 37.

27. A November 2, 1945, report describes the inadequacies of the IEJ building and the benefits of the OAD. Leslie I. Poste to Chief, Monuments, Fine Arts and Archives Section, Internal Affairs Branch, "Report of Inspection of Offenbach Collection Point," November 2, 1945, NARA, RG 260, M1942, reel 3.

28. Poste, "Development of US Protection of Libraries," 337–38.

29. Ibid., 335–39. Kurtz, *America*, 130.

30. Waite, "Returning Jewish Cultural Property," 214–15. Schidorsky, *Gevilim Nesraphim*, 225, listing the countries and libraries whose books were deposited at the Offenbach Depot. Sutter, "Lost Jewish Libraries," 229–32.

31. Chiméne I. Keitner, "Introductory Note to the United States Second Circuit Court of Appeals: *Koibel v. Royal Dutch Petroleum Co.*," *International Legal Materials* 49, no. 6 (2010), 1522. See, generally, *Law Reports of Trials of War Criminals: Selected and Prepared by the United Nations War Crimes Commission*, vol. 10: *The I. G. Farben and Krupp Trials* (London: His Majesty's Stationery Office, 1949).

32. Poste, "Development of US Protection of Libraries," 340–41. The official date of the order is March 2, 1946. "Monthly Report, March 1946," March 31, 1946, NARA, RG 260, M1942, reel 9. Poste was an officer assigned to the Seventh Army and tasked with surveying the status of the books and other items at the Rothschild Library. His article and dissertation remains the most detailed account of creation of the OAD. Poste, "Development of US Protection of Libraries," 339–44. By January 8, 1946, all the looted property at "the Repository at Hungen . . . has been evacuated recently to the Central Collection Point at Offenbach." William C. Baker to Director, Economic

Division, Office of Military Government for Germany (US) (Attn: Monuments, Fine Arts and Archives Section, Restitution Branch), January 8, 1946, NARA, RG 260, M1941, reel 21.

33. Poste, "Development of US Protection of Libraries," 340. For additional biographical information, see Glickman, *Stolen Words*, 198–99. On February 14, 1946, the director of the MFA&A wrote to the Office of Military Government for Greater Hesse and described the necessary requirements for the director position at the OAD. "Administration and Operations of the OAD," February 14, 1946, NARA, RG 260, M1942, reel 3.

34. NARA, RG 260, M1942, reels 9 and 10.

35. Poste, "Development of US Protection of Libraries," 340. "Monthly Report, March 1946," March 31, 1946, NARA, RG 260, M1942, reel 9 (a list of the German employees appears in enclosure 4). Generally, the MFA&A was severely understaffed. There were only forty MFA&A personnel in the American Zone from November 21, 1945 to March 1, 1946. "MFA&A Organization in U.S. Zone (Including Personnel Distribution) 21 November 1945—1 March 1946," NARA, RG 260, M1944, reel 4.

36. "Monthly Report, March 1946," March 31, 1946, 6 and enclosure 5 ("Work-Plan for Sorting"), NARA, RG 260, M1942, reel 9; Dawidowicz, *From That Place*, 315.

37. "Monthly Report, March 1946," March 31, 1946, 6, NARA, RG 260, M1942, reel 9.

38. Ibid.

39. Ibid. Major D. P. M. Graswinckel was the "key person" in the restitution of the Netherlands' materials. Seymour Pomrenze, "Offenbach Reminiscences: The Netherlands' Experiences," *Spoils of War*, no. 2 (July 15, 1996): 18–20, https://pdfsecret.com/download/spoils-of-war_5a13158ad64ab24772a2d315_pdf. F. J. Hoogewoud, "The Return of the Bibliotheca Rosenthliana—But Not without Damage," in *Bibliotheca Rosenthaliana: Treasures of Jewish Booklore: Marking the Two Hundredth Anniversary of the Birth of Leeser Rosenthal, 1794-1994*, ed. Adri K. Offenberg (Amsterdam: Amsterdam University Press, 1996), 116–17. The Rosenthalia Library originally belonged to a rabbi in Hamburg, Germany, Lesser Rosenthal. At his death in 1868, his collection contained approximately six thousand volumes and thirty-two Hebrew manuscripts. Afterward his son offered the library as a gift to the German government and the Royal Library in Berlin. The Germans declined his gift. His children then approached the city of Amsterdam, where they were residents, and proposed giving the library to the city, on the condition that the city maintain the library and continue to provide funds for its expansion. The city agreed. A catalog was made of the collection. Meijer Marcus Roest, *Catalog der Hebraica und Judaica: Aus der L. Rosenthal'schen Bibliothek* (1875, repr. Amsterdam: B. M. Isräel, 1966); see also Shimeon Brisman, *A History and Guide to Judaic Bibliography* (Cincinnati: Hebrew Union College Press, 1977), 54–57; Adri K. Offenberg, "From Lesser Rosenthal to Today's Bibliotheca Rosenthaliana," in *Bibliotheca Rosenthaliana*, introduction, xi-xii. The Ets Hayyim Library was established in the early seventeenth century. The Nazis plundered the entire library, and much of it was discovered at the OAD. Unfortunately, the Nazis stored the library's rarest materials separately, and they were never located after the Holocaust. See Raphael Weiser and Joseph Kaplan, eds., *Treasures from the Library Ets Haim/Livraria Montezinos of the Portugees Israëlietisch Seminarium*

Ets Haim, Amsterdam (Jerusalem: Jewish National and University Library, 1980). The Ets Hayyim Library received an additional ten cases in April. "Monthly Report, April 1946," April 30, 1946, 6, NARA, RG 260, M1942, reel 9.

40. We have been unable to identify exactly when and from where the Strashun Library books made their way to the OAD. They may have been among those discovered at Hungen or remained somewhere in Frankfurt and brought directly to the OAD. But by at least April 1946, the Strashun Library books were at the OAD. See "Monthly Report, April 1946," April 30, 1946, NARA, RG 260, M1942, reel 9.

41. That the Strashun Library remained undetected because of confusion regarding the acronym arguably began with Mattityahu and his proclivity to use obscure abbreviations. For example, Mattityahu's commentary on *Midrash Rabba*, *Mattat Yah* was published posthumously by his nephew Samuel Strashun. While Samuel was preparing the manuscript for print, he wrote to Judah Bahak requesting assistance in deciphering book titles that appeared in the manuscript. Bahak's reply is preserved at the YIVO Archives. Judah Bahak to Samuel Strashun, 15 Elul, 1890 [August 31, 1890], YIVO Archives, RG 223.2, folder 82.3. Bahak used the opportunity to request Samuel's assistance in publishing one of Bahak's works. Bahak's notes and decryptions of titles are included in *Mattat Yah*. Mattityahu Strashun, *Mattat Yah* (Vilna: Widow and Brothers Romm, 1893), 4. For biographical information regarding Bahak, see his entry in the Jewish Encyclopedia. Herman Rosenthal, "Behak, Judah," in *Jewish Encyclopedia*, ed. Isidore Singer et al. (New York: Funk and Wagnalls, 1901–1906), vol. 2, 641. The use of arcane abbreviations is common throughout Jewish literature and consistently resulted in decoding errors. See Yaakov Samuel Spiegel, *Amudim be-Toldot ha-Sefer ha-Ivri: be-Sha'arei ha-Defus* (Petah Tikvah: [Ya'akov Shemu'el Spiegel], 2014), 304–8, 319–21; Yaakov Shemuel Spiegel, "The Use of Uncommon Abbreviations," *Yeshurun* 10 (2002): 814–30; *Yeshurun* 11 (2002): 919–31; *Yeshurun* 12 (2003): 802–14; *Yeshurun* 13 (2003): 828–43.

42. Poste, "Development of US Protection of Libraries," 354. Bencowitz arrived on April 13. "Monthly Report April," April 30, 1946, 3, NARA, RG 260, M1942, reel 9.

43. Colonel Seymour J. Pomrenze, "Personal Reminiscences of the OAD, 1946–1949, Fulfilling International and Moral Obligations," November 30, 1998, https:// www.ushmm.org/information/exhibitions/online-exhibitions/special-focus /offenbach-archival-depot/establishment-and-operation. A diagram of the revised workflow appears in "May Monthly Report," May 31, 1946, encl. 3, NARA, RG 260, M1942.

44. Leslie Poste describes Bencowitz's process in detail. Poste, "Development of US Protection of Libraries," 354–58. See also Gallas, *Leichenhaus*, 47–49 (providing examples demonstrating that the ex libris are themselves an expression of the diverse book culture of Europe before the Nazis).

45. Bencowitz's catalogs are retained in the National Archives, RG 260, M1942, reels 11–13, accessed January 13, 2017, https://www.fold3.com/browse/115/hea6C18mG.

46. The Strashun Library stamps appear both in volumes 3 and 6, "Miscellaneous Jewish" under "Straschun." Both volumes reproduce the same eleven stamps. Some of the stamps, however, are incorrectly associated with the Strashun Public Library. For example, two stamps (nos. 4 and 6) are from the Strashun synagogue and one

(no. 7), from the Strashun kloyz. A reproduction of Strashun's personal stamp appears in vol. 5, "Wilno," no. 69, NARA, RG 260, M1942, reel 12. Regarding the Strashun kloyz, see Cohen-Mushlin, *Synagogues in Lithuania N-Z*, 323n89.

47. Weinreich asserted in an affidavit that YIVO was officially incorporated in 1940, the same year he arrived in New York. Indeed, in YIVO's tax filings it indicates a 1940 formation date. But according to the New York Department of State records, incorporation occurred in 1942.

48. After receiving the report, Weinreich was unsure who best to contact — Bencowitz or the State Department — regarding "libraries [that] rightfully belong to this Institute [(YIVO)]." Weinreich requested the advice of Marcus Cohn, the American Jewish Committee's Washington representative. Max Weinreich to Marcus Cohn, July 2, 1946, Lucy S. Dawidowicz Papers, P-675, box 51, folder 9, American Jewish Historical Society, New York, and Boston. Henceforth, "Dawidowicz Papers, box no., folder no." Cohn's advice was to write "Captain Bencowitz in Offenbach." See Max Weinreich to Marcus Cohn, July 24, 1946, Dawidowicz Papers, box 51, folder 9.

49. Max Weinreich to Captain Isaac Bencowitz, July 9, 1946, NARA, RG 260, M1942, reel 5. Five separate archival collections contain many of the documents related to YIVO and restitution: the Lucy S. Dawidowicz Papers, P-675, American Jewish Historical Society, New York, and Boston; records of the YIVO Institute for Jewish Research, New York, RG 100, Administrative Records; uncataloged "Files Relating to Restitution of YIVO Property"; Max Weinreich Papers, YIVO Archives, RG 584; and NARA, RG 260, M1942. I have reviewed four of the five. YIVO RG 100 records were closed to this researcher. The chief archivist at YIVO, Dr. Lyudmila Sholokhova, explained the access restrictions: "The bulk of YIVO Administrative Records are private records and as a matter of policy, are not part of the research archives which are available." Dr. Lyudmila Sholokhova to Dan Rabinowitz, November 17, 2016 (copy in the possession of the author). Numerous researchers, however, have made extensive use of these records. See, e.g., Fishman, *Book Smugglers*; Nancy Sinkoff, "From the Archives: Lucy S. Dawidowicz and the Restitution of Jewish Cultural Property," *American Jewish History* 100, no. 1 (January 2016), 117–47; Cecile Esther Kuznitz, *YIVO and the Making of Modern Jewish Culture: Scholarship for the Yiddish Nation* (New York: Cambridge University Press, 2014); Kalman Weiser, "Max Weinreich and the Emergence of YIVO's American Center," *Choosing Yiddish: New Frontiers* (Detroit: Wayne State University Press, 2012). Dr. Sholokhova provided no explanation regarding the past use of the RG 100 records. To the extent that copies of documents appear in multiple archives, I have cited those that are contained in the National Archives. The National Archives documents are the official United States Government records and best represent the historical record. Inherent in the private archives of YIVO and Dawidowicz are chain of custody and other evidentiary issues.

50. Shor, *Likutei Shoshanim*, 32. The responsibility for the library changed over time. Some of those changes were a consequence of governmental policies that dissolved communal boards, such as the Tzedakah Gedolah, but at all time remained under some form of communal organization. Shor, *Likutei Shoshanim*, 40–47.

51. Kruk, *Last Days*, 108, 138, 155, 196–97, 358; Abraham Sutzkever, *Vilner Ghetto* (Tel Aviv: Sekhvi, 1946), 97–100,

52. S. M. Dubnow, "Ob izuchenii istorii russkikh evreev i ob uchrezhdenii russkoevereiskago istoricheskago obshchestav," *Voskhod* 4, no. 9 (April–September 1891), 1–91. Dubnow also published a Hebrew version of his article. Simon M. Dubnow, *Nahpesa ve-Nahkora: Kol Kore el ha-Nevonim be-Am ha-Mitnadvim Le'esof Homer le-Binyan Toldot Bene Yisrael be-Polin ve-Rusiya* (Odessa: Ha-Pardes, 1892). For a bibliography of works discussing Dubnow, see Dan Haruv, "Simon Dubnow: An Annotated Bibliography," *Writer and Warrior: Simon Dubnow: Historian and Public Figure*, eds. Abraham Greenbaum, Israel Bartal, and Dan Haruv (Jerusalem: Zalman Shazar Center for Jewish History, 2010), 213–66 (Heb. section).

53. Even prior to Dubnow, views regarding the use of Yiddish and its role in Jewish life shifted over time. Indeed, especially among Orthodox Jews, by the late eighteenth and early nineteenth centuries Yiddish was no longer treated with disdain. Katz, *Words on Fire*, 153–63.

54. Simon Rabinovitch, *Jewish Rights, National Rites: Nationalism and Autonomy in Late Imperial and Revolutionary Russia* (Redwood City, CA: Stanford University Press, 2014), 1.

55. Ibid. The literature regarding Jewish Diaspora Nationalism is far too large to provide a complete bibliography. Some recent treatments include Robert Seltzer, *Simon Dubnow's "New Judaism": Diaspora Nationalism and the World History of the Jews* (supplement to the *Journal of Jewish Thought and Philosophy*) (Leiden: Brill, 2013); Simon Rabinovitch, *Jewish Rights, National Rites: Nationalism and Autonomy in Late Imperial and Revolutionary Russia* (Redwood City, CA: Stanford University Press, 2014); Joshua Karlip, *The Tragedy of a Generation: The Rise and Fall of Jewish Nationalism in Eastern Europe* (Cambridge: Harvard University Press, 2013); Simon Rabinovitch, ed., *Jews and Diaspora Nationalism: Writings on Jewish Peoplehood in Europe and the United States* (Waltham, MA: Brandeis University Press, 2012); James Loeffler, "Between Zionism and Liberalism: Oscar Janowsky and Diaspora Nationalism in America," *AJS Review* 34, no. 2 (November 2010), 289–308; Zohar Segev, "Diaspora Nationalism: The World Jewish Congress, American Jewry and the Rehabilition of European Jewry after the Holocaust," *Zion* 75 (2010), 153–82.

56. Kuznitz, *Making of Modern Jewish Culture*, 17–19.

57. Fishman, *Embers*, 2. In 1918 Lunski, the Strashun Library librarian, wrote a history of the Vilna Ghetto as an act of preservation of what otherwise might be lost forever. Kuznitz, *Making of Modern Jewish Culture*, 25. Lunski wrote other histories. Shor, *Likutei Shoshanim*, 146–58.

58. Only in 1929 was "YIVO" established as a legal entity. Prior to that, "activities had been carried out under the auspices of the Society of the Friends of the Yiddish Scientific Institute." Kuznitz, *Making of Modern Jewish Culture*, 128–29.

59. Eventually, some of his students, most prominently many YIVO leaders, broke with Dubnow and his philosophy. Joshua Karlip, *The Tragedy of a Generation: The Rise and Fall of Jewish Nationalism in Eastern Europe* (Cambridge: Harvard University Press, 2013), 186–205.

60. Fishman, *Embers*, 2.

61. Kuznitz, *Making of Modern Jewish Culture*, 63.

62. Ibid., 113–16, 139–40.

63. Ibid., 134. Ran, *Jerusalem of Lithuania*, vol. 1, 264 (photograph of opening events at the Wiwulski Building). Other "modern" organizations chose to site their locations outside the ghetto for reasons similar to YIVO's. Kuznitz, "On the Jewish Street," 77-79.

64. Dawidowicz, *From That Place and Time*, 77-79, quoted in Kuznitz, *Making of Modern Jewish Culture*, 132.

65. Kuznitz, *Making of Modern Jewish Culture*, 133-34.

66. Beyond the question of YIVO and its connection to the historic Jewish Vilna, there may also be a linkage between the Vilna Gaon and Yiddish. See Joshua A. Fishman, "The Gaon of Vilne and the Yiddish Language," in *The Gaon of Vilnius and the Annals of Jewish Culture*, 18-26.

67. Kuznitz, *Making of Modern Jewish Culture*, 135 (quoting Shmuel Niger).

68. Ibid., 134-35.

69. Dawidowicz, *From That Place and Time*, 77-79.

70. Kuznitz, *Making of Modern Jewish Culture*, 131.

71. Ibid., 137.

72. *Der Yivo Nokh Draytsn Yor Arbet* (Vilna: 1938). The cover is reproduced in Kuznitz, *Making of Modern Jewish Culture*, 138.

73. Dawidowicz, *From That Place and Time*, 79.

74. Kuznitz, *Making of Modern Jewish Culture*, 137.

75. Sutter, "Lost Jewish Libraries," 224n22.

76. Shor, *Likutei Shoshanim*, 72-76, 181.

77. Kuznitz, *Making of Modern Jewish Culture*, 131.

78. Fishman, *Rise of Modern Yiddish Culture*, 96. The library at Hebrew University began using the system in 1924. Zvi Baras, *A Century of Books: The Jewish National and University Library 1892-1922* (Jerusalem: Jewish National and University Library, 1992), 10.

79. Kuznitz, *Making of Modern Jewish Culture*, 137.

80. Max's son, Uriel, also traveled to Copenhagen with his father as a thirteenth birthday present. The family referred to the thirteenth birthday as a "bar mitzvah" but "without for a moment attributing any religious significance to it." Gabriel Weinreich, *Confessions of a Jewish Priest: From Secular Jewish War Refugee to Physicist and Episcopal Clergyman* (Cleveland, OH: Pilgrim Press, 2005), 35.

81. The theory regarding the reason for Reyzen's arrest and ultimate execution was suggested by Noah Pryłucki, the director of YIVO during the 1940-1941 Soviet occupation of Vilna, who was appointed as a lecturer of Yiddish at Vilna University. At the time, Pryłucki was an ardent communist, and he likely provided this theory to justify the Soviets' treatment of Reyzen. Weiser, "Coming to America," 248n4; Weiser, "The Jewel in the Yiddish Crown," 250. In reality, immediately upon the Soviets' entrance into Vilna, on September 9, 1939, the front page of *Der Tog* carried the headline, "Jewish Vilna Receives Red Army Festively." Moreover, the rest of that issue contains a number of positive articles regarding the Red Army and its arrival in Vilna. Nevertheless, the Soviets closed the newspaper immediately because it was

not a government-sponsored publication. Levin, *Lesser of Two Evils*, 117. Reyzen was a central figure within YIVO. In January 1940, Zelig Kalmanovitch was despondent after Reyzen's arrest and questioned how YIVO could continue to live when the "head and heart of YIVO is gone." Weiser, "The Jewel in the Yiddish Crown," 240-41 (quoting Kalmanovitch).

82. Abramowicz, *Profiles*, 313-20; *YIVO Encyclopedia*, s.v. "Reyzen, Zalman," accessed January 2, 2018, http://www.yivoencyclopedia.org/article.aspx/Reyzen_Zalmen.

83. Weiser, "Coming to America," 234.

84. Approximately 70 percent of the immigrants were from Nazi-occupied territories, with the remaining number from the Soviet-occupied territories. Levin, *Lesser of Two Evils*, 200, and table 9.1, "Refugees Listed with the Refugee Committee by the Vilna Kehilla"; Weiser, "Coming to America," 243; Weiser, "The Jewel in the Yiddish Crown," 224 (the immigration of so many Jews raised the percentage of Jews in Vilna from 6.4 percent to 8.4 percent).

85. Weiser, "Coming to America," 243.

86. Levin, *Lesser of Two Evils*, 112-13.

87. See "Bericht vom dem Arbeitsergebnis der juedischen Arbeitsgruppe beim Einsatzstab RR Wilna," February 18-June 8, 1942, Lithuanian Central State Archive, f. 633, op. 1., d. 5. That report states that YIVO received ten thousand volumes during the Soviet occupation. But many of the inventories in the report appear to be inexact and likely based on rough estimates rather than actual counts.

88. Levin, *Lesser of Two Evils*, 113.

89. Ibid., 113-14. Weiser, "The Jewel in the Yiddish Crown," 247. The chair was held by Noah Pryłucki, a member of YIVO (albeit not without controversy). Pryłucki held the chair until the Nazis dismissed him on June 27, 1941. His scholarship led to his arrest and forcible conscription in the ERR's project to loot Jewish Vilna institutions. Like Lunsky, daily, Pryłucki was taken from his cell to the Strashun Library to prepare lists of incunabula for shipment to Germany. On August 18, 1941, he was shot by the Nazis. Weiser, "The Jewel in the Yiddish Crown," 251-52.

90. "Bibliothek der Hohen Schule in Vorbereitung," September 29, 1941, Central State Archive, Ukraine, f. 3673, op. 1, d. 136, 397 ("Von der grossen Anzahl der *wissenschaftlichen* Bibliotheken" [emphasis added]).

91. Kruk, *Last Days*, 231; Fishman, *Embers*, 4; Schidorsky, *Gevilim Nesraphim*, 183.

92. Fishman, *Book Smugglers*, 59, 267n11.

93. Kruk, *Last Days*, 296.

94. For a list of some of the other collections, see "Bericht vom dem Arbeitsergebnis der juedischen Arbeitsgruppe beim Einsatzstab RR Wilna," February 18-June 8, 1942, Lithuanian Central State Archive, f. 633, op. 1., d. 5.

95. Many accounts conflate the Strashun Library and YIVO smuggling efforts into a single episode. See, e.g., Shavit, *Hunger*, 95-96.

96. Fishman, *Book Smugglers*, 67-89.

97. In addition to moving materials into the ghetto, the Paper Brigade also hid materials in the YIVO building itself. Fishman, *Book Smugglers*, 87.

98. Fishman, *Embers*, 5.

99. Fishman, *Book Smugglers*, 69–74.

6. A Transatlantic Crossing

1. NARA, RG 260, M1942, reel 5. The exact number of Strashun Library books that left the OAD is discussed following.

2. This was not YIVO's first request for assistance from the government. Rather, since June 1942, Weinreich made repeated inquiries to the American government about whether it had received information regarding the state of YIVO's building and library in Vilna. See, e.g., Max Weinreich to Green H. Hackworth, August 3, 1944, Dawidowicz Papers, box 51, folder 57, (referencing a June 10, 1942, letter from Weinreich to the State Department's legal adviser); Max Weinreich to Dr. Summer Crosby, July 19, 1944, Dawidowicz Papers, box 51, folder 57; Max Weinreich to Green H. Hackworth, August 3, 1944, Dawidowicz Papers, box 51, folder 57, (requesting that the US government contact the Soviets for information on whether YIVO's building "at 18 Wiwulski Street, is still intact or has it been destroyed" and the fate "of the tremendous library, archive, and museum collections"); Max Weinreich to John Walker, September 29, 1944, Dawidowicz Papers, box 51, folder 57 (YIVO received reports that indicated its property was removed "to one of the German so-called research institutes on Jewish problems, probably in Frankfurt"). For a detailed history of YIVO's efforts to transfer the Vilna materials to New York, see Bilha Shilo, "'Funem Folk, Farn Folk, Mitn Folk': The Restitution of the YIVO Collection from Offenbach to New York," *Moreshet* 14 (2017): 362–412; Bilha Shilo, "'Funem Folk, Farn Folk, Mitn Folk': Historiah shel Asufei YIVO le-ahar milhemet ha-olam ha-shniyah" (master's thesis, Hebrew University of Jerusalem, October 2016). The author wishes to express his gratitude to Bilha for her generously sharing the conclusions of her research and providing copies of archival materials.

3. *Guide to YIVO Archives*, comp. and ed. Fruma Mohrer and Marek Web (New York: YIVO Institute for Jewish Research, 1998), 176n685.

4. By the end of the hostilities in Europe in 1945, Weinreich was sufficiently familiar with the details of Rosenberg's plan of plunder and looting on behalf of IEJ's library in Frankfurt and its operations in Vilna that he was requested to draft a summary of the operation for the Nuremberg trials. Abraham G. Duker to Max Weinreich, July 26, 1945, YIVO Archives, Territorial Collection, RG 116, Germany II, box 4a. Weinreich, within a week, responded with a lengthy description of the ERR's operations. Max Weinreich to Abraham G. Duker, August 1, 1945, YIVO Archives, Territorial Collection, RG 116, Germany II, box 4a.

5. "Memorandum to Dr. Eugene N. Anderson, Division of Cultural Cooperation, Department of State, by the Delegation of the Yiddish Scientific Institute—YIVO (Professor Sol Liptzin, Secretary of the Academic Council of YIVO, and Chairman of the German Department of City College, New York, and Dr. Max Weinreich, Research Director of the Yiddish Scientific Institute—YIVO) on May 7, 1945," NARA, RG 260, M1941, reel 9. That day a second meeting was held at the State Department. See Shilo, "Funem Folk," 371.

6. Grimsted, "Roads to Ratibor," 407 (citing Schonfeld Report, NARA, RG 94, box 6779).

7. Lt. Col. Hammond to Director RD&R Div., August 2, 1945, NARA, RG 260, M1941, reel 15.

8. On June 6, 1945, Maj. Gen. Hilldring forwarded the May 7, 1945, memorandum to Lt. Gen. Clay, "for any action you feel appropriate." J. H. Hilldring to Lt. Gen. Lucius Clay, June 6, 1945, NARA, RG 260, M1941, reel 9.

9. Major Mason Hammond to Director, RD&R Division, Memorandum, "Subject: Library of the Yiddish Scientific Institute," June 23, 1945, NARA, RG 260, M1941, reel 9. On July 4, 1945, Lt. Gen. Clay forwarded Buchman's report to Maj. Gen. Hilldring, and assured him that "[t]he necessary steps are being taken to preserve these materials and make them available for examination." Lucius D. Clay to Maj. Gen. J. H. Hilldring, July 4, 1945, NARA, RG 260, M1941, reel 9. On June 24, 1945, Lt. Buchman attempted to visit the Hungen repository in search of any YIVO materials. But "Lt. Buchman was informed . . . that the repository is a G-2 Intelligence Target and cannot be visited without G-2 authorization." From Mason Hammond, Chief, MFA&A Branch to Dir., RD&R Division, "Insitut zur Erforschung der Judenfrage," June 24, 1945, NARA, M1941, reel 9.

10. Abraham Aaroni to Celia Aaroni, June 20, 1945, Dawidowicz Papers, box 51, folder 6. Soon afterward, on July 24, 1945, Lt. Col. Judah Nadich, the senior Jewish chaplin in the army, notified Weinreich that YIVO property was at Frankfurt. See Max Weinreich to Seymour Pomrenze, March 21, 1946; Max Weinreich, Affidavit, March 12, 1946 (Weinreich attests that Nadich, "in a letter dated July 24, 1945, informed the institute that the YIVO Library had been found at Frankfort."), NARA, M1942, reel 5. Regarding Nadich's continuing efforts on behalf of YIVO, see Shilo, "Funem Folk," 373. In late August 1945, Nadich was appointed as special adviser on Jewish Affairs to Gen. Eisenhower, responsible for interfacing with Jewish DPs. Zeev W. Mankowitz, *Studies in the Social and Cultural History of Modern Warfare: Life between Memory and Hope: The Survivors of the Holocaust in Occupied Germany* (Cambridge: Cambridge University Press, 2002), 64.

11. George W. Baker to Max Weinreich, July 23, 1945, Dawidowicz Papers, box 51, folder 6.

12. Repeatedly, the US government emphasized in its 1944 and 1945 correspondence with Weinreich that the issue of restitution of any Jewish property was under discussion and still pending resolution. For example, in September of 1944, the State Department informed Weinreich that the issue of restitution was the topic of an Allies' conference in London, and that "difficult legal and diplomatic issues are involved." The department pledged to notify Weinreich of the outcome of the London conference and "whatever procedure is set up by the Allied Nations for the restitution or replacement of the invaluable material belonging to cultural institutions." John Walker to Max Weinreich, September 14, 1944, NARA, RG 260, M1944, reel 18. The resolution of the issue of the distribution of Jewish property remained unsettled until 1947. Gallas, *Leichenhaus*, 134–40; Herman, "Hashevat Avedah."

13. Saul Kagan to Max Weinreich, September 14, 1945, Dawidowicz Papers, box

51, folder 6. According to Shilo, Kagan was suggesting that YIVO should receive property it never owned—"everything from Vilna"—and that in fact is the policy which was ultimately implemented, giving YIVO non-YIVO property. Shilo, "Funem Folk," 380, 388. But that interpretation ignores the next sentence in which Kagan provides the justification for why "everything" should go to YIVO. Not because YIVO never owned those items, but because even if the items in question contained private markings, the YIVO library itself in large part comprised exactly those sorts of books, donated from those individuals, and those items were previously part of the library. In the first OAD report after the books were moved from the Rothschild Building to the OAD, YIVO property is labeled "JIWO Scientific Institute NYC." "March 31, 1946, Monthly Report." NARA, RG 260, M1946, reel 6.

14. Koppel Pinson to Leibush Lehrer, November 30, 1945 (cable), Dawidowicz Papers, box 52, folder 4 ("Large part of YIVO Library Vilna now in Frankfurt [. . .] please cable authorization to me as YIVO Director to allow release of some of the less valuable books here promise to use such authorization with great caution and respect for YIVO aims and rights."); Pinson was in Frankfurt on behalf of the Joint Distribution Committee. In November 1945, he proposed a loan program under which unidentifiable books would be distributed to DPs. After he received authorization, he began sorting through the looted books, and in the process, came across YIVO books. The success of his project is the subject of considerable debate. Indeed, in 1947 the Army questioned whether Pinson adhered to the terms of the loan program and selected only unidentifiable books, and even if the books he selected were distributed to the DPs or were diverted elsewhere. Sinkoff, "From the Archives," 130–32, 142.

15. Max Weinreich and Leibush Lehrer to Koppel S. Pinson (cable), December 4, 1945 (cited in Sinkoff, "From the Archives," 130); Shilo, "Funem Folk," 30–31. There is a discrepancy as to the exact date Pinson learned of the appointment and whether he received the December cable. On March 18, 1946, Weinreich wrote to Pinson (again) appointing him YIVO representative at the OAD and indicating that he had already sent Pinson the authorization back in December of 1945. On March 11, 1946, however, seven days before Weinreich sent his letter, Pinson wrote to Pomrenze that Weinreich had already agreed to appoint Pinson as YIVO's representative. Koppel Pinson to Seymour Pomrenze, March 11, 1946, NARA, RG 260, M1942, reel 5.

16. YIVO was not the only organization to contact Jewish servicemen in Germany seeking their assistance in locating and transferring Jewish books and property. The Hebrew University was regularly in contact with chaplains in Europe to press its cause. Herman, "Hashavat Avedah," 58.

17. Some of Weinreich's letters are written in Yiddish and others in English. The reason for the selection of one language over another for any particular letter is not entirely clear. In some instances, we can speculate that because of the sensitive nature of the contents of the letters, he elected to use Yiddish to keep unauthorized persons from reading the letters. In at least one instance, Weinreich explicitly indicates as much. Max Weinreich to Lucy Schildkret, February 15, 1947, Dawidowicz Papers, box 52, folder 1. Here, Weinreich may have written in Yiddish because of

his references to Seymour's personal connection to YIVO. Indeed, when Weinreich writes Pomrenze three days later in English, he makes no mention of any relationship between YIVO and Chaim, or Seymour. Rather, Weinreich states, without further explication about the source, that "we have been informed that YIVO Library, together with other Jewish book collections confiscated by the Nazis and brought to Frankfort, is not in the American Zone in your custody," without any mention of Chaim's role. Max Weinreich to Captain S. J. Pomrenze, March 21, 1946, NARA, RG 260, M1942, reel 5.

18. On March 22, 1946, Chaim personally cabled Seymour and requested that he assist in the transfer of the YIVO library to New York. Shilo, "Funem Folk," 376.

19. For a description of its history under the Nazis, see Herman de la Fontaine Verwey, "The Bibliotheca Rosenthaliana during the German Occupation," *Studia Rosenthaliana* 38-39 (2005-2006): 60-72; F. J. Hoogewoud, "An Introduction to H. de la Fontaine Verwey's 'The Bibliotheca Rosenthaliana during the German Occupation,'" *Studia Rosenthaliana* 38-39 (2005-2006): 49-59.

20. Max Weinreich to Seymour Pomrenze, March 19, 1946 [Yiddish], NARA, RG 260, M1942, reel 6.

21. An internal YIVO report regarding its work during 1938-1939 seems to contradict Weinreich. Instead, that report indicates that the YIVO collection saw de minimis growth. The report records that the "library received over 1,000 books from the Danzig Jewish community, and another 300 or so from two other donors," a total of thirteen hundred volumes. "Report of the Work of YIVO during the year 1938-39 through December 31, 1939" [Yiddish], YIVO Archives, RG 584, 292a.

22. In 1938 YIVO celebrated its thirteenth year with a small pamphlet that described its growth and accomplishments since its founding in 1925. Its library and archive receive mention, and the library is reported to be at forty thousand volumes. *Der Yivo Nokh Draytsn Yor Arbet (YIVO after Thirteen Years of Work)* [Yiddish] (Vilna, 1938).

In the late 1960s, YIVO librarian Dina Abramowicz surveyed YIVO's history and quoted the forty-thousand-volume statistic as authoritative. Dina Abramowicz, "YIVO Library," *Jewish Book Annual* 25 (1967-1968), 89. Likewise, external reports suggest that as late as October 1939, the library maintained approximately forty thousand volumes. After Lithuanian independence in October 1939, the government surveyed the state of Vilna cultural institutions, YIVO among them. The subsequent report lists the library's holdings in October 1939, standing at forty thousand volumes. "Žinia apie veikusię 1939 m. spalio men. 10 d. Vilniaus mieste ir jo srityje draugija," November 28, 1939, YIVO Archives, RG 584, folder 293b. Similarly, ERR reports estimate from forty to fifty thousand volumes. "Bericht," April 28, 1942, Central State Archive, Ukraine, f. 3767, op. 1, d. 136; "Bericht," February 18-June 8, 1942, Lithuanian Central State Archive, f. 633, op. 1, del. 5. The eighty-five-thousand-volume estimate for the YIVO collection is still widely cited. See Laila Hussein Moustafa, Joshua Harris, and Bethany Anderson, "Lessons from World War II and the Holocaust: What Can Be Done to Save Cultural Heritage and Memory during Times of War," *What Do We Lose When We Lose a Library?: Proceedings of* the Conference Held at the KU Leuven 9–11 September 2015, ed. Mel Collier (Leuven: University Library KU Leuven, 2016), 154; e.g., Schidorsky, *Gevilim Nesraphim*, 219n** (listing the YIVO Library at eighty-five thousand volumes). Schidorsky is inconsistent in his accounting for YIVO Library. Elsewhere he states that YIVO Library consisted of approximately fifty thousand volumes. Schidorsky, *Gevilim Nesraphim*, 181. Schidorsky's estimates for the library are provided without citation. Similarly, his estimate, again without citation, that the Strashun Library held thirty-five thousand volumes prewar is flawed. In 1940 the Strashun Library held approximately fifty thousand volumes. Shor, *Likutei Shoshanim*, 75–77. In subsequent years, the estimates of YIVO library's prewar holdings continued to rise. In 1951 the *News of the YIVO* stated that the library held one hundred thousand books. "YIVO Library Is Back at Home," *News of the YIVO* 40 (March 1951). Similarly, in 2000 YIVO sought money from a settlement with Swiss banks regarding Holocaust-era assets. YIVO asserted that it lost "a minimum of $2 million . . . in World War II." Those losses are divided among three asset classes, and prewar YIVO is described as having "amassed a specialized library of over 100,000 volumes." Carl J. Rheins to Honorable Judah Gribetz, September 5, 2000, http://www.swissbankclaims.com /pdfs_eng/YivoInstitute.pdf. No citation for this sum is provided. Nonetheless, regarding YIVO Archives, the claim cites and relies on the 1946 article "The Tentative List of Jewish Cultural Treasures in Axis-Occupied Countries" in *Jewish Social Studies* as an accurate representation of the archive. That article, however, states that YIVO held eighty-five thousand volumes. Research Staff of the Commission on European Jewish Cultural Reconstruction, "Tentative List of Jewish Cultural Treasures in Axis-Occupied Countries," *Jewish Social Studies* 8 (1946), H. 1, supplement, entry 249. In 2004 YIVO filed a supplement to its 2000 claim, without any adjustment to the pre–World War II YIVO library holdings. Carl J. Rheins to the Honorable Edward R. Korman, January 27, 2004, http://www.swissbankclaims.com/DOCUMENTS_NEW /YIVOENG_0076_084.pdf.

23. Research Staff of the Commission on European Jewish Cultural Reconstruction, "Tentative List of Jewish Cultural Treasures in Axis-Occupied Countries," *Jewish Social Studies* 8 (1946), H. 1, supplement, entries 248–49. Regarding the genesis and compilation of the "Tentative List," see Elisabeth Gallas, "Documenting Cultural Destruction: The Research Project of the Commission on European Jewish Cultural Reconstruction, 1944–1948," in *Als der Holocaust noch keinen Namen hatte: Zur frühen Aufarbeitung des NS-Massenmordes an Jüdinnen und Juden* (*Before the Holocaust Had Its Name: Early Confrontations of the Nazi Mass Murder of the Jews*), ed. Regina Fritz, Éva Kovács, and Béla Rásky (Vienna: New Academic Press, 2016), 45–61.

24. Herman, "Hashavat Avedah," 51 (citing a letter from Koppel Pinson to Hannah Arendt, April 12, 1946).

25. "Members of the Commission" in "Tentative List," 3. Weinreich's involvement was also because of his role as director of YIVO. Ibid., 4 ("By maintaining direct contact with several hundred former rabbis, educators, social workers and communal leaders of the formerly Axis-occupied countries who now reside in the United States [. . .] the personnel of the Joint Distribution Committee and others now active in the European countries, the staff of the Commission has been able to accumulate a

considerable body of valuable materials concerning both the former and the present status of these cultural treasures."); ibid., 8 ("Certain significant data have also been secured from former officials of the institutions here listed."). Gallas, "Documenting Cultural Destruction," 54 ("Most of the information [on Polish collections were] . . . collected from YIVO New York members.").

26. Max Weinreich to Sumner McK. Crosby, July 19, 1944, NARA, RG 260, M1941, reel 6; Max Weinreich to Sumner McK. Crosby, June 23, 1944. NARA, RG 260, M1941, reel 6.

27. Max Weinreich to Captain Isaac Bencowitz, July 9, 1946, NARA, RG 260, M1942, reel 5.

28. Max Weinreich to Captain S. J. Pomrenze, March 21,1946, NARA, RG 260, M1942, reel 5. Pomerenze later wrote a brief review of the "Tentative List." Seymour Pomrenze, "Review," *American Archivists* 10, no. 1 (Jan. 1947), 68–69.

29. "Yiddisher Visenshaftlecher Institut (YIVO) in Vilna (Yiddish Scientific Institute)," in "Tentative List," 246n249.

30. The actual number was over fifty thousand. That inventory, however, was completed by the Soviets after the start of the war. The last published estimate was in Lunski's 1935 article, where he counts thirty-five thousand volumes. Lunski, "Di Strashun Bibliotek," 282.

31. Marcus Cohn to Max Weinreich, August 14, 1946 ("In the early part of this year it would have been possible to have YIVO material sent to the United States," but intervening events thwarted that.). Max Weinreich to Lucy Schildkret, February 15, 1947 [Yiddish], Dawidowicz Papers, box 52, folder 1 (Weinreich explained that in March 1946, the State Department was ready to approve YIVO's request for the property at the OAD.).

32. Max Weinreich to Captain Isaac Bencowitz, July 9, 1946, NARA, RG 260, M1942, reel 5.

33. On July 24, 1946, Weinreich wrote to Marcus Cohn, who suggested that Weinreich contact Bencowitz directly regarding the Strashun Library. Weinreich complained that he had not received any reply to his July 9 letter. Max Weinreich to Marcus Cohn, July 24, 1946, Dawidowicz Papers, box 51, folder 9.

34. "Monthly Report," October 31, 1947, NARA, RG 260, M1942, reel 10.

35. Max Weinreich to Seymour Pomrenze, February 8, 1947, Dawidowicz Papers, box 52, folder 1.

36. Kurtz, *America*, 92.

37. Max Weinreich to Lucy Schildkret, February 15, 1947 [Yiddish], Dawidowicz Papers, box 52, folder 1.

38. Affidavit of Max Weinreich, March 12, 1946, NARA, RG 260, M1942, reel 5; Affidavit of Max Weinreich, February 8, 1947, NARA, RG 260, M1942, reel 5; Affidavit of Markus Uveeler, February 1, 1947, NARA, RG 260, M1942, reel 5.

39. Max Weinreich to Lucy Schildkret, February 15, 1947 [Yiddish], Dawidowicz Papers, box 52, folder 1.

40. Shilo, "Funem Folk," 376–77.

41. Max Weinreich to Lucy Schildkret, February 15, 1947 [Yiddish], Dawidowicz Papers, box 52, folder 1.

42. Max Weinreich to Lucy Schildkret, March 15, 1947, Dawidowicz Papers, box 52, folder 1. The State Department approved the language of the injunction between February 15 and 18. Summary of M. Uveeler and Major Pomrenze Telephone Conversation, February 18, 1947 ("The cablegram to Germany has been approved by the State department and will now go to the War Department for approval."). Shilo, "Funem Folk," 376–77.

43. Indeed, Horne later reported to his superiors that "the subject materials at the Depot are easily identifiable as to ownership. This applies equally to YIVO and Strashun Collections." Joseph A. Horne to the Attention of the MFA&A Section, March 17, 1947, NARA, RG 260, M1942, reel 5.

44. Max Weinreich to Captain Isaac Bencowitz, July 9, 1946, NARA, RG 260, M1942, reel 5.

45. Luther E. Evans to General Hilldring, February 25, 1947, Dawidowicz Papers, box 55, folder 5. From Pomrenze's appointment as director of the OAD until late 1946, he supported the creation of a single restitution policy for Jewish assets, under the responsibility of a single umbrella Jewish organization, rather than a piecemeal division of the property among the various Jewish organizations, including YIVO. Gallas, *Das Leichenhaus der Bücher*, 122; Herman, "Hashevat Avedah," 72–75. In December 1946, Pomrenze's views shifted, and he began advocating on behalf of YIVO. Shilo, "Funem Folk," 376.

46. Max Weinreich to Seymour Pomrenze, February 14, 1947 [Yiddish], Dawidowicz Papers, box 52, folder 1.

47. Shor, *Likutei Shoshanim*, 46–47. At that time Lunski wrote that the merger would destroy the soul of the Strashun Library.

48. Levin, *Lesser of Two Evils*, 113–14.

49. Kruk, *Last Days*, 212–13, 223, 267–68, 296.

50. Kruk's diary entry for February 19, 1942, records that he learned that the Strashun Library collection point, at 3 University, would act as a central collection and sorting location for "all the Jewish material—from YIVO, the Strashun Library, and all others." Kruk, *Last Days*, 212–13. The Nazis determined that the floor of the building at 3 University Street, the Strashun Library collection, was unable to support the weight of the YIVO Library. Sutter, "Lost Jewish Libraries," 226; Fishman, *Embers*, 4. The 2005 English translation of Kruk's diaries includes an editorial note that erroneously reports that "many of [the Strashun Library books] were gathered at YIVO under the German occupation." Kruk, *Last Days*, 138n54.

51. Sutzkover, *Vilna Ghetto*, 99.

52. Kruk, *Last Days*, 212–14.

53. Joseph Horne to Office of Military Government for Germany (US) Economic Division, Restitution Branch, "The Yiddish Scientific Institute (YIVO)," March 17, 1947, NARA, RG 260, M1942, reel 5.

54. Max Weinreich to John Walker, September 29, 1944, NARA, RG 260, M1942, reel 5 (Weinreich responds to Walker's "letter of September 22nd, addressed to [Dawidowicz] in [Weinreich's] absence"); Sinkoff, "From the Archives," 125n31.

55. Dawidowicz, *From That Place and Time*, 294.

56. Ibid., 313–14.

57. Ibid., 313, 318.

58. Ibid., 318.

59. Ibid.

60. Ibid., 318–19.

61. Cable from Lucy Schildkret to Max Weinreich, February 14, 1947, Dawidowicz Papers, box 52, folder 4.

62. The exact timing of her discovery and subsequent discussions with Horne is unclear. Accounting for that the discovery occurred a "matter of days" after her return to the OAD on February 11; and because she continued to review and discover additional books "each day thereafter" *prior* to receiving Horne's approval, her description of the timeline is most likely imprecise.

63. Dawidowicz, *From That Place and Time*, 318.

64. Well before she arrived at the OAD, Dawidowicz was included in YIVO's endeavors to obtain the YIVO library. Sinkoff, "From the Archives," 128.

65. Thus, the affidavit only attests to the aggregate of the prewar YIVO library.

66. Affidavit of Max Weinreich, March 12, 1946, NARA, RG 260, M1942, reel 5.

67. Sinkoff, "From the Archives," 125n31.

68. Marcus Cohn to Dr. John Slawson, June 4, 1946, Dawidowicz Papers, box 52, folder 1; Max Weinreich to Lucy Schildkret, February 15, 1947 [Yiddish], Dawidowicz Papers, box 52, folder 1; Herman, *Hashavat Avedah*, 112–26, 155–60.

69. Weiser, "Coming to America," 239–46. Prior to the Holocaust, the Amopteyl's activities were, in the main, raising money on behalf of YIVO. Ibid., 235–36.

70. Ibid., 237–39, 245.

71. Ibid., 237–46. YIVO's 1990 catalog of its Yiddish holdings correctly places the move from Vilna to New York on the shoulders of the Amopteyl. Zachary M. Baker, "The Yiddish Collections of YIVO Library: Their History, Scope, and Significance," *The Yiddish Catalog and Authority File of YIVO Library*, ed. Zachary M. Baker and Bella Haas Weinberg (Boston: G. K. Hall, 1990), viii ("[I]n October 1940 the American Section of YIVO decided to reconstitute itself as YIVO's headquarters.").

72. The reason that Dawidowicz describes this story as "strange" is unclear. Although those in Vilna may have fought off efforts to ship the library, that was still within the realm of the possible and was in fact what many Jews were pursuing at that time.

73. Weiser, "Coming to America," 246–47.

74. Lucy Schildkret to Max Weinreich, February 16, 1947, Dawidowicz Papers, box 55, folder 3.

75. Ibid.

76. This version is quoted in Sinkoff, "From the Archives," 131n52, and is from the YIVO RG 100 archive. This author was denied access to that archive by YIVO because this archive is closed to researchers, as mentioned earlier. Dawidowicz's preference was to write this letter in Yiddish; however, she could not because "the Central Committee has borrowed all the Yiddish typewriters (they wanted to publish a book and are mimeographing it instead because they are a bunch of jerks) and because [she was] working from home." Lucy Schildkret to Max Weinreich, February 16, 1947, Dawidowicz Papers, box 55, folder 3.

77. Lucy Schildkret to Max Weinreich, May 25, 1947, Dawidowicz Papers, box 55, folder 4. Schildkret even questioned Horne's work ethic: "The Director of the Depot has, of course, nothing to do, except look at art books and drink tea twice a day." Lucy Dawidowicz to the Conference of the General Historical Society, May 16, 1947, Dawidowicz Papers, box 55, folder 4.

78. Lucy Schildkret to Max Weinreich, May 25, 1947, Dawidowicz Papers, box 55, folder 4. In February 1947, Weinreich expressed his uncertainty regarding the degree of Dawidowicz's relationship with Horne. Max Weinreich to Lucy Schildkret, February 15, 1947. But by May he was confident that "she had the full support of Mr. Horne." Max Weinreich to Seymour Pomrenze, May 2, 1947, Dawidowicz Papers, box 52, folder 1.

79. Max Weinreich to Lucy Schildkret, February 15, 1947 [Yiddish], Dawidowicz Papers, box 52, folder 1.

80. Lucy Schildkret to Max Weinreich, February 16, 1947, Dawidowicz Papers, box 55, folder 3.

81. Max Weinreich to Lucy Schildkret, February 28, 1947 [Yiddish], Dawidowicz Papers, box 52, folder 1.

82. Max Weinreich to Lucy Schlidkret, February 22, 1947, Dawidowicz Papers, box 52, folder 1.

83. Astrinsky, *Mattityahu Strashun 1817–1885*, i (preface) ("[The] YIVO building in Vilna, located outside the ghetto, was converted into a processing center for ransacked Jewish libraries and archives from Vilna and the surrounding area. This was where almost all of the Strashun books were crated and shipped by rail to Germany.").

84. Lucy Schildkret to Max Weinreich, cable, March 15, 1947, Dawidowicz Papers, box 55, folder 1.

85. The Strashun Library books at the OAD were known to include a significantly higher number of volumes, then estimated at over 24,000, which is confirmed in the "Monthly Reports." The 4,500 count is likely a result of a typographical error, the leading "2" was inadvertently left off.

86. Joseph A. Horne, Director OAD, to Office of Military Government for Germany (US), Economic Division, Restitution Branch, March 17, 1947, NARA, RG 260, M1942, reel 5. Dawidowicz provided Horne with a partial translation of Weinreich's February 14, 1947, letter, a copy of which was attached to Horne's letter.

87. Ibid.

88. In early May, Weinreich anticipated Pomrenze's imminent departure for the OAD. Max Weinreich to Seymour Pomrenze, May 2, 1947, Dawidowicz Papers, box 55, folder 2. ("It is self-understood that we cannot rush you excessively, but for a number of reasons we would very much like — at the last meeting, we discussed this once again — that, to the extent possible, you not lose another day. I also ask that as soon as the date of your journey is set, you let us know immediately.")

89. Uveeler asserts that "a synopsis of the enclosed description was submitted to the Department of State in connection with [the] YIVO claim of 76,482 volumes." Uveeler does not specifically identify when the synopsis regarding YIVO's associ-

ated libraries was provided to the State Department. The extant correspondence between YIVO and the State Department, however, never mentions the concept of associated libraries.

90. Max J. Uveeler to Seymour Pomrenze, June 5, 1947, NARA, RG 260, M1942, reel 5.

91. Lucy Schildkret to Max Weinreich, June 17, 1947, Dawidowicz Papers, box 55, folder 4.

92. NARA, RG 260, M1942, reel 5. The original inventory is also preserved at YIVO's archives. See Restitution of YIVO Property, folder 17. The sum of the YIVO and Strashun books does not align with 34,204. The discrepancy is attributable to a last-minute addition of books to the shipment that were from neither the YIVO nor the Strashun libraries. At the time the shipment was ready, it consisted of only 414 crates, yet YIVO had authorization for 420 crates. Thus, "Horne told the loaders to take six cases at random to fill the quota." Dawidowicz, *From That Place and Time*, 325. The extra six crates contained other books from Vilna. The detailed inventory accounts for the contents of the 414 crates, but the cover sheet provides the total number of books, including the extra Vilna books. Comparing the inventory with the cover sheet indicates that the six crates contained a total of 1,653 books. NARA, RG 260, M1942, reel 5. The October 1946 monthly report inventoried those books and their respective former owners. "List of Wilna Collection," Monthly Report, October 31, 1946, enclosure 9, NARA, RG 260, M1942, reel 10.

7. Ex Libris and Obscurity in Postwar America

1. For a discussion regarding the exact number of Strashun Library books, see the previous discussion at the end of chapter 6.

2. Lucy Schildkret to Max Weinreich, June 17, 1947, Dawidowicz Papers, box 55, folder 4 (all caps in original).

3. Sinkoff attributes the need for secrecy to the additional six crates of Vilna books that were not from either the YIVO or the Strashun Library collection. Sinkoff, "From the Archives," 140. But those books numbered only 1,653, as compared to the 23,709 Strashun Library books, a seemingly inconsequential number to justify Dawidowicz's plea for secrecy and her radical solution.

4. OAD, "Ex-Libris Found among Looted Books in the Archival Depot," vol. 1, NARA, RG 260, M1949, box 778; "Library Markings Found among Looted Books in the Archival Depot," vol. 1, Eastern, NARA, RG 260, M1949, box 779; "Library Markings Found among Looted Books in the Archival Depot," vol. 2, Western, NARA, RG 260, box 780; Dovid Katz, *Windows into a Lost Jewish Past: Vilna Book Stamps* (Vilnius: Versus Aureus, 2008), 54–55 (discussing YIVO's pre–World War II ex libris).

5. Lucy Schildkret to Max Weinreich, June 17, 1947, Dawidowicz Papers, box 55, folder 4.

6. In August 1947, Julius Uveeler, the corporate secretary of YIVO, relayed to Seymour Pomrenze that YIVO was still "keeping the matter" of Strashun "secret." Julius Uveeler to Seymour Pomrenze, August 21, 1947, Dawidowicz Papers, box 55, folder 4.

7. Kuznitz, *YIVO and the Making of Modern Jewish Culture*, 184–89; Fishman, *Mod-*

ern Yiddish Culture, 135–37. (Over time, however, Weinreich's views on YIVO's role and mission evolved.)

8. The "Vilna Collection" includes not only books but also archival documents. Nevertheless, the previous examples are instances in which the Vilna Collection books were singularly discussed.

9. "The Reading Room of the Strashun Library," *News of YIVO* 36 (February 1950). The caption also provides that "the librarian I. Strashun [. . .] perished during the last war at the hands of the Germans." According to one source, in 1895, when he was fifteen, he was appointed a trustee of the Strashun Library. That year he also began serving as a librarian in the library. When the Nazis began looting the library, he was overcome with grief and committed suicide, hanging himself by his teffilin straps. Shor, *Likutei Shoshanim*, 30.

10. "YIVO Library Is Back at Home," *News of YIVO* 40 (March 1951) (all caps in original).

11. Ibid. (emphasis added).

12. "Vilna Collection Augmented: Library Acquires Rare Jewish Periodicals," *News of YIVO* 41 (June 1951).

13. "YIVO Library Is Back at Home," *News of YIVO* 40 (March 1951) (all caps in original).

14. Noam Zadoff, *Gershom Scholem: From Berlin to Jerusalem and Back*, trans. Jeffrey Green (Waltham, MA: Brandeis University Press, 2017), 134–41. Nearly all of those books and manuscripts were identifiable, including some that belonged to YIVO.

15. "Censored Books in the Vilna Collection," *News of YIVO* 46 (1952). Each of the fourteen appears in the catalog of Mattityahu's personal library, *Likutei Shoshanim* (Berlin: Ittskovski Printing, 1889): *"LS." Bachya's Commentary on the Bible* (Pesaro, 1514), LS 550; *Sefer ha-Terumot* (Venice, 1523), LS n. 1451; *Sefer Hasidim* (Bologna, 1538), LS 1804; *Mahzor Minhag Roma* (Bologna, 1541), LS 2750; *Abudraham* (Constantinople, 1514), LS 1; *Pirush Ibn Ezra al ha-Torah* (Constantinople, 1514), LS 3865; *Shulhan shel Arba* (Mantua, 1514), LS 5105; *Pirush ha-Ketubah* (Constantinople, 1516), LS 3837; *Derekh Emunah* (Constantinople, 1522), LS 999; *Mesorat ha-Talmud* (Constantinople, 1523), LS 2961; *Sefer ha-Hinukh* (Venice, 1523), LS 1221; *She'elot ue-Teshuvot Binyamin Ze'ev* (Venice, 1539), LS 4519; *She'elot ue-Teshuvot ha-Rivash* (Constantinople, 1547), LS 4519. The remaining three are early Yiddish imprints, the types of books that the YIVO Library specifically collected and that are more likely to be from its library. The article states that the Vilna Collection was comprised of forty thousand volumes.

16. "Catalogue of the Vilna YIVO Library," *News of YIVO* 54 (1954); "YIVO Activities in 1954," *News of YIVO* 55 (1955).

17. "Rabbinical Collection Now Open to the Public," *News of YIVO* 86 (1963).

18. "YIVO Library," *News of YIVO* 4 (March 1951).

19. The Monthly Report records that on May 8, 1946, "Captain S. J. Pomrenze left for the States." May 31, 1946, NARA, M1942, reel 9 (emphasis added).

20. In December 1946, at the request of YIVO, Pomrenze wrote a history of his role as director of the OAD, and the larger history of "Operation Offenbach." Seymour J. Pomrenze, "'Operation Offenbach,'—The Salvage of Jewish Cultural Treasures in Germany" [Yiddish], *YIVO Bleter* 29 (Summer 1947), 282–85.

21. NARA, RG 260, M1942, reel 5. In August 1948, YIVO received an additional sixty books from its associated libraries. Receipt from the Commanding General European Command, August 19, 1947, NARA, RG 260, M1942, reel 5. Between July 1, 1949, and November 30, 1950, an additional 3,290 books were given to YIVO by Jewish Reconstruction, Inc., as part of its distribution of unidentifiable heirless Jewish property. Those books were entirely unrelated to the prewar YIVO library and the return of YIVO property in New York in 1947, the subject of the article in *YIVO News*. See Dicker, *Of Learning and Libraries*, appendix B. Even assuming, *arguendo*, that the article's description of the composition of the YIVO collection, versus that of the Strashun Library, included the entire number of the restituted books, 37,413, the 23,709 Strashun Library books remain the overwhelming majority of the total books that YIVO received.

22. Those involved in the transfer of YIVO books to New York tended to minimize or ignored Dawidowicz's role entirely. Sinkoff, "From the Archives," 141–45.

23. Lisa Moses Leff, *The Archive Thief*, 126; Gallas, *Das Leichenhaus der Bücher*, 58n84. (Gallas, in addition to citing Dawidowicz, also cites Weinreich's February 14, 1947, and Uveeler's June 5, 1947, conflicting descriptions of YIVO's "associated libraries" without comment. In an earlier article, Gallas cites only Weinreich's and Uveeler's renditions; Dawidowicz's is omitted.) Elisabeth Gallas, "Preserving East European Jewish Culture: Lucy Dawidowicz and the Salvage of Books after the Holocaust," *Simon Dubnow Institute Yearbook* 11 (2012): 82n28; Sutter, "Lost Jewish Libraries," 231; "US Restitution of Nazi-Looted Cultural Treasures to the USSR, 1945-1959: Facsimile Documents from the National Archives of the United States," compiled with an introduction by Patricia Kennedy Grimsted, 46–47, accessed February 12, 2017, http://www.archives.gov.ua/Eng/NB/USRestitution.php.

24. *Mattityahu Strashun, 1817–1885: Scholar, Leader, and Book Collector*, ed. Yermiyahu Ahron Taub (New York: YIVO Institute for Jewish Research, [2001]) (New York: YIVO Institute for Jewish Research, [2001]).

25. Aviva E. Astrinsky, "Preface," in *Mattityahu Strashun, 1817–1885: Scholar, Leader, and Book Collector*, i.

26. Max Weinreich to Lucy Schildkret, February 26, 1947, Dawidowicz Papers, box 52, folder 1.

27. Astrinsky, "A Brief History of the Strashun Library," iv. The two accompanying citations tagged to her are unhelpful; neither discusses the Strashun Library's transfer to New York, instead focusing on the return of the YIVO Library from Vilna to New York. See Astrinsky, "A Brief History," ivn1, citing David E. Fishman, *Embers Plucked from the Fire: The Rescue of Jewish Cultural Treasures in Vilna* (New York: YIVO Institute for Jewish Research, 1996) and Dina Abramowicz, "Guardians of a Tragic Heritage: Reminiscences and Observations of an Eyewitness," *Judaica Librarianship* 11, no. 1-2 (2003) 62–66. There are a number of inaccuracies in her history. She indicates that Americans discovered three million books at the OAD. Instead, the OAD functioned as a collection point for most of the books the Americans recovered—no books were recovered at the OAD. The OAD processed three million books, but those books were uncovered all over Germany. See Waite, "Returning the Jewish Cultural Property," 215; Kurtz, *America*, 136–46 (discussing the multiple collection points

within the American Zone in Germany); Schidorsky, *Gevilim Nesraphim*, 222–25 (detailing the sorting and identification process at the OAD).

28. Jonathan Brent, "The Last Books," *Jewish Ideas Daily*, May 1, 2013, accessed August 11, 2017, http://www.jewishideasdaily.com/6413/features/the-last-books/. Brent appears to conflate the two distinct libraries, Mattityahu's private library and the public Strashun Library. According to Brent, "Shortly before the war broke out, the library of Mattityahu Strashun, the first Jewish public library ever established, consisted of some 50,000 volumes, many unique and rare and hundreds of years old." But "the library of Mattityahu Strashun" neither was "the first Jewish public library ever established" nor consisted of "some 50,000 volumes." Rather, "the library of Mattityahu Strashun" formed the core of and was the first to be incorporated into Vilna's Strashun Library, which was indeed "the first Jewish public library ever established" and eventually held "some 50,000 volumes."

29. Sinkoff, "From the Archives," 140.

30. *The History and Future of the Strashun Library: Conference Program* ([New York: YIVO Institute for Jewish Research, 2017]), preface. One of the presentations was "The Strashun Library in War Time, 1939–1941"; however, the specifics of YIVO's claim to the Strashun Library were not discussed.

31. Ibid.

32. Ibid.

33. David Fishman recognizes that the basis of Weinreich's claim to the Strashun Library books "was rather dubious" and that "there was no documentary evidence to support it." Fishman, *Book Smugglers*, 196. But Fishman does not discuss any of the evidence that appears contrary to Weinreich's claim or Dawidowicz's history of the Strashun Library books, the latter of which Fishman does not mention at all. Shilo is the first to challenge YIVO's entitlement to the Strashun Library based on the extant evidence. Unlike Fishman, she acknowledges that the Strashun Library books "were known [by Weinreich] not to belong to YIVO." Shilo, "Funem Folk," 386. Shilo considers the transfer of the Strashun Library books to YIVO a "grey area of restitution." Ibid., 388. As David Fishman has recently shown, the Strashun Library books are not the only example in which YIVO received materials that it likely had no legal entitlement to and then first kept secret their existence; and when it finally revealed them, YIVO then obfuscated the details of the acquisition. Fishman, *Book Smugglers*, 218–19.

34. Lyudmila Sholokhova, director of the YIVO Archives and Library, e-mail to the author, August 17, 2016, copy on file with the author. According to some reports, prior to YIVO's move to the Center for Jewish History building, the Strashun Library books were kept in a separate area in the stacks. But those stacks were closed to researchers, and the public was unaware that there was any distinction between the Strashun Library books and the others in the Vilna Collection. Moreover, the Strashun Library cataloging system was difficult to use, and librarians and staff had difficulty locating the books.

35. Leff, "Rescue or Theft," 30. See also Shilo, "Funem Folk," 388, who discusses Leff and the Strashun Library books.

36. Leff, "Rescue or Theft," 5.

37. Ibid., 30.

38. Ibid., 4.

39. Gallas, "Preserving East European Jewish Culture," 80–81.

40. Gallas, "Locating the Jewish Future," 31–32. In 1944 Weinreich expressed his fear that YIVO materials might return to Lithuania. Leff, *Archive Thief*, 125.

41. Gallas, "Locating the Jewish Future," 32 (quoting Pomrenze).

42. Gallas, *Das Leichenhaus der Bücher*, 134–72; Kurtz, *America*, 151–73.

43. Waite, "Returning Jewish Cultural Property," 215.

44. Max Weinreich to John Slawson, May 16, 1946, Dawidowicz Papers, box 51, folder 9.

45. NARA, RG 260, reel 3.

46. Echols to John Slawson, May 21, 1946, Dawidowicz Papers, box 51, folder 9.

47. Max Weinreich to John Slawson, June 1, 1946, Dawidowicz Papers, box 51, folder 9.

48. Koppel Pinson to Joseph Schwartz, July 29, 1946, JDC Archives, Records of the Geneva Office of the American Joint Distribution Committee, 1945–1954, http://search.archives.jdc.org/multimedia/Documents/Geneva45-54/G45-54_Count/G45-54_GR_022/G45-54_GR_022_0294.pdf#search=.

49. Max Weinreich to Jerome Michael, December 6, 1946, Restitution of YIVO Property, folder 5; Seymour Pomrenze to Max Weinreich, December 6, 1946, Restitution of YIVO Property, folder 5.

50. Leff, "Rescue or Theft," 17.

51. Leff, *Archive Thief*, 179–200.

52. Leff, "Rescue or Theft," 26.

53. The Library of Congress, for example, has created a virtual library, the "Holocaust-Era Judaic Heritage Library," of the heirless Jewish books it received. Library of Congress, African and Middle Eastern Reading Room, accessed January 28, 2018, https://www.loc.gov/rr/amed/hs/hsspecialcollections.html.

8. Another Port of Call

1. Harkavy, *Le-Heker Mishpahot*, 47–48.

2. Tzvi Harkavy [and Israel Ta-Shema], *Autobibliographia: Kol ha-Pirsumim, ke-1, 200 'arakhim: Sefarim, Kuntresim, Mehkarim, u-Ma'amarim, Mahadurot, Tirgumim ve-Arikhah; be-Ivrit, be-Yiddish, be-Ladino, u-be-Laaz* [. . .] (Jerusalem: Erets-Yisrael Press, 1970).

3. David Tidhar, *Entsiklopedyah le-halutse ha-yishuv u-vonav* (Tel-Aviv: David Tidhar, 1947–1970), vol. 16, cols. 4990–94. The entry for Gershon Harkavy erroneously incorporates some of Tzvi's biographical details. Ibid., vol. 3, col. 1326. Shaul Shimon Deutsch, *Larger than Life: The Life and Times of the Lubavitcher Rebbe Rabbi Menachem Mendel Schneerson*, vol. 2 (New York: Chasidic Historical Productions, 1997), 6.

4. For example, in a 1961 article, Harkavy simply reports that a "remnant of a remnant of the great Strashun Library, after many twists and turns, ultimately ended up in Jerusalem at the Central Torah Library for Israel at Hechal Shlomo." Tzvi Harkavy, "Rabbi Matisyahu Strashun," *Areshet* 3 (1961), 429. Harkavy follows

that statement with a cryptic allusion to something larger, yet "now is not the time to reveal all the details of the library's journey or how the library ended up at YIVO." Ibid., n15. Shor's history of the Strashun Library and Shilo's treatment of the restitution of YIVO/Strashun property make only brief mention of this episode but do not provide much information beyond Harkavy's own statements. Shor, *Likutei Shoshanim*, 204-5; Shilo, "Funem Folk," 388-89.

5. *Herut*, October 23, 1955; *Ha-Mishmar*, Oct. 20, 1955. These articles describe the purpose of Dina's trip generically as a "public mission." She is identified as publisher; she was a partner with her husband in the Erets Yisrael Press, possibly indicating that the trip was somehow connected to the book trade. A. M. Haberman was in the United States at the same time as Dina, on a mission on behalf of the bibliographical society. Dina likely was a member of the same organization and may also have been part of Haberman's delegation. Indeed, Haberman was the one who first reported that the Strashun Library was at YIVO, evincing that he too had visited YIVO and overlapped with Dina. "How Did the Strashun Library End Up in New York?," *Herut*, November 25, 1955, 6. The trip was also for personal reasons. Dina brought her son, Yehuda, with her on the trip. Because the Harkavy family was very close with the Lubavitcher Rebbe, he participated in Yehuda's *upsherin* (haircutting ceremony, which occurs when boys are three years old). Harkavy, *Mekorei Ha-Rambam*, 3. Dina was the daughter of Reuven Katz, the chief rabbi of Petakh Tikvah. Tidhar, *Entsiklopedyah le-halutse ha-yishuv u-vonav*, vol. 3, cols. 1490-91. For a photograph of Dina, her husband, and her son, see ibid., vol. 16, col. 4991.

6. Tzvi Harkavy states that she specifically went to YIVO at his behest, but offers no information how he already knew the manuscript was at YIVO. Harkavy, *Im ha-Madurah*; Strashun, *Mekorei ha-Rambam*, 4.

7. The book was published in 1957. Harkavy's edition received some unfavorable reviews. Tuvia Preshel, *The Tuvia's Articles: Indices and Lists* (Jerusalem: Mossad Harav Kook, 2016), 91-94 (reprinted from *Ha-Darom* 9 (1959)); K. Kahana, "Mekorei ha-Rambam," *She'arim*, April 20, 1957. Unsurprisingly, Harkavy responded to both reviews. Tzvi Harkavy, "Regarding K. Kahana's Criticism of *Mekorei ha-Rambam*," *She'arim*, May 24, 1957; Tzvi Harkavy, "A Response by Tzvi Harkavy," *Ha-Darom* 10 (1959), 181-83.

8. "How Did the Strashun Library End Up in New York?," *Herut*, November 25, 1955, 6.

9. Ibid.

10. Lucy Schildkret to Max Weinreich, June 17, 1947, Dawidowicz Papers, box 55, folder 4; Julius Uveeler to Seymour Pomrenze, August 21, 1947, Dawidowicz Papers, box 55, folder 4.

11. Harkavy, *Autobibliographia*, 8.

12. Harkavy completed his edition of Samuel's commentary on January 13, 1957. Harkavy, *Mekorei ha-Rambam*, 3. That volume includes Harkavy's assertion that "members of [Mattityahu's] family" had sought to remove the books to Israel. "Toldot ha-RaSha-Sh," 58n19. Harkavy does not specifically refer to himself, but refers generically to "members of [Mattityahu's] family." Nonetheless, he is most likely referring to himself. Throughout the rest of this episode, no other family members

are mentioned. Moreover, Harkavy reported at a June 20, 1956, board meeting of the Library of the Ministry of Religion that he was already taking steps to secure the Strashun Library books. "Protocol," June 20, 1956, Mossad Harav Kook Archive (copy on file with the author). Harkavy wrote an article under a pseudonym, in advance of the release of *Mekorei ha-Rambam*, declaring that the Strashun Library "that currently resides in New York, at YIVO, will be sent to Israel soon." "Mekorei ha-Rambam," *Ha-Tzofeh*, February 3, 1956. The article's byline is Gimel, but in Harkavy's bibliography he is identified as the author. Harkavy, *Autobibliographia*, no. 480.

13. "Meeting Minutes of the Administration of the Library," June 6, 1956, Mossad Harav Kook Archive (copy on file with the author) (reporting that "proceedings are ongoing regarding the Strashun Library that is being held by YIVO in New York to remove the books" to Israel); Harkavy, "Toldot ha-RaSha"Sh u-Ketavav," 58n19; B.G. [Tzvi Harkavy], "Gilgulei Sifriat Strashun," *Ha-Tsofeh*, November 14, 1958. Harkavy is identified as the author in his *Autobibliographia*, no. 592.

14. Harkavy, "Toldot ha-RaSha"Sh," 58n19; "Meeting Minutes of the Administration of the Library," June 6, 1956, Mossad Harav Kook Archive (copy on file with the author).

15. "Meeting Minutes of the Administration of the Library," June 6, 1956, Mossad Harav Kook Archive.

16. Gish Amit, *Ex-Libris: Chronicles of Theft, Preservation, and Appropriating the Jewish National Library* (Jerusalem: Hakibbutz Hameuchad, 2014), 72–74. Previously, the Hebrew University, through the organization Otzrot ha-Golah, was responsible for retrieving European Jewish property. In 1952 the Ministry of Religion and the Hebrew University agreed to partner in that endeavor, and they jointly returned to Europe until the late 1960s. Schidorsky, *Gevilim Nesraphim*, 263–64 esp. n72, 268–70, 276, 280, 435–63 (appendices 12–13). By 1958, with Harkavy's claim still pending, the library of the Ministry of Religion, which was created from heirless Jewish books, was transferred to what became known as the Central Rabbinical Library.

17. Gallas, *Das Leichenhaus*, 82, 188–98; Schidorsky, *Gevilim Nesraphim*, 239–42. The Israeli institutions made other pragmatic arguments that confirmed their view that Israel was the sole destination for Holocaust books. Ultimately, the Israeli argument for sole heirship of all heirless Jewish assets was rejected. The heirless books at the OAD were distributed throughout the world. The Hebrew University, however, was first in line for that global distribution. See Schidorsky, *Gevilim Nesraphim*, 242. Beyond the heirless books at the OAD, the Israelis were the sole recipients of collections located in other European countries. Gallas, *Das Leichenhaus*, 198–207; Schidorsky, *Gevilim Nesraphim*, 254–86; Shilo, "Funem Folk," 382–85.

18. Kuznitz, *Making of Modern Jewish Culture*, 184–86. Kuznitz questions whether YIVO in Europe or America ever succeeded in its quest for worldwide dominance. Ibid., 190–95.

19. Draft April 1957 [untitled], Chief Rabbis Yizhak Nissim and Isaac Halevy Herzog, Israel State Archives, Chief Rabbinate, 0005ot5.

20. "Protocol," 2 Adar, 5718 [February 22, 1958], Israel State Archives, Chief Rabbinate, 0005ot5; Moshe Yaffo to Chief Rabbi Yitzhak Nissim, February 2, 1958, Israel State Archives, Chief Rabbinate, 0005ot5 (Yaffo was the director of the institute).

Ultimately, when Hechal Shlomo opened to the public on May 8, 1958, it dropped the "Supreme" and "World" from its title and letterhead and satisfied itself with just "The Religious Centre." Nonetheless, Hechal Shlomo continued to claim that it operated as the supreme worldwide religious center. See, e.g., "Third Annual Report," March 1961 ("[T]oday one no longer hears the question: 'Will Hechal Shlomo really become a world religious center?' Its position as such has been firmly established."), Israel State Archives, Chief Rabbinate, 00050t5.

21. Draft [untitled], April 1957, Israel State Archives, Chief Rabbinate, 00050t5.

22. "Third Annual Report," March 1961, Israel State Archives, Chief Rabbinate, 00050t5.

23. "Hechal Shlomo" undated brochure, Israel State Archives, Chief Rabbinate, 00050t5. The assumed amount was "100 dollars for a large congregation" and "50 [dollars] for individuals and small congregations." Undated donation card, Israel State Archive, Chief Rabbinate, 0050t5.

24. Moshe A. Yaffo to Chief Rabbi Yitzhak A. Nissim, March 26, 1957, Israel State Archives, Chief Rabbinate, 00050t5; "Minutes of Ministry of Religion," April 17, 1952, Israel State Archives, Chief Rabbinate, 00050t5 (reporting that the decision to discontinue the planned Chief Rabbinate building was because of, in part, the inability to solicit donations from Jews abroad since they "viewed such an endeavor as the responsibility of the government or the communities" the Rabbinate served).

25. "Record of Meeting," December 10, 1957, Israel State Archives, Chief Rabbinate, 00050t5; "Meeting Minutes," January 28, 1958, Israel State Archives, Chief Rabbinate, 00050t5; "Meeting Minutes," 2 Adar, 5718 [February 22, 1958], Israel State Archives, Chief Rabbinate, 00050t5. The agreement was not always followed to the letter; and the font size for "Seat of the Chief Rabbinate" is smaller, and in other instances it is the same size font as "Hechal Shlomo."

The Chief Rabbinate and Hechal Shlomo's agreement notwithstanding, that did not end the debate. Many ultra-Orthodox Jews objected to the very notion of a single supreme religious center that controlled and represented the entire Jewish people, a de facto reconstitution of the Great Sanhedrin (that operated as the highest religious, political, and judicial body in Palestine before, during, and after the destruction of the temple until c. 425 CE). In their minds, unilaterally asserting authority over all religious Jews was entirely unacceptable. Proclamation, 12 Kislev, 5718 [December 5, 1957], Israel State Archives, Chief Rabbinate, 00050t5. (The document is signed by Rabbis Yitzhak Ze'ev Solovetchik, Dov Berish Weinfeld, Eliezer Yehuda Finkel, Yehezkel Abramsky, Akiva Sofer, Zalman Soroskin, Yehezkel Sarna, and Shabbati Yagel.) American rabbis also separately objected to Hechal Shlomo's claim to lead all of religious Jewry. Simha Elberg, "Ha-'Arot le-Be'ayot: Rabbanut ha-Rashit u-Merkaz Ruhani Olami," *Ha-Pardes* 32, no. 8 (1958), 2–4; Israel State Archives, Chief Rabbinate, 00050t5. The Hechal Shlomo board decided that any dialogue with the naysayers was pointless and proceeded with its plan and did not even respond to these objections. Consequently, Hechal Shlomo remained adamant that it served as and should be recognized as the Supreme Religious Center for all Jews in Israel and abroad. "Meeting Minutes," 2 Adar, 5718 [February 22, 1958], Israel State Archives, Chief Rabbinate, 00050t5. In addition, some Orthodox Jews were opposed to an office of a chief rabbi. Their opposition reached a high point in 1963, when during a protest outside Jerusalem, the chief rabbi was burnt in effigy. Israel State Archives, Chief Rabbinate, 000i79k.

26. Lea Ben Dor, "Parliamentary Report, Debate in a Hurry," *Jerusalem Post*, April 3, 1959.

27. Executive Director-Hechal Shlomo to Editor of the *Jerusalem Post, Jerusalem Post*, April 13, 1959. See also the editor's response, which asserts that there is an unstated connection between the Mizrachi and Hechal Shlomo. Ibid.

28. "Third Annual Report," March 1961, Israel State Archives, Chief Rabbinate, 00050t5.

29. Ibid..

30. "Meeting Minutes," 2 Adar, 5718 [February 22, 1958], Israel State Archives, Chief Rabbinate, 00050t5; Tzvi Harkavy, "Hechal Shlomo, ha-Sifri'ah ha-Torani be-Yisrael, Hadashot be-Sifri'ah No. 1," Menachem-Av 5,718 [July-August 1958], Israel State Archives, Chief Rabbinate, 00050t5.

31. "Hechal Shlomo: The Seat of the Chief Rabbinate of Israel—The Religious Centre," [undated], Israel State Archives, Chief Rabbinate, 00050t5.

32. "Meeting Minutes," 2 Adar, 5718 [February 22, 1958], Israel State Archives, Chief Rabbinate, 00050t5. Warhaftig's survey of library holdings is limited to religious libraries, but does not account for the Hebrew University Library, which held substantially more Jewish legal texts than either the Rambam Library or Hechal Shlomo. Nonetheless, Warhaftig does not discuss the Y. L. Maimon Rabbinical Library at the Mossad Harav Kook Institute in Jerusalem either. That library held an estimated forty thousand volumes in total. Shlomo Shunami, *Al Safriut ve-Safranim* (Jerusalem: Reuven Mass, 1979), 79–80.

33. The library was dedicated on May 11, 1958, but until July only members of the Chief Rabbinate had access. "Hazmanah: Le-Hanukat ha-Sifri'ah ha-Torani ha-Merkazi le-Yisrael 'A"S M. Pollak," Israel State Archives, Chief Rabbinate, 00050t5; "Meeting Minutes," June 29, 1958, Israel State Archives, Chief Rabbinate, 00050t5; Tzvi Harkavy, "Hechal Shlomo, ha-Sifri'ah ha-Torani be-Yisrael, Hadashot be-Sifri'ah No. 1," Menachem-Av 5,718 [July-August 1958], Israel State Archives, Chief Rabbinate, 00050t5.

34. Tzvi Harkavy, "Hechal Shlomo, ha-Sifri'ah ha-Torani be-Yisrael, Hadashot be-Sifri'ah No. 1," Menachem-Av 5,718 [July-August 1958], Israel State Archives, Chief Rabbinate, 00050t5.

35. "Meeting Minutes," June 29, 1958, Israel State Archives, Chief Rabbinate, 00050t5. The Ministry of Religion had participated in earlier trips to Eastern Europe in search of heirless Jewish books and assets. Schidorsky, *Gevilim Nesraphim*, 263–80.

36. Tzvi Harkavy, "In the Largest Judaica Libraries in the World," *Ha-Sefer: A Bibliographic Journal* 7/8 (1959): 61. "[Draft] Agreement between the Board of Hechal Shlomo in Jerusalem and Dr. Tzvi Harkavy," Jerusalem, July 31, 1960, Archive of the Institute for the Study of Religious Zionism, Bar Ilan University, Jerusalem, Dr. Zerach Warhaftig, PA/16.

37. B. G. [Tzvi Harkavy], "Gilgulei Sifriat Strashun," *Ha-Tsofeh*, November 14, 1958. Harkavy is identified as the author in his *Autobibliographia*, no. 592.

38. A copy of the settlement agreement, written in Yiddish, appears in Tzvi Harkavy, "Be-Sifriot ha-Yehudiot ha-Gedolot be-Olam," *Ha-Sefer* 7/8 (1959): 61. Harkavy also described the terms of the settlement at a board meeting of the Central Rabbinical Library. "Meeting Minutes, The Central Rabbinical Library," March 1, 1959, Israel State Archives, Chief Rabbinate, 0005ot5. A few newspapers also reported on the settlement agreement. Chaim Lieberman, "A Yid un a Schmechil," *Forverts*, December 5, 1958; S. Izban, "Dr. Tzvi Harkavy," *Der Amerikaner*, January 2, 1959; "Famous Library for Jerusalem," *Jewish Chronicle*, January 16, 1959.

39. Shor, *Likutei Shoshanim*, 143–45.

40. "Toveah Hatzi Million Lira Temurot Sifriah she-hushmedah al yedi ha-Nazim," *Davar*, February 26, 1959. Harkavy raised his claim with the Ministry of Religion in 1956. At a later date, exactly when remains unclear, he also filed a complaint with the Rabbinical Court. See "Meeting Minutes of the Administration of the Library," June 6, 1956, Mossad Harav Kook Archive.

41. The archives of the Rabbinical Court are accessible to only the members of the family who were involved in the lawsuit, in this instance the Harkavy family. The author unsuccessfully attempted to receive permission from that family.

42. Harkavy, *Leheker Mishpahot*, 48–49; Harkavy, "Toldot RaSha"Sh u-Ketavav," 56.

43. Antokolski, *Evel Kaved*, 19.

44. For biographical information, see Tidhar, *Entsiklopedyah le-halutse ha-yishuv u-vonav*, vol. 11, col. 3860.

45. "Toveah Hatzi Million Lira Temurot Sifriah she-hushmedah al yedi ha-Nazim," *Davar*, February 26, 1959.

46. Klausner, "Batei Eked Sefarim," 75–78. Harkavy, however, took issue with Klausner's portrayal of Mattityahu as fully aligned with the more radical maskilim in Vilna and as signing a petition in favor of forcing Jews to wear contemporary clothing. Harkavy, *Mishpahat Harkavy*, 47. Upon Klausner's death, Dr. Johannes Pohl, the Nazi responsible for the plunder of the Strashun and YIVO Libraries, sent a letter of condolence to the president of Hebrew University. Pohl also requested medical advice from a specialist at the university. Noah Zevulani, "Ha-Nazi Y. Pohl Shalah Mivrak Tanhumim 'al Moto shel [Professor] Klausner," *Herut*, January 18, 1961.

47. "Strashun Will," Lithuanian State Historical Archive, f. 450, op. 7, d. 125.

48. Tzvi Harkavy to Moshe A. Yafe, 7 Tishrei, 5721 [September 7, 1960]; Moshe A. Yafe to Tzvi Harkavy, 9 Tishrei, 5721 [September 29, 1960], reproduced in [Harkavy], "Seridei Sifri'at Strashun," *Ha-Sefer* 9 (1961): 60–61. In a letter dated July 13, 1960, to the minister of internal affairs, Haim-Moshe Shapira, Harkavy indicates that he had already ceded his rights to the Strashun Library. Yet a draft agreement, dated July 31, 1960, between Hechal Shlomo and Harkavy, is preserved in the Dr. Zerach Warhaftig's archives, implying that an agreement was still pending. Archive of the Institute for the Study of Religious Zionism, Bar Ilan University, Jerusalem, Dr. Zerach Warhaftig, PA/16. Perhaps Harkavy, prior to July 13, 1960, agreed in principle to donate the Strashun Library books, but the formal agreement was not finalized until after July 31. Warhaftig is credited for successfully concluding the negotiations with Harkavy. Hechal Shlomo, "Third Annual Report," Israel State Archives, Chief Rabbinate, 0005ot5.

49. Tzvi Harkavy to Moshe Yaffa, Administrator of Hechal Shlomo, 7 Tishrei, 5720, reprinted in *Ha-Sefer* 9 (1961). Another reason for including the marks on the cover potentially mitigated the confusing ex libris inside the books (and may also have been intended to downplay the YIVO period of ownership).

50. "[Draft] Agreement between the Board of Hechal Shlomo and Dr. Tzvi Harkavy, Jerusalem," July 31, 1960, Archive of the Institute for the Study of Religious Zionism, Bar Ilan University, Jerusalem, Dr. Zerach Warhaftig, PA/16. The draft settlement agreement also required the Strashun Library books to be displayed in the reading room. That condition too is lacking in the final agreement. Ibid.

51. Despite Harkavy's donation to the Central Rabbinical Library, he was not rewarded in kind. He complained that a year and a half after his trip to America, he was still waiting on reimbursement. Dr. Tzvi Harkavy to the Board of Hechal Shlomo, 16 Tammuz, 5720 [July 11, 1960], Israel State Archives, Chief Rabbinate, 00050t5; Dr. Tzvi Harkavy to Minister Haim-Moshe Shapiro, July 13, 1960, Archives of Mossad Harav Kook.

Harkavy's donor stamp appears on only lthe books originating from the Strashun books that were sent to the Central Rabbinical Library. Because Harkavy was heir to only the Strashun Library books, books from other Vilna libraries, which were sent by YIVO to the Central Rabbinical Library, bear YIVO's donation stamp and not Harkavy's.

52. The author has thus far been unable to locate the exact date that Harkavy received the ruling in his favor. The decision may have been rendered after January 19, 1959, when Harkavy returned to Israel, and prior to the end of February 1959, when Harkavy is first reported to have exercised his rights as sole heir to Strashun. As a result of the Bet Din declaring Harkavy the heir, he is said to have filed a claim against the German government for a half-million lira for the loss of the Strashun Library. "Toveah Hatzi Million Lira Temurot Sifriah she-hushmedah al yedi ha-Nazim," *Davar*, February 26, 1959, 3; "The Individual and the Community," *Herut*, January 19, 1959 (reporting on Harkavy's return). In March 1959, however, Harkavy related the details of the YIVO settlement to the Hechal Shlomo board and made no mention of any personal claim to the books, casting doubt that the court issued an opinion in February. "Meeting Minutes: The Central Rabbinical Library," March 1, 1959, Israel State Archives, Chief Rabbinate, 00050t5. Perhaps Harkavy filed his claim against the German government based on his personal opinion rather than a final decision of the court.

53. Indeed, in 1958, immediately after the settlement between YIVO and Hechal Shlomo, Harkavy and Hechal Shlomo's administration feared that without representation in New York, the terms of the agreement might not be met. "Protocol," March 1, 1959, Israel State Archives, Chief Rabbinate, 00050t5.

54. Noah Zevulan, "Higiu Seridei Sifrei Strashun," *Herut*, October 4, 1960; Harkavy, "Rebi Mattityahu Strashun," 429n15; Tzvi Harkavy, "Rebi Mattityahu Strashun," *Hokmat Yisrael be-Europa*, ed. Shimon Federbusch (Israel: Agon, 1965), vol. 3, 353n41; [Harkavy], "Seridei Sifri'at Strashun," *Ha-Sefer* 9 (1961), 60. In July 1960 an article in *YIVO News* reported that the first shipment of 997 books from the Vilna Collection had left port for Hechal Shlomo in Jerusalem, and explained that

this was a result of Harkavy's visit to the YIVO library when Harkavy "was promised a gift of all duplicates of rabbinica in YIVO Library, particularly of those in the rescued Vilna collection." *News of YIVO* 75 (July 1960). There is a small deviation regarding the number of books contained in the first shipment. The YIVO report lists 997 books. But after the shipment arrived in Haifa, Harkavy inventoried 1,140 books. "[Draft] Agreement between the Board of Hechal Shlomo and Dr. Tzvi Harkavy, Jerusalem," July 31, 1960, Archive of the Institute for the Study of Religious Zionism, Bar Ilan University, Jerusalem, Dr. Zerach Warhaftig, PA/16; Tzvi Harkavy, "Letter to the Editor Regarding the Strashun Library," *Herut*, October 9, 1960.

55. Noah Zebulan, "Dr. Devorzky at the Opening of the Strashun Library: The Nazi Academic Johannes Pohl Sold Countless Books from the Strashun Library to a Paper Factory," *Herut*, December 26, 1960.

56. Avraham Brodis, "Geulat Gevilin u-Mezuzah," *Davar*, December 27, 1960; [Tzvi Harkavy], "Sereidei Sifri'at Strashun," *Ha-Sefer* 9 (1960): 60. Farber was in the Vilna Ghetto and kept a diary that was later published. The diary does not discuss his rescue of the mezuzah. Farber does, however, briefly discuss the Strashun Library, and specifically, meeting Lunski soon after the Nazis conscripted him to select books from the library. Kalman Farber, *Olkeniki*, 184–85.

57. [Harkavy], "Seridei Sifri'at Strashun," 60; Tzvi Harkavy [Israel Ta-Shema], *Autobibliographia*, no. 691. In a later biography of Mattityahu, Harkavy lists the exhibits at the opening, but omits the settlement agreement. Harkavy, "Rebi Mattityahu Strashun," 353n41.

58. [Noah Zebulani], "Sifrei Strashun le-Yerushalayim," *Herut*, August 2, 1962. When Harkavy visited YIVO in 1958, he estimated that close to 60 percent of the rabbinic books from the Strashun Library were duplicates. If that is the case, or even close to the correct number, five hundred books appear to conflict with his estimate. "Protocol," March 1, 1959, Israel State Archives, Chief Rabbinate, 00050t5. Prior to the war, approximately 30 percent, fifteen thousand, of an estimated fifty thousand total books were duplicates. Lithuanian National Archives, f. 401, op. 2, d. 518, list 16. How many of those were rabbinic is not recorded in that last survey. But Lunski's 1935 article estimates that of the then thirty-five thousand books, approximately half were rabbinic. Lunski, "Di Strashun Bibliotek," 282.

59. Klausner, "Bate-Eked Seforim," 82. According to Klausner, the Association of Vilna Jews was requesting that the books be sent to the Israeli National Library. Harkavy's last article discussing Mattityahu, in 1965, mentioned that he was pressing to send the remaining books to Israel. Harkavy, "Rebi Mattityahu Strashun," *Hokmat Yisrael be-Europa*, 353n41. For earlier reports of ongoing efforts to obtain additional books, see H. S. Levi, "Seridei Sifri'at Strashun," *Herut*, January 13, 1961; "Derushim Ha'varat Sifri'at Strashun," *Ha-Boker*, January 8, 1961.

60. The WJC, in 1942, was the first organization that publicized the Nazis' plan to exterminate the Jews, and it was heavily involved in documenting other atrocities. Zohar Segev, *The World Jewish Congress during the Holocaust: Between Activism and Restraint* (Berlin: Walter De Gruyter, 2014), 23–35.

61. Herman, "Hashavat Avedah," 49–65, esp. 54–57. In the 1990s, the WJC again

played a similar role in the restitution of heirless Jewish assets, in this instance Swiss bank accounts. Here too successful restitution required that the WJC cooperate with other NGOs and the US government. This effort received support at the highest level. President Clinton appointed Stuart Eizenstat, then the US ambassador to the European Union, to serve as the president's special envoy for property restitution in Central and Eastern Europe. In 1998 Eizenstat orchestrated a $1.25 billion global settlement with the Swiss banks. See Stuart Eizenstat, *Imperfect Justice: Looted Assets, Slave Labor, and the Unfinished Business of World War II* (New York: PublicAffairs, 2003).

249

62. Herman, "Hashavat Avedah," 129.

63. Shimon Federbusch, *Hekhrei Yahadut* (Jerusalem: Mossad Harav Kook, 1965), 319-24.

64. Federbusch, *Hekhrei Yahadut*, 324.

65. Pomrenze's brother, Chaim, was associated with YIVO; and Weinreich, in his first letter to Seymour, referenced his brother's relationship with YIVO. Neither Bencowitz nor Horne had any familial connections with YIVO. Pomrenze, however, was fluent in Hebrew, and it is unclear why Federbusch claims that he had a lack of literacy. Perhaps he was attempting to cast Pomrenze in a poor light.

66. Sinkoff, "From the Archives," 127-28.

67. Salo Baron to Jerome Michael, November 11, 1946, Department of Special Collections, Stanford University Library, M0508, Salo W. Baron Papers, box 39, folder 2.

68. Leff discusses other institutions that also acquired property recovered from Europe under less than clear circumstances to bolster their self-perceived roles in the aftermath of World War II. See Leff, *Archive Thief*, 189-98.

Postscript

1. Iakerson, *Hebrew Incunabula*, no. 66.

2. Giuseppe Veltri, *Renaissance Philosophy in Jewish Garb: Foundations and Challenges in Judaism on the Eve of Modernity* (Leiden: Koninklijke Brill, 2009) (supplements to the *Journal of Jewish Thought and Philosophy*, vol. 8), 44-59.

3. Generally, printers of Hebrew books did not explain why certain images were included on title pages; the assumption is that it was simply for aesthetic purposes. At least in one case, this was made explicit. The *Shu"t Ma-harit"z*, Venice, 1684, by Yom Tov Tzalahon, includes an illustration of the temple on the title page. The publisher, Tzalahon's grandson, explained that this was included because "it makes it more beautiful"; he was so enamored with the illustration—even though it is very rudimentary—that he included it three times in the book (this likely speaks more about the publisher's exposure—or lack thereof—to art in general).

4. Richard I. Cohen, *Jewish Icons, Art and Society in Modern Europe* (Berkeley: University of California Press, 1998), 127.

5. Heller indicates that the first Hanau print to use this title page is R. Aaron Samuel ben Moses Shalom of Kremenets's *Nishmat Adam*. Marvin J. Heller, *Further Studies in the Making of the Early Hebrew Book* (Leiden: Brill, 2013), 52. That is incorrect. *Nishmat Adam* was published in 1611, whereas *She'elot u-Teshuvot Mahril* was published in

1610. See Yeshayahu Vinograd, *Otsar Sefer ha-Ivri: Reshimat ha-Sefarim she-nidpesu be-Ot Ivrit me-Reshit ha-Defus ha-Ivri be-Shenat RKh"T* (1469) *'ad Shenat TRKh"G* (1863) (Jerusalem: Hamachon le-bibliographia me-muhshevet, 1994), "Hanau" nos. 8 and 23, 162–63.

6. There is the possibility that the title page was reused from a non-Jewish book. If that was the case, it may explain the Christological elements. The top of the title page depicts the binding of Isaac. Regarding the use of this motif on Hebrew title pages, see Heller, *Further Studies*, 35–56.

7. Because of the image's obvious connection with the Hebrew title, it was unlikely to have been borrowed from a non-Jewish source.

8. Very little is known about Sirkes's biography or the history and reception of the pamphlet. See in general Joseph Bar-El, "R. Yoel ben Hazzan, "Re'ah Neho'ah," (Ramat Gan: University of Bar Ilan Press, 1979).

9. Ibid., 1.

10. Aron Freimann, "Tadel der Kantoren, Ein Flugblatt," *Zeitschrift für Hebräische Bibliographie* 15 (1911), 155–58.

11. Yitzhak Yudlov, *Ginzei Yisrael*, no. 1753.

12. Carl Rheims to Dan Rabinowitz, September 8, 2016, e-mail (copy on file with the author).

13. Kestenbaum, *Catalogue of Fine Judaica: Hebrew Printed Books, Manuscripts and Graphic Art: Featuring: Duplicates from the Rare Book Room of YIVO Library, New York and the Library of the Late Dr. Max Kimche, Zürich: Part II*, September 10, 2009 (New York: Kestenbaum, 2009).

14. The exact number of Strashun Library books included in the auction is opaque. As with the YIVO Vilna Collection, the catalog collectively describes YIVO and the Strashun Library books as "YIVO Copy" and does not differentiate based on provenance. Nevertheless, some books are identifiable as belonging to either Mattityahu's library or the larger Strashun libraries.

15. *A Brief Encounter with Archives* (New York: YIVO Institute, 2005), 13–14; "Materials of a Famous Hebrew Library," *News of the YIVO* 194 (2002), 19; Astrinsky, *Mattityahu Strashun*, 9, 18.

16. The 2009 auction results are available at https://www.kestenbaum.net/prc _0909.php.

17. None of these books are included in the online collection of Hebrew books from the YIVO library, accessed August 23, 2017, http://yivolibrarybooks.org/. The current director of the YIVO library was unable to provide any information regarding any preservation efforts applied to the auctioned books or to any of the previously deaccessioned books. Lyudmila Sholokhova to Dan Rabinowitz, June 1, 2016 (e-mail) (copy on file with the author).

18. Dawidowicz, *From That Place and Time*, 326.

19. Max Weinreich, "Der yivo in zayn finftn tsendling," *Yediyes fun YIVO* 98 (1965), 6 (quoted and translated in Fishman, *Modern Yiddish Culture*, 137).

20. Quoted in Poste, "Books Go Home," 1703.

21. For some of the recent discussions specifically regarding books, see Anders

Rydell, *The Book Thieves: The Nazi Looting of Europe's Libraries and the Race to Return a Literary Inheritance*, trans. Henning Koch (New York: Viking, 2015); Leff, *Archive Thief*; Patricia Kennedy Grimsted, "The Road to Minsk for Western 'Trophy' Books: Twice Plundered but Not Yet 'Home from the War,'" *Libraries and Culture* 39, no. 4 (Fall 2004), 351-404; Grimsted, "Roads to Ratibor"; Grimsted, "Postwar"; Markus Kirchhoff, *Häuser des Buches: Bilder Jüdischer Bibliotheken* (Leipzig: Reclam, 2002).

22. Waite, "Returning Jewish Cultural Property," 213.

23. Giselle Barcia, "Comment: After Chabad: Enforcement in Cultural Property Disputes," *Yale Journal of International Law* 37 (2012): 463, 464.

24. Margaret M. Mastroberardino, "Comment: The Last Prisoners of World War II," *Pace International Law Review* 9 (1997): 315, 342.

25. "Tentative List," entry 2. The number of manuscripts is based on the revised estimate that was included in "Addendum and Corrigenda." Dr. Richard Fuchs, who was in Germany until March 1939, is the source of the correction. Richard Fuchs, "The Hochschule für die Wissenschaft des Judentums in the Nazi Period—Some Personal Reflections," *Leo Baeck Institute* 12 (1967), 3.

26. Section 7 of RHSA, the section responsible for confiscating Jewish libraries, was not established until 1939 and was the successor to the German Security Services (Sicherheitsdienst, SD), which had plundered Jewish libraries since 1933. Nonetheless, for simplicity we have used "RHSA" to refer collectively to the entities that engaged in the looting of Jewish libraries, which were not included in Rosenberg's ERR. Schidorsky, "The Library of the Reich Security Main Office and Its Looted Book Collections," *Libraries and the Cultural Record* 42, no. 1 (2007), 22-23.

27. Schidorsky, "Library of the Reich," 27.

28. Dov Schidorsky, "Confiscation of Libraries and Assignments to Forced Labor: Two Documents of the Holocaust," *Libraries and Culture* 33, no. 4 (Fall 1998), 355.

29. Schidorsky, "Library of the Reich," 37.

30. Schidorsky, *Gevilim Nesraphim*, 233-35.

31. Ari Kinsberg, "The Modern Trial and Tribulations of a Medieval Hebrew Manuscript (Mahzor Catalonia, NLI Heb 8°6527)," *The Catalan Mahzor: MS Heb 8°6527, Treasure of the National Library of Israel* (London: Facsimile Editions, 2016), 14.

32. Douglas McGill, "Ohio Professor Says He Was Smuggler of Hebrew Books," *New York Times*, August 16, 1984.

33. Rita Reiff, "AUCTIONS; 1400's Bible from Prague," *New York Times*, April 13, 1984.

34. Kinsberg, "Modern Trial," 19n8.

35. Zafren, "From Hochschule," 51-53; Glickman, *Stolen Words*, 172-73.

36. Kinsberg, "Modern Trial and Tribulations," 12-13; Zafren, "From Hochschule," 51-53.

37. Anglea Joy Davis, "Comment: Beyond Reparations: A Proposal for the Equitable Restitution of Cultural Property," 33 *UCLA Law Review* 642, 647-62 (1985).

38. This was not JTS's only questionable acquisition of Holocaust property. Leff, *Archive Thief*, 170-72.

39. Zafren, "From Hochschule," 51-52; Glickman, *Stolen Words*, 171-72. Although

in this instance HUC acted with caution regarding the acquisition of suspect materials, HUC may have purchased a substantial number of materials whose provenance was less than clear. Leff, *Archive Thief*, 179–81.

40. Jesselson's substantial role in the Hochschule auction has only recently been made public in an article accompanying a limited-edition facsimile of the Mahzor Catalonia. Kinsberg, "Modern Trial and Tribulations," 8–26.

41. Ibid., 12.

42. Ibid., 13 (quoting, Robert Abrams, "Memorandum of Law in Support of Plaintiffs' Motion for Preliminary Injunction").

43. Carla Hall, "Judaica Recall at Sotheby's: Court Orders Recall of Rarest Items from Sale," *Washington Post*, July 18, 1985; Kinsberg, "Modern Trial and Tribulations," 13.

44. Douglas McGill, "Sotheby's Told to Hold Hebrew Book Proceeds," *New York Times*, Aug. 28, 1984.

45. Kinsberg, "Modern Trial and Tribulations," 17 (quoting Bonnie Burnham and Linda E. Ketchum, "World War II Art Losses Still Surfacing," *Stolen Art Alert* 5, no.8 (October 1984), 2).

46. "Scholar Called a Hero in Judaica Controversy," *New York Times*, September 3, 1984.

47. For a list of the current location of many of the books, see Zafren, "From Hochschule," 65.

48. Kinsberg, "Modern Trial and Tribulations," 15–16. The dispersal provided the Leo Baeck Institute with its oldest book, a 1490 edition of the *Kol Bo*, a collection of medieval laws. David Hulbert, "Battle for Three Books," *European Judaism* 41, no. 2 (2008), 67.

49. Rita Reif, "Ohio College Dismisses Seller of Hebrew Books," *New York Times*, August 7, 1985; Zafren, "From Hochschule," 58; Kinsberg, "Modern Trial," 16. Even before the final settlement, the HUC's president condemned Guttmann. Herbert Zafren, the director of libraries for HUC, published an article regarding the auction, in which he admits that he carried a personal bias against Guttmann. Zafren, "From Hochschule," 46.

50. Kinsberg, "Modern Trial and Tribulations," 21n24.

51. Douglas McGill, "Sweeping Reassessment in the Auction Trade," *New York Times*, July 31, 1985.

52. Kinsberg, "Modern Trial and Tribulations," 17.

53. The Prague Bible, accessed August 28, 2017, https://www.yu.edu/Libraries/Digital-Projects/Prague-Bible;the Catalonia Mahzor, accessed August 28, 2017, http://web.nli.org.il/sites/NLI/Hebrew/digitallibrary/pages/viewer.aspx?presentorid=MANUSCRIPTS&docid=PNX_MANUSCRIPTS000042450-1#FL10352114.

54. This was not the only controversy regarding the ownership of the Chabad Library. An earlier controversy has parallels to some of the post–World War II dispute regarding the Strashun Library. The portion of the Chabad Library that made its way to the United States was the subject of litigation between a grandson of the sixth Lubavitcher Rebbe, Barry Gurary, and the Chabad organization. Gurary alleged that

the library was the personal property of his grandfather and not the organization. Thus, he was entitled to the books. The organization argued that the library was communal property. The court ruled in favor of the organization. The ruling was significant enough to warrant a new holiday, Didan Notzach (we prevailed in our case), held on the date of the court's decision. *Hei Teves Didan Notzach: The Victory of the Seforim: A Synopsis of Events Relating to the Retrieval of Seforim, the Court Battle, the Legal Decisions and the Rebbe's Perspective*, comp. R. Moshe Bogomilsky (Brooklyn: R. Moshe Bogomilsky, 2007).

55. For a history and discussion of this case, see Talya Levi, "Note: Russia and the Stolen Chabad Archive," *Georgetown Journal of International Law* 915 (2015); Michael J. Bazyler and Seth M. Gerber, "Litigating the Pillage of Cultural Property in American Courts: Chabad v. Russian Federation and Lessons Learned," 32 *Loyola of Los Angeles International and Comparative Law Review* 45 (January 22, 2010).

56. Barcia, "Comment," 465-67.

57. Kurtz, *America*, 210-31.

58. Aron Freimann, *Stadtbibliothek Frankfurt a.M. Katalog der Judaica* (Frankfurt: M. Lehrberger, 1932).

59. Samuel H. Dresner, "The Second Private Library of Aron Freimann," *Studies in Bibliography and Booklore* 10, no. 3/4 (Winter 1973-1974), 73-79. Rachel Heuberger, *Bibliothek des Judentums: Die Hebraica- und Judaica-Sammlung der Stadt- und Universitätsbibliothek Frankfurt am Main — Entstehung, Geschichte und heutige Aufgaben* (Frankfurt: V. Klostermann, 1996), 45-84.

60. Rachel Hueberger, Laura E. Leone, and Renate Evers, "The Challenges of Reconstructing Cultural Heritage: An International Digital Collaboration," *International Federation of Library Associations and Institutions* 41, no. 3 (2015), accessed December 25, 2016, http://sammlungen.ub.uni-frankfurt.de/freimann.

61. Much of the discussion regarding the postwar history of the materials discovered in Vilna relies on David Fishman's recently published book and his earlier treatment. See Fishman, *Book Smugglers*, 137-52, 156-63, 171-83; Fishman, *Embers*, 7-10, 13.

62. Sutzkever, *Vilner Ghetto*, 229.

63. M. [sic] Kaczerginski, "A yor arbet funem yidishn muzey in Vilne," *Eynikayt* (Moscow), October 2, 1945, cited in Fishman, *Embers*, 9.

64. On May 23, 1946, Sutzkever wrote Weinreich that among the items smuggled out of Vilna were "very important manuscripts, documents, and books — from [. . .] the Strashun Library" and other Vilna institutions. Quoted in Fishman, *Embers*, 28.

65. A translation of the text of the council's resolution appears in Fishman, *Embers*, 31-32.

66. Fishman, *Book Smugglers*, 235.

67. Ibid., 246. For the testimonies of some of those who participated in these efforts, see Fishman, *Embers*, 32-34.

68. Fishman, *Book Smugglers*, 244-48. Fishman, *Embers*, 10. Ulpis also saved an untold number of Hebrew and Yiddish materials from the University of Vilnius that otherwise would have been consigned to the trash. Fishman, *Book Smugglers*, 245.

69. Emanuelis Zingeris, "Bikher un mentshn: vegn dem goyrl fun yidishe un

hebreishe bikher-fondn in Lite" [Books and People: Concerning the fate of Yiddish and Hebrew book collections in Lithuania], *Sovietish Heymland* 7 (1998): 70–73 (cited in Baker, "Librarians Visit," 65n6). Regarding the magazine and its effect on Soviet Jews and the preservation of Yiddish, see Katz, *Words on Fire*, 372–73. The article in *Sovietish Heymland* was the first account in Yiddish. The first published description of the collection of Jewish books at the Book Chamber actually appeared in 1987 in a Lithuanian journal. See Emanuelis Zingeris, "Knygu hebraju ir jidis kalbomis fondai Lietuvoje" [Collections of Hebrew and Yiddish books in Lithuania], *Knygotyra* 13, no. 2 (1987): 86–103 (cited in Baker, "Librarians Visit," 65n6).

70. Fishman, *Book Smugglers*, 250–51.

71. In 2001 YIVO mounted its exhibition, "Mattityahu (Mathias) Strashun (1817–1885): Scholar Leader and Book Collector," which displayed some of his books. Nonetheless, neither the exhibition nor the accompanying collection of articles made any mention of the more than one thousand of Mattityahu's books "that were miraculously saved in their home town." Esfir Bramson-Alperniené, "Die YIVO-Bibliothek in Wilna: Ein Sammelpunkt der jiddischen Kultur," in *Jüdische Kultur(en) im Neuen Europa, Wilna 1918–1939*, ed. Marina Dmitrieva and Heidemarie Petersen (Wiesbaden: Harrassowitz, 2004), 10.

72. Zachary Baker, Pearl Berger, and Herbert C. Zafran, "Vilnius Judaica: Still Portrait — Dynamic Reality: Report of the CARLJS Delegation on Its Survey of 'Judaica' in Vilnius, 19-26 March 1997" (May 12, 1997), app. A, 19–20, app. C, 23.

73. Ibid., 27.

74. Ibid.

75. Ibid., 27–33.

76. Quoted in Joseph Berger, "Split Up by Holocaust, Top Collection of Yiddish Works Will Reunite Digitally," *New York Times*, October 2, 2014.

77. Quoted in Berger, "Split Up by Holocaust."

78. UNESCO, *Memory of the World* (1992), accessed August 21, 2017, http://en.unesco.org/programme/mow.

79. Berger, "Split Up by Holocaust."

80. This information was kindly provided by Lempertiené to the author. We assume that many of these books are those that were hidden in the ghetto library, which according to Kruk's inventory numbered 2,464 books. Because the current accounting includes only the books that originally belonged to Mattityahu, and those from the Strashun Library have yet to be inventoried, the possibility remains that all or nearly all of those books are in the National Library.

Bibliography

Archives

ISRAEL

Archive of the Institute for the Study of Religious Zionism, Bar-Ilan University, Ramat Gan
    PA/16, Zerach Werftig Papers
Israel State Archives, Jerusalem
    0005ot5, Chief Rabbinate Papers
Mossad Harav Kook Archives, Jerusalem
    Meeting Minutes of the Ministry of Religious Affairs

LITHUANIA

Lithuanian Central State Archive, Vilnius
    F. 401, op. 2, d. 518, Ministry of People's Education of the Lithuanian Soviet
        Socialist Republic
    F. 633, op. 1, d. 5; Einsatzstab Reichsleiter Rosenberg
Lithuanian State Historical Archive, Vilnius
    F. 450, op. 1, d. 1143, Mattityahu Strashun Last Will and Testament
    F. 450, op. 7, d. 125, Mattityahu Strashun Informal Last Will and Testament

UKRAINE

Central State Archive of the Organs of Higher Power (TsDAVO), Kyiv
    F. 3676, Einsatzstab Reichsleiter Rosenberg

UNITED STATES

American Jewish Historical Society, New York
    P-675, Lucy S. Dawidowicz Papers
National Archives, College Park, MD
    RG 260, general records of US military government in Germany
Stanford University, Stanford, California
    M0508, Salo W. Baron Papers
United States Holocaust Memorial Museum
    RG 20.021M, Records of the Einsatzstab Reichsleiter Rosenberg, f. R-633/1
YIVO Institute for Jewish Research, New York
    RG 58, Khaykl Lunski, Papers, 1855–1941
    RG 116, Territorial Collection, Germany
    RG 223, Abraham Sutzkever and Szmerke Kaczerginski Collection of Literary
        and Historical Manuscripts

RG 453, Mendel Elkin Papers
RG 584, Max Weinreich Papers, 1930s–1968

Published Materials

Abramowicz, Dina. "Guardians of a Tragic Heritage: Reminiscences and Observations of an Eyewitness." *Judaica Librarianship* 11, nos. 1–2 (2003): 62–66.
——. "The Library in the Vilna Ghetto." *The Holocaust and the Book: Destruction and Preservation*. Edited by Jonathan Rose. Boston: University of Massachusetts Press, 2001.
——. "YIVO Library." *Jewish Book Annual* 25 (1967–68): 87–102.
Abramowicz, Hirsz. *Profiles of a Lost World: Memoirs of Eastern European Jewish Life before World War II*. Translated by Eva Zeitlin Dobkin. Edited by Dina Abramowicz and Jeffrey Shandler. New York: YIVO Institute for Jewish Research, 1999.
Agranovskii, Genrikh. *Evreiskie stranitsy litovskikh arkhivov*. [Jewish pages from Lithuanian Archives] [Vilna]: VsI "Saugi Pradzia" and Green Prints Tipografiia, 2017.
Agranovskii, Genrikh, and Guzenberg, Irina. *Vil'nius. Po sledam Litovskogo Ierusalima. Pamiatnye mesta evreiskoi istorii i kul'tury. Putivoditel'*. 2nd edition. Vilnius: Gos. Evreiskii muzei im. Vilenskogo Gaona, 2016.
Aharon ben Abraham ha-Kohen. *Perah Mateh Aharon*. Amsterdam, 1703.
Allony, Nehemya. *Ha-Sifri'ah ha-Yehudit bimei ha-Beinayim: Reshimot Sefarim me-Genizat Kahiyr*. Edited by Miriam Frankel and Haggai Ben-Shammai. Jerusalem: Machon Ben Tzvi le-Heker Kehilot Yisra'el be-Mizrach, 2006.
Ambrulevičiūtė, Aelita. *Houses That Talk: Sketches of Vokiečiu Street in the Nineteenth Century*. Vilnius: Auko žuvys, 2015.
Amit, Gish. *Ex-Libris: Historiah shel Gezel, Shimur u-Nehus be-Sifriah ha-Liumit be-Yerushalayim*. Jerusalem: Hakibbutz Hameuchad, 2014.
Antokolski, Moshe Simon. *Evel Kaved*. Vilna: Abraham Tzvi Katzenellenbogen, 1886.
Asher ben Yehil. *Besamim Rosh*. Edited by Saul Berlin. Berlin: Hevrat Hinukh Ne'arim, 1793.
Assaf, David. *Untold Tales of the Hasidim: Crisis and Discontent in the History of Hasidism*. Waltham, MA: Brandeis University Press, 2012.
Assaf, Simha. *Batei ha-Din ve-Sidurehem 'Aharei Hatim'at ha-Talmud*. Jerusalem: Defus ha-Po'alim, 1924.
——. "Professor Y. N. ha-Levi Epstein." In *Brisk de-Lita: Entsyklopedia shel Galuyot*. Edited by Eliezer Steinman. Jerusalem: Hevrat Entsyklopedia shel Galuyot, 1954.
Astrinsky, Aviva, Mordekhai Zalkin, and Yermiyahu Ahron Taub, eds. *Mattityahu Strashun, 1817–1885: Scholar, Leader, and Book Collector*. New York: YIVO Institute for Jewish Research, 2001.
Avrutin, Eugene M. "The Politics of Jewish Legibility: Documentation Practices and Reform during the Reign of Nicholas I." *Jewish Social Studies* 11, no. 2 (2005): 136–69.

Azulai, Hayyim Yosef David. *Ma'agal Tov ha-Shalem*. Edited by Aron Freimann. Jerusalem: Mekitsei Nirdamim, 1921.

Bacon, Gershon. "Rubinstein vs. Grodziński: The Dispute over the Vilnius Rabbinate and the Religious Realignment of Vilnius Jewry, 1928–1932." In *The Gaon of Vilnius and the Annals of Jewish Culture*, edited by Larisa Lempertiené, 295–305. Vilnius: Vilnius University, 1998.

Baker, Zachary M. "Judaica Librarians Visit Vilnius." *Spoils of War* 4 (August 1997): 61–65.

———, and Bella Haas Weinberg, eds. *The Yiddish Catalog and Authority File of YIVO Library*. Boston: G. K. Hall, 1990.

Baras, Zvi. *A Century of Books: The Jewish National and University Library 1892–1922*. Jerusalem: Jewish National and University Library Press, 1992.

Bar-El, Joseph. *R. Yoel ben Hazzan: "Re'ah Neho'ah."* Ramat Gan: University of Bar-Ilan Press, 1979.

Barit, Jacob. *Toldot Ya'aqov*. Vilna: Abraham Tzvi Katzenellenbogen, 1883.

Bartal, Israel, and Chaya Naor. *Jewish Culture and Context: The Jews of Eastern Europe, 1772–1881*. Philadelphia: University of Pennsylvania Press, 2011.

Barzilay, Isaac. *Shlomo Yehudah Rapoport [SHI"R] and His Contemporaries: Some Aspects of Jewish Scholarship of the Nineteenth Century*. Jerusalem: Masada Press, 1969.

Beinfeld, Solon. "The Cultural Life of the Vilna Ghetto." *Simon Wiesenthal Center Annual* 1 (1984). http://motlc.wiesenthal.com/site/pp.asp?c=gvKVLcMVIuG&b=394971.

Benayahu, Meir. *Rabi Hayim Yosef David Azulai: Helek Rishon: Toldot Hayyav*. Jerusalem: Mossad Harav Kook, 1959.

Benedictsen, Æge Meyer. *Lithuania: "The Awakening of a Nation": A Study of the Past and Present of the Lithuanian People*. Copenhagen: Egmont H. Petersen, 1924.

Berger, Joseph. "Split Up by Holocaust, Top Collection of Yiddish Works Will Reunite Digitally." *New York Times*, October 2, 2014.

Berger, Mira. "Sifriat Strashun be-Vilna." In *Ha-Hinnukh ve-ha-Tarbut ha-Ivrit be-Eiropah Bein Shetei Milhamot ha-Olam*, edited by Zevi Scharfstein, 511–19. New York: Ogen Publishing House of Histadrut Ha-Ivrit Be-America, 1957.

Bernfeld, Simon. *Toldot ShI"R (R' Shlomo Yehuda Rapoport): Tsiur Kulturi me-Hayya'v, Zemano, u-Po'aluto ha-Ma'ada'it*. Berlin: Ahiasaf, 1899.

Bramson-Alperniené, Esfir. "YIVO-Bibliothek in Wilna: Ein Sammelpunkt der jidischen Kultur." In *Jüdische Kultur(en) im Neuen Europa, Wilna 1918–1939*, edited by Marina Dmitrieva and Heidemarie Petersen. Wiesbaden: Harrassowitz, 2004.

Breuer, Edward. *The Limits of Enlightenment: Jews, Germans and the Eighteenth-Century Study of Scripture*. Cambridge: Harvard University Press, 1996.

Briedis, Laimonas. *Vilnius: City of Strangers*. Vilnius: Baltos Lankos, 2012.

Brisman, Shimeon. *A History and Guide to Judaic Bibliography*. Cincinnati: Hebrew Union College Press, 1977.

Broides, Isaac. *Vilna ha-Tsiyonit ve-'Askaneha: Sefer Zikhronot ve-Te'udot 'al Pe'ulot*

Hovevei Tsion veha-Tsionim be-Vilna mi-Shenat 1881–1924. Tel Aviv: Histadrut 'Olei Vilna veha-Galil be-Tel Aviv, 1939.

Brown, Violet, and Walter Crosby. "Jew Finds Hebrew Collection Nazis Stole in Lie Drive: Boro Lieutenant's Discovery of Manuscripts, Paintings Avenges His Flight from Vienna." *Brooklyn New York Eagle*, April 9, 1945.

Canpaton, Isaac ben Jacob. *Darkhei ha-Talmud.* Venice, 1565.

Chamiel, Ephraim. *The Middle Way: The Emergence of Modern-Religious Trends in Nineteenth-Century Judaism: Responses to Modernity in the Philosophy of Z. H. Chajes, S.R. Hirsch, and S. D. Luzzato.* Jerusalem: Carmel, 2011.

———. *"The Dual Truth": Studies on Nineteenth-Century Modern Religious Thought and Its Influence on Twentieth-Century Jewish Philosophy.* Jerusalem: Carmel, 2016.

Cholawski, Shalom. *So Much Longing, So Much Charm: Nesvizh, Vilna, Rakov.* Translated by Margalit Rodgers. [Israel]: S. Cholawski, 2005.

Cohen, Israel. *Vilna.* Philadelphia: Jewish Publication Society, 1943.

Cohen, Richard. *Jewish Icons, Art and Society in Modern Europe.* Berkeley: University of California Press, 1998.

Cohen-Mushlin, Aliza, Sergey Kravtsov, Vladimir Levin, Giedrė Mickūnaitė, and Jurgita Šiaučiūnaitė-Verbickienė, eds. *Synagogues in Lithuania N-Z: A Catalog.* Vilnius: Vilnius Academy of Arts, 2012.

Cygielman, Shmuel Arthur. *The Jews of Poland and Lithuania until 1648 (5408): Prolegomena and Annotated Sources.* Jerusalem: Zalman Shazar, 1991.

Cyprus, Nathan. "Shlomo Yehuda Rapoport (ShI"R), 1790–1867: Torah, Haskalah ve-Hokhmat Yisrael, ve-Reshitah shel ha-Leumiut ha-Yehudit ha-Modernit." PhD diss., Hebrew University, Jerusalem, 2012.

Cytron, Barry D. *Fire!: The Library Is Burning.* Minneapolis: Lerner Publications, 1988.

Davar. "Toveah Hatzi Million Lira Temurot Sifriah she-hushmedah al yedi ha-Nazim." February 26, 1959.

Dawidowicz, Lucy S. *From That Place and Time, A Memoir, 1938–1947.* New York: Bantam Books, 1991.

Der Tog. "Jewish Vilna Receives Red Army Festively." *Der Tog,* September 9, 1939.

Der Yom. "At the Strashun Library in Vilna, a Short Survey of the Library." *Der Yom,* January 31, 1936.

Deutsch, Shaul Shimon. *Larger than Life: The Life and Times of the Lubavitcher Rebbe Rabbi Menachem Mendel Schneerson,* vol. 2. New York: Chasidic Historical Productions, 1997.

Dicker, Herman. *Of Learning and Libraries: The Seminary Library at One Hundred.* New Jersey: Ktav, 1988.

Dinur, Ben-Zion. "Yerushalaim de-Lita." In *Jerusalem of Lithuania: Illustrated and Documented,* collected and arranged by Leyzer Ran, vol. 1, xiv–xvi. New York: Vilna Ferlag, 1974.

Dresner, Samuel H. "The Second Private Library of Aron Freimann." *Studies in Bibliography and Booklore* 10, no. 3/4 (Winter 1973/1974): 73–79.

Dubnow, Simon M. *Nahpesa ve-Nahkora: Kol Kore el ha-Nevonim be-'am* ha-Mitnadvim Le'esof Homer le-Binyan Toldot Benei Yisra'el be-Polin ve-Rusiya. Odessa: Ha-Pardes, 1892.

———. "Ob izuchenii istorii russkikh evreev i ob uchrezhdenii russkoevereiskago istoricheskago obshchestav." *Voskhod* 4, no. 9 (April–September 1891): 1–91.

Duschinsky, Charles. "Rabbi David Oppenheim: Glimpses of His Life and Activity, Derived from His Manuscripts in the Bodleian Library." *Jewish Quarterly Review* 20, no. 3 (January 1930): 217–47.

Eizenstat, Stuart E. *Imperfect Justice: Looted Assets, Slave Labor, and the Unfinished Business of World War II*. New York: Public Affairs, 2003.

Elbaum, Jacob. *Petihut ve-histagrut: ha-Yitzirah ha-Ruhanit-ha-Sifrutit be-Polin u-be'Artzot Ashkenaz be-shelhei ha-me'ah ha-Shesh-Esrei*. Jerusalem: Magnes Press, 1990.

Eliakh, Dov. *HaGaon: Le-Toldot Ha'yav u-Beirur Mishnato shel Morenu ve-Rabbenu HaGR"A HaGaon Rebi Eliyahu me-Vilna ZTsUK"L*, 3 vols. Jerusalem: Moreshet Hayeshivot, 2002.

Eliasberg, Yehuda Betzalel. *Marpeh le-'Am*. Vilna: R' Menahem Mann ben R' Barukh Z"L, 1834.

Elberg, Simha. "He-'Arot le-Be'ayot: Rabbanut ha-Rashit u-Merkaz Ruhani 'Olami." *Ha-Pardes* 32, no. 8 (1958): 2–4.

Englman, Shua. "Ha-Rav Shmuel Strashun (HaRaShSh) ve-Hagahotav le-Talmud Bavli." Ph.D. diss., Bar-Ilan University, Ramat Gan, 2008.

Etkes, Immanuel. *The Gaon of Vilna: The Man and His Image*. Translated by Jeffery M. Green. Berkeley: University of California Press, 2002.

———. "Teudah beYisrael—Bein Temurah le-Mesorot." In Isaac Ber Levinsohn, *Teudah beYisrael*, edited by Immanuel Etkes. Jerusalem: Merkaz Zalman Shazar, 1977.

Eynhorn, Dovid. "Yerushalaym de-Lite." In *Vilne: A Zamelbukh*, edited by Yefim Yeshurun. New York: Vilna Branch, 1935.

Farber, Kalman. *Olkeniki, Radin, Vilna: mi-Yomano shel Ben Torah ba-Sho'ah ule-faneha*. Jerusalem: n.p., 2006.

Federbusch, Shimon. *Hokreih Yahadut*. Jerusalem: Mossad Harav Kook, 1965.

Feigelmanas, Nojus. *Lietuvos Inkunabulai*. Vilnius: Vilniaus valstybinio V. Kapsuko universiteto Mokslinė biblioteka, 1975.

Feigensohn, Samuel Shraga [Safan ha-Sofer]. "Defus Romm be-Vilna," parts 1 and 2. *Ha-Sefer* 1 (1954): 27–33; 2–3 (1955): 46–57.

———. "Toldot Defus Romm." In *Yahadut Lita*, edited by Dov Lipas, vol. 1, 268–96. Tel Aviv: Am-Hasefer, 1959.

Feiner, Shmuel, ed. *RSH"Y Finn: Me-Haskalah Lohemet le-Haskalah Mishameret*. Jerusalem: Merkaz Dinar, 1993.

Fishburn, Matthew. *Burning Books*. Houndsmills, Basingstoke: Palgrave, Macmillan, 2008.

Fishman, David, E. *Embers Plucked from the Fire: The Rescue of Jewish Cultural Treasures in Vilna*. New York: YIVO Institute for Jewish Research, 2009.

———. *The Book Smugglers: Partisans, Poets, and the Race to Save Jewish Treasures from the Nazis*. Lebanon, NH: ForeEdge, 2017.

———. *The Rise of Modern Yiddish Culture*. Pittsburgh: University of Pittsburgh Press, 2005.

———. "The Strashun Library in War Time, 1939-1941." In *The History and Future of the Strashun Library: Conference Program*. New York: YIVO Institute for Jewish Research, 2017.

Fishman, Joshua A. "The Gaon of Vilne and the Yiddish Language." In *The Gaon of Vilnius and the Annals of Jewish Culture*, edited by Larisa Lempertienė, 18-26. Vilnius: Vilnius University, 1998.

Flanner, Janet. "Annals of Crime: The Beautiful Spoils." *New Yorker*, February 22, 1947, 31-36.

———. *Men and Monuments*. New York: Harper, 1957.

Fontaine Verwey, Herman de la. "The Bibliotheca Rosenthaliana during the German Occupation." *Studia Rosenthaliana* 38/39 (2005/2006): 60-72.

Freeze, ChaeRan Y., and Jay M. Harris, eds. *Everyday Jewish Life in Imperial Russia: Select Documents, 1772-1914*. Waltham, MA: Brandeis University Press, 2013.

Freidberg, Chaim. *Toldot ha-Defus ha-Ivri be-Polin*. Tel Aviv: Gutenberg, 1950.

Freimann, Aron. *Stadtbibliothek Frankfurt a.M. Katalog der Judaica*. Frankfurt: M. Lehrberger, 1932.

———. *Thesaurus Typographiae Hebraicae Saeculi*, 15 ed. Berlin: Marx, 1924-1931.

Frick, David. "Jews and Others in Seventeenth-Century Wilno: Life in the Neighborhood." *Jewish Studies Quarterly* 21, no. 1 (2005): 8-24.

Friedman, Herbert A. *Roots of the Future*. Jerusalem: Gefen, 1999.

Friedman, Phillip. *Their Brother's Keeper*. New York: Crown, 1957.

Fuchs, Richard. "The Hochschule fur die Wissenschaft des Judentums in the Nazi Period: Some Personal Reflections." *Leo Baeck Institute* 12 (1967).

Fuenn, Samuel Joseph. *Kiryah Ne'emanah: Korot 'Adat Yisra'el be-'Ir Vilna YTz"V*. Vilna: Yosef Reuven ben R' Menahem Romm, 1860.

———. *Kiryah Ne'emanah: Korot 'Adat Yisra'el be-'Ir Vilna YTz"V*. Edited by Hillel Noah Maggid-Steinschneider. Revised edition. Vilna: Yitzhak Funk, 1905.

Gallas, Elisabeth. *Das Leichenhaus der Bücher: Kulturrestitution und jüdisches Geschichtsdenken nach 1945*. Göttingen: Vandenhoeck and Ruprecht, 2016.

———. "Documenting Cultural Destruction: The Research Project of the Commission on European Jewish Cultural Reconstruction, 1944-1948." In *Als der Holocaust noch keinen Namen hatte: Zur frühen Aufarbeitung des NS-Massenmordes an Jüdinnen und Juden (Before the Holocaust Had Its Name: Early Confrontations of the Nazi Mass Murder of the Jews)*, edited by Regina Fritz, Éva Kovács, and Béla Rásky, 45-61. Vienna: New Academic Press, 2016.

———. "Preserving East European Jewish Culture: Lucy Dawidowicz and the Salvage of Books after the Holocaust." *Simon Dubnow Institute Yearbook* 11 (2012): 73-89.

Ginzburg, A. "Di Neshome fun Yiddisher Vilne." *Der Vilner*, 27.

Glick, Shmuel, ed. *Kuntres ha-Teshuvot ha-Hadash: Otsar Bibliografi le-Sifrut ha-She'elot ve-ha-Teshuvot me-Reishit ha-Defus ve'Ad shenat TSh"S (1470-2000)*. 4 vols. Jerusalem: Bar-Ilan University, Faculty of Law, 2006-2010.

Glickman, Mark. *Stolen Words: The Nazi Plunder of Jewish Books*. Philadelphia: Jewish Publication Society, 2016.

Goitein, S. D. *A Mediterranean Society: The Jewish Communities of the World as Portrayed in the Documents of the Cairo Geniza*. 1996; reprint, Berkeley: University of California Press, 1999.

Goldstein, Bernard. *Twenty Years with the Labor Bund: A Memoir of Interwar Poland*. Translated by Marvin S. Zuckerman. West Lafayette, IN: Purdue University Press, 2016.

Gottesman, Itzik Nakhmen. *Defining the Yiddish Nation: The Jewish Folklorists of Poland*. Detroit: Wayne State University Press, 2003.

Grade, Chaim. "The Seven Little Alleys." In *My Mother's Sabbath Days: A Memoir by Chaim Grade*. Translated by Channa Kleinerman Goldstein and Inna Hecker Grade. New York: Knopf, 1986.

———. *Di Kloyz un di Gas*. New York: Schulsinger Brothers, 1974.

Green, Warren. "The Fate of the Crimean Jewish Communities: Ashkenazim, Krimchaks and Karaites." *Jewish Social Studies* 46, no. 2 (Spring 1984): 169–76.

Greenbaum, Masha. *The Jews of Lithuania: A History of a Remarkable Community, 1316–1945*. Jerusalem: Gefen, 1995.

Gries, Zeev. *The Book in the Jewish World, 1700–1900*. Oxford: Littman Library of Jewish Civilization, 2010.

Grimsted, Patricia Kennedy. "Roads to Ratibor: Library and Archival Plunder by the Einsatzstab Reichsleiter Rosenberg." *Holocaust and Genocide Studies* 19, no. 3 (Winter 2005): 390–458.

———. "The Postwar Fate of Einsatzstab Rosenberg Archival and Library Plunder, and the Dispersal of ERR Records." *Holocaust and Genocide Studies* 20, no. 2 (Fall 2006): 278–308.

———. "US Restitution of Nazi-Looted Cultural Treasures to the USSR, 1945–1959: Facsimile Documents from the National Archives of the United States." http://www.archives.gov.ua/Eng/NB/USRestitution.php.

Guzenberg, Irina. *Vilnius: Sites of Jewish Memory, A Concise Guide*. Translated by Svetlana Shatalova and edited by Geoff Vasil. Vilnius: Pavilniai, 2013.

Haberer, Erich. *Jews and Revolution in Nineteenth-Century Russia*. Cambridge: Cambridge University Press, 1995, 73–75.

Habermann, Abraham Meir. "He'arot ve-Hashlamot." In Nathan Nata Rabinovich, *Ma'amar 'al Hadpasat ha-Talmud: Toldot Hadpasat ha-Talmud*, edited by Abraham Meir Habermann. Jerusalem: Mossad Harav Kook, 1952.

Hamburg, Binyamin Shlomo. *Meshihei ha-Sheker u-Mitnagedeihem*. Benei Brak: Machon Moreshet Ashkenaz, 1989.

Hanau, Shlomo Zalman. *Binyan Shlomo*. Frankfurt: Mattias Andrea, 1708.

Harkavy, Tzvi. "Tagvuah ma-et Tzvi Harkavy." *Ha-Darom* 10 (1959): 181–83.

———. *Le-Heker Mishpahot*. Jerusalem: Hotza'at Hasefarim Erets Yisraelit, 1953.

———. *Autobibliografiah: Kol ha-Pirsumim, ke-1,200 'arakhim: Sefarim, Kuntresim, Mehkarim, u-Ma'amarim, Mahadurot, Tirgumim ve-Arikhah; be-Ivrit, be-Yiddish, be-Ladino, u-be-La'az*. Jerusalem: Hotza'at Hasefarim Erets Yisraelit, 1970.

———. "Be-Sifriot ha-Gedolot ba-Olam." *Ha-Sefer: A Bibliographic Journal* 8 (1960): 59–62.

———. "Ha-Korim el ha-Arukh: Be-Inyan Seredi Sifriat Strashun." *Herut*, October 9, 1960.

——— [Gimmel, pseud.]. "Mekorei ha-Rambam." *Ha-Tsofeh*, February 3, 1956.

———. "Rabi Matityahu Strashun." *Areshet* 3 (1961): 426–29.

———. "Rabi Matityahu Strashun (1816–1885)." In *Hokhmat Yisrael be-Europa*, edited by Shimon Federbusch, vol. 3, 345–55. Jerusalem: Agon, 1965.

———. "Regarding K. Kahana's Criticism of *Mekorei ha-Rambam*." *She'arim*, May 24, 1957.

———. "Seridei Sifri'at Strashun." *Ha-Sefer* 9 (1961): 60–61.

———. "Toldot ha-RaSha"Sh u-Ketavav." In *Mekorei ha-Rambam: Samuel Strashun*, edited by Tzvi Harkavy, 53–58. Jerusalem: Hotza'at Hasefarim Erets Yisraelit, 1957.

Harris, Jay M. *How Do We Know This? Midrash and the Fragmentation of Modern Judaism*. Albany: State University of New York Press, 1995.

Harshav, Benjamin. *The Polyphony of Jewish Culture*. Redwood City, CA: Stanford University Press, 2007.

Haruv, Dan. "Simon Dubnow: An Annotated Bibliography." In *Writer and Warrior: Simon Dubnow: Historian and Public Figure*, edited by Abraham Greenbaum, Israel Bartal, and Dan Haruv, 213–66. Jerusalem: Zalman Shazar Center for Jewish History, 2010.

Havlin, Shlomo Zalman. "'Ha- Kloyz' shel ha-Gaon me-Vilna ZTs"L, Helek shel 'Pinkas ha-Kloyz.'" *Yeshurun* 6 (1999): 678–85.

Hayyim of Volozhin. *Nefesh ha-Hayyim*. Vilna: Menahem Mann ben Barukh Romm, 1837.

———. "Ha-Pinkas shel Kloyz ha-Gaon." *Yeshurun* 16 (2005): 746–60.

Henkin, Eitam. "Me-Hibbat Tzion le-Anti-Tzionut: Temurot be-Orthodoksiah ha-Mizrah Europit—Ha-Rav Dovid Friedman me-Karlin (1915–1928) ke-Mikreh Mivhan." PhD diss., University of Tel Aviv, 2013.

Herman, Dana. "Hashavat Avedah : A History of Jewish Cultural Reconstruction, Inc." PhD diss, McGill University, Montreal, 2008.

Herskovics, Mayer. *Maharats Chayot: Toldot Rabi Tzvi Hirsch Chayot u-Mishnato*. Jerusalem: Mossad Harav Kook, 1972.

Heschel, Abraham Joshua. "Yerushalayim de-Lita." In *Jerusalem of Lithuania: Illustrated and Documented*, collected and arranged by Leyzer Ran, vol. 1, xxi. New York: Vilna Ferlang, 1974.

Heuberger, Rachel. *Bibliothek des Judentums: Die Hebraica- und Judaica-Sammlung der Stadt- und Universitätsbibliothek Frankfurt am Main—Entstehung, Geschichte und heutige Aufgaben*. Frankfurt: V. Klostermann, 1996.

———, Laura E. Leone, and Renate Evers. "The Challenges of Reconstructing Cultural Heritage: An International Digital Collaboration." *International Federation of Library Associations and Institutions* 41, no. 3 (2015). http://sammlungen.ub.uni-frankfurt.de/freimann.

Hildesheimer, Meir. "Moses Mendelssohn in Nineteenth-Century Rabbinical Literature." *Proceedings of the American Academy for Jewish Research* 55 (1988): 79–133.

Holdheim, Samuel. *Ma'amar ha-Ishut*. Berlin: Julius Sittenfeld, 1861.

Hoogewoud, F. J. "An Introduction to H. de la Fontaine Verwey's 'The Bibliotheca Rosenthaliana during the German Occupation.'" *Studia Rosenthaliana* 38/39 (2005/2006): 49–59.

——. "The Return of the Bibliotheca Rosenthaliana—But Not without Damage." In *Bibliotheca Rosenthaliana: Treasures of Jewish Booklore: Marking the Two Hundredth Anniversary of the Birth of Leeser Rosenthal, 1794–1994*, edited by Adri K. Offenberg, 116–17. Amsterdam: Amsterdam University Press, 1996.

Hundert, Gershon David. *Jews in Poland-Lithuania in the Eighteenth Century: A Genealogy of Modernity*. Berkeley: University of California Press, 2004.

Hutner-David, Bruria. "The Dual Role of Rabbi Zvi Hirsch Chajes: Traditionalist and 'Maskil.'" PhD diss., Columbia University, New York, 1971.

Ilya, Menashe. *Alfei Menashe*. Vilna: Ha-Meshutafim ha-Negidim, 1815.

International Dictionary of Library Histories. Edited by David H. Stam. Chicago: Fitzroy Dearborn, 2001.

Kaczerginski, Szmerke. *Partizaner geyen! . . . fartseykhenungen fun Vilner Ghetto*. Buenos Aires: Tsentral-Farband fun Poylishe Yiden in Argentinei, 1947.

Kagan, Berl. *Sefer Prenumeranten: Vegvayzer tsu Prenumerirte Hebreishe Sefarim un Zayere Hotmim fun 8,767 Kehiles in Eyrope un Tsofn-Afrike*. New York: Ketav, 1975.

Kahana, K. "Mekorei ha-Rambam." *She'arim*, April 20, 1957.

Kamenetsky, Dovid. "Ha-Gaon Rabi Menashe me-Ilya ZTs"L." *Yeshurun* 20 (2008): 729–81.

——. "Ktav Yad Kodesh shel Rabbenu ha-Gra." *Yeshurun* 19 (2007): 705–26.

Kaplan, Ze'ev Shraga. *Edut be-Ya'akov*. Warsaw: Ha-Tsefirah, 1904.

Karlip, Joshua. *The Tragedy of a Generation: The Rise and Fall of Jewish Nationalism in Eastern Europe*. Cambridge: Harvard University Press, 2013.

Karpinowitz, Abraham. "Tall Tamare." In *Vilna My Vilna*. Translated by Helen Mintz. Syracuse, NY: Syracuse University Press, 2015.http://www.yiddishbookcenter .org/sites/default/files/downloads/PT59_tall_tamare_sm.pdf.

Katz, Dovid. *Lithuanian Jewish Culture*. Vilnius: Baltos Lankos, 2010.

——. "Vilne, Vilno, Vilna: Three Alphabet Spellings (and Pronunciations) for the Name of Vilnius" [Hebrew]. *Keepsakes of Old Jewish Vilna* (16). http:// defendinghistory.com/keepsakes-of-old-jewish-vilna-16.

——. *Windows into a Lost Jewish Past: Vilna Book Stamps*. Vilnius: Versus Aureus, 2008.

——. *Words on Fire: The Unfinished Story of Yiddish*. New York: Basic Books, 2007.

Katzenellenbogen, Rafael. "RaSh"Sh le-Shitato." In *Mekorei Ha-Rambam Le-RaSh"Sh*, edited by Tzvi Harkavy, 60–64. Jerusalem: Ha-Sefarim ha-Erets Yisra'elim, 1957.

——. "Ha-Rashash le-Shitato," *Moriah* 10–12 (1972).

——. "Ha-Rashash le-Shitato," in Ya'akov Gershon, *Be'er Ro'ei*. Jerusalem: Midrash Rabbi Rafael, 1981.

Katzenellenbogen, Zvi Hirsch. *Netivot 'Olam*. Vilna: R' Yosef Reuven ben R' Menahem Mann Romm, 1853.

Katzman, Asher. "Zikhronot me'Hakloyz' shel Hagaon Mevilna ZTsUK"L." *Yeshurun* 6 (1999): 685–90.

Katzman, Eliezer. "Le-Demut ha-Gaon R' Yehoshua Heshel Levine ZTs"L." *Yeshurun* 5 (1999): 742–83 and *Yeshurun* 6 (1999): 700–27.

Kaye, Lawrence M. "Looted Art: What Can and Should Be Done." *Cardozo Law Review* 20, no. 2 (December 1998): 657.

Keitner, Chiméne I. "Introductory Note to the United States Second Circuit Court of Appeals: Koibel v. Royal Dutch Petroleum Co." *International Legal Materials* 49, no. 6 (2010): 1522.

Kestenbaum and Co. *Catalogue of Fine Judaica: Hebrew Printed Books, Manuscripts and Graphic Art: Featuring: Duplicates from the Rare Book Room of YIVO Library, New York and The Library of the Late Dr. Max Kimche, Zürich*, part 2, September 10, 2009. New York: Kestenbaum, 2009.

Kirchhoff, Markus. *Häuser des Buches: Bilder Jüdischer Bibliotheken*. Leipzig: Reclam, 2002.

Klausner, Israel. "Batei-Eked Sefarim be-Yerushalim di-Lita." In *Sefer Refa'el Mahler, Kovetz mehkarim be-Toldot Yisrael*, edited by Shmuel Yevin. Merhavyah: Sifriyat Poalim, 1974.

———. *Korot Beit ha-Almin ha-Yashan be-Vilna*. Vilna: ha-Kehillah ha-'Ivrit be-Vilna, 1935.

———. *Toldot ha-Kehillah ha-Ivrit be-Vilna*. Vilna: ha-Kehillah ha-'Ivrit be-Vilna, 1938.

———. "Ha-Gezerah al Tilboshot ha-Yehudim, 1844–1850." *Gal-Ed* 6 (1982): 11–26.

———. "Ha-Tenuah ha-Tzionit be-Lita." In *Yahadut Lita*, edited by Dov Lipas, vol. 1, 508–29. Tel Aviv: Am-Hasefer, 1959.

———. *Vilna, Yerushalayim d'Lita: Dorot ha-Aharonim 1881–1939*. Edited by Shmuel Barantchok. Israel: Ghetto Fighters' House, 1983.

———. "Vilna." In *Yahadut Lita*, vol. 3, 257–327. Tel Aviv: ha-Agudah le 'Ezrah ha-Dadit le-Yotsei Lita be-Yisra'el, 1967.

Knuth, Rebecca. *Burning Books and Leveling Libraries: Extremist Violence and Cultural Destruction*. Westport, Conn.: Praeger, 2006.

———. *Libricide: Regime Sponsored Destruction of Books and Libraries in the Twentieth Century*. Westport, Conn.: Praeger, 2003.

Kohn, Pinhas. "Le-Tolodot ha-Defus Romm be-Vilna." *Kiryat Sefer* 12 (1935): 109–14

Kotik, Abraham Hirsch. "Dos Bukh un Der Leyzer." *Der Fraynd*, July 8, 1911.

Krinsky, Carol Herselle. *Synagogues of Europe: Architecture, History, Meaning*. New York: Architectural History Foundation and Massachusetts Institute of Technology, 1985.

Kruk, Herman. "The Library and Reading Room in the Vilna Ghetto, 6 Strashun Street." Translated by Zachary M. Baker. In *The Holocaust and the Book: Destruction and Preservation*, edited by Jonathan Rose. Boston: University of Massachusetts Press, 2001.

———. *The Last Days of the Jerusalem of Lithuania: Chronicles from the Vilna Ghetto and the Camps, 1939–1944*. Edited by Benjamin Harshav and translated by Barbra Harshav. New Haven, CT: Yale University Press, 2002.

Kulbak, Moyshe. "*Vilne*." Vilna, 1926.

Kuntres Ahavah be-Ta'anugim: Be-'Inyan Darkhei ha-Zivug ve-haKravah bein Ish le-Ishto. Edited by Tzvi Malachi. Lod, Israel: n.p., 1991.

Kurtz, Michael J. *America and the Return of Nazi Contraband: The Recovery of Europe's Cultural Treasures*. New York: Cambridge University Press, 2006.

———. *Nazi Contraband: American Policy on the Return of European Cultural Treasures, 1945–1955*. New York: Garland, 1985.

———. "Resolving a Dilemma: The Inheritance of Jewish Property." *Cardozo Law Review* 20, no. 2 (December 1998): 625.

Kuznitz, Cecile E. "An-sky's Legacy: The Vilna Historic-Ethnographic Society and the Shaping of Modern Jewish Culture." In *The Worlds of S. An-sky: A Russian Jewish Intellectual at the Turn of the Century*, edited by Gabriella Safran and Steven J. Zipperstein, 32–45. Redwood City, CA: Stanford University Press, 2006.

———. "On the Jewish Street: Yiddish Culture and the Urban Landscape in Interwar Vilna." In *Yiddish Language and Culture: Then and Now*, edited by Leonard Jay Greenspoon, 65–92. Omaha, NE: Creighton University Press, 1998.

———. *YIVO and the Making of Modern Jewish Culture: Scholarship for the Yiddish Nation*. New York: Cambridge University Press, 2014.

Lachmann, Renate. *Memory and Literature: Intertextuality in Russian Modernism*. Translated by Roy Sellars and Anthony Wall. Minneapolis: University of Minnesota Press, 1997.

Law Reports of Trials of War Criminals: Selected and Prepared by the United Nations War Crimes Commission, vol. 10: *The I. G. Farben and Krupp Trials*. London: His Majesty's Stationery Office, 1949.

Leff, Lisa Moses. "Rescue or Theft? Zosa Szajkowski and the Salvaging of French Jewish History after World War II." *Jewish Social Studies* 18, no. 2 (2012): 1–39.

———. *The Archive Thief: The Man Who Salvaged French Jewish History in the Wake of the Holocaust*. New York: Oxford University Press, 2015.

Leiman, Shnayer Z. "A Note on R. Bezalel Alexandrov's [*Mishkan Betzalel*] and Its *Prenumeranten*." *Seforim Blog*, November 28, 2016. http://seforim.blogspot .com/2016/11/a-note-on-r-bezalel-alexandrovs-and-its.html.

———. "R. Moses Schick: The Hatam Sofer's Attitude toward Mendelssohn's Biur." *Tradition* 24, no. 3 (Spring 1989): 83–86.

———. "The New Encyclopaedia: Some Preliminary Observations." *Seforim Blog*, June 5, 2007. http://seforim.blogspot.com/2007/06/shnayer-leiman-new -encyclopaedia.html.

Lempertienė, Lara. "The Transformations in the Culture of Reading amongst Lithuanian Jews in the Second Half of the Nineteenth Century–First Half of the Twentieth Century." *Straipsniai* (online journal), http://straipsniai.lt.

Levin, Dov. *The Lesser of Two Evils: Eastern European Jewry under Soviet Rule, 1939–1941*. Philadelphia: Jewish Publication Society, 1995.

———. *The Litvaks: A Short History of the Jews in Lithuania*. Translated by Adam Teller. Jerusalem: Yad Vashem, 2000.

Levin, Hillel. "'Should Napoleon Be Victorious': Politics and Spirituality in Early Modern Jewish Messianism." *Jerusalem Studies in Jewish Thought* 17 (2001): *65–*84.

Levine, Yeshoshua Heschel. *Sefer Aliyot Eliyahu: Toldot ha-Adam ha-Gadol be-Anakim . . . Gaon me-Vilna*. Vilna, 1856.

Levinsohn, Isaac Baer. *Be'er Yitzhak: Sefer ha-Kolel Igerot Ratso' ve-Shov bein Yitzhak Be'er Levinzon u-Vein Hakhmei Doro*. Warsaw: Dov Baer Nathanson, 1899.

———. *Teudah beYisrael*. Vilna: Menahem Mann ben Barukh Romm, 1828.

Liekis, Šarūnas, and Antony Polonsky. "Introduction." *Polin: Studies in Polish Jewry*, edited by Šarūnas Liekis, Antony Polonsky, and ChaeRan Freeze. Oxford: Littman Library of Jewish Civilization, 2013.

Liftz, Dov. "Ha-Kara'im be-Lita." In *Yahadut Lita*, edited by Dov Lipas, vol. 1, 138-50. Tel Aviv: Am-Hasefer, 1959.

Litvak, Olga. *Haskalah: The Romantic Movement in Judaism*. New Brunswick, NJ: Rutgers University Press, 2012.

Loeffler, James. "Between Zionism and Liberalism: Oscar Janowsky and Diaspora Nationalism in America." *AJS Review* 34, no. 2 (November 2010): 289-308.

Lunski, Khaykl. "Der 'Sefer haZahav' ein der Strashun Bibliotek." In *Vilner Almanakh: unter der redaktsye fun A. Y. Grodzenski*, edited by Aaron Isaac Grodzenski. Reprint, edited by Isaac Kowalski, 37-46. Brooklyn, NY: Moriah Offset, 1992.

———. "Di Strashun Bibliotek un Vilne." In *Vilne*, edited by Yefim Yeshurun, 267-72. New York: Vilner Brentsh, 1935.

———. "Ha-'Kloyzim' be-Vilna, Hatzer Beit ha-Kneset ve-Rehov ha-Yehudim." *Ha-Tsefirah*, July 4, 1921.

———. *Me-ha-Ghetto ha-Vilna'i: Tipusim u-Tzlalim*. Vilna: Agudat ha-Soferim veha-Zhurnalistim be-'Vilna, 1921.

Mankowitz, Zeev W. *Life between Memory and Hope: The Survivors of the Holocaust in Occupied Germany*. Cambridge: Cambridge University Press, 2002.

Mark, Jacob. *Be-Mehi'tsatam shel Gedolei ha-Dor: Biographiot, Sofrim, Amerot ve Sihot Hulin shel Gedolei Yisrael be-Dor ha-Kodem*. Translated by Samuel Haggai. Jerusalem: Gevil, 1958.

———. *Gedoylim fun Unzer Tsayt*. New York: Arium Press, 1925.

Mark, Zvi. "Madness, Melancholy and Suicide in Early Hasidim." *Kabbalah: Journal for the Study of Jewish Mystical Texts* 12 (2004): 27-44.

Marten-Finnis, Susanne. *Vilna as a Centre of the Modern Jewish Press, 1840-1928: Aspirations, Challenges, and Progress*. Oxford: Peter Lang, 2004.

Marx, Alexander. "Some Jewish Book Collectors." In *Studies in Jewish History and Booklore*, 198-237. New York: Jewish Theological Seminary of America, 1941.

———. "Some Notes on the History of David Oppenheimer's Library." *Revue des Études Juives* 82 [Israel Lévi Festschrift] (1926): 451-60.

———. "The History of David Oppenheimer's Library." In *Studies in Jewish History and Booklore*, 238-55. New York: Jewish Theological Seminary of America, 1944.

Mashberg, Tom. "Not All Monuments Men Were Men." *New York Times*, January 29, 2014.

Mevorakh, Barukh, ed. *Napoli'on ve-Tekufato: Reshumot ve-Eduyot Ivriot shel Bene ha-Dor*. Jerusalem: Bialik Institute, 1968.

Meyer, Michael A. *Response to Modernity: A History of the Reform Movement in Judaism*. Detroit: Wayne State University Press, 1995.

Mickūnaitė, Giedrė. *Making a Great Ruler: Grand Duke Vytautas of Lithuania.* Budapest: Central European Press, 2006.

Milosz, Czeslaw. *A Year of the Hunter.* Translated by Madeline G. Levine. New York: Farrar, Straus and Giroux, 1994.

———, and Tomas Venclova. "A Dialogue about Wilno." In Tomas Venclova, *Forms of Hope: Essays.* New York: Sheep Meadow Press, 1999.

Mohrer, Fruma, and Marek Web, comp. and eds. *Guide to YIVO Archives.* New York: YIVO Institute for Jewish Research, 1998.

Mondshein, Yehoshua. "Ktav Yad ve-Hahanot le-Defus be-Beit ha-Almanah ve-ha-Ahim Romm." *Alei Sefer* 6–7 (1979): 187–97.

———. "Ketav Yad ve-ha-Khanot le-Defus be-Beit ha-ʾAlmanah ve-ha-ʾAhim Ramm." *Alei Sefer* 8 (1980): 124–36.

Morgenstern, Arie. "Bein Banim le-Talmeidem: Ha-Mavak ʾal Moreshet Ha-Gra ve-ʾal ha-Ideologiah Torah mul Eretz-Yisrael." *Daat: A Journal of Jewish Philosophy and Kabbalah* 53 (2004): 82–124.

Moustafa, Laila Hussein, Joshua Harris, and Bethany Anderson. "Lessons from World War II and the Holocaust: What Can Be Done to Save Cultural Heritage and Memory during Times of War." In *What Do We Lose When We Lose a Library?: Proceedings of the Conference Held at the KU Leuven 9–11 September 2015*, edited by Mel Collier. Leuven: University Library KU Leuven, 2016.

Nadler, Allan. *The Faith of Mithnagdim: Rabbinic Responses to Hasidic Rapture.* Baltimore: Johns Hopkins University Press, 1997.

Nathans, Benjamin. *Beyond the Pale: The Jewish Encounter with Late Imperial Russia.* Berkeley: University of California Press, 2004.

Nathanson, Dov Baer. *Sefer ha-Zikhronot.* Warsaw: Y. Eletin Nathanson, 1878.

Offenberg, Adri K. "From Lesser Rosenthal to Today's Bibliotheca Rosenthaliana." In *Bibliotheca Rosenthaliana: Treasures of Jewish Booklore*, edited by Adri K. Offenberg, Emile G. L. Schrijver, and F. J. Hoogewoud, xi–xii. Amsterdam: Amsterdam University Press, 1996.

Perl, Gil S. *The Pillar of Volozhin: Rabbi Naftali Zvi Yehuda Berlin and the World of Nineteenth-Century Lithuanian Scholarship.* Boston: Academic Studies Press, 2013.

Pludermacher, Shalom. "Shirei Minhah." In Mattitayhu Strashun, *Mattat-Yah*, edited by Shalom Pludermacher, 39–80. Vilna: Ha-ʾalmanah ve-ha-ʾAchim Romm, 1893.

———. "Zikaron le-Hakham: Zeh Sefer Toldot ha-Rav ha-Gaʾon, he-Hakham ha-Kolel Rabi Mattityahu Strashun ZʾʹL." In Mattityahu Strashun, *Mattat-Yah*, edited by Shalom Pludermacher, 7–38. Vilna: Ha-ʾalmanah ve-ha-ʾAchim Romm, 1893.

Polastron, Lucien X. *Books on Fire: The Destruction of Libraries throughout History.* Translated by Jon E. Graham. Rochester, NY: Inner Traditions, 2007.

Pomrenze, Seymour. "Offenbach Reminiscences: The Netherlands' Experiences." *Spoils of War*, no. 2 (July 15, 1996): 18–20. http://www.lostart.de/Content/07_Publikationen/EN/SpoilsOfWar/Spoils%20of%20War%202.pdf?__blob=publicationFile.

———. "'Operation Offenbach'—The Salvage of Jewish Cultural Treasures in Germany." *YIVO Bleter* 29 (Summer 1947): 282–85.

———. "Personal Reminiscences of the OAD, 1946–1949, Fulfilling International and Moral Obligations." https://www.ushmm.org/information/exhibitions/online-exhibitions/special-focus/offenbach-archival-depot/establishment-and-operation.

Porat, Dina. *The Fall of a Sparrow: The Life and Times of Abba Kovner.* Translated and edited by Elizabeth Yuval. Redwood City, CA: Stanford University Press, 2009.

Poste, Leslie I. "The Development of U.S. Protection of Libraries and Archives in Europe during World War II." PhD diss., University of Chicago, 1958.

———. "Library Books Go Home from the Wars." *Library Journal* 73, no. 21 (December 1, 1948): 1699–1704.

Preschel, Tovia. *Ma'amrei Toviah.* Jerusalem: Mossad Harav Kook, 2016.

Rabinovitch, Simon. *Jewish Rights, National Rites: Nationalism and Autonomy in Late Imperial and Revolutionary Russia.* Redwood City, CA: Stanford University Press, 2014.

———, ed. *Jews and Diaspora Nationalism: Writings on Jewish Peoplehood in Europe and the United States.* Waltham, MA: Brandeis University Press, 2012.

Ran, Leyzer. *Jerusalem of Lithuania: Illustrated and Documented.* 3 vols. New York: Vilno Album Committee, 1974.

Rapoport, Solomon Judah Leib ha-Kohen. *Erekh Milin: 'Al Seder A"B, Kolel Bi'ur Kol Shemot 'Atzmiyim shel Anashim. . . .* Prague: Shlomo Yehuda Rapoport, 1852.

———. *Erekh Milin.* Warsaw: Ha-Tsefirah, 1915.

———. *Mikhtevei Bikoret: Asher Heritz ha-Rav Shi"r z"1 'el RSD"L z"1.* Edited by Eisig Gräber. Przemysl: Zupnick, Knoller, and Hammerschmidt, 1885.

———. *Nahlat Yehuda.* Krakow: Carl Budweiser, 1868.

Raven, James, ed. *Lost Libraries, The Destruction of Great Book Collections since Antiquity.* London: Palgrave, Macmillan, 2004.

Ravid, Benjamin C. I. "The Venetian Ghetto in Historical Perspective." In *The Autobiography of a Seventeenth-Century Venetian Rabbi: Leon Modena's "Life of Judah,"* translated and edited by Mark R. Cohen, 279–83. Princeton, NJ: Princeton University Press.

Research Staff of the Commission on European Jewish Cultural Reconstruction. "Tentative List of Jewish Cultural Treasures in Axis-Occupied Countries." *Jewish Social Studies* 8, no. 1, supp. (1946).

———. "Addenda and Corrigenda to Tentative List of Jewish Cultural Treasures in Axis-Occupied Countries." *Jewish Social Studies* 10, no. 1 (January 1948).

Richards, Pamela Spence. "'Aryan Librarianship.'" *Journal of Library History (1974–1987)* 19, no. 2 (Spring 1984): 249–50.

Richler, Binyamin. *Hebrew Manuscripts: A Treasured Legacy.* Cleveland, Ohio: Ofeq Institute, 1990.

Roest, Meijer Marcus. *Catalog der Hebraica und Judaica: Aus der L. Rosenthal'schen Bibliothek.* 1875; reprint, Amsterdam: B. M. Isräel, 1966.

Roth, Cecil. "Famous Jewish Book Collections and Collectors." In *Essays in Jewish Booklore,* 330–35. New York: Ktav, 1971.

Rubin, Y. "Unzer Vilne." *Unzer Tog,* 9.

Rydell, Anders. *The Book Thieves: The Nazi Looting of Europe's Libraries and the Race* to *Return a Literary Inheritance*. Translated by Henning Koch. New York: Viking, 2017.

Saks, A. S. *Worlds That Passed*. Philadelphia: Jewish Publication Society of America, 1943.

Samet, Moshe. *Hadash 'Asur min ha-Torah: Perakim be-Toldot ha-Orthodoksi'ah.* Jerusalem: Carmel, 2005.

Sandler, Peretz. *Ha-Bi'ur le-Torah shel Moses Mendelssohn ve-Si'ato Hithavut ve-Hashpa'ato.* Jerusalem: Mekor, 1984.

Sarna, Jonathan D. "Jewish Culture Comes to America." *Jewish Studies* 42 (2003–2004): *45–*57.

Schacter, Jacob J. "R. David Friedman: The Ban on Secular Study in Jerusalem." *Tradition* 26, no. 4 (1992): 102–5.

Schick, Barukh ben Jacob of Shklov. *Sefer Euklidos*. The Hague, 1780.

Schidorsky, Dov. *Gevilim Nesraphim ve-Otiot Porakhat: Toldotehem shel Asufei Sefarim ve-Sifriot be-Eretz Yisrael ve-Nesiyonot le-Hatzalat Sredeihem l'ahar ha-Shoah.* Jerusalem: Magnes Press, 2008.

———. "The Emergence of Jewish Public Libraries in Nineteenth-Century Palestine." *Libri* 32, no. 1 (1982): 1–40.

Schiffman, Lawrence H. "The Vilna Gaon's Methods for the Textual Criticism of Rabbinic Literature." In *The Gaon of Vilna and the Annals of Jewish Literature*, compiled and edited by Izraelis Lempertas and Larisa Lempertienė, 116–27. Vilnius: Vilnius University, 1998.

Schischa, Abraham. "Rabbinic Writings from the Collection of Rabbi David Oppenheim." *Yeshurun* 31 (2014): 781–94.

Schnold, Rachel. "Elijah's Face: The Portrait of the Vilna Gaon in Folk Art." In *The Gaon of Vilna—The Man and His Legacy*, edited by Rachel Schnold. Tel Aviv: Beit Hatefutsoth, 1998.

Schönblum, Samuel. *Catalogue d'une Collection anconienne dont la plus grande partie dérive de la Bibliotheque appartenant aux célébres C. J. D. Azulai et son fils Rafael, Rabbin à Ancone.* [Lemberg]: Poremba, 1872.

Schreiner, Stefan. "The Vilner Gaon as a Biblical Scholar (A Reappraisal)." In *The Gaon of Vilna and the Annals of Jewish Literature*, compiled and edited by Izraelis Lempertas and Larisa Lempertienė, 128–36. Vilnius: Vilnius University, 1998.

Schwarzfuchs, Simon. *Napoleon, The Jews and the Sanhedrin*. London: Routledge and Kegan Paul, 1979.

Segev, Zohar. "Diaspora Nationalism: The World Jewish Congress, American Jewry and the Rehabilitation of European Jewry after the Holocaust." *Zion* 75 (2010): 153–82.

Seltzer, Robert. *Simon Dubnow's "New Judaism": Diaspora Nationalism and the World History of the Jews*. Supplements to the *Journal of Jewish Thought and Philosophy*. Leiden: Brill, 2013.

Shalit, Moshe. "Vilner Bibliothekn." *Vilne Zamelbukh* 2, no. 1 (1916): 30–52.

Shapiro, Moshe Samuel. *R' Moshe Shmuel ve-Doro: Kovetz Ma'asot ve-Iggerot.* New York: Sons of the Author and His Good Friends, 1964.

Shavit, David. *Hunger for the Printed Word: Books and Libraries in the Jewish Ghettos of Nazi-Occupied Europe*. Jefferson, N.C.: McFarland, 1997.

Shepard, Richard F. "Rejoining the Chapters of Yiddish Life's Story." *New York Times*, August 30, 1989.

Shilo, Bilha. "'Funem Folk, Farn Folk, Mitn Folk': The Restitution of the YIVO Collection from Offenbach to New York." *Moreshet* 14 (May 2017).

———. "Funem Folk, Farn Folk, Mitn Folk: Historiah shel Asufei YIVO le-ahar milhemet ha-olam ha-shniyah." Master's thesis, Hebrew University, 2016.

Shor, Frida. *Me-Likute Shoshanim 'ad Brigadat ha-neyar: Sipuro shel Bet Eked ha-Sefarim 'al shem Strashun be-Vilna*. Ariel, West Bank: Ha-merkaz ha-universitai Ariel be-Shomron, 2012.

Šimaite, Ona. "Letters from a Librarian: Lost and Found in Vilna." Introduction and translation by Julija Šukys. *Proceedings of the Modern Language Association* 118, no. 2 (March 2003).

Sinkoff, Nancy. "From the Archives: Lucy S. Dawidowicz and the Restitution of Jewish Cultural Property." *American Jewish History* 100, no. 1 (January 2016): 117–47.

Smolenskin, Perets. "Ma'asa be-Rusya." *Ha-Shahar*, August 19, 1870, 285.

Spiegel, Ya'akov Shmuel. *'Amudim be-Toldot ha-Sefer ha-Ivri: Be-Sha'arei ha-Defus*. Jerusalem: Bar-Ilan University Press, 2014.

———. "The Use of Uncommon Abbreviations." *Yeshurun* 10 (2002): 814–30; 11 (2002): 919–31; 12 (2003): 802–14; 13 (2003): 828–43.

———. *Amudim be-Toldot ha-Sefer ha-Ivri: Hagahot u-Magihim*. Ramat Gan: Bar-Ilan University Press, 1996.

Stampfer, Shaul. *Families, Rabbis and Education: Traditional Jewish Society in Nineteenth-Century Eastern Europe*. Oxford: Littman Library of Jewish Civilization, 2010.

———. "The Image of the Ga'on." In *Ha-GRA u-Beit Midrasho*, edited by Moshe Halamish et al. Ramat Gan: Bar-Ilan University Press, 2003.

———. *The Lithuanian Yeshiva, Revised and Expanded Edition*. Jerusalem: Zalman Shazar Center for Jewish History, 2005.

Stanislawski, Michael. *A Murder in Lemberg: Politics, Religion, and Violence in Modern Jewish History*. Princeton, NJ: Princeton University Press, 2007.

———. "The 'Vilna Shas' and East European Jewry." In *Printing the Talmud*, edited by Sharon Mintz and Richard Goldstein, 97–102. New York: Yeshiva University Museum, 2005.

———. *Tsar Nicholas I and the Jews: The Transformation of Jewish Society in Russia, 1825–1855*. Philadelphia: University of Pennsylvania Press, 1983.

Starr, Joshua. "Jewish Cultural Property under Nazi Control." *Jewish Social Studies* 12, no. 1 (1950): 27–48.

Steinmetz, Shimon. "Yated Ne'man on R. Solomon Judah Rapoport (Shir) and Wissenschaft des Judentums." *On the Main Line*, October 23, 2011. http://onthemainline.blogspot.com/2011/10/yated-neeman-on-r-solomon-judah.html.

Steinschneider, Hillel Noach. *Ir Vilna*, edited by Mordechai Zalkin, vol. 2. Jerusalem: Hebrew University Press, 2003.

———. *Ir Vilna.* Vilna: Almanah ve-Ha'achim Romm, 1900.

Stern, Eliyahu. *The Genius: Elijah of Vilna and the Making of Modern Judaism.* New Haven, CT: Yale University Press, 2013.

Strashun, David. *Likutei Shoshanim: Reshimat Seforim.* Berlin: H. Itzkowski, 1889.

Strashun, Mattityahu. "Be-Shem D! Shenat ve-he-Tsidku'et ha-Tzadik." *Ha-Maggid,* August 28, 1862.

———. "Divrei hokhma: Mikhtav 'al Davar R. Shem Tov Ba'al ha-'Emunot ve-'Rasha"t ben Falaquera." *Pirkhei Tsafon,* part 1 (1841): 46–48; part 2 (1844): 77–89.

———. "He-'Arot Shonot." *Ha-Levanon,* February 26, 1868.

———. *Mattat-Yah.* Edited by Shalom Pludermacher. Vilna: Ha-'almanah ve-ha-'Achim Romm, 1893.

———. "Note." *Ha-Maggid,* March 4, 1858, 35.

———. *Rabi Mattityahu Strashun: Mivhar Ketavim.* Edited by Tzvi Harkavy. Jerusalem: Mossad Harav Kook, 1969.

———. "Rehovot Kiryah." In *Kiryah Ne'emanah,* edited by Samuel Joseph Fuenn. Vilna: Yitzhak Funk, 1915.

Sutter, Sem C. "Polish Books in Exile: Cultural Booty across Two Continents, through Two Wars." *The Holocaust and the Book: Destruction and Preservation.* Amherst: University of Massachusetts Press, 2001.

———. "The Lost Jewish Libraries of Vilna and the Frankfurt Institut zur Erforschung der Judenfrage." In *Lost Libraries: The Destruction of Great Book Collections since Antiquity,* edited by James Raven, 219–35. London: Palgrave, Macmillan: 2004.

Sutzkever, Abraham. *Vilner Ghetto.* Tel Aviv: Sekhvi, 1946.

Teplitsky, Joshua. "Between Court Jew and Jewish Court: David Oppenheim, The Prague Rabbinate, and Eighteenth-Century Jewish Political Culture." PhD diss., New York University, 2012.

Treasures from the Library Ets Haim (*Livraria Montezinos of the Portugees Israëlietisch Seminarium Ets Haim, Amsterdam*). Jerusalem: Jewish National and University Library Press, 1980.

United Press. "Jewish Art Cache Found in Germany; Third Army Seizes Collection Used for Propaganda by Reich Government Army to Hold Treasures." *New York Times,* April 9, 1945.

Veidlinger, Jeffrey. *Jewish Public Culture in the Late Russian Empire.* Bloomington: Indiana University Press, 2009.

Vinograd, Yeshayahu. *Thesaurus of the Books of the Vilna Gaon: Detailed and Annotated Bibliography of Books by and about the Gaon and Hasid R. Eliahu b. R. Shlomo Zalman of Vilna.* Jerusalem: Kerem Eliahu, 2003.

———. *Otsar Sefer ha-Ivrei: Reshimat ha-Sefarim she- nidpesu be-Ot Ivrit me-Reshit ha-Defus ha-Ivri be-Shenat* (1469) (1863). Jerusalem: Hamachon le-bibliographia me-muhshevet, 1994.

Waite, Roger. "Returning Jewish Cultural Property: The Handling of Books Looted by the Nazis in the American Zone of Occupation, 1945 to 1952." *Libraries and Culture* 37, no. 3 (Summer 2002): 213–28.

Weinberg, Joanna. "Translator's Introduction." In Azariah de' Rossi, *The Light of the Eyes*, translated by Joanna Weinberg. New Haven, CT: Yale University Press, 2001.

Weiner, Samuel. *Kohelet Moshe Aryeh Leyb Friedland: Reshimat Kol ha-Sefarim ha-Ivrim Nidpasim be-Kitve-Yad, ha-Nimtsa'im be-Asefat-Friedland be-Otsar Muzeom ha-Aziaici shel ha-Akademia le-Mada'im be-St. Peterburg*, vols. 1–7. Petropolis: Commission for the Imperial Academy of Sciences, 1893–1902.

Weiser, Kalman. "Coming to America, Choosing Yiddish: Max Weinreich and the Emergence of YIVO's American Center." *Choosing Yiddish: New Frontiers of Language and Culture*, edited by Lara Rabinovitch, Shiri Goren, and Hannah Pressman, 233–52. Detroit: Wayne State University Press, 2012.

———. "'The Jewel in the Yiddish Crown': Who Will Occupy the Chair in Yiddish at the University of Vilnius?" *Polin* 24 (2012): 223–55.

Wesseley, Naftali Hertz. *Divrei Shalom ve-'Emet*. Berlin, 1781–1783.

Wetsch, Robert. "Besuch in Frankfurt." *Mitteilungsblatt des Irgun Olej Merkaz Europa* (January 11, 1946): 10.

Willensky, Ya'akov. *Daltei Teshuvah*. Vilna, 1890.

Yavetz, Ze'ev. *Toldot Yisrael: Metukun 'al pi Mekorot ha-Rishonim*. Berlin: [Eitshkavski], 1906.

Yeshurun. "A Collection of Letters from Jewish Scholars to ShZH"H." *Yeshurun* 33 (2000).

YIVO Institute. *The History and Future of the Strashun Library: Conference Program*. New York: YIVO Institute for Jewish Research, 2017.

———. "Catalogue of the Vilna YIVO Library." *News of YIVO* 54 (1954).

———. "Censored Books in the Vilna Collection." *News of YIVO* 46 (1952).

———. "Rabbinical Collection Now Open to the Public." *News of YIVO* 86 (1963).

———. "The Reading Room of the Strashun Library." *News of YIVO* 36 (1950).

———. "Vilna Collection Augmented: Library Acquires Rare Jewish Periodicals." *News of YIVO* 41 (1951).

———. "YIVO Activities in 1954." *News of YIVO* 55 (1955).

———. "YIVO Library Is Back at Home." *News of YIVO* 40 (1951).

———. *Der Yivo Nokh Draytsn Yor Arbet*. Vilna: YIVO Institute, 1938.

Yudels, A. "In der Alter Strashun Bibliotek." *Literarishe Bletter*, December 17, 1926.

Yudlov, Isaac. *Ginzei Yisrael: Sefarim, Hoverot, ve-Alonim Me'osef Dr. Yisrael Mehlman asher be-Bet ha-Sefarim ha-Leumi veha-Universitah*. Jerusalem: Bet Hasefarim Haleumi ve-Universitah, 1985.

Zadoff, Noam. *Gershom Scholem: From Berlin to Jerusalem and Back: An Intellectual Biography*. Translated by Jeffrey Green. Waltham, MA: Brandeis University Press, 2017.

Zalkin, Mordechai. *Be-Alot ha-Shahar: Ha-Haskalah ha-Yehudit ba-Impiriah ha-Rusit be-Meah ha-Tesha Esrei*. Jerusalem: Magnes Press, 2000.

———. "Bet ha-Midrash le-Rabbanim be-Vilne — Bein Dimui le-Metsiut." *Gal-Ed: On the History and Culture of Polish Jewry* 14 (1995): 59–72.

———. "Ir shel Torah — Torah ve-Limudeha be-Merhav ha-'Ironi ha-Lita'i be-Me'ah ha-Tesha-esrei." In *Yeshivot u-Batei Midrashoth*, edited by Immanuel Etkes. Jerusalem: Merkaz Zalman Shazar, 2007.

———. "Samuel and Mattityahu Strashun: Between Tradition and Innovation." In *Mattityahu Strashun, 1817–1885: Scholar, Leader, and Book Collector*, edited by Yermiyahu Aharon Taub and Aviva E. Astrinsky, 1–28 . New York: YIVO Institute for Jewish Research, 2000.

———. "The Periodical 'Pirhei Tsafon' and Its Role in the Social System of the Haskalah Movement in the Russian Empire." *Kesher* 35 (2007): 63–69.

———. "Who Wields the Power? The Kahal and Chevrot in Vilna in the 19th Century." In *The Gaon of Vilnius and the Annals of Jewish Culture*, edited by Larisa Lempertienė, 354–60. Vilnius: Vilnius University, 1998.

———. "Wilno/Vilnius/Vilne: Whose City Is It Anyway?" In *Insiders and Outsiders: Dilemmas of East European Jewry*, edited by Richard I. Cohen, Jonathan Frankel, and Stefani Hoffman, 221–30. Oxford: Littman Library of Jewish Civilization, 2010.

Zevulani, Noah. "Dr. Devorzky at the Opening of the Strashun Library: The Nazi Academic Johann Pohl Sold Countless Books from the Strashun Library to a Paper Factory." *Herut*, December 26, 1960.

———. "Ha-Nazi Y. Pohl Shalah Mievrak Tanhunim 'al Moto shel [Professor] Klauzner." *Herut*, January 18, 1961.

———. "Hegeihu Seridei Sifrei'at Strashun." *Herut*, October 4, 1960.

———. "Sifrei Strashun le-Yerushalayim." *Herut*, August 2, 1962.

Zinberg, Israel. *A History of Jewish Literature: The Haskalah Movement in Russia*. Translated and edited by Bernard Martin. Cincinnati, Ohio: Hebrew Union College Press, 1978.

Zlotkin, Menahem Mendel. *Shemot ha-Sefarim ha-Ivrim: Lefi Sugehim ha-Shonim, Tokhnatam u-Te'dudotum*. Neuchâtel: Dalchaux and Niestelé, 1950.

Zweifel, Eliezer Tsevi Hakohen. "Kina LeMoto." *Ha'Asif*, 1887.

Zunz, Leopold. "Toldot Rabi Azariah min ha-Adumim." *Kerem Hemed* 5 (1841): 131–58.

———. "Tosefot le-Toldot R' Azariah min ha-'Adumim." *Kerem Hemed* 7 (1843): 119–24.

Index

Note: Page references in *italics* refer to photos and illustrations.